W9-CLA-039

A Manual on BOOKSELLING

How to Open and Run a Bookstore

Fourth Edition

Edited for the
American Booksellers Association by
Robert D. Hale
with
Allan Marshall
and
Ginger Curwen

This edition is specially prepared for distribution to members of the American Book-sellers Association, 137 West 25th Street, New York, New York 10001. A trade edition with identical contents is available from Harmony Books, a division of Crown Publishers, Inc.

Copyright © 1987, 1980, 1974, 1969 by the American Booksellers Association, Inc.

All rights reserved. No part of this book may be reproduced or transmitted in any form or by any means, electronic or mechanical, including photocopying, recording, or by any information storage and retrieval system, without permission in writing from the publisher.

First edition published in 1969; second edition in 1974; third edition in 1980; fourth edition in 1987. Inquiries should be addressed to Harmony Books, a division of Crown Publishers, Inc., 225 Park Avenue South, New York, New York 10003 and represented in Canada by the Canadian MANDA Group.

HARMONY and colophon are trademarks of Crown Publishers, Inc.

Manufactured in the United States of America

Library of Congress Cataloging-in-Publication Data

A manual on bookselling.

   Bibliography: p.
   1. Booksellers and bookselling—United States.
2. Booksellers and bookselling—Handbooks, manuals, etc.
I. Hale, Robert D. (Robert David), 1928–
II. Marshall, Allan.   III. Curwen, Ginger.
IV. American Booksellers Association.
Z476.M35 1987   070.5'0973   87-419
ABA ISBN 0-517-56888-8

10 9 8 7 6 5 4 3 2 1
Fourth Edition

Contents

Foreword

The Climate of the Book Industry Today

BERNARD E. RATH

Increased competitiveness is probably the single biggest change in the book industry in recent history, as more of those who have been successful in other careers as merchants and/or professionals bring much of the experience they have gleaned with them. The rift that existed at one time between those who are affectionately known as "bookpeople" (who sell books because they love books) and those often disparagingly known as "businesspeople" (who sell books to make money) has been bridged to some extent. There is an attempt at coexistence and an understanding that a respect for finance, profitability, and inventory turns and a respect for books and authors are not necessarily mutually exclusive.

The bitterness felt by many independents, prompted by the belief that chain stores were attempting to put them out of business, has abated as independents have come to realize that there is a niche in the marketplace in which they can successfully compete with chain booksellers.

Certainly one such area is specialty bookselling; another is the general independent bookstore, which provides a level of community service and support that often (but not necessarily) cannot be duplicated by the chains. In spite of their fears in times of heavy competition for the walk-in frontlist business, many booksellers have found that they can in fact survive and, in some cases, prosper. However, just as everyone knows someone who was killed or wounded in Vietnam, most retailers can point to a bookseller or booksellers who went out of business in the face of price wars conducted across the country by national chain stores and regional discount operations. Successful independents have remained solvent by building what has been referred to as "back-door business" through such ventures as school book fairs, rental libraries, corporate sales, frequent buyer clubs, targeted mailings, and, most important, by employing "guerrilla marketing," as characterized by Jay Levinson. As a result, these independent booksellers have amassed lists of proven book buyers numbering, cumulatively, in the thousands and tens of thousands and maintained by microcomputers, both inside and outside the bookstore.

As much as it had been decried and disliked by many booksellers, price discounting (offering primarily frontlist books at discounts up to 30, 40, or even 50 percent) has become a way of life for bookselling, as it has for merchants in many other retail businesses. Although selling hundreds or even thousands of books on the *New York Times* Bestseller List for little or no profit galls many retailers, most booksellers have found that these books actually represent a relatively small proportion of their overall annual sales. In the final analysis, the profit contribution of these books had been a relatively small percentage of the total. Meanwhile the consumer, who has been bombarded by off-price advertising in electronics, automobiles, airline tickets, shoes, and even designer clothing, is less accustomed to paying full retail. Still, many booksellers do not match off-price retailers in every respect, since the demographics and customer loyalty in one's trading area continue to be significant factors in determining correct retail strategy.

The wholesalers, both national and regional, having enjoyed tremendous growth in the late 1970s and 1980s, continue to change the nature of book distribution by providing benefits of price and service to retailers. This has grown to the point where an ever-greater percentage of many booksellers' business is no longer carried on directly with publishers, and some booksellers have chosen not to order books from publishers at all, except when there is no alternative.

The installation of hundreds of computerized management and inventory systems in bookstores in the middle 1980s has resulted in a new level of sophistication among booksellers, who are now able to know what their requirements are for any given title in any given period of time at the push of a few buttons. As a result, booksellers are buying fewer books more often, which results in more frequent inventory turns, in and of itself a major contributor to increased profitability. However, when coupled with ordering books from wholesalers or from electronic buying mechanisms, bookselling has the capability of becoming much more financially rewarding than it has been in recent memory, all the while requiring that those who venture into it be prepared to work harder at the business of selling books than at the pleasure of living with them.

Preface

ROBERT D. HALE

In his book *The Successful Bookshop* (1926), Frederic G. Melcher wrote, "To be a successful bookseller one needs an innate fondness for books, an infinite capacity for pains in handling details, a certain poise and self-confidence which is the basis of selling ability. Beyond these one must cultivate business ability, for successful bookstore management is based fundamentally on the same principles as any other retail business: aggressive merchandising and sound financial control."

The purpose of *A Manual on Bookselling* is to help prospective booksellers accomplish exactly what Mr. Melcher outlined in the paragraph above.

Anyone who is not already a bookseller, or determined to become one, may wonder upon reading this manual what keeps a person in a business that is so encumbered with details and produces a profit that seems pitiful compared to the required investment of time, money, and effort. This is not to say you cannot become financially well off in the retail book business. There are those who have, but many more have found it only modestly rewarding in dollars, if enormously enriching in innumerable other ways.

A professional bookseller can become an integral part of a community to an extent achieved by no other merchant. A real bookstore is part of the educational process, a source for every kind of information, providing access to every type of experience, vicarious or actual. The bookseller who does more than shelve books, who helps people find the books they need and want, who brings books to the attention of customers who may have special appreciation for those particular books, whose accumulated knowledge of what has been published and what is to be published is used in the service of his community, is as valuable to that community as the teacher or librarian, priest or rabbi.

Booksellers have the means to enchant or enrage. They are selling intangibles, ideas, entertainment, amusement, enlightenment, inspiration, insight. No technological advance has reduced an iota the impact a book can have on a reader. Books can reduce pressure or strengthen resolve. There are books for every purpose—and readers for every book. Books are mysterious and magical or shatteringly real. Gathering them together in a bookstore is an experience beyond that of any other kind of retailing.

Booksellers have existed since the beginning of the written word, in many forms in many places on the planet. In Western tradition there are known booksellers dating back to ancient Egypt and Rome, several of them recording complaints not dissimilar to those voiced by booksellers today. For most of history, books were sold primarily in bookstores, but now they are sold everywhere in all kinds of stores. As late as World War II, the would-be book buyer might have had to drive fifty miles or more in some parts of the United States to find a book to buy. Now books are ubiquitous. It is impossible to escape them, even if one wanted to—and this in spite of television and VCR and all those other technological advances that were possibly going to stop people from reading.

While those who run drugstores with a paperback rack next to the front door might well benefit from this book, the effort that has gone into its publication is dedicated to those who mean to make the selling of books the mainstream of their business life. I say "life" because it easily becomes that. Bookselling tends to carry over into all the other parts of a true bookseller's existence. Which leads us back to that initial comment after Frederic Melcher's quotation: Why does one become a bookseller?

I stumbled into it, as is usually the case. Very few children reply, "A bookseller!" when asked, "What do you want to be when you grow up?" Now I am a bookseller because I could not be happy as anything else. Nothing would be as satisfying or as stimulating. No matter how many years I am at it, I cannot know everything, I cannot anticipate all the questions, I will not be able to read all the books I want to. If I live forever, there will still be things to do tomorrow. Isn't that reason enough?

Others might answer in varying ways. Perhaps bookselling allows a person to make a statement while also making a living—if the bookstore is cause-oriented. Maybe it's because it's a great way to meet interesting people—not just the well educated and affluent, but people of all backgrounds with every type of need. "I like to talk," one bookseller once reported, "and because people who buy books also like to talk, I engage in a constant exchange of ideas in my store."

I suspect "people" would be a major reason many of us become booksellers. Book buyers tend to be precise and exacting. Even if they don't know the title of the book they want, they know what *kind* of book and offer a challenge to the bookseller to put that kind of book in their hands. Because they are buying words rather than something to wear, book buyers tend to talk more openly to a bookseller about things that are important to them. If you are interested in really knowing people, the bookstore is a great place to be.

"I'd like to write a book someday, so maybe if I work with those others have written, something will rub off," is a reason given with some freqency. Being a bookseller is also a way to meet writers. Watching which books writers buy to read is a fascinating pursuit. Having writers as customers—and even the most remote bookstore might have at least one—is a marvelous experience for a bookseller.

"Bookselling is providing a service, and being of service to my community is very rewarding," a bookseller might respond. "Bookselling isn't a job, it's the pursuit of pleasure," says another. "Where else could I have so much fun?" replies a third.

Bookselling can be all of these things and more. Loving books is not sufficient justification for becoming a bookseller, though it's a vital ingredient. Along with that love must go dedication and energy and patience and fortitude and all the other good things we were brought up to admire. While we are having fun and being stimulated and enriched, we must also pay strict attention to sound business practices.

Booksellers tend to romanticize things, and that's all right, so long as we know we're doing it. Knowing we are a link in the chain that transforms the thoughts of writers of all times into the awareness of multitudes of individuals is a glorious feeling—made better if we are also solvent. It is the hope of all those who contributed to this book that all who read it will achieve glorious success.

One Bookseller's Credo

Bookselling was and is for me a cultural and political expression, an expression of progressive change, of challenge to oppressive authority, of a search for a community of values that can act as an underpinning of a better world. The true profit in bookselling is the social profit; the bottom line, the measure of the impact of the bookshop on the community.

A. DAVID SCHWARTZ
Milwaukee, Wisconsin

Acknowledgments

Each contributor to this edition of A *Manual on Bookselling: How to Open and Run a Bookstore,* whose experience and knowledge has been so generously shared, has my individual and collective thanks. While booksellers can be fiercely competitive, they are also historically free with advice and assistance to colleagues, as this volume attests.

Thanks also to Ginger Curwen and Allan Marshall, who not only provided much-needed materials when the well went dry, but also pushed and prodded. They have been both coach and shepherd.

And to Joan Ripley and Bill Banks, who read portions of the manuscript at various stages and made positive suggestions.

Last, thanks and by now gratitude to the good people at Harmony Books, whose patience may not be endless but is ever gracious.

Robert D. Hale, Editor

I
Beginning

Chapter 1

Opening a Bookstore

CYD ROSENBERG

When prospective booksellers are asked, "Why do you want to open a bookstore?" they generally respond with answers such as "I like to read," "I want to fulfill a need in my community," or "I want to operate my own business and be my own boss." Let's begin with that word "business." A retail bookstore is a business just as is any commercial enterprise, be it a shoe store, grocery store, or clothing store. What makes the book business unique is the product being sold—books, which contain worlds and centuries of thought and ideas, each title unique unto itself. That uniqueness is both the challenge and the reward. Bookselling is a joy when the right book is found for a customer or when the bookseller is a conduit for growth, new experiences and pleasures through books. This is all extremely satisfying. It can and should also be profitable. But profit and satisfaction come only after you have mastered a complicated retail business with endless detail and paperwork that require hours of labor. Unfortunately, even with all of this effort and attention to detail, bookselling too frequently provides little financial reward and small return on investment.

This chapter will answer some questions that should be asked early on if one is thinking of becoming a bookseller.

What personal preparation should I make for opening a bookstore?

After spending a considerable amount of time thinking about what is involved in running a retail business—such as the initial financial investment, the time and labor, and the ongoing fiscal responsibility—you should proceed to discover what it is actually like to work in a bookstore by getting practical experience. This means persuading a bookseller to hire you, even if it is only as temporary help at Christmastime. If the bookseller cannot afford to hire another person, and your budget will allow it, volunteer to put in regular hours doing those tasks that are part of every bookseller's daily routine. These include receiving and unpacking books, which most booksellers enjoy, shelving books, which isn't always as much fun, doing whatever is required for the store's inventory-control system, selling, working at the register, gift wrapping, setting up and dismantling displays, and cleaning. It doesn't take long to understand the daily routine and to know whether the pleasurable aspects offset the drudgeries. Such an experience will either confirm your desire to become a bookseller or make you think twice about proceeding with plans for a bookstore.

The next logical step is to attend a Prospective Booksellers School, sponsored by American Booksellers Association. Taught by booksellers who have successfully opened stores, this three-and-a-half-day seminar is conducted on a regular schedule in various parts of the United States, depending upon demand. Classes are given in the mechanics of financing, site selection and lease negotiation, layout, inventory selection (as well as ordering and receiving procedures), advertising and promotion techniques, selling, and financial and staff management. ABA staff members and the teaching faculty are available for individual counseling at these schools. Much useful information results from the exchange between registrants based on individual and varying in-store experiences and their own store-planning progress to date.

While financial management is offered at the school, it is very brief. An extension course in small-business management or accounting is always useful. The Small Business Administration regional office has information on business-related courses available in their area. SBA also offers many courses of its own and has valuable printed material, much of it free.

Planning a retail book business is usually a lengthy process, during which prospective booksellers can enhance their knowledge of what lies ahead by attending workshops and panel discussions at regional bookseller association meetings, as well as at the national American Booksellers Association convention. Regional schedules and locations are available from the ABA office in New York City. The national ABA convention, the largest book show in the Western Hemisphere, is held annually during the last weekend in May or the first weekend in June. Further information on regional associations and the national convention can be found in later chapters.

Where should I open a bookstore?

You must ask yourself: Where will my bookstore succeed? A good location is critical to the success of the venture. Collect as much information as possible about your chosen community. Obtain U.S. Census figures and statistics from the state, county, township, or municipality regarding the age, income, and occupational and educational brackets of the community. Talk to the Chamber of Commerce and other local merchants about the business outlook for the community in general and your chosen neighborhood in particular. Speak to librarians and leaders of community organizations about the reading habits of those who live or work in your area. Talk specifically with the librarian about circulation figures and the types of books and materials that are most popular in your area. Read local magazines and newspapers, if they exist. Analyze all your findings to determine whether the location you desire will support a bookstore.

ABA offers assistance in researching demographic data for potential locations through the Bookstore Site Analysis Service. This program provides statistical data, regarding your specific potential site, on population, income levels, number of households, education levels, and types of occupations, that will help you in your planning and in your financial projections. The demographic data should be an integral part of the business plan you present to a banker when securing either a loan or line of credit. The service is available to both members and nonmembers, but there is a substantial discount for ABA members.

You should obtain a copy of the most recent *Abacus Financial Profile*, which is sent free to all ABA members, and is available at a nominal fee for nonmembers.

The Abacus Group is a group of forty-three member stores representing fifty-three locations that have agreed to be surveyed annually as to the fiscal health of their businesses. The forty-three stores in the 1985 Abacus Group have total retail sales of $46 million, for the most part individually they fall into the $250,000–$500,000 annual gross sales volume category, and are geographically evenly distributed across census areas. The figures used in this report are taken from the above-mentioned group survey. Readers should be cautioned that The Abacus Group figures do not represent a profile of the "average" bookstore, and that the figures of the forty-three stores may not be representative of the industry as a whole. The Abacus Group stores appear to be generally successful, and, in order to complete the detailed survey, they had to possess a general business sophistication, as well as accurate financial knowledge and records.

You should examine the current study's statistics on bookstore profitability, as well as operating ratios. Using these figures, project the sales volume necessary to provide the gross sales and net profit you hope to earn from the business. If this is to be your chief source of income, decide how much, or how little, you absolutely need to take home, and then, starting from that point, work back to the required sales. Will it be possible to generate that desired amount of sales in your chosen location?

Choosing a location is the most critical decision you will make, for it directly relates to the potential profitability and future success of your business. The single most important factor is foot traffic. Is the space in a shopping area with substantial foot traffic? Is there easy access to nearby parking? For a sufficient volume to support your business, you need many customers making comparatively small purchases.

Many retail bookstores are located in malls or other kinds of shopping centers. While these locations are desirable for the foot traffic they offer, the operating costs make many of them prohibitive for booksellers. While everything depends on the particular circumstances of your community, you should bear in mind that shopping centers and malls are not the only ideal locations for retail bookstores. Many successful stores have located in downtown business districts, renovated historic districts, and neighborhood shopping streets or strip malls.

According to the *Abacus Financial Profile* for 1985, on average, stores reported spending 6 percent of gross sales for total occupancy expense. Stores surveyed with sales of less than $250,000 spent 7.7 percent of gross sales in this area. This category includes rent, mortgage payment, building depreciation, real estate taxes, insurance, utilities, repair, maintenance, and cleaning. Store rental and occupancy costs must be kept in line with projected sales; 6–8 percent is excellent, and by not overspending on rent and related expenses, more dollars are available to the owner for other expenses. Rental charges should never exceed 10–12 percent of gross sales, and, as mentioned previously, 6–8 percent is ideal. You may consider the possibility of paying higher rent on a space with an excellent location, but you must be certain that the location truly is an excellent one, one that will bring you added traffic and sales to offset the high rental charge. By the same token, you should not necessarily choose the cheapest space—it may be in a bad location without adequate foot traffic or parking facilities. This principle holds true, whether talking about a downtown location, a strip shopping center, or an enclosed mall. Just renting a space in an enclosed regional mall does not ensure traffic; there are both good and bad locations in malls, depending on the relation to the anchor stores, traffic patterns, and access to parking facilities.

The square footage, or store size, has a direct relationship to projected sales. According to the 1985 *Abacus Financial Profile*, the average store produced $243.53 in sales per square foot of total space, as opposed to $299.73 in sales per square foot of selling space. The stores with sales of less than $250,000 generated $86.62 and $104.10 respectively. For the middle group of stores, those doing between $250,000 and $500,000, the figures were $180.89 and $221.92. Bear in mind that you will be paying rent on more space than actual selling space. Your rent includes back room, office, lavatory, and possibly even basement. As you are paying rent on space not actually involved in sales, you must be certain to take maximum advantage of whatever actual selling space you do have. An average ABA member bookseller has approximately 1,500–1,800 square feet of selling space, although we do have member stores with as little as 500 square feet, as well as member stores with square footage in excess of 17,000 square feet. A specialty store, for example, requires less space than a full-line general trade bookstore and can often locate in a seemingly less desirable retail space. The figures cited above can be used in making sales projections. It is wise to do a series of projections with varying sales-per-square-foot figures, ranging from a projection around $150.00 per square foot to perhaps $200.00 per square foot. Your sales projection can determine whether a space is large enough to generate the necessary volume, or too large—causing you to consider stocking other merchandise besides books to generate the needed volume.

Analyze all aspects of a site, its psychological suitability as well as its business potential, and work out financial details with the help of an accountant, preferably one with a background in small business. Before signing any lease, have all of its provisions carefully examined by your attorney, again preferably one with a background either handling small businesses or, more important, negotiating leases for retail space.

Should I have a books-only store, or will I sell nonbook merchandise as well?

Most bookstores sell other merchandise as well; calendars, cards, and magazines are the most common. Nonbook merchandise is usually referred to as "sidelines" and is described in greater detail in chapter 46.

Sidelines are attractive to a bookseller for two basic reasons: they increase the gross profit margin, and they act as a lure for increased in-store traffic. Most sidelines are purchased at 50 percent of selling price. Books are purchased at every conceivable percentage of selling price, the average being 60 percent. The 10 percent difference on top of the added sales make sidelines essential parts of most retail bookstores.

How do I know what discounts I will get on the books and nonbook merchandise I buy for the bookstore?

Legally there cannot be a standardized set of terms among suppliers of merchandise to bookstores or any other retail business. Each producer of merchandise establishes its own terms of doing business, from initial discount on merchandise—or the wholesale price—to dates of payment, whether or not freight is included, and so on. Generally, gift and stationery merchandise, including cards, is sold to retailers at half the suggested retail price. Other sidelines vary.

Publishers list their terms in the *ABA Book Buyer's Handbook.* Most trade discounts from suggested retail are based on quantity ordered. Discounts on textbooks, educational books, scholarly and reference books, and the like can be anything from nonexistent up to regular trade. Unfortunately it is impossible to list every publisher in the *ABA Book Buyer's Handbook.* Those not listed have to be contacted directly for their specific terms.

Wholesalers have their own terms. Some of these are listed in the handbook, and some are not.

For purposes of initial planning, both inventory costs and profit ratios, the prospective bookseller can use a basic 40 percent discount from selling price, plus a percentage for freight, which booksellers generally pay. The specifics of buying from publishers and wholesalers is dealt with in depth in chapters 19 and 20.

What is a book wholesaler? Will I find one in my area?

Wholesalers, independent distributors, and jobbers are in the order-fulfillment business, stocking titles from a number of publishers and then reselling them to retail bookstores. A wholesaler generally stocks both hardback and paperback books, current (or frontlist) titles and backlist books. An independent distributor, frequently referred to as an ID, is often a newspaper and magazine distributor who deals primarily in mass-market paperbacks, though a limited selection of hardback books may be carried. A jobber is either a wholesaler or an independent distributor who adds the service of title selection, inventory maintenance, and returns. This is called "jobbing" and is a service usually utilized by nonbookstore outlets with a very limited display of books, such as drugstores, supermarkets, and newsstands.

There are several types of wholesalers: national wholesalers, with regional warehouses throughout the country; regional wholesalers, who service a particular geographic area; and specialty wholesalers, who deal with titles relating to a specific subject such as religious books or children's books. In addition, there are several wholesalers who specialize in small press titles. Independent distributors can be found throughout the United States and generally service a specific geographic area.

Terms for most of the above will be found in the *ABA Book Buyer's Handbook*. Most established booksellers use wholesalers and occasionally independent distributors as well as publishers for obtaining their books.

What happens to the books I buy for my store and then can't sell?

Contrary to a popular misconception, books are sold by publishers and other distributors on a final basis. They are not shipped to bookstores on consignment. They must be paid for according to the terms of sale. However, recognizing the risk factor in the unknown title, publishers instituted return policies. These vary as greatly as do sales policies, but in general the concept is that a bookseller may, within each publisher's specific policy, return unsold books for credit against future purchases.

This cooperation between publisher and bookseller allows books to be displayed before the public, the ultimate consumer. A successful bookseller knows the public that patronize his or her bookstore and displays those books that will be of interest to that public. Mistakes are inevitable. The cost of the mistakes is shared by the publisher who printed enough books to be sent out to the stores to be displayed and by the bookseller who has paid freight to get the books into the store and will also pay freight to return them. No intelligent bookseller buys books just because they can be returned. However, that intelligent bookseller does frequently take a chance because of the partial escape clause—partial, because many publishers have a returns penalty of varying percentages.

All of these returns policies are outlined in the *ABA Book Buyer's Handbook*.

How can I set up accounts with publishers and other sources of supply?

A most effective way to establish accounts is to attend a booksellers regional meeting where publishers are exhibiting and where their representatives can be approached, both for information about opening an account and for catalogs of their lists. Having the publisher's representative assist in the opening of an account, as well as in writing an initial order, can save weeks of waiting. Most sales reps carry their publisher's new account application forms. Wholesalers are also present at these meetings and can similarly be of help in opening an account. An added advantage of this method is that it establishes personal contact at once between the representative who serves the territory and the new bookseller.

If this is impossible, then each publisher and each wholesaler must be contacted individually either over the telephone or through the mail. Unfortunately there is no single credit clearinghouse for a new bookseller. Using information in the *ABA Book Buyer's Handbook*, each prospective source for books should be asked to send credit applications and catalogs with opening order forms. It is also a good idea to ask for an early visit from their local salesperson. When returning the completed application, include a copy of your financial statement and an outline of your store's projections. These documents should be presented in the most professional manner possible; it is worth the investment of time and money to have them properly prepared and reproduced.

Because all this takes a great deal of time, start applying for credit and establishing accounts months in advance of the planned opening of your store. Also be prepared to pay in advance for initial orders. However, even prepayment does not speed up delivery of books to a new account. Because each publisher's terms and systems differ, expect a variety of responses to both applications and orders. Once credit is established, payment terms are generally net thirty days, though some publishers do offer discounts for early payment.

How do I know which books to order for my initial inventory?

No one can tell you exactly which books to order. There is no tried-and-true formula because every bookstore is different in some way from other established stores. Attention must be paid to the kind of store you want, the public you expect to serve, the location of your store, and all the other factors that went into the establishment of the business. If there is any rule of thumb, it is to be conservative. It is far better to begin slightly underinventoried and then build. A store should give the impression of being fully stocked without having stacks of books that may not sell. Extreme attention to selection and caution in quantities is a good guide to follow.

There are tools that can be useful—the *ABA Basic Book List*, for instance, which is a selection of titles in subject categories cross-referenced by publisher. The list is compiled by a committee of established retail booksellers and can be of great help to the neophyte. More information on this list is available in chapter 9, "Trade Tools for a Bookstore."

Publisher's representatives are also helpful in setting up an inventory, since they are familiar with the sales record of titles from their house. However, you should apply whatever standard you've adopted to each title selected no matter how strongly it is touted by a salesman. The test, of course, is "Will it sell in my store?"

Wholesalers have knowledge of titles that are currently selling and can be very helpful to the beginning bookseller, either through simple assistance with initial orders or by providing materials especially created to recommend an opening store inventory. While other booksellers will not be able or willing to provide complete lists, few are averse to suggesting basic titles or to letting the neophyte spend time examining their inventory, especially if the new bookstore will not be in direct competition. This familiarity with books that should be on the shelves is best obtained by working in a bookstore similar to the one you want to open. Only in that way can you learn which titles sell constantly, frequently, or from time to time and so be able to judge what quantities might be needed.

How much should I plan to spend on opening inventory?

The amount of money to be spent on opening inventory depends upon sales projections and space occupied. If a sales projection of $150,000 is estimated, and an inventory turn (the total sales per year divided by the average inventory at retail) of three is anticipated, then the starting inventory should be approximately $50,000 at retail. If purchased at an average 40 percent discount, inventory cost would be $30,000. Inventory turns are dealt with fully in chapter 14, "Budgeting."

At least as important as the dollars to be spent on opening inventory are those the bookseller should keep in reserve to cover costs during the first months of operation. Study chapter 2, "Financing the New Bookstore."

How do I plan the fixtures for a bookstore?

The physical planning for a bookstore is such an important element of success or failure that much time should be spent at the drawing board before any decisions are made. More important than the type of wood or other material to be used is the efficiency of a fixture combined with its contribution to the overall look you want to create. If you have no experience at all in store planning or retail expertise, it is wise to use a professional for assistance. Consider an architect or a store planner. Many commercial fixture companies have store planners. Be aware when using representatives of fixture companies that part of their purpose is to sell their company's product, so it is well to respond positively to a line of fixtures before becoming too involved with a planner from that fixture firm. Custom fixtures are usually more expensive, though costs can be cut if you know how to build your own or can call on the services of a skilled carpenter.

Chapter 7, on store planning and layout, will tell you points to consider, not the least of which is the image you want your store to convey. Because the investment in fixtures and equipment for a store is major and long term, it is always best to take as much time as needed to make the right decisions before proceeding with purchase or installation. It is impossible to say what might be spent on fixturing a store because there are so many variables. A professional can take all these variables and come up with estimates.

There is a listing of commercial fixture companies in the *ABA Sidelines Directory,* and most commercial fixture companies specializing in bookstores exhibit at the national ABA convention. Used fixtures are sometimes advertised in *ABA Newswire* or *American Bookseller.*

What are some of the other start-up expenses I'll need to consider?

In addition to the basic costs of construction, fixturing, and inventory, there are the costs of whatever equipment is deemed essential, such as computer, cash register, adding machine, and typewriter. Then there is the cost of installing telephones, the expense of dues and subscriptions, deposits on utilities, assorted licenses depending upon state and local requirements, and whatever professional fees have been accumulated.

Money should be set aside for advertising and promotion expenses for your opening and for supplies: bags, wrapping paper, order forms, gift certificates, and accounting materials. Chapter 8, "Behind the Scenes," lists many items that may not come immediately to mind but will be needed.

What are some of the reference tools I should begin to use in planning the store?

This book is an excellent first tool. The *ABA Book Buyer's Handbook,* which comes with membership in ABA, provides information of publishers' terms. The *ABA Basic Book List* is important for the beginner. *American Bookseller* magazine and the *ABA Newswire* are also useful tools (these are described at length in chapter 9, "Trade Tools for a Bookstore"), as are *Books in Print, Publishers Weekly, Forthcoming Books, Subject Guide to Books in Print,* and other R. R. Bowker publications.

If I am serious about becoming a retail bookseller, what should I do first?

Read this book. Then, if you are still serious, join the ABA and get all the materials that come with membership. You can join as a provisional member prior to the actual opening of your store. Contact the ABA to talk with staff members employed to aid prospective as well as established booksellers; either telephone the office (212-463-8450) or visit the ABA directly at 137 West 25th Street in New York City. Appointments must be made in advance to assure time for proper discussion. And, plan to attend a booksellers school, preferably the ABA Prospective Booksellers School mentioned earlier in this chapter and discussed in greater detail in chapter 62.

Chapter 2

Financing the New Bookstore

ELIOT LEONARD

So, you want to open a bookstore, or you may want to move and expand your present store. You will need to do a lot of thinking and planning and set many merchandise and financial goals as you prepare for this venture. You should commit all your thoughts and goals to paper in an organized manner that will provide you with a successful course to follow and also create a business plan that can be used to sell your concept to a bank or to anyone else from whom you may need to borrow money.

This business plan should be detailed but stated simply so that it can be easily understood. The more information you include about ideas and expectations, and how you hope to realize them, the more impressive your plan will be and the more you will project a knowledgeable image.

Begin with a summary, and do a table of contents. Then explain your concept of the market and your store's place in that market, using figures and reasons, backup material, and any other exhibits that demonstrate why the new business might be successful. Make it honest and believable by including well-thought-out growth, profit, and return-on-investment figures. Do not try to hide potential problems, major or minor. Edit and organize the whole package to show the maximum professionalism. If help from an experienced consultant, banker, attorney, accountant, or others is needed, get it. It will be well worth what you pay for their services.

Along with your business plan, be prepared to submit a complete personal financial statement that any prospective lender will most likely request.

Someone opening a bookstore does not usually want to give up part of the ownership by selling shares of the new business (equity financing). It is more common for the new bookseller to use some of his or her own money and other assets, borrow the balance needed, and pay the loan back with interest over several years. A Small Business Administration loan might be available under certain conditions. It is always impressive when applying to borrow funds to include a repayment proposal and timetable as part of the business plan.

The following is a suggested format for such a business plan, with the kinds of information that should be included:

1. *Table of Contents.* List briefly the main areas of the plan. Include page numbers at which those areas begin.

2. *Concept.* Specify what type of bookstore you contemplate. Will it be a general trade bookstore or one specializing in certain subject areas? What will be the merchandise mix of books and sidelines? Explain how your proposed customer services and great book selection compare with those of competing stores. How do you plan to promote the store, to draw customers from your market? Try to compare your projected store to a model, successful, noncompeting bookshop in another region.

3. *Product.* Report on the growth of the bookselling industry, of reading and book buying; explain that books are not luxury items. Tell how readers use books for how-to purposes and for self-education and how increasingly they buy books as gifts. Obtain statistics from industry periodicals, the library, and other sources, and expand on the many elements that may contribute to a continuing growth of bookselling in the future. Add any conditions that make the forecast especially bright for your market area. Describe your main sources of supply.

4. *Location.* Describe the space in which you intend to establish your store. Is it in a central business district or a residential, financial, or educational area? What other kinds of retail stores are nearby? Describe the advantages that result from their proximity. If you are considering opening in a shopping center, is it a regional, community, or strip center? Tell about the store site, its visibility to passing traffic, the convenience for walking and/or driving customers. Is there ample parking space?

5. *Demographics.* Who are your potential customers? Where will they come from? Give population numbers; age, education, and income levels; and information on ethnic backgrounds and family formation. List the cities and towns in the market area and how far away they are. State the value range of homes, and

evaluate trends in the condition of local property. Estimate the growth of the general market.

6. *Organization.* Give details about the ownership and management of the projected store. Include letters of recommendation about yourself and people who will be in charge of important functions such as buying and management. State their prior experience in bookselling and/or retailing. Stress management knowledge of expense control. If a spouse or other family member is to be involved, describe his/her responsibilities and authority.

7. *Competition.* Name all the bookstores or book outlets already established in your intended customer market; include their sizes, volumes, types, and how you will compare with them. What will be your main differences in advertising, promotion, merchandising, customer services?

8. *The Lease.* This element of a business plan is very important to a lender and to you as you create budgets to be included in the business plan. Presumably you and the landlord have reached agreement on a definite lease, contingent on your obtaining adequate financing. Spell out the important lease details, including rent and other costs, length of lease with options, and who pays for preparing the space.

9. *The Loan.* Spell out how much money you will need to get the new store going, how much of your own funds you will use, and how much you are requesting in a loan. List and define major costs in construction and leaseholder improvements, fixtures, equipment, merchandise inventory, supplies, preopening expenses, licenses, fees, and so on. Be sure to include the cash reserve fund that will help you get through the first few months before sales generate enough money to pay all the bills.

10. *Appendix.* Include as many exhibits as possible to back up your statements, such as:

> Maps of the complete market area and of your store location, with adjacent businesses.
>
> A picture of the storefront.
>
> A diagram showing your planned layout of fixtures and aisles.
>
> Your lease proposal.
>
> Information provided by the Chamber of Commerce, your city's planning department, the library, and other sources.

A planned timetable from lease signing to opening.

Your preoperating expense budget (see chart), a complete profit and loss projection for the first year, plus P & L summaries for two to four more years and a cash-flow projection for the first year.

An impressive business plan can open the pockets of prospective lenders. Bankers are conservative, especially toward a retail business such as bookselling, about which they know little. Your chances of obtaining the loan are much better if you are already doing business with that bank. If a knowledgeable person has helped you prepare the plan, he or she should also attend the loan meeting. Another important factor: how much of your own money are you ready to commit to the project? If your statements and your financial and merchandise budgets are realistic, you will have a good chance to convince the lender to come through for you.

The Preopening Budget

Think out, plan, and chart all the expenses you will incur before opening for business. The initial financial needs of your proposed business may result in the largest expenditures you will make in your first years of bookselling.

Your budget could consist of a simple list of all items and services to be purchased and used, with amounts. The more notes of explanation you include for the larger amounts, the better. For example, make clear what will go into preopening advertising; stipulate what kinds of fixtures and equipment you will use; note that you will not draw any salary until the store is open for business. The following is a sample preopening budget. The figures used are only examples; they do not have any bearing on percentages to be expected, except where noted.

PREOPENING BUDGET

Cash on Hand (personal & borrowed)	$40,000

Projected Payouts	
Cost of merchandise purchased	$20,000[1]
Wages—miscellaneous	2,000
Payroll taxes	200
Outside services—professional	400
Supplies—store & office	2,000
Leaseholder improvements	1,000
Advertising	750
Auto/travel	200
Rent	[2]
Telephone	150
Utilities	150
Repairs & maintenance	
Insurance	150
Taxes & licenses	200
Interest (on loan)	[3]
Capital purchases (fixtures & equipment)	10,000
Miscellaneous expenses	500

Total Payouts	($37,700)
Reserve Balance	$2,300

[1]Cost of merchandise purchased equals about 60 percent of beginning inventory and includes transportation.

[2]This presumes you have negotiated a lease whereby rent does not start until opening day.

[3]Attempt to secure a loan on which first payment, including interest, is not due until after the first month of business.

Chapter 3

Location and Lease

ELIOT LEONARD

The prospective bookseller, having decided to open a bookstore, usually has an idea of the community where the store is to be located and has perhaps even spotted one or two available spaces that are "just right for a bookshop." A little looking around in familiar areas has probably comprised the full extent of location analysis.

Because a good location is essential to success, much more considered thought should go into choosing the site for a retail store unless the book dealer is already an experienced merchant. Professional help should be brought in—a consultant, real estate adviser, local banker, another retailer, or a combination of these people— because "perfect" locations are not easy to find, and those that are available are frequently difficult to analyze.

Two questions should be asked: Is there a need for a bookstore in this business section of this community in this city? Will the people in this market area support a bookshop (or an additional bookstore, if one is already established nearby)?

Studying the demographics of the area and any marketing research that has previously been done is one step toward the answers. Figures should be compiled about the customers who come to adjacent stores for goods and services. Are they potential book buyers? From what radius do they come—one, three, five, or more miles? In sparsely populated regions a shopping area might serve customers from twenty or thirty miles in all directions. A densely populated market might be concentrated within a single mile of its center. Demographics for whatever area the considered location serves should be studied in detail.

Don't just depend upon studies that have been made. Drive up and down all the streets of the area. Notice the condition not only of businesses in the area, but of the residences as well. Does it seem to be a thriving neighborhood, one that is perhaps "coming back," or are there signs of deterioration? Are there vacancies? Do they look as if they've been vacant long? Is there foot traffic? Are people walking about in the area, or is it all automobile traffic? If the latter, is there plenty of parking space? Subjective observations added to quantitative market figures will present a picture of the potential clientele and suggest what the store's image should be as well as its inventory mix.

Retail locations

Regional shopping centers or malls are usually very large groups of specialty stores of all sizes, with one to five department stores. Most are enclosed, and many of sufficient size contain two general trade bookstores. It is difficult for an independent operator to lease space in these malls because the owners/developers prefer chains that have proven profitable in other centers and whose payment of rent over a number of future years is guaranteed by the considerable assets behind them. Occasionally a local bookseller who has built a reputation with a large volume and significant selection of books is able to lease a second or third bookshop space in these regional centers. However, total occupancy costs in large malls are usually the highest of any type of business location because of their powerful attraction for throngs of shoppers. These costs are usually beyond the means of the beginning independent bookseller.

Neighborhood and community-center malls are smaller groups of stores, ranging from fifteen or twenty up to fifty plus, which provide a multitude of merchandise and services. These centers usually have one department store, a supermarket, drugstore, bank, restaurant, home-improvement store, and a collection of smaller specialty stores. Depending on the demographics of the region, the larger of these shopping centers could probably support one bookshop. Rents are lower than in regional shopping malls. National book chains are now locating more and more branches in these community centers because fewer large regional malls are being built. It is easier, however, for the independent to secure space in this type of center than in the large regional mall. Because these smaller centers are almost always open air, they are subject to the vagaries of weather, which can have an effect on foot traffic. Foot traffic is a major ingredient in high volume and should always be considered in any location.

Strip centers are most often located along busy major thoroughfares exposed to heavy automobile traffic. These contain between three and a dozen stores on average with no major or very large shops. Convenience stores are frequent tenants of strip centers. Each outlet in such a center pulls its own customers. People drive in for definite merchandise and, having obtained it, depart. There is not much shopping or browsing, not much impulse buying, in a strip center. Because there is little or no foot traffic and because of the independence of each tenant, occupancy costs are generally lower in strip centers than in either regional or community malls.

Free-standing stores are single stores. If they have good visibility along a major highway or on a busy street, and if the access to them is easy with plenty of parking, they are a viable location. Many large retail chains choose this type of location for their branches. Large companies rent or build their own buildings, devoting the entire space to their operation. A small independent bookseller should probably rent in the beginning, especially if this is a first business venture, though there are advantages to owning one's own property. Free-standing store space has to be large enough for the best selection of books in the area in order to attract customer traffic all by itself. It has to look good enough to bring in people driving past. A reputation for inventory and knowledgeable staff is essential to pull customers into a free-standing location. Because so much depends upon the business acumen of the retailer in a free-standing store, rents are usually on a par with those of the community or strip centers. If purchasing the building is the only way to obtain it, and if that is indeed the best location for the proposed bookstore, then professional guidance is needed for the investment of capital as well as for the potential success of the business.

Central business districts in cities and towns, large and small, are the "downtown" areas that were the major shopping areas in America before the development of malls. With that development, many central business districts deteriorated and many of the major stores moved out and into malls. There were those that survived the change in shopping habits and have continued to thrive. Others have been rehabilitated and revitalized in varying ways, adapting some of the merchandising style of the malls while maintaining their own individuality. These districts, especially those that have either kept shopper attraction or have redeveloped it, should be explored by the prospective bookseller. Notice if the other specialty stores in the area appear to be successful. Pay attention to the other buildings in the area. Are they office buildings with large populations of potential customers? Are there residential areas nearby? Popular restaurants? Rents in these central business districts run the gamut from very low to almost as high as the regional malls, depending upon the traffic and the profitability of stores already established there.

Specialized locations can be anywhere. Booksellers have opened stores in extraordinary locations that for a number of reasons appeal to large groups of buyers who get to that store by whatever means is necessary. These stores are in office buildings (and not just in the lobby, but on high-up floors), in apartment complexes, amusement and entertainment areas, and national parks. Some of them serve as tourist attractions as well as catering to a permanent population.

What are the kinds of demographic statistics one should accumulate when analyzing potential market areas?

Numbers of people. The more people residing or working in the region, the more potential readers and buyers there are.

Ages, income, and education levels. These give clues to the percent of the population that might be buying books. Market studies show that most book buyers are between the ages of twenty and fifty, in the medium- to high-income level, with some years of college education and higher. Obviously all statistics are only guidelines. The caliber of a local school system, the support of the public library, and the interests of a population can have as much bearing on book buying as income and age. There are book markets of only fifty thousand people that support two bookstores better than other communities of a hundred thousand or more. Knowing the people in one's market area is exceedingly important, first as a group and then as individuals.

Market trends. Is the community or market area growing? What kinds of people are moving in? Do people seem to stay for a long time in the area, or is it a transient community? Are the prices of real estate increasing? Is the overall feeling one of improvement or deterioration? What kinds of businesses are opening nearby? Where do the people in the area do their major shopping, their specialty shopping?

Type of market. Is it mainly a residential community, a college or university city, an area of office buildings, or a combination of these? Is it a daytime-only or a round-the-clock business area? Does it have a high percentage of executive-, professional-, managerial-type people? What is the local library situation?

The answers to these questions can give evidence of the need (or lack of need) for a bookshop, how large such a store might be, and the kind of books and other merchandise it should stock. If one is going to specialize, data showing the need for books in the proposed specialization should be sought. Specialization implies a greater market area than that usually served by the general store. This is explored in some depth in chapter 27.

Demographic information can be obtained from many sources: the Department of Commerce at both state and federal levels, the public library, regional planning departments, the local Chamber of Commerce, real estate offices, banks, and other community sources. Magazines and periodicals are also helpful, especially when relating to a specialized market. Local newspapers will reveal not only local concerns, but the level of sophistication in an area as well. Talking to the people who are already a part of the community is extremely useful. They can relate how they feel about what is available at the moment, what more should be available, and how they view the future for the immediate community.

The wide range of rents (from very low to very high, usually based on dollars per square foot leased, depending upon the type of market and shopping area and always on supply and demand) will have a bearing on where the prospective bookseller looks for space. As a rule, space costs increase annually. It is not always easy to find a good location at an affordable rent. Time should not be wasted looking at high-priced locations if money is limited. Assets to be used for investing in the enterprise plus the experience of the owner usually determine the class of store that might be opened. If money is no problem, every kind of location can be explored, including the high-rent districts. But with limited means, the classiest business locations and regional shopping malls are probably out of the question, and the search should be concentrated in neighborhood and community centers, business districts, free-standing stores, or strip centers. The specialist has greater freedom of choice with another set of traffic-building tools.

Usually the higher the rent, the greater the sales potential, all other factors being equal. An established bookseller with a solid reputation might open almost anywhere and pull people to that store. But a new entrepreneur should open in the best available, affordable, visible space that has foot traffic, easy access for automobiles, and a preestablished level of trade. Time is needed to build a clientele that may change its shopping pattern once it gets to know and appreciate the new store but has to be enticed in the beginning by convenience. Convenience means being where shoppers come for other things or where there is no problem parking, where they can easily "just run in."

Costs may dictate acceptance of a second or third choice rather than what appears to be the best-available site. It is important that the new bookseller not put most of the available money into rent, fixtures, and equipment. Inventory is what will be sold; investment in inventory is essential. A third-choice site that allows for a first-rate inventory would be the desirable option.

When evaluating locations, the number-one figure to bear in

mind is "estimated annual sales." What is the volume potential in a specific space of a specific size in a specific location? All planning and budgeting of cost of merchandise that will produce gross profit that will pay operating expenses and leave a net profit is based on the money produced by sales made during the year.

The next factor to keep in mind is the amount of space needed to achieve that volume. The two figures are matched against the total occupancy costs requested by the owner. Although some landlords charge a straight monthly total for rent, most retail space now has additional occupancy costs attached, such as taxes, mall and parking maintenance, center promotion, security, and so on. All of these shared costs, if they apply, are based on the square feet leased.

There is a tendency for new booksellers to overestimate the sales potential of a new bookstore, which leads quickly to cash-flow problems. The bookshop does not reach the sales projections, and the owner finds it difficult or impossible to pay expenses and buy new merchandise. It is best to be conservative when projecting sales for a considered site. Following are some examples of the relationship of sales to the cost of space on an annual basis:

SPACE SQ. FT.	SALES $	SALES $ SQ. FT.	RENT $	RENT $ SQ. FT.	RENT % TO SALES	REMARKS
900	125,000	139	7,200	8	5.8	Excellent
1,000	75,000	75	7,000	7	9.3	Fair
1,200	150,000	125	12,000	10	8.0	Good
1,200	100,000	83	12,000	10	12.0	Too high
1,800	200,000	111	25,200	14	12.6	Too high
2,500	500,000	200	50,000	20	10.0	Fair

A first-year rent goal depends on many factors, but a cost of 10 percent or less on sales is reasonable. Volume increases planned in the second and third years should reduce the percent figure. The first three examples in the table show acceptable figures. The fourth and fifth stores would have to struggle to come down to more reasonable and profitable ranges, while the largest operation will be in a safe range in a short time. Large-volume bookstores can usually increase sales much faster than small stores in the early years.

Some of the examples are straight rent with no extra charges. Two include additional-occupancy charges in the rent per square foot. Before figuring the rent percent to sales, one should be sure to know and include *all* costs for the space, which should be spelled out and itemized in exact detail in the lease.

When looking at possible locations, visit, inspect, and analyze existing competition in the area. Do not discard a location because there are other bookstores already in the market area—*if* the community being considered has the potential to support another store. You might feel you can provide a better bookstore or a different kind of bookstore. As a prospective bookseller, you might be thinking of a better selection of titles than that carried by the existing store, or customer service that would be superior, or greater book knowledge, or a specialty that would do quite well in that area. There are many reasons to open a bookstore in a market where another bookstore is already in operation. If three, six, or even more bookstores are already thriving in a large market, it is obvious they have helped each other develop book buyers, many of whom may come some distance just because of the variety of bookstores that exist there. Additional stores might open profitably in such an area. This is especially true in university locations with vast populations of students and academics.

There is no finite formula, but in regions of twenty to sixty thousand people, one to three stores would seem to suffice, depending upon demographics. In more densely populated areas, the number of possible bookstores increases.

A bookstore should be located with its potential customers in mind. Is it easy for them to reach when they want to? Is it safe after dark if the store is open in the evening as well as the day? Are adjacent stores open the same hours as the bookstore, so customers can accomplish several shopping errands at one time? Similarly, do other stores offer a variety of merchandise to fulfill multiple customer needs? Do your neighboring merchants do a good job of promotion, or if you are in a mall, is the mall professional at sales promotion? There are many desirable and undesirable characteristics in almost every site—and each should be considered.

While there is difference of opinion, it is generally believed a bookshop has a greater chance for success if it is located in a middle-class mall, center, or group of stores, rather than in an area that is exclusively high fashion, classy specialty and department stores. There are greater numbers of shoppers in the middle-class mall than in carriage-trade areas, and thus many more opportunities to sell books that are comparatively low-ticket items.

When the right site seems to have been located, walk into several nearby retail stores, ask for the manager or owner, introduce yourself, explain what you are considering, and ask for honest opinions. Also ask questions about that person's experience in the community, with customers, trends that have been observed in shopping habits, or the successes and failures of businesses. Ask what happened to the business that vacated the space you are considering. Obtain any and all information that will not only help make the decision on the location, but also be useful in negotiating with the landlord. Always go into any negotiation armed with as much information as possible.

Be patient when selecting the best site for a proposed bookstore, and be inexhaustible in determining its assets and liabilities. Location is critical to success. It is an early decision that most retail merchants must live with for a very long time. Wrong assumptions, incorrect analysis of demographics, the wrong type of store for a particular area, a combination of problems that conspire to reduce traffic and therefore sales—all can cause store failure or an early move that may be expensive and is certainly undesirable. Time and effort spent before the lease is signed can save money, time, and effort later. The right decision can be the first step toward a successful, profitable bookstore.

Chapter 4

Negotiating the Lease

ELIOT LEONARD

After you have chosen one or two good, affordable locations for a bookstore, the next step is to return to the owner or leasing agent of the preferred site to review earlier discussions, ask further questions, and enter into serious and exacting negotiation. The landlord's terms and conditions will be stated as the prospective tenant's requirements are explained. Initial landlord conditions and all of the tenant's requirements are seldom met, but the two parties working in good faith can usually understand each other's needs and come to mutually agreeable terms. If this agreement appears impossible, or if the landlord refuses to compromise in any way and the prospective tenant is being forced to forgo all of his or her specifications, it would be wise to put the discussion on hold and move into negotiation with the second-choice location. After all the discussions with both the first and second parties have been held, the decision has to be made as to which is going to be the better location for the store, considering the terms demanded by both landlords.

Once the decision has been made and agreement has been reached between landlord and tenant, a written lease is prepared by the owner or an agent. Because of its long-term impact on the business, this lease is the single most important legal document presented to a bookseller. It has to be inspected and analyzed with extreme care. This requires knowledge and experience. Investing in the services of a lease attorney, specialized accountant, or consultant should be considered part of the cost of beginning your business.

One presumes in such analysis that a lease will cover all the salient points discussed between lessor and lessee in reaching a verbal agreement, but it is surprising how many items may have been missed or misunderstood. Offer the professional an explanation of what is supposed to be in that lease, and he or she will be able to spot errors and omissions and help correct any mistakes. A formal lease is highly detailed and written in legalese. It should be checked out word by word, clause by clause. Once it is signed, changes cannot be made. Occupancy costs and the landlord's rules of operation become fixed and noncontrollable. Leases usually protect the landlord more than the tenant. This document, therefore, will weigh heavily on the potential profit of the bookstore.

It is important to keep in mind when inspecting the lease, before it is signed, that one can still negotiate. According to the old cliché, "The three most vital things to a bookstore are location, location, location." This overstates the case somewhat, and could be adapted to read, "The three most important things to do when working on a lease are negotiate, negotiate, negotiate." If the landlord has gotten to the point of offering a lease, he wants, and perhaps needs, that bookstore in his space. This helps the bookseller strive for more advantageous terms. It also helps to know how the owner/agent negotiates, so you might know how much to ask for and how realistic some concessions might be. Having a second location in mind is an asset at this time because it makes the tenant bolder in negotiating and the landlord aware that the bookseller is not dealing from weakness or desperation nor quite signed-up.

Owners cannot always be flexible on rental costs, but they can adjust leasehold improvements and renovations, starting date for rent, tax and utility charges, and so on. Rarely should the prospective tenant accept these clauses as they appear in the first draft of the lease.

Following are a number of items and terms that should be covered in most leases. If they are not in the written document offered by the landlord, the bookseller should decide the importance of each and which should be included in the revised lease.

Make sure you have a description of the location, its exact location, and its size and space configuration (preferably with a site plan, dimensions, and indicated relationships to adjoining stores). A tenant has to know the exact square footage if rent and other charges are to be based on space used. Be sure no part of the space to be rented is to be used by others. Be sure areas such as hallways, outside stairs, restrooms and the like, which are used by others, are not included in the leased square footage. Space should be measured from inside the site walls, not the outside dimensions. Do *not* allow an alternate space clause in case the desired space is not ready on time. Try not to rent space next to tenants who might play loud music continually, which would be disturbing to book browsers. Stay away from space under or over a restaurant, where the potential for water or smoke damage is above average.

Time of lease is essential. The starting and ending dates for a bookstore occupancy must be listed. When does the rent start, and are you to be charged the full rent if the space is in a location where all construction is not completed? What are the options for renewal? How much notice is required for renewal and nonrenewal? Consider how much notice is necessary for the bookseller if the landlord does not intend to renew the lease. Rent should not begin until the day the bookstore opens, which means make-ready time should be spelled out in the lease. Beware of penalty clauses if the bookstore does not open on schedule. Have a clause to cover the extra expense involved if the owner does not turn over the space on the date promised. This cost can be considerable if inventory has to be received elsewhere and transported. Try not to have the lease expire on December 31 or June 30, because both December and June are good selling months and should not be spent preparing a move. Two final thoughts on time of lease: First, the tenant should not have to pay a penalty if the store is closed by fire or flood or even sales lower than expectation. Second, there should be a clause protecting the tenant's occupancy rights if the property is sold.

Total occupancy costs should be spelled out, item by item and figure by figure. These include basic monthly and annual rent, all other payments to be made to the landlord for services provided, and other prorated charges. The tenant should know at the beginning if an extra percentage of rent is to be paid when the business reaches a certain volume. The tenant should aim in this case for a low-percentage and a high-percentage break so that future total rent paid annually will decrease as a percent of projected sales. It is also imperative that both landlord and tenant agree on the definition of gross sales. Discounted employee purchases, charitable donations of merchandise, and credits and refunds to customers should be deducted from gross sales.

The rent due date should be spelled out, as should the tenant's responsibility for real estate taxes. If the tenant does have to pay a portion of those taxes, the lease should state how that portion is figured. Similarly, merchant association fees if there is such in a mall and charges for upkeep of the mall, its parking areas, and other public facilities should all be clearly spelled out in a lease. All such charges should be based on actual square footage used as a percent of the owner's total space and not as a percentage of the owner's total occupancy.

Avoid a C.P.I. (Consumer Price Index) clause or an inflation clause that would increase the rent as the index rises; if such a clause is insisted upon by the landlord, it is wise to have a maximum figure stated in the lease. This is especially important if there are other rent increases built into the lease, such as real estate taxes. After compiling all charges, it is a good idea to figure the total estimated occupancy cost for the next three years in relation to planned sales, to know that these costs are acceptable and reasonable. A last tip on rent: When locating in a new center that is not yet fully occupied, it is sometimes possible to put off paying full rent until the center is 80 or 90 percent occupied and open for business.

Effective, efficient use of space is essential if a business is to thrive. Prospective tenants should check before signing any lease for restrictions on space use. The business should be able to receive, process, sell, display, and store any merchandise to be sold. In the case of a bookstore, sidelines such as magazines, calendars, and other book- and communication-related items frequently sold in bookstores should be allowed. Be sure the lease allows the sale of both new and used books. The lease should not preclude the use of the store space for book fairs, authors' parties, meetings, and other promotional events. The lease should not restrict the space to be used within the rented area for office and storage, though of course the bookseller will maximize selling space. The rules regarding signs and their placement, both within the store and on the storefront, should be detailed if there are any restrictions that might hamper the bookseller's need.

Insurance and liability will be covered by both the lessor and lessee; therefore the lease should state exactly what responsibility lies with which party. Specific areas to be considered include fire, flood, personal and public accident, store interiors and common areas, building walls, and roof. The bookseller will need insurance on merchandise, vandalism, business interruption, and theft of money. Both personnel and customers should be insured for in-store accidents. Have the lease state who pays for a leaky roof, damage caused by adjacent tenants, and damage due to natural causes.

Leasehold improvements are, among other things, what the bookseller will do to make the store space ready for the merchandising of books and other items. As an addendum to the paragraph above, the lease should explain the warranty of leasehold improvements, those provided and paid for both by the landlord and the tenant. These would include plumbing, air conditioning, electrical work, and so on. If the location is newly constructed, the landlord might offer anything from a space ready for fixtures to a bare slab and equally bare walls, or part of the necessary leasehold improvements, sometimes including partial utilities. No matter how much the landlord will do, or what has been done already, the new tenant will have to spend money to bring the site up to desired specifications. The important point in this discussion is to know what is needed to operate the store and who will pay for it. This is one of the most highly negotiable areas of leasing, and the prospective bookseller should always take full advantage of it.

If the tenant has to plan and pay for space renovation and construction, the landlord might negotiate on a dollar allowance per square foot. The landlord might be happy to be rid of the actual work and, pleased at the prospect of a successful new tenant, might come through with a sum to help toward the work. If this is the case, he will want to approve the working plans. In any event, the landlord will want to know what renovation plans the tenant has for the space being rented. The tenant should always have a good idea of the total costs of planned leasehold improvements before signing a lease.

Other lease items to be checked include restrictions on subleasing, zoning restrictions, use of common areas, change of bookstore ownership, and change of ownership of building. A lease may be as simple as two or three pages, especially if it is a free-standing building, or a storefront in a block of stores, in which case there would not be the need for as many of the items that have to be covered in a mall or shopping center lease. But it is always important to include in writing as much information as possible in all areas of potential conflict. Therefore, even a basic lease could run for ten or twenty or more pages. All facts relating to financial matters are significant and should be put in writing. Who, for instance, approves and pays for future increases in common-area charges or for general building improvements? Are there caps on increases of any kind or maximums stated? How are prorated charges related to store space? It could make a great difference.

What deposits are required (for security, for instance), and are they refundable? Who holds these deposits, and is interest paid on them? What financial records must the bookseller keep for the landlord, and how often will they be inspected? Conversely, will the owner's records relating to pro-rata and special assessments be open for the bookseller's inspection?

Is the landlord committed to promoting the stores in the mall, strip, or business area? How often? Is the tenant bound by the lease to advertise, and to what extent? If there is a real estate broker's commission involved in obtaining the space, who pays it?

If you are not totally positive about a location, it is wise to insist on an "out" clause during negotiations. This would state that the tenant can leave without penalty after one or two years if sales and/or profit do not reach an agreed-upon level. The landlord in turn may want a clause allowing the bookseller's removal if the bookstore does not seem to fit into the retail property plan or is not producing sufficient income after an agreed-upon period of time. A first lease should not be for more than three or a maximum of five years anyway, with an option to renew under reasonable rental terms.

Contracting for store space is a detailed and time-consuming project. It must not be hurried, and professional assistance should be sought. The landlord usually has the advantage, unless you are looking to locate in a declining business area or one that for a variety of reasons has numerous vacancies. However, the bookseller should be looking for the best space affordable and therefore should not hesitate to inform an owner that bookstores, according to national surveys, lead all other specialty-type retail stores in attracting people to a business area. Although a bookstore may not be able to reverse a decline in an area, it can speed up renewal. The bookseller should look for the best space for the type of bookstore desired, and then go after it.

A final tip: Do not spend any money on a location, or on any of the leasehold improvements, until the lease is signed, no matter how firm an oral agreement might seem. Once the lease is signed the race can begin, and it will usher in the busiest six months in the new bookseller's experience.

Chapter 5

Legal Concerns

MAXWELL LILLIENSTEIN

Because of the differences in the laws of each state and the proliferation of new laws both on state and federal levels, only an outline of legal concerns is possible. Although this chapter explores typical questions involving the opening and operating of a bookstore, it is not intended to be a substitute for legal counsel. Only your lawyer can supply the legal specifics applicable in your state and to your particular situation.

This chapter has been designed to help the independent bookseller with the problems of opening a first or second store. For that reason, many considerations that would be applicable to a chain or a department store have been omitted from this discussion.

To Buy or to Start from Scratch

Presumably, the reader will not be ready to consider legal questions until the decision is made, hopefully after attendance at an ABA Prospective Booksellers School, that he or she has sufficient capital, motivation, and knowledge for the successful operation of a bookstore. The aspiring bookseller must then make a definite decision—whether to start from scratch or to buy an existing business.

A novice in any business is all too likely to make critical mistakes regarding such preliminary concerns as site location, length of start-up period during which the business will operate at a loss, and amount of capitalization necessary in order to reasonably ensure profitability at a future date. Nevertheless, building a business from scratch is certainly the most satisfying way of succeeding, and many do take this approach. In such an event, the prospective bookseller will wish to consider the following before determining the location:

- The applicable state and local income taxes (or their equivalent)
- Applicable personal property taxes, if any
- Applicable sales or occupancy taxes
- The possibility of obtaining the right kind of lease, maximizing tenant protection on a long-term lease, and minimizing liability in the event the venture fails (see section below on obtaining a lease)

For those wishing to purchase an existing business, with built-in goodwill, customer base, inventory, employees, and (it is hoped) profit, the following are questions that the bookseller in conjunction with his or her lawyer must ask.

Should I purchase assets or shares of stock in the corporation that presently operates the business?

Although there are certain advantages in purchasing shares of an existing corporation, these are, in the case of a small retail operation, invariably outweighed by the dangers inherent in such an approach. Anyone who purchases the shares of a corporate enterprise is also purchasing the liabilities of that enterprise—including some that may not be known to the existing owner. In such an event, it is best to provide limited protection to the purchaser by having the seller set aside a portion of the purchase price as a reserve against unknown liabilities (such as potential tax claims against the corporation). In addition, the seller of the shares should be asked to indemnify the purchaser against any such claims.

If I purchase assets, are those assets owned free and clear?

It is not uncommon for a retailer to purchase fixtures, racks, cash registers, and the like on terms that impose a lien on those items. The purchaser's lawyer will wish to make a search pursuant to the Uniform Commercial Code of that particular state to determine what liens may exist. The contract of sale of the assets should also contain representations and warranties by the seller to the effect that all assets are being sold free and clear of all liens except those specifically described in the contract.

*What are my rights and obligations under existing contracts
applicable to the store? Does the lease to the bookstore permit
the tenant to assign the lease or to sublet the space occupied
by the bookstore?*

If you are purchasing shares of a corporate tenant, the problem will
not exist since the corporation will continue as a tenant. However, as
it is more likely that you are purchasing assets, you will wish to be
certain that the lease contains a provision allowing the tenant to
assign it or to sublet the space. If the lease requires the written
consent of the landlord, as is often the case, you will wish to assure
yourself that the landlord will give such consent before entering into
the contract to purchase. After you are satisfied regarding the
transferability of the lease, you will wish to examine any other
service contract or contracts relating to assets being sold that affect
the bookstore.

What would be the best way for me to pay the purchase price?

If you are one of the lucky few who can buy a going business for cash
at no great financial sacrifice, do it. In most cases, you will wish to
purchase the business on an installment basis, presumably with a
down payment in the first year of less than 30 percent of the total
purchase price. In most cases where the business is being sold at a
profit, the seller will insist upon this approach. The balance of the
payout period will depend greatly upon the amount of the purchase
price, the respective bargaining positions of purchaser and seller,
and the profitability of the business.

In some cases, the payout may be partially contingent upon the
amount of future earnings. A purchaser who obtains such a provision in the contract of purchase has gained a valuable assurance that
the seller's representations regarding the profitability of the business
are reasonably accurate. Where possible, a purchaser should attempt to obtain the seller's personal assistance in connection with the
business for a reasonable transition period. You will then be taking
advantage of the seller's knowledge of the business and customer
contacts.

*Have I complied with the state laws requiring notice to
creditors?*

Your lawyer will seek to include in the contract purchase provisions
requiring compliance with the Bulk Sales Act as it applies to your
state (usually a section of the Uniform Commercial Code). The
principal requirements of such laws are to provide notices to the

creditors of the business that such sale is pending. If they do not assert claims against the assets being transferred within a specified period of time, your right to title to assets being conveyed is not endangered. Sometimes the provisions of the Bulk Sales Act are circumvented. However, in such event, an adequate percentage of the purchase price should be held in escrow for a reasonable period of time to be used to satisfy claims of existing creditors.

Should I obtain a noncompetition covenant from the seller?

If at all possible, the purchaser should obtain a provision in the contract restricting the seller from entering into a similar business in a geographical area within which the seller might effectively attract some of his old customers. Such a restrictive covenant should contain a provision setting forth the length of time as well as the geographical area in which the seller may not enter into a similar business.

Proprietorship, Partnership, or Corporation

The manner in which you structure your new business will have an effect on your financial liability, the type and amount of taxes you will pay, your credit rating, the continuity of the business after death, and many other important matters. Obviously, an enterprise that is started as a sole proprietorship or as a general partnership possesses the benefit of simplicity. Except for the requirement of filing a simple document (usually with the county clerk), reflecting the name of the bookstore and the name of the sole proprietor or partners, no other legal formalities are normally required. Unfortunately the potential cost of this simplicity may be greater than the aspiring bookseller suspects. For this reason, after you review with your lawyer the pros and cons of a proprietorship, general partnership, limited partnership, and incorporation, it is my guess that in three cases out of four you will decide to incorporate. These are some of the reasons:

Limited liability. When you run a business through the artificial personality of a corporation, you are limiting your liability to the assets owned by the corporation. If the corporation should become insolvent, its creditors may not look to you for payment. If, on the other hand, you operate as a sole proprietor or as a general partnership, you may be exposed to unlimited personal liability in the event of such insolvency. Of course, if the corporation does not have sufficient assets, creditors may insist upon personal guarantees from the principal shareholders before extending credit to the corporation. However, after a reasonably good track record has been established, creditors will generally be willing to extend credit to the corporate entity without requiring a personal guarantee.

Continuity. A sole proprietorship usually ends when the proprietor dies. By law, a general partnership ends when a partner dies or withdraws from the partnership. A corporation can be created so as to go on forever, despite the death of an owner or the sale of all his or her shares. Furthermore, if the principal of the corporation wishes to bequeath the bookstore to certain individuals, the corporate structure provides maximum flexibility for the bookseller wishing to divide the interest in his store among relatives, business associates, or employees.

Tax advantages. If you are starting from scratch, your attorney or accountant will probably advise you to form a Subchapter S corporation. Under the Internal Revenue Code, such a corporation may be permitted if it has fewer than ten shareholders at the outset. The advantage is that the income or losses of the corporation flow directly to the shareholders, permitting them to include the inevitable first-year losses of a new business on their income tax returns. After the lean years have passed, the corporation may elect to be taxed as most corporations are. Keep in mind that taxable corporate income is defined as that profit remaining after the payment of all salaries, including the salaries of the principals. Thus, in most instances, a small corporation engaged in retail business will rarely be left with any significant taxable income at the end of the corporate fiscal year. It is possible, however, that after consulting with your accountant and/or attorney, you will retain the Subchapter S structure indefinitely so as to avoid a double tax, first on corporate income and then on your own corporate salary.

Transferability of shares. One of the major advantages of a corporation is the ease of transferring interests in such an entity. A shareholder need only sell some or all of his or her shares and deliver endorsed stock certificates, reflecting such sale, to convey his interest. If there is to be more than one principal in the corporation, you will unquestionably wish to discuss with your lawyer the advisability of a shareholder buy-out agreement. Such an agreement typically deals with the terms of any eventual buy-out, possible options to the surviving principal or principals to purchase the shares of the decedent from the estate of a deceased shareholder, an employment agreement relating to the terms of employment of the principals, and provisions ensuring that the principals will continue to remain as directors and officers of the corporation.

What to Look for in a Lease

Booksellers opening a new store will in most cases be doing so as a tenant. These are the lease provisions that you and your attorney should be concerned with when negotiating a lease or taking an assignment or sublease from an existing tenant.

Rental. The rental provision is of primary interest. Obviously, the amount of the base rental must not exceed the bookseller's budget. However, in many store leases, you will find provisions that increase the basic rent under certain circumstances. One of the most common provisions, in this inflationary era, is an escalator clause that will increase the rental to the tenant in proportion to future increases in the landlord's obligations to pay real estate taxes and/or labor costs and/or other operating costs relating to the maintenance of the building. Such escalator clauses must be examined very carefully by an attorney since they are typically phrased in such convoluted legal jargon that even experienced real estate lawyers must review the provisions with extreme care. If a store is located in a shopping center or like location, the rental may be based in part upon gross receipts of the store, gross sales, or some similar formula. Such a percentage lease is loaded with potential legal snares and must be examined carefully by an experienced lawyer. Finally, there are various obligations imposed upon a tenant that, under the terms of the lease, may be defined as "additional rent." These may include the obligation to name the landlord as "additional insured" on the tenant's liability and/or fire and extended coverage policies, an obligation to pay the landlord's real estate taxes, an obligation to make certain repairs (typically the landlord will agree to make only structural repairs), and an obligation to pay for plate glass insurance coverage. The list of items that may be included in a lease as "additional rent" is not exhaustive. The bookseller and lawyer should scrutinize the terms of a proposed lease to be sure that the basic rent and all items of "additional rent" fit within the bookseller's budget.

Use clause. Every lease contains a section, usually in the beginning, defining the use to which the space may be put. In the case of a lease to a bookstore, the landlord will normally insert a provision permitting the use as "a bookstore and related purposes." At first blush this may seem perfectly satisfactory. However, since bookstores have been merchandising an increasingly large number of wares other than books, the ideal use clause would be one reading substantially as follows: "Bookstore and related purposes or any other use not inconsistent with applicable zoning laws and landlord's certificate of occupancy." If you cannot get such a broad clause, make sure to obtain a provision enabling you to use the premises for the sale of a wide variety of products other than books (such as records, cassettes, computer software, gifts, greeting cards, novelty items, and games).

Terms. Ideally you should seek a reasonably long-term lease coupled with limited liability to you in the event your business fails. One way to accomplish this is to incorporate and refuse to sign any personal guarantee that the corporation shall perform its obligations under the terms of the lease. Another way to achieve the same end is to insert a clause permitting the tenant to terminate upon some reasonable notice. Frequently the landlord will favorably consider such a clause only if the tenant agrees to pay a penalty (usually referred to as "liquidated damages") in the event such option to terminate is exercised.

If possible, you should seek an option to renew, especially if the landlord is reluctant to give you a long lease. Understandably, landlords are reluctant to grant such options to renew and will only do so if they have a weak bargaining position or if the basic rental for the renewal term is set at a substantially higher rate. So long as the amount of the basic rental for the renewal period involves an increase of not more than 6 to 8 percent per year of the primary term, you may consider the rental for the option period as reasonable. Remember, it is an option that you need not exercise unless you wish to. Remember also that the rate of inflation was in double digits not long ago.

Sublet and assignment. You will wish to pay careful attention to this clause, especially if the lease is long-term and you are personally liable on it. If your business goes sour, you will want the opportunity to sublet or assign the lease, thereby relieving yourself of the burden of paying rent for the balance of the term of the lease. If the landlord refuses you the right to sublet or assign indiscriminately, at the very least you should insist upon a clause that provides that the landlord will not "unreasonably withhold its consent to a sublet or assignment." You should also strive to insert a clause giving you the right to assign the lease in the event of the sale of the business. Otherwise, when the time comes to sell and a purchaser insists on purchasing the assets rather than the shares of your corporation (for reasons set forth above), you may lose a possible sale of the business if the lease does not contain a provision enabling you to assign it or sublet.

Miscellaneous. Entire books have been written on the subject of commercial leases: this section cannot be exhaustive. Other clauses that should be considered in a proposed lease are those dealing with fire and other casualties, security deposits, tenant's obligations to make repairs, tenant's right to install fixtures and make other interior and exterior changes with or without the landlord's consent, and tenant's right to reasonable notice in the event landlord alleges a default on the part of tenant.

Insurance

Whether or not the lease requires you to do so, you should carry adequate fire and extended coverage, general liability, and plate glass insurance. In selecting a liability insurance policy, you should discuss with your insurance broker a policy broad enough to protect you against the claims unique to the book business. For example, be sure that the policy protects you against claims based upon the allegedly libelous contents of the books you sell and claims to the effect that a purchaser following the instructions in a do-it-yourself book may have sustained injuries. Such claims are unusual, but they do occur.

Opening a Second Store

Almost everything discussed above is equally applicable to the opening of a second store. With respect to the desirability of incorporating, however, I cannot urge too strongly the incorporation of the second store as a separate corporation. Remember, the second store will most likely be run in whole or in part by you, an absentee owner. This increases the risk of an early demise. Without incorporating, you may find yourself in the shattering position of having established an extremely profitable first store only to see it being sold at auction to pay the creditors of the second store, which has not been structured as a separate corporation.

The foregoing is intended only to give the reader a working knowledge of the principal legal problems to be faced when opening a bookstore. It is no substitute for sound legal advice, tailored to your individual needs. When you are ready to open a store, see your lawyer. It may be the most important investment you make in your new business.

Chapter 6

Insurance and Protection

ADRIEN V. LORENTZ

Every bookstore needs protection from loss resulting from theft, fire, burglary, illness, accident, embezzlement, or even death. The kinds of insurance policies necessary to cover all these contingencies are numerous, perplexing, and sometimes expensive. The purpose here is to give the bookseller an overall view of the types of policies that are available, pointing out the necessity of some policies, the advisability of several others, and the comparative value of those discussed. Not every bookstore will need, or be able to afford, all the types of insurance described in this chapter, but having more knowledge than necessary never hurt anyone.

Property Coverage

Property can mean a whole list of things: the building in which your store is located, inventory, fixtures, machinery, office equipment, personal property of the insured, or personal property of others. The perils to be insured against likewise can encompass a whole list of eventualities: fire, smoke, wind, water, lightning, vehicle explosion, riot, strikes, or malicious mischief.

When you consider property coverage, the value of your property is important. There are three ways to assess this value: you can have the work done by a professional appraiser; you can employ the services of the insurance company's appraiser; or you can do it yourself (perhaps with the help of your accountant) on the basis of your own records. Choose the method that is most advantageous to you, but be sure that your agent is in agreement before you proceed. With regard to book inventory, it should be decided whether to insure at retail or at cost, and that decision should be specified in your policy. It is also a good idea to recalculate the value of your inventory at least once a year so that you know whether to increase your coverage. Just after you have taken inventory or while your accountant is working on your tax returns is a good time for such a reevaluation. Also, consideration should be given to increasing your coverage during your peak seasons—before Christmas, for example, or during the summer months if you happen to be in a beach resort community.

Standard fire policies insure for the actual cash value of the property at the time of the loss. That means the cost of the repair or replacement, less any depreciation.

Fire and property damage policies often contain a *coinsurance clause*, which specifies that the amount of insurance must be equal to a specified percentage of the full property value. With this clause—usually 90 percent of full value—any covered loss will be paid up to the face value of the policy. You have the option to be covered by a lesser amount, but payment will be made for only that portion of the loss determined by the ratio of insurance carried as against the maximum amount that could have been carried.

For example, if your property were valued at $100,000 with a 90 percent coinsurance clause, you could recover up to $90,000. If, however, you elected not to pay for so much insurance and were covered for 60 percent, your recovery in case of loss would be six-ninths of the loss up to $60,000. It is usually wise, if you can afford it, to be insured for the maximum amount allowed in the clause.

Another valuable clause to understand is the *waiver of subrogation*. Simply stated, this means that should a fire or similar damage occur on your premises and spread to another property adjacent to yours, your insurance would cover that loss also. In case of rental, such as in a shopping center, the landlord will sometimes cover you for this. Check to be sure you are covered one way or another. If possible, at the time you are negotiating your lease, try to convince the landlord to provide the coverage, and have it written into the lease. Like so many other things in this world, you don't get what you don't ask for, and it never hurts to try. (See chapter 4, "Negotiating the Lease.")

Extended coverage. This clause is also important. We have been addressing the subject of fire insurance, but if you desire more extensive protection, you can add other perils, such as windstorm, hail, smoke or water damage, explosion, vandalism, and malicious mischief. These, and more, are all included in the extended coverage clause and can be added to the basic fire insurance at a relatively small additional cost. Your best buy may be one of the all-risk contracts that offer the broadest-available protection for the money.

Glass insurance. This is another type of coverage to be considered. In fact, the requirement to have this kind of insurance may be part of your lease. If possible, insist that your landlord have such coverage added to his insurance policy on your behalf at no added expense to you. It is, after all, his property he wishes to be assured will be repaired in case of damage. If that fails, you can purchase, and have added to your property insurance, special glass insurance that covers all risk to plate glass windows, glass signs, glass brick, glass doors, showcases, countertops, and insulated glass panels. You will be covered not only for the replacement cost of the glass itself, but also for the labor to install it, any damage to merchandise, and any costs incurred in boarding up the window until the repair is made.

Liability Insurance

The basic comprehensive general public liability policy covers the legal liability to any member of the public having cause to show bodily harm or property damage as a result of occurrences arising out of the operations, ownership, or use of someone's premises—a type of protection that is absolutely essential.

Although the policy is called comprehensive, certain situations are not covered by the basic policy unless they are specifically added by endorsement . . . and by additional payment, though this is usually a nominal additional premium:

Personal injury. This includes liability for claims resulting from false arrest, detention, or imprisonment, malicious persecution, libel, slander, or defamation of character, invasion of privacy, wrongful eviction, or wrongful entry.

Elevator collision. This provides coverage in cases of damage to elevator cars and property in an elevator as the result of the car's fall down the shaft or of supply trucks colliding with the elevator.

Automobile liability. This insurance is necessary if any automobiles or trucks are used in your business, whether you own, rent, or borrow them. Medical coverage is also recommended as part of this package. Although it is possible to get this coverage under a single automobile policy, it is definitely preferable to request that it be added to your comprehensive liability policy, thereby saving some money.

Contractor's operation. This will cover the bookseller's liability arising from operations performed by painters, window cleaners, or other independent contractors, if this liability is not covered by the contractors themselves. It is therefore important to obtain "certificates of insurance" from all contractors, covering not only their general liability, but also their workers' compensation and automobile liability.

In order to avoid increasing the limits of liability in all your primary policies, an *umbrella* policy can be purchased. Such a policy is designed to provide $1 million or more (no longer considered high or unreasonable even for a small business) per loss of the excess over all underlying policies. Moreover, it covers nearly all exposures to loss that are not included in the underlying policies, but this feature is subject to a deductible of $1,000 or more.

The advisable amount of liability coverage varies with your net worth and the amount of your financial exposure. The large sums awarded recently in some bodily injury cases suggest it is wise to carry a high limit in this policy. The cost of higher protection is not great compared to the risk involved.

Miscellaneous Coverages

There are numerous other forms of insurance that cover risks the bookseller may encounter. Often budget restrictions will limit your ability to buy these policies, but it is good to know what is available, should the need present itself.

Loss of earning and extra expense. Loss of earning will pay for loss of net profits owing to damage from such things as fire, sprinkler leakage, and vandalism. Extra expenses coverage allows a bookseller to operate in another location without loss of income but at a greater cost.

Valuable papers and records. Accounting records, contracts, and general business papers can be covered if damaged or destroyed. This usually pays only for the blank material or labor required to transfer damaged records, not for the cost of research and preliminary work, which may be covered by an all-risks valuable papers and records policy.

Crime insurance. This includes burglary, robbery of monies, forgery, and embezzlement whether by employees, customers, or professional thieves.

Accounts receivable records. Loss of income resulting from inability to collect outstanding accounts because of damage or destruction of the records of accounts receivable from almost any cause may be covered under a special policy.

Fine arts. Some stores have rare books or valuable paintings and other art objects that would be insured partially under business fire insurance policies. Frequently such objects have enhanced value beyond the actual cost of reproduction (in case of fire loss) and may also be subject to other perils, such as breakage and water damage, that are not covered by the basic fire insurance contract.

Package Policy

It is often advisable to incorporate into one package policy all the necessary insurance protection of fire, extended coverage, and general liability. This one policy can also include crime, vandalism, sprinkler leakage, water damage, and valuable papers and records insurance. Many of these extras are included at little cost in this type of package, whereas if purchased separately, they could easily be too expensive to consider. Not only may the coverages overlap, but some of the charges to you might be duplicated.

Parcel Insurance

One other type of insurance used by bookstores, and until recently not questioned, is postal or delivery insurance, incoming and outgoing. Most publishers ship FOB their warehouses. This means that the bookseller is responsible for the package after it leaves a publisher's warehouse. Publishers usually add the cost of insuring the package to the freight costs. Some leave you an option to refuse this additional cost, but you are then responsible if the books are not delivered.

The high cost of the U.S. Postal Service book rate plus insurance costs have caused booksellers to look for alternative sources in private insurance companies. There are companies that will insure all shipments with a blanket policy.

Workers' Compensation

Workers' compensation is legally required by most states. The standard workers' compensation policy is divided into two sections.

Coverage A offers statutory weekly indemnity, medical reimbursement, and other benefits according to the workers' compensation and occupational disease laws of the various states. These benefits are payble if the employee becomes involved in an accident arising out of and in the course of employment, whether such accidents occur in or out of the employer's premises.

Coverage B offers coverage of the employer's legal liability for work-connected injuries that are not compensable under the various state laws, such as a permanent injury that does not prevent the employee from pursuing his normal work. It also covers suits against the employer by third parties who may have been held responsible for injuries to an employee, contending that the employer was negligent. Coverage B normally has a limit of $100,000, except in certain states where the insurance companies are not permitted to limit this to a fixed amount. Wherever it is so limited, it is suggested that the basic $100,000 be increased to $500,000 for an additional premium.

Employee Benefits

Employee benefits are an aid to keeping qualified personnel. Included are:

Group life insurance. This coverage is usually written as annual renewable term insurance and can be combined with accidental death and dismemberment insurance. When written at group rates, it is very reasonable. It should be noted that if you pay group insurance premiums and cover all employees up to $50,000, the cost to you is deductible for federal income tax purposes, yet the value of the benefit is not taxable income to your employees.

Medical benefits. With the high cost of medical and hospital bills, a group plan covering such expenses is an incentive for acquiring and retaining good personnel. A basic hospital-surgical benefit plan with supplemental Major Medical coverage, as represented by the standard Blue Cross/Blue Shield plan, is the most common.

There is also available comprehensive medical coverage, usually with a $100 deductible, that offers protection against the potential financial drain of a long or serious disability. Many commercial companies offer these plans. Explore this field in depth; coverages and costs vary greatly. Any benefits should be carefully integrated with the benefits payable under Social Security or workers' compensation to avoid excessive benefits and keep costs at a minimum.

Accident and sickness insurance. Some states have mandatory nonoccupational disability benefit laws that require employers to provide basic benefits for lost time caused by accident or sickness. If your state does not have such laws, voluntary group accident and sickness policies are commercially available and recommended.

Business life insurance. A business life policy covering key personnel, whether a corporate officer, a partner, an individual proprietor, or a manager, should be considered as an additional protection of your investment. The proceeds can be used to help bolster the firm's credit, retire the stock interest of the deceased executive, and finance the search, selection, and training of an adequate replacement. Proceeds of this type of policy are not subject to income tax, but premiums are not a deductible business expense. Also, the cash value of business life insurance (also known as "key-man" insurance) accumulates as an asset of the business and can be borrowed against, and the interest and dividends are not subject to income tax as long as the policy remains in force.

Key-man insurance covering business expenses incurred by the absence of a proprietor due to illness should also be investigated.

Pensions and Profit Sharing

A pension plan assures employees that when they reach the end of a productive career, there will be adequate retirement benefits to permit them to live out their retirement with financial security. Pensions and profit-sharing plans are helpful if the business is large enough to support and sustain the expense. Any incentive like this is definitely a plus for employees. Here again, the advice of an expert in the field is essential in the formation of a good plan. Individual Retirement Accounts (IRA) can be established by an employer if employees are not covered by a qualified retirement plan.

How and Where to Buy Insurance

With all the aforementioned insurance policies and benefit plans, you may wonder how much insurance you, the bookseller, should buy to get protection and how much you can afford. Don't become insurance poor. Insurance is a gamble, and any amount purchased is based on expectation of the possibility of a loss. Your decisions should be made in light of all your particular circumstances and with the advice of competent experts.

Insurance agents, as mentioned before, are a variable. Know your agent and the companies to which he assigns you. There are two kinds of agents. One is the independent insurance agent, who is actually a broker representing several companies; the other is the company agent, who is employed by a single company or insurance group and sells policies only from that one company. The agent broker has the advantage of being able to concentrate on your needs by placing your policies with whichever company offers the best deal for you. If you are now buying from a company man, ask an independent agent to detail a plan for you and compare.

Insurance companies have gained great wealth from betting the right way. They have the advantage of the fine-print clauses drawn up by experienced lawyers to protect their financial interests. In case of a loss, the home office expert will interpret the fine print for you. Will your agent be sufficiently knowledgeable and willing to protect your interest in case of a dispute on interpretation? Did he prepare a plan for you initially, and has he kept up with proper coverage based on any changes in your business? Is he actually aware of you and your business, or did he just take the order and collect the yearly commissions? Did he oversell you on nonproductive insurance? These are important questions to consider in your appraisal of an agent and your insurance program.

Insurance binders, usually verbal agreements of insurance coverage while a policy is being written, are useful when needed but are potentially dangerous. You are at the mercy of your agent if a loss should occur during the binder period. You are not sure of the conditions of your policy, which company covers you, and even if the policy was written before your loss. The obvious answer is to use the binder for as short a time as possible. Get your policy, and read the fine print before signing.

It is to be hoped that you will gamble correctly and have no losses; if not, remember the adjuster is not necessarily independent. He has worked with the insurance company before, not with you, so be sure your agent sees that you get a just and quick settlement. Lengthy settlements usually favor the company. It can wait, while you need the money at once to rebuild your business.

Get several bids on your insurance. There are plenty of agents looking for your business. Let the agent prove to you that he can give the best coverage at the best price. Don't necessarily go to a member of your club or a friend, for it is often difficult to do business with him when a loss occurs. He has loyalty to his company as well as to you, and more often than not his company will come first.

Don't hesitate to change agents or to ask for bids from other agents even if you have dealt with one person for many years. You are using insurance as a protection and are entitled to the most protection you can get for the least money. Shopping for insurance is like shopping for a new automobile. Remember that the price is important, but service is more so, and the cheapest deal is not always the best. Past history of quality service and mutual trust is difficult to match. If you are totally secure with your agent and have full confidence in him, don't change just for the sake of change.

Insurance, like most things, requires specialists. The best coverage in all fields cannot necessarily be obtained from one agency. Property damage, life, auto, liability and casualty, and health insurance are separately classified and require special knowledge in widely differing fields. Get your insurance from the person who has studied and mastered his field. Forget the part-time agent. Most insurance agents, like other businesspeople, are honest and sincere in their relations with their clients; however, their knowledge and connections vary widely. For life insurance, get an agent who has met the professional requirements for the Certified Life Underwriter (CLU) designation; for casualty, seek out the agent who has been awarded the Certified Liability and Casualty Underwriter (CLCU) designation. These people are pledged to a strict professional code of ethics and are respected by their companies and fellow agents as leaders in their respective fields. One last note: Read the fine print, and have it explained before you sign any policy. This can be tedious, but it is truly a necessity.

Business Security

Another form of protection other than insurance is business security. This is the basic commonsense application of measures to prevent break-ins and thefts. To secure your building and equipment properly, install modern dead-bolt locks on all outside doors, install bars on the insides of side and rear doors, provide adequate night lighting both inside and out, keep your safe secured to the floor and well lighted, keep a record of serial numbers of all equipment, and consider the installation of a burglar alarm.

The theft of books and money are serious problems and any measures, both passive and active, taken to prevent these occurrences are worthwhile. Such simple things as stamping all checks when received "For deposit" and keeping only small amounts of cash on hand should be obvious. The proper screening of employees for honesty is necessary; far too many books leave the premises out the back door with dishonest employees. The use of large mirrors or in-store television cameras to cover blind spots is sometimes a deterrent. However, the best form of theft protection is an alert staff attentive to everyone entering your store.

With carefully selected insurance and proper security measures, the bookseller can feel secure and devote his time and efforts to the problems that arise daily in this unique business.

Chapter 7

Bookstore Layout

KEN WHITE and CYD ROSENBERG

The overall appearance of a bookstore results from a number of factors, with the owner's desired image being only one of them. The final design will reflect the bookseller's personal taste as well as the image the bookseller wants the store to convey to potential customers. The physical aspects of the space to be occupied have to be considered, the dimensions both inside and out as well as the relationship of that space to other stores nearby. A site in a modern shopping mall offers very different challenges and possibilities from a site in a historic district. There are ordinances, local, state, and perhaps federal, that govern signs, exits and entrances, and many other things having to do with a retail store. These ordinances and all restrictions must be investigated before the first decisions are made affecting the design of the store.

In the pages that follow, Ken White, a professional designer, has much to say about all the considerations that go into planning a store's effective and efficient layout, the treatment of areas for different kinds of merchandise, and so on. But before anyone gets inside your store, what they see as they approach should have made it clear to them what they will find there. If a bookstore is to succeed, it should make an instant statement, a positive impact, both on the outside and on the inside. "Here is a store with a wide selection of the best current books in all categories!" Or "This is an intimate bookshop specializing in children's books!" Or "Here are books you might not find in most bookstores!" Whatever the bookseller's calculated plan to sell books may be, an important part of that plan is designing a storefront that will imprint itself upon the minds of prospective customers and pull them inside.

Everything about a storefront says something to passersby, from the color it is painted to its windows, sign, and entrance. All aspects contribute to or detract from its effectiveness as that store's most important, most constant, and probably longest-lasting advertisement. A storefront that is not kept clean and neat—even though it may be beautifully designed—says something negative to a customer. An old front gussied up with bright colors, an awning, perhaps, and maybe window boxes, says something positive. It isn't the investment that counts as much as imagination and attention to all the details that make up what your customers will see when they approach your store.

It is a common and valuable practice for a business to have its own logo, a design that has been created to become the established mark of that business. The logo is used in advertising and on store bags and stationery, and it should be incorporated in some way into the storefront, either as part of the sign or in some other fashion. The bookseller wants to obtain recognition of the logo early on, so that it will serve as a reminder whenever and wherever it is seen. McDonald's golden arches is a highly successful logo.

The outside of the store should reflect what is to be found inside. An old-fashioned front with flowers isn't going to lead successfully to a state-of-the-art store specializing in software and high-technology books. A glass-and-chrome exterior can lead to classic literature, if the inside is also glass and chrome and if with signs and effective window displays a customer is made aware that classics may be found within. Period is not as important as adaptation to the purpose. With imagination, either the bookseller's or that of professional designers, almost any materials can be used to attract the customers you want to attract—if it is all carefully planned in advance.

Once the customers have come inside, it is important that the exterior message conveyed be maintained and fulfilled. If the exterior has a strong personal stamp, then the interior should extend that personality, whether it be the personality of the owner or the special aspect of the merchandise. It is well to remember in every phase of planning a store that the more you can do not only to bring customers in, but to bring them back again and again, the greater your chances for success. In planning the physical plant, the exterior and the interior, make it a store that customers will want to come to. Make it a store they will think of first when they think of buying a book.

A simplified diagram of a bookshop would be a cube with two open ends: one would be for book and merchandise inflow; the other to attract customers. If the store is well planned, books and customers meet in the middle. The inflow of books and their control hold no mysteries that can't be solved by fluent organization. The inflow of customers, on the other hand, is a fine art involving not only planning ability, but also showmanship and psychology. The problems are the same for the smallest bookshop and the largest store; only the scale and emphasis vary. Specialized booksellers must not overlook the fact that there are basic planning principles that apply to every store.

Planning Principles

The basic function of a bookstore is to sell books. Plan from the inside out. It is only after interior spaces and equipment have been plotted and organized that a logical background exists for the design of a store's facade and entrance.

The customer's attention, however, as stated earlier, is first caught by the storefront. He is not exposed to the attractions of the sales floor until he is inside. Nor are customers aware of hidden service areas that are essential from the store owner's point of view.

The store planner's objectives, then, are

(1) to create an efficient, attractive environment within the bookstore in order to promote maximum sales;
(2) to integrate sales space with behind-the-scenes functional service areas that supply the merchandise;
(3) to attract customers into the sales space by means of an inviting storefront.

Unique Bookstore Planning Problems

Bookstores present unique planning problems because their customers are always browsing and on the move except at the actual point of sale and at the cash register. Store planners must give them a clear route from store entrance to interior sections of the sales floor. This central traffic artery should be planned so that customers can easily enter, browse, select, buy, check out, and leave. The whole pattern of sales departments should be arranged so that an attractive visual effect is obtained from any point in the interior as customers move through the store.

Each type of book requires its unique place in the bookstore plan, properly related to customer traffic routes, service departments, and other functional facilities. The first step in planning layout is to divide and locate the merchandise to be sold into three fundamental divisions on the basis of *impulse, convenience,* and *demand.*

As a rule, impulse items (including new arrivals and best-sellers) should be up front or in heavy traffic spots; convenience merchandise (such as backlist books) should be centrally located; and demand merchandise (reference books) should be at the rear. Store layout should require the customer to walk through as much of the store as possible to reach the item he plans to purchase. This will give the customer the opportunity to see other books and merchandise.

Impulse Buying

Although more and more attention in general retailing is being given to capturing impulse sales, the average bookstore barely scratches the surface of this opportunity to increase volume. Scientific store planning and merchandising take full advantage of every square foot of sales space to capitalize on impulse buying. The economic success of a store can depend on how well it stimulates impulse sales. If a store sold only demand or convenience merchandise that its customers planned to buy before they entered the store, it could soon be bankrupt. Buying surveys by one major bookselling chain have shown that more than 50 percent of all the book sales it rang up were impulse sales. This means that their customers made more than half their purchases without having planned to do so before entering the store.

Location of Merchandise

To make it easy for the customer to find a book or to shop for related merchandise, book categories and nonbook departments should be placed in logical relation to each other, in a shopping pattern that does its own suggestion selling: art near photography, history near sociology, cooking near hobbies and home repair, and so forth. The store planner can also increase sales by cross-merchandising departments—for example, athletic equipment in the sports book department, and live plants or packaged seeds in the gardening book department. There is an interesting and effective trend in the direction of minishop or boutique locations—a particular group of books or style of merchandise is collected from several departments in a visual merchandising presentation to appeal to a particular kind of customer. Even the smallest shop can be planned with this visual merchandising principle in mind. In larger stores it is one of the cornerstones of successful retailing.

Aisles and Circulation

The amount of aisle and circulation space planned for customers and staff depends on the type of bookstore. The size of the
sales floor will determine whether there has to be a single aisle or
several aisles. In a small bookstore, a straight, dead-end aisle may be
all that is possible. In bookstores with a larger floor area and more
complex merchandising programs, a centralized main aisle may
have branch aisles to disperse shoppers through the sales areas. If the
store is very large, the main aisle should be paralleled on one or both
sides by other aisles. These should be connected by a pattern of cross
aisles and by one or more main cross aisles.

Main aisles should allow some degree of aisle merchandising.
When this space exists, a sale table or tables can be placed in the
middle of the aisle. Aisles should be from three to five feet wide,
though they are frequently narrower by about 10 to 15 percent.

Customer comfort must be carefully considered when aisle
widths are determined. It is good for a bookstore to be crowded at
times, but a customer who is jostled and feels closed in will usually
want to get out of the bookstore as quickly as possible and may not
come back!

Vertical Movement

The problem of air circulation is of utmost importance for
stores having sales areas on several levels. Well-designed and inviting
stairs can overcome customer objections to walking up or down. One
device is to use mirrors in such a way that sales displays on the other
floors are visible all the way up or down. It is preferable that
stairways be placed about two-thirds of the way back in the selling
area, thus exposing most of the main floor before the customer leaves
it for another level. Local building codes and ordinances governing
stairs should be checked before any plan is finalized. Fire exits must
be planned so they lead directly to the exterior.

Cashier Stations

If at all possible, cashiers should be placed on the left side of the
entrance for small bookstores. Remember that traffic flows to the
right on the way in and does the same on the way out. Cashier
stations and service desks can create a lot of traffic disturbance
during rush hours if they aren't carefully planned. Bookstore policy
will dictate the functions and services of the cashier, but when the

basic function is to ring up transactions and make charges, small L-shaped minicheckout units or straight counters are satisfactory. Bookmarks and pickup sideline impulse sales can be handled at the cashier station if the bookstore retails any of these specialties.

Other service functions, such as receiving payment on charge accounts, making charges, special ordering, accepting telephone orders, layaway, and gift wrapping, require larger cashier stations. Very large stores may relegate these other activities to service desks located elsewhere in the bookstore.

Service Desks

Some nonselling functions, such as special order and information desks, can act as a magnet, drawing customer traffic to interior locations in the bookstore. Knowledgeable store planners purposely locate these customer services in the rear or even on upper or lower floors. Provisions must be made at service desks for microfiche readers, reference books, and all other necessary tools, as well as storage space for books and merchandise awaiting customer pickup, telephone, and the like.

Receiving and Stockrooms

The relationship of the receiving and marking room to the sales area is of utmost importance. It may be contiguous in a small bookshop or located three selling levels away in a very large store. Wherever possible, stockrooms, like receiving rooms, should be located immediately adjacent to the selling area.

Determining the size of the receiving room. If the receiving room is larger than necessary, space and equipment are wasted; if it is too small, errors, short tempers, and any number of crises are inevitable. How much receiving room space to allow will vary with the amount of inventory to be processed, the size of the bookstore, the variety of its merchandise, and the frequency of deliveries.

Since receiving room space is non-income-producing, it is essential to keep it to a minimum, but adequate space must be provided to open, unpack, count, check, and verify the price of incoming books and other merchandise. Provisions must be made to file shipping documents and process return shipments. A "hold" area for books and merchandise awaiting pricing or other processing is essential, as is storage space for a reasonable quantity of store bags, supplies, and used shipping cartons kept to facilitate returns.

Staff Lounge and Rest Rooms

Small bookshops generally have one rest room, a drinking fountain, and a coatrack or bank of employee lockers. Larger stores require greater amenities. A properly sized employee lunchroom, often with a kitchenette, drinking fountain, pay telephone, and coat lockers, is routine. Separate men's and women's toilet rooms with an employee nap or rest room are required by some local health and building codes. Few bookshops build special public rest rooms.

Basic Bookstore Plans

The concept for formulating the overall interior layout of the bookstore selling areas is based on statistical data, merchandise requirements, intuition, and professional experience. The most popular types of bookstore plans are the *open grid plan* and the *zone and cluster plan*.

The open grid plan. This consists of a completely open sales space surrounded by perimeter wall fixtures with center floor sales fixtures laid out in parallel and repetitive arrangements. Department divisions and selling fixtures are usually kept at or below eye level. If any of the sales equipment is high, it should be of a see-through type to permit visibility throughout the bookstore. The open grid plan concept is most commonly used by mall, chain, and general bookstores.

The main advantage of this concept is that it provides flexibility, lower building cost, good visibility, and an opportunity for merchandise exposure, cross-merchandising, and security for the entire selling floor. The main disadvantage of the open grid plan is that it restricts the opportunity to create a sense of place and atmosphere for book departments. As a result, we see disconnected merchandise relationships.

Raised galleries and podiums. The visual problem of the open grid plan, however, can be reduced by raising selected departments and merchandise classification to an appropriate height and onto a raised gallery, with levels varying from eight inches to four feet. Consecutive galleries, raised one level above the floor of the store, can also be used for greater efficiency in the use of space and to create more interesting plan arrangements. Merchandise capacity is increased and security is improved when a raised department is clearly separated from its neighbors. In large stores, galleries at the far ends of the space let you know where shoppers are. Customers on

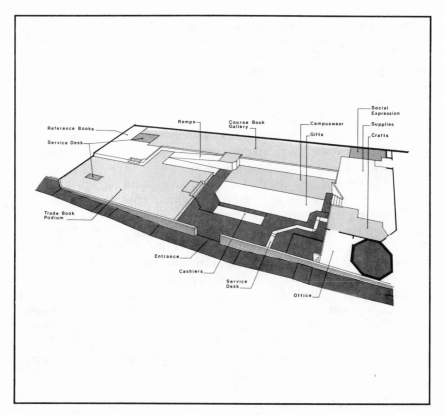

Fig. 7-1.   Raised galleries and podiums.
(Courtesy of Ken White Associates, Inc.)

the gallery also see the store and its merchandise from a different perspective, and the potential for visual selling is upgraded.

A side note on levels: Federal and many state laws require that wheelchair access be provided to all selling and service levels of some stores. It is a matter of consideration to use incline ramps with a ratio of one-inch rise to twelve-inch lengths and steps with safety handrails. This meets federal guidelines and provides functional customer access to the galleries. (See figure 7-1.)

The zone and cluster plan. The need for larger stores to provide some definition between major book categories and nonbook merchandise departments has led to the popularity of the zone and cluster plan. The concept is to cluster each major category of merchandise in zones around a central area threaded together by aisles moving traffic in a counterclockwise direction. Within each zone, related product categories are clustered to create special visual merchandising situations. This concept permits greater flexibility and latitude of design treatments in the individual zones. The concept works well with either perimeter or centralized service core stockroom plans.

The decision to locate merchandise in the front, center, rear, or sides of the store in the zone and cluster plan should be based on the need for the item to be exposed in a primary location for customer convenience, stock and capacity requirements, and the item's impulse sale value. High-impulse merchandise is best located in areas around entrances, service desks, and cashier stations, which are the most heavily trafficked and the places where customers congregate.

Departments with greater area demand and support requirements are usually placed farther from the entrance and on either lower or higher levels. The location of large departments or of convenience categories would fall into this consideration.

Nonselling facilities, such as administrative offices, service desks, employee facilities, and related areas, are always placed in secondary locations. The receiving department and stockrooms should relate to the sales area and to the accounting office to facilitate the flow of paperwork. The placement of nonselling areas will have a considerable effect on the shape and use of the selling departments that surround them.

Modernization Planning

The initial step in preparing a floor plan for existing space is to measure the exterior shell of the space, the location of the entrance, stairs, utility room, and so on. These measurements should be reduced to an existing condition drawing, rendered to scale. Where existing fixtures are to be used, they must be measured, surveyed, and plotted in on the plan drawing. Thus, the plan prepared will provide a clear view of the layout.

With careful, imaginative planning, extra stock capacity can usually be found for books and merchandise. Several of the techniques employed extend wall cases to the ceiling, thus increasing shelf capacity. Book and merchandise gondolas may be double-decked, and glass cubes can be built around columns. The use of book beams, the technique of extending stock shelving down from the ceiling to a height of seven or eight feet above the floor, adds an increased capacity and contributes to the character and image of the bookshop interior. (See figure 7-2.)

Occasionally wall cases are placed against the face of wall projections, such as HVAC (heating, ventilation, and air condition-

Fig. 7-2. Book beams.
(Courtesy of Ken White Associates, Inc.)

ing) ducts, building pilasters, pipes, and so forth, and considerable space can be gained by moving them flush against the building wall between the projections. Spaces between the fixtures can be equipped with appropriately selected slot-wall or slat-wall merchandise displays, which add to the selling power of the area. In other situations, these spaces can be covered with mirrors to stretch the size of the space visually.

It is occasionally feasible to develop additional storage space in a bookstore with a high ceiling by building a mezzanine stockroom directly above areas occupied by existing stockrooms. Constructing a balcony space over part of the selling area is another option.

How I Plan a Bookstore

I have given you a picture of how space is apportioned, methods for locating categories and departments within the store, and types of bookstore plans. The most practical way to help you understand the principles of the store planning process is to explain how I set about the job of planning a bookstore and, in passing, to say whether my methods differ greatly from others I know.

Block merchandise planning. I begin by making a breakdown of the space. This involves deciding how much area will be assigned to each selling and functional space within the overall area. This important step in the planning process involves the determination of the amount of wall shelving or hanging capacity that the blocked-out area will accept. The remaining space in the department is then calculated mathematically to determine the number of appropriate store fixtures the remaining area will contain, after provisions are made for customer and service aisles. This is where properly sized modular building column bays become so important. There is a school of planning that skips this step and goes directly to the layout and arrangement of store fixtures and service facilities from the block plan. Using that approach, however, the planner might find himself without adequate capacity at the end of the plan and be forced to start over again.

The final sizes of departmental areas are then sketched and blocked out onto several building plans drawn to one-sixteenth-, one-eighth-, or one-quarter-inch scale. These plans relate the adjacency of one merchandise department to the other, in several combinations, to determine the best visual and operational flow. And naturally, they relate the nonselling and service areas with the sales area.

An efficient overall design is based on a smooth, workable traffic layout. A floor plan that is structured only to secure a particular motif can turn into an operational nightmare. Unfortunately there are many examples of poor bookstore planning in which the novelty of an idea seen elsewhere was adopted and resulted in wasted space and unnecessary footsteps.

Several block plan layouts are always prepared, all drawn to scale. It is then possible to review and discuss several planning solutions. When the block plan has been established in the horizontal plane of the store, I study the possibility of dramatizing the selling area by raising or lowering one or more departments. The changes in level will finally be accomplished by building raised galleries or sinking plaza areas by normal construction methods in specially selected departments.

Although the element of cost is most important, before moving on to the preliminary store fixture planning, I find it advisable first to seek the ideal solution, almost without regard to eventual costs. Adjustments can then be made to keep within the limits of a reasonable cost budget.

Preliminary store fixture plan. With the departmental adjacencies established on the block plan and the ideas reviewed with my client, the next step in the planning process is to lay out and arrange the preliminary store fixture plan. This is the plan on which store selling fixtures, equipment, and service requirements are drawn in merchandising arrangements within the shapes and boundaries of the selling departments determined by the block plan. It is, of course, necessary to take care to order, arrange, and draw the preliminary store fixture plan so the distances are correct to accommodate customer aisles, the required number of appropriate sales fixtures, and the quantity of shelving required to accommodate the amount of stock planned.

Overlays. In thinking out a plan for a bookstore, I try to imagine the people who will be using the store, and I ask myself how they will perceive it. I begin sketching the preliminary store fixture layout by working out the main areas—first with little rough plans one-sixteenth inch to the foot in scale on buff-colored sketching tissue and then at one-eighth- or one-quarter-inch scale. These sketches are known as overlays.

As the preliminary overlays are worked out, a judgment must be made to determine the height of any selling area to be raised onto galleries and any changes in the height of ceilings. Since you can't always visualize measurements exactly, I have a two-inch-wide surveyor's rod (rule) running up the wall beside the door of my drafting room. This is divided into one-foot sections in alternating colors, and the footage is nicely numbered. It is tremendously helpful in deciding such things as whether a cornice or an overstock fixture should be seven or ten feet high. The rod also helps us visualize the comparative height of the store fixtures that will border the raised galleries. Because more merchandise is visible and accessible there, main merchandising action usually takes place deep in the store at the point where major customer aisles intersect. These points become locations for planning imaginative visual merchandising concepts such as endcaps, steps, slot wall, or similar features. All the best ideas on the overlays are collected and neatly sketched and lettered on a single finished plan drawing.

The preliminary plan drawing. With the basic merchandising plan concept set and the sales and service areas established, thoughts and efforts turn to the coordination of the overall ceiling, with changes in ceiling height, valances, curtain walls, lighting, HVAC outlets, sprinklers, and the store fixture plan. This will incorporate the order and merging of ramps, galleries, store fixture arrangements, and major traffic arteries into a single statement.

Models. As the preliminary plan is developed and drawn, I find it useful to make a study model of the bookstore interior and occasionally of the exterior. These study models are often very rough, made of cardboard with departmental spaces and aisles colored in, but they are useful in many ways. They help verify the concepts we have and give an idea of what the store will look like from a bird's-eye view. (See figure 7-3.) They are particularly handy for studying traffic flow and the relationship of sales equipment to the structure of the building, particularly if the space is populated with a forest of columns.

Because models bring the plan into three-dimensional form, they help achieve good planning balance and aid in the study of the visual design composition. Later, in the natural flow of the planning process as the design development proceeds, I like to have these study models brought up-to-date and incorporate into them the final motifs and design elements.

Frequently, larger-scale models are made to study special types of store fixtures, graphics, and complex and sensitive design problems.

Rendering and perspective sketches. Design perspective sketches are a part of the process and a means to an end. Store planners and designers constantly collect and sketch out informal ideas as they travel—at meetings, at lunches, or, in my case, often on

Fig. 7-3. A bookstore model.
(Courtesy of Bill Mitchell Photography)

airplanes as I fly from one project to the next. These little "noodle" sketches are drawn on whatever is at hand—napkins, business cards, flight coupon jackets, or notebooks or journals—for later reference.

As the plan is developed, I find it helpful to make a number of bird's-eye-view and normal-view perspective sketches of the principal aspects of the store. The sketches are made to visualize the way the elements of the plan and the design will relate to the program and to one another. Many design sketches are simple line drawings, but others are a combination of ideas and the contrasting qualities of each of the bookstore design elements. They preview the development of the character and ambiance of a portion of the bookstore or department.

Perspective sketches are drawn in a variety of art media. Black line shadow and tone sketches are most commonly made because they are easily reproduced and can be used for advertisements, publicity, and a host of other purposes once the final design is established. Some designers prefer to draw with colored ink, pens, markers, and washes. Still others work with Conte crayons on colored paper or make full-color illustrations with pastels, water-colors, or tempera colors. These types of illustrations, made to capture the spirit of the design, are often imaginative, and are always impressive. Some design drawings are works of art.

Some bookstore projects require detailed perspective sketches with every shelf drawn in place in order to convey to the client the scope of activity that will occur in the scene that is illustrated. These sketches are often reproduced and used by booksellers to "assign bays and shelves" and to plan the location for basic book categories.

Updating preliminary estimates. With the preliminary store fixture plan, the model, and sketches made, the next important step is to review and update the estimate of costs and the time scheduled to complete the planning and build and open the new bookstore. This is serious work and often requires securing preliminary esti-mates of both the cost and time from reliable fixture and specialty contractors. The procedure is a safeguard both to control the cost and keep the project on target. If the cost is excessive, this is the time to adjust the preliminary plans and scope of the work to bring the whole thing back onto budget.

Presenting the plan. When the preliminary plan has been concluded and agrees with the planning program, it is presented to the client along with the model or sketches, the finished schedule describing the materials contemplated, the updated budget, the time schedule, and status reports.

The presentation sometimes requires the presence of the project architect and always requires the bookseller's planning team. This meeting is important. Decisions are made here that will affect the store's well-being for a long time. At the conclusion of the meeting the bookseller should be able to advise the store planner, architect, and others to proceed with the design of both the exterior and interior of the new bookstore. This is also the time and place to make any suggestions or changes that will affect the plan and to be certain of the budget and the proposed construction schedule of the project.

Each bookstore planning project is a unique undertaking. Final, definite plans, specifications, and details may be simple or complex, but they are necessary in order to obtain competitive estimates and to start actual construction. The final plans and specifications will incorporate and specifically detail all the elements of the bookstore design.

Who needs a professional store planner?

The answer to this question depends on what changes the space or department requires. Will it be a major job, such as fixing bad plaster and resurfacing floors, moving electrical outlets, or relocating walls? If the job involves a major overhaul, by all means consult an experienced professional bookstore planner. If the project entails building platforms, installing complicated lighting, or designing built-in store fixtures, a bookstore planner can save you needless heartache. Conversely, if it is simply a question of deciding on a suitable loose fixture arrangement or choosing a color scheme, most bookstore people feel that they can tackle the project themselves—especially if they have done the homework outlined in this book.

When you hire an experienced store planner, you pay him for his familiarity with craftspeople, contractors, and resources; you also pay him for experience, imagination, and a selective eye. If you knew what he knows, you could plan, design, renovate, equip, and decorate bookstore interiors yourself. The difference between saving or spending money on decoration hinges on the way you envision the design possibilities or alternatives of a given space. Because designers are specifically trained to do this, they save enormous sums of time and money on store fixture equipment, graphics, and decoration. Discuss your budget freely and openly to avoid any future misunderstandings; if it is very limited, say so. If the designer cannot work within such limited means, he should also be truthful in a tactful manner. The budget should never be left a mystery. Get it out in the open.

With this cooperative planning approach, you will come away with the basis for a complete trade bookstore—advice on what kinds of fixtures to buy, what colors to use, where to place the fixtures, and how to save money and plan for the future. The professional's fee is a bargain if it allows you to pick the brains of the experts—and thereby save a bagful of mistakes.

It never hurts to obtain the advice of experts, even if you don't end up hiring them. As we stated earlier, they earned their stripes through practical experience, solving most of those "insurmountable" problems that every novice encounters the first time.

Chapter 8

Behind the Scenes: Supplies and Equipment

JOAN RIPLEY

Books and fixtures are the two major initial purchases when opening a bookstore. But there are other items needed to make that store a smooth-running, efficient operation. Many of them are small and seem unnoteworthy until you find you don't have them on opening day. That's when you'd give your right arm for some Scotch tape or a paper clip. Since the "best laid schemes o' mice an' men" can fail, it is better to anticipate the supplies necessary for your retail business. All these items are additions to those having to do with tools of the trade, decoration, display, and so on. They range from the smallest, that paper clip, to the largest, a cash register. Remember that these supplies cost money. Start small and be innovative rather than purchase large quantities or expensive items in the very beginning.

To illustrate how these supplies pertain to an overall business operation, I have grouped them below in broad categories: utilities, ordering books, receiving books, sales and revenue, wrapping and handling, returns, accounts payable and receivable, and, finally, general supplies.

Utilities—gas, electricity, water, and telephone listings

You may not consider utilities as items except on an expense ledger, so think of them here as a checklist. In most areas, the earlier you notify the utility companies of when you want service, the better off you will be. They will probably require credit forms to be filled out and deposits paid. By getting in touch with the phone company early, you can have a number reserved and then have this number printed on all your forms and use it in your advertising. The most important reason for contacting the phone company as soon as you can is to have your name included in the next printing of the directory and in the Yellow Pages. Every day you are open without your store's name in these two publications may mean lost sales. Directory deadlines are fixed and unalterable, so call and obtain these dates early in the game.

Ordering books—order forms and window envelopes, special order forms, STOP forms, and files for each

The ABA has available for purchase a combination order-invoice form that is well designed and recognized by all publishers. If you want to print your own form with additional instructions on it, make certain that it has your correct billing name and address as well as your SAN (standard address number). These forms should be consecutively numbered and consist of at least two parts: the part that gets sent to the publisher and a file copy for yourself.

STOP forms, which are also available from the ABA, are used when you wish to prepay the order for a single title to receive a higher discount than you would ordinarily receive for an invoiced order of a single title in small quantities.

Copies of all orders must be filed in a systematic fashion so they can be processed when you receive orders or can be checked if necessary. Use a separate accordion file, a box file, or a simple folder to keep track of purchase orders. If you are going to accept customer special orders, again, you must maintain an ordering system for them, with appropriate forms and files.

Receiving books—carton opener, clipboard, red pencil, price stickers (make sure they are not permanent), inventory cards or notebooks, and files for invoices and packing slips

We have to open the boxes in which the books arrive, and it is amazing how difficult this can be without a sharp cutter. (Be careful not to slice the books in the process.) The invoice or packing slip has to be checked, and putting it on a clipboard reminds you not to use a book for backing—impressions of funny circles and initials on the book's glossy dust jacket reduce a book's salability. Since some invoices are written in pen, it is best to use a colored pencil (we like bright red) so your marks clearly show what did and didn't come in and discrepancies become very obvious. Price stickers are used for items not already priced, such as most sidelines or special promotion books. At the receiving point, records should be kept for inventory control; appropriate cards or forms must be available. Don't forget files (accordions will do) for packing slips and invoices.

*Sales and revenue—cash register and tapes, cash box, change,
credit card forms, credit card imprinter, charge pads, and gift
certificates*

The receptacle for storing money received after the sale of a book
can range from the simplest cigar box to the most sophisticated
electronic cash register. A cash register can be an expensive item.
Even a secondhand one costs money, but it has more than enough
benefits to justify the expense. First of all, your sales can be read or
totaled at any time of the day, which can help you determine peak
and slow hours. If the register has separate categories that can be
totaled, this is an invaluable aid in inventory control because you
will know just what you are selling each day in each category. The
more people there are handling money in the store, the more
important it is to have a cash register.

New electronic cash registers have caused the price of older
types to decrease. Beware of purchasing a used machine without
first investigating the availability of a maintenance contract for it;
the eventual cost of repairs might well exceed the purchase price.
There's not much that new electronic registers cannot do, but it may
not be prudent to purchase one unless you are sure your new business
can justify the initial expenditure. A cash storage box will be needed
for cash on hand kept for the next day's operation. Do not keep
money in the cash register overnight.

If you are going to use credit cards, you must have an imprinter
and charge forms, available from your bank. Similarly, if you are
going to have your own charges, you must have charge pads, charge
cards for each customer, and a file for same as well as statements and
window envelopes for sending out bills at the end of each month.

Gift certificates (these are also available from the ABA) are a
valuable aid when just the right book can't be found or if you are
temporarily out of a particular title.

*Wrapping and handling—wrapping paper, ribbon, bows, or
seals, gift enclosure cards, bags, mailers, mail forms, mail
insurance, labels, and logo*

Gift wrapping is important for personal service. In bookstores,
fifteen-inch and eighteen-inch rolls of wrapping paper are the sizes
generally used. You'll probably need to purchase at least one roll of
each and cutters to mount them on. There are many designs
available from paper supply houses that also carry accessories to
make attractive and effective packages. These supply houses may
also be a good source for your store's bags. Two sizes are usually
necessary, seven by fifteen inches and a larger size to be used as a

shopping bag for multiple purchases or nonbook merchandise if you stock it. Specially designed bags, and some other supplies, are available at relatively low cost through the ABA. Ask for samples.

If mailing books for customers is one of your services, you'll need book mailers—again available from your paper supply house and through the ABA. When you mail books, it is essential to keep a record of what you sent and to whom. Index cards and a simple card file can be used for this purpose, or printed forms might be designed if you desire. You can write the address directly on the mailer with a permanent marking pen or use printed labels. It is a good idea to inquire about blanket mail insurance policies instead of purchasing post office insurance for each package you send. The blanket policy is also very helpful for returns to publishers.

Logo-imprinted promotional items, such as bookmarks or bookplates, need to be ordered well in advance. Your logo should be designed very early to be available for use in all your initial advertising.

Returns—heavy-duty tape and dispenser, charge-back forms (two parts), permission forms (two parts), and wrong-shipment or damaged-book forms (two parts)

You don't sell every single book you purchase, so it is necessary to have forms and packaging for returning books to the publisher or wholesaler. Strapping tape or some form of heavy-duty tape is required for sealing cartons. A dispenser for it makes life much easier. Remember to include in every return shipment a charge-back form with your name and account number so that you will receive proper credit. Any forms you design can be typed up once and taken to your local copy service to be printed in quantity. Remember to use a carbon so you will have a copy for your file.

Accounts receivable and accounts payable—calculator or adding machine and tape, statements, customer charge file and payment record, window envelopes, accounts payable file, ledgers, a daily register, time sheets, government forms, and checkbook

Depending on the sophistication and volume of your business, some or all of the above will be needed. If you have your own charge accounts, you'll need some sort of adding machine with a tape. A simple calculator is also useful for balancing at the end of the day or for making up the bank deposit if an adding machine is unavailable.

Staff records will be needed—such as time cards for hours worked, amount paid, taxes withheld, and so on.

Your accountant will assist you in recommending what kinds of ledgers and journals to purchase for bookkeeping, accounts payable, receivable, and so forth, and the government will supply you with the forms needed to comply with its regulations *after* you inform it that you are opening a business. Your lawyer should help you in filing the proper papers, applying for resale numbers, and the like.

General supplies—scratch pads, pencils and pens, stapler and staples (regular and heavy-duty for mailing), paper clips, rubber bands, rubber cement, thumbtacks, Scotch tape and dispenser, Magic Markers, stationery, envelopes, postcards and carbon paper, "Speedy Memo 2" (a two-part correspondence form for every occasion), big clips (to hold orders or inventory cards), business cards, notebooks (if necessary), file cabinets, stamps and ink pad—store stamp with name and address, deposit stamp with account number for checks, date stamp, receiving stamp, book rate, and special handling stamps— postage stamps or stamp meter, and typewriter (if necessary)

All stores won't require everything discussed in this chapter, while others will need more items than have been mentioned. These lists should simply serve as a guide and to remind you of the many items needed to function as a retailer. The essential thing is to plan ahead so that you are prepared to be a professional bookseller beginning on opening day and to eliminate as many minor frustrations as possible.

P.S. Don't forget cleaning equipment and supplies to keep that new store sparkling.

Chapter 9

Trade Tools for a Bookstore

CYD ROSENBERG

The three primary title reference tools for a bookstore are: *Books in Print,* published by R.R. Bowker Co., the *ABA Book Buyer's Handbook,* published for its members by American Booksellers Association, and microfiche subscription services available from wholesalers.

Books in Print

Books in Print is an annual listing of well over half a million titles currently available from publishers in the United States. These are books considered of interest to the general trade that are available in cloth and/or paper binding. Not included in the listing are elementary or high school textbooks, government publications, professional law books, or books available only to members of an organization.

Approximately fourteen thousand publishers and their hundreds of imprints are represented in this basic reference tool. However, each year dozens of small publishers and hundreds of self-published authors enter the scene, many of whose books will not appear in *Books in Print* simply because they are unknown to *BIP's* publisher. Therefore, while *Books in Print* is the basic work, it is not infallible. Errors of omission do occur, and because of the time lag between the collection of information and its publication, many books that do not appear will be on the market and many others that did appear will have gone out of print.

Bowker has attempted to alleviate this problem for booksellers by offering *Books in Print* on microfiche, which can be updated four times each year. This is a great advance, but one that is more costly than the basic seven-volume bound edition. The seven volumes that are published each October consist of three containing alphabetical lists by title and three alphabetical lists by author. Each entry contains all pertinent data, including coauthors (or editors, if the book has an editor rather than an author as such), publisher, price, year of publication, number of volumes if part of a series, Library of Congress catalog number, and the very important *International Standard Book Number* (ISBN), which many publishers require when books are ordered.

All publishers cited in *Books in Print* are listed alphabetically, with full address and telephone number, in a separate volume. No terms of purchase for resale or any other trade information is given in this listing.

ABA Book Buyer's Handbook

It is to the *ABA Book Buyer's Handbook* that booksellers turn for all information pertaining to ordering books from publishers. Compiled by the editor of publications on the staff of American Booksellers Association, it is updated annually and sent to ABA members automatically. Detailed listings of hundreds of publishers contain discount schedules, addresses for ordering and returning, policies governing that publisher's returns, co-op advertising allowances, cash discounts, *STOP* participation, telephone numbers (frequently 800 numbers) for customer service as well as ordering, names of key personnel, and much other vital information. Many publishers include in their listing a small space advertisement listing key backlist titles. These can be very helpful when a bookseller wants to add books to an order to achieve the next level of discount.

Space is provided within each listing for the bookseller to record the account number for that company as well as the name and address of the publisher's local sales representative.

Wholesalers, independent distributors, and remainder companies are also listed within the handbook. The supplementary section contains such information as cross references for all imprints reported by publishers, importers of foreign language materials, catalog suppliers, sources for books in braille and large type, an annotated list of book trade reference tools and a bibliography of books about the book business, a list of related trade associations, and much other material of interest and concern to booksellers. Many experienced booksellers consider the *ABA Book Buyer's Handbook* the bible of the business.

Microfiche

A microfiche is a small (usually four-by-six-inch) piece of plastic that resembles a negative, on which several hundred book citations can be imprinted. The fiche is placed in a microfiche reader, which can be either purchased or leased and manipulated so pertinent data on a sought-after title is magnified and readable. Most general, and many specialty, book wholesalers offer their customers a microfiche service. Obtained by subscription at varying costs, the fiches are usually updated weekly.

While the information contained on the fiche differs with each service, most of them contain a listing of the books in stock, or on order, at that particular wholesaler, along with price and order number. Sometimes this order number is the International Standard Book Number, and sometimes it is the wholesaler's applied order number.

Because it is updated weekly in most cases, this service provides invaluable current information—for a bookseller trying to obtain books for special order, for instance. In most instances it forestalls the disappointment of unfulfilled orders because of an out-of-stock situation. Most providers of a microfiche service include merchandising information as well, such as media tie-in titles, author tours, promotion suggestions, capsule reviews, best-seller lists, and other useful items.

Other Tools from R. R. Bowker

While *Books in Print* is the basic tool from Bowker, it is by no means the only one to be considered by a bookseller. However, before investing in the others it is wise to think well about how each is to be used and about how valuable it might be to the business.

Paperbound Books in Print is perhaps second in usefulness to a bookseller, because while the *Books in Print* is supposed to contain information on all books available in paperback as well as cloth, this isn't always the case. Part of the reason is that *Paperbound Books in Print* is issued twice each year, in the spring and again in the fall, which makes it at least half the year more current than *Books in Print*.

Published in three volumes, it comprises a title index, author index, and subject index. The third is especially useful in helping customers find a book when they do not have a specific title in mind. Because it is concise, *Paperbound Books in Print* can also save a bookseller time in finding the paperbound edition of a book. However, if one does not find a book listed in *Paperbound Books in Print*, it is always wise to check *Books in Print* as well, in case there was a slip and a paperbound edition was not included as it should have been. This kind of cross- and double-checking is very much a part of the bookseller's customer service.

Subject Guide to Books in Print is a four-volume companion to *Books in Print* and is published about the same time each fall. All of its listings are by subject category, as the name implies. Using the list of subject headings, it is a fairly simple matter to track down customer requests for books of which neither the author nor the title is known—unless the book is fiction, in which case it will not be listed. The subject guide is also of use in expanding a category selection of books within a store. Caution has to be exercised, however, if nothing is known by the bookseller about a title, author, or publisher's reputation for that particular kind of book.

Forthcoming Books appears six times each year on subscription from Bowker and is considered by most booksellers to be as essential as *Books in Print*, simply because it supplies information on titles, in both hardcover and paperback, that are about to be published or have been published since the last edition of *Books in Print*. This information is cumulative throughout the six issues. It is a way of constantly updating *Books in Print*. This publication is especially good about information on academic, technical, and esoteric titles, as well as regular trade books, but is weak on mass-market information.

The *Books in Print Supplement* is a two-volume work that is published in the spring and is intended to update the previous *Books in Print* with new titles, price changes, and information on titles that have gone out of print since publication of the last *BIP*. Although its price change and *o.p.* information is helpful to a bookseller, most do not think this tool is as essential (if a choice has to be made) as *Forthcoming Books*.

Publishers Weekly has been the publishing industry's journal for over a century. It continues to be of both interest and importance to retail booksellers because of the information it contains on new titles, through its advertisements, and through its pages of mini-reviews called "Forecasts." Knowledgeable buyers pay attention to the comments in Forecasts and to the *PW* best-seller lists. Spring and fall announcement issues and other special issues on children's books, religious books, technical books, and so on can be of great assistance to a bookseller.

PW, as it is called within the industry, also contains much publishing industry news as well as articles on retail bookselling.

Additional ABA Tools

American Bookseller magazine is targeted specifically to retail booksellers and bookselling. Issued monthly, it features articles of practical instruction on all aspects of retailing as well as describing specific booksellers' successes. Published by Booksellers Publishing, Inc., a wholly owned subsidary of American Booksellers Association, the magazine brings readers monthly reports on the activities of the association and of regional bookseller associations, as well as putting into perspective publishers' activities as they affect retail booksellers. Through its columns it has become a forum for booksellers as well as an instrument of education.

The magazine is supported by publishers advertising their books and services. It is distributed to members of ABA as part of their membership and is available to all others by subscription.

Newswire is a weekly ABA publication in newsletter format. It was created to keep booksellers informed about author appearances and book reviews so they could more successfully merchandise specific titles. However, its original purpose has been broadened considerably; it now contains the latest information on whatever is of most immediate concern to booksellers. This can be anything from the most recent publisher discount changes, to changes of address or telephone number, to censorship battles and bookseller/publisher litigation. It has become the medium for instant communication in retail bookselling.

Basic Book List is a publication prepared by a committee of practicing booksellers. It is a listing of books, both by subject and by publisher, of titles deemed by members of the committee to be basic salable stock. Each title has been discussed and approved by booksellers actually selling those books. No title is included through publisher submission.

The *Basic Book List* is exceedingly useful to the neophyte bookseller as a stock selection guide, though the warning must be given that no bookseller should just automatically stock every title in *Basic Book List*. It is intended to help establish or add to a category of books within the inventory. It is also meant to help educate a bookseller and the staff on books considered worthwhile within a category. Booksellers also use it, through the publisher listings, to add titles when attempting to achieve the next level of discount.

Sidelines Directory is published periodically by ABA as an aid for booksellers looking for information on sources for nonbook merchandise. It contains listings of manufacturers or distributors by product type. An introductory section before each type of merchandise gives general information about buying and merchandising that type of item. This directory also contains data on major gift and stationery shows, merchandise marts, and trade publications.

Supplementary Tools from Bowker

Publishers, Distributors and Wholesalers of the United States contains address information on over forty-five thousand of those listed in the title, many of which are not listed in either *Books in Print* or *ABA Book Buyer's Handbook.* The volume also has a listing of publisher International Standard Book Number prefixes in numerical order.

Literary Market Place is a more detailed annotated directory of the publishing industry, with all of the above plus agents, media, exporters and importers, sales reps, and so on. While this tool is of use primarily to those booksellers who need to know the names and numbers of publishers' promotion people, it should be noted that the book, published annually in paperback, can be purchased for resale. It does have a modest market.

American Book Trade Directory is an annotated listing of retail bookstores in the United States and Canada, by state or province and then city or town. It describes succinctly each bookstore, giving name, address, telephone number, owner, manager, buyers, and types of books carried. This information is solicited annually and should be supplied by booksellers because it makes them available not only to publishers, but to potential customers as well.

Publishers' Trade List Annual is a four-volume compilation of publishers' catalogs. In theory the information within these catalogs should be the most accurate available as to title, price, and the like. However, some publishers submit short lists rather than fully annotated catalogs, and because so many change prices after their catalogs are published, *PTLA* is of limited usefulness. It has fallen from being an essential directory in a good bookstore to a supplemental tool.

Of the special reference publications published by Bowker, *Children's Books in Print, Subject Guide to Children's Books in Print, British Books in Print, Large Type Books in Print, Religious Books in Print, Medical Books in Print, Scientific and Technical Books in Print* are useful to those catering to the markets indicated. A general bookseller should be aware of them and, if depth in a category or actual specialization is desired, acquire the proper volume.

An Assortment of Other Tools

Most booksellers find it useful to keep publishers' catalogs from the current season as well as from a previous season or two. Current-season titles are often postponed, and customers frequently want information on a "new" title that came out last year.

Reviews are also tools, not only to stimulate sales, but also to expand a bookseller's own awareness and knowledge of books. Of the national book review publications, *The New York Times Book Review* has the most impact for newspapers, while *Time* and *Newsweek* continue to stir response among magazine readers. But the bookseller must also be aware of regional publications that affect sales and of specialized magazines, both local and national. Customers expect booksellers to know about "that book" they read about in their favorite magazine or newspaper. It is impossible to know them all, but awareness of as many as possible is important.

Television sells books, as every bookseller knows. Although it isn't an absolute, having an author on "The Today Show," "Good Morning America," "The Phil Donahue Show," "60 Minutes," or any number of others is almost certain to precipitate a rush of people into bookstores looking for "that book." The same is true for radio talk shows. Even better is to have the author or the book talked about on a news program.

Specialty stores should know about specific publications or programs that will stimulate sales. Children's booksellers need to communicate with the Children's Book Council, subscribe to *The Horn Book* and perhaps *Parent's Choice*. A Christian bookstore would be familiar with *Bookstore Journal* and *Christian Bookseller*. Similarly, a Judaica store would use the Jewish Book Council and *Jewish Book News*. There are special tools for every specialization. They just have to be sought out and utilized.

Chapter 10

Hiring and Staff Training

FRANK LOWE

Even the person who wants to "do it all myself so I know it will be done right" cannot handle all the work involved in running a bookstore alone. No matter how small a beginning or modest the projection, help will be required. How much help depends upon physical space and financial capability. A five-hundred-square-foot store probably does not need more than one person at a time in the store, but is the one person going to be the same person six days a week from early opening to late closing? Is the one person going to do all the ordering, receiving, shelving, selling, returning, bookkeeping, advertising, wastebasket emptying, and so on? In the very beginning, perhaps, but not for long.

Financial capability simply means, How do I pay people to work for me, even at minimum wage, which is a sad standard for most beginning employees in bookstores? Statistics suggest that 1.6 full-time people (which obviously means the second one is not really full-time) are the norm in a bookstore grossing $50,000; 2.7 people in a store grossing $100,000; 3.7 people for $150,000; and 4.7 people for $300,000. These same statistics imply that a total salary/wage percentage of 17 percent of gross sales would, after the owner/manager's wage had been deducted, leave in the $50,000 store 4 percent for staff; 6 percent in the $100,000 store; 8 percent in the $150,000 store; and up to 10 percent in the $300,000 store.

If the need exists, and the financial capability is there, how do you select an employee for a bookstore? Generally there will be a sizable pool of eager applicants because a bookstore seems to many people an idyllic place to work. This pool isn't a bad place to begin, since those who have asked to leave their name in case you need help have taken the first step in expressing their interest. However, each of these would-be applicants must be scrutinized carefully. Just loving books isn't enough. Degrees in literature aren't enough. The ideal is the tireless, intelligent worker who loves books, knows all there is to know about them, and is a whiz at systems.

If there aren't several such paragons in the pool, look for an applicant who appears to have good basic sense, a fair knowledge of authors and titles, an ability to learn quickly, and the capacity to retain what has been learned, because bookselling is an accumulation, over decades, of detailed information. The person who can direct a customer who has requested a book similar to "that one Alice Walker wrote" to several that will fulfill the request is a true bookseller. Getting to know what those others are, assuming one knows about the "one Alice Walker wrote," is knowledge acquired, accumulated each day one works in a bookstore. This kind of knowledge is essential in a bookstore with personalized service and, as much as the books themselves, is what attracts customers.

It is important to match the employee to the need, whether it be the other person in a two-person bookstore or the twenty-third receiving person in a massive retail bookstore. Matching the need includes everything from skills required to appearance desired. Appearance desired can be as diverse as matching the looks of those already there, so as to keep a uniform look, to finding somebody far distant from those already there to stimulate a different kind of customer. Knowing what you expect the staff member to do beyond the actual duties assigned is an important part of planning for and finding the right person. New people on a staff should add something by their presence. They should enrich the image of the business in whatever way enrichment is desired.

The new person should know from the beginning of the interview what the bookstore is meant to be, what purpose the bookseller has in mind for the store, what function it is to fulfill in the community. As important as teaching the new employee how to run the cash register is to share with that employee the bookseller/owner's philosophy of bookselling—if the employees are to be extensions of the bookseller, if they are to make real the aspirations the bookseller had when establishing the bookstore.

Beyond dreams is detail. Bookselling is a most detailed occupation. Any potential employee must have the capacity for detail in all aspects of the business. And, of course, a bookstore employee should have an interest in people and be able to relate to them and their needs. The most brilliant individual with vast knowledge and endless patience with detail is useless in dealing with the public if that individual hates people or simply can't get along with them. The customer who wants a book the bookseller loathes is as worthy of service as is the groupie who only reads what the bookseller recommends. Getting books to people is what bookselling is all about. The person who doesn't like one or have patience with the other does not belong in a bookstore.

If a pool full of eager applicants does not exist, spreading the word among customers and fellow businesspeople, placing an advertisement in the local newspaper, or perhaps asking local employment agencies are all things that might be tried. Experiences vary so from place to place that a bookseller has to decide after trial and error which method results in the best employee applications. One must always be wary of taking the easiest route, that of hiring relatives or close friends just because they are there. If that is their only qualification, don't do it. If they have all the others, then go one step farther and ask yourself if working together will enhance or ruin whatever the relationship is already, and then decide if you can work with this person in spite of this relationship. Be more cold-blooded in analyzing friends and relatives than total strangers because you have more to lose.

Once a decision is made, and someone has been hired, that person has to be trained. Successfully training staff is like winning at Catch-22: a reliable staff depends upon proper training, yet there is never enough time to train "properly." Training sessions are always begun with the best intentions, but interruptions commence, and from the first one onward, the most frequently asked question to the new employee is, "Now, where was I?" This is obviously not the case in large business operations with formal staff training and indoctrination sessions. Very few bookstores fit into that category in their early days.

Since interruptions can't be stopped, they should be used. A training outline should have been drawn up prior to the commencement of staff training, so that all areas are covered. If these facets are dealt with in small segments, the trainer can utilize the interruption as an example of "such and such as outlined on page whatever." In other words, use the interruption to put into practice right at that moment something that is detailed in the outline.

Although this method may lengthen the time devoted to training a new staff member, it does allow information to be assimilated and used. Questions will arise during the practice session that can be answered right then and thus instill in the trainee's mind exactly how something is to be handled. Covering material thoroughly and slowly, and with practical application, can save much time later on and lessen chances for misinterpretation.

This may seem like beginning at the end, but by using the detailed outline so everything is eventually covered, those interruptions that cannot be avoided in a small store become exercises and are very useful as such. This is as true for explanation of store policy as for instruction in systems. It is understood that all facets of the operation must be covered, so one cannot simply wait for an interruption that will serve as an example of something important. It is merely suggested that the interruptions be turned to advantage.

Because policies and procedures reflect the image of the store— how you want your store to serve and appear to the public—they must be explained thoroughly to the new staff member so the reasons behind everything are as well understood as the way things are done. It is too easy to be casual with these explanations, forgetting that what seems obvious and self-evident to the bookseller may not be comprehensible to a newcomer.

This method of "stop and go" training does require careful structuring of material so that the trainee can be led through the assorted responsibilities of the job in a logical order, understanding how each new duty arises out of the previous segment. The written outline prepared in advance will make sure nothing is omitted in the training process, no step left out that would confuse and perhaps create problems in the future. Think of all these facets as pieces of a puzzle presented to the new employee one at a time. All the pieces must fit if the picture is to be complete. This will lessen the temptation to hasten the training, to cover only the mechanics of the job.

Structure is the key. Putting together the structure is important not only in training, but in organizing the daily routine of any and all staff members. It has been proven that productivity can be increased measurably with a carefully structured daily schedule that allots specific times for specific responsibilities, with plenty of time for each but none to be wasted. This is essential if all facets of a bookstore operation are to be adequately covered by a minimum staff.

Explain the whole operation to the new employee, not only what their schedule will be, but what the schedule of the whole store is. It is a grand scheme. Explain it, and let the new employee know where he or she will fit into that scheme. This requires an overview of everything about the store: store coverage, stock and inventory control, receiving and processing merchandise, shipping, special orders, mail and telephone sales, store hours, days off, and on and on and on.

Let them know that you will explain each responsibility of their specific job separately and will give them periods of practical application. Make sure they know your ultimate goal for them, and assure them you will instruct them carefully in the steps they will need to take to reach that goal. If there are other staff members already in place, explain the authority scale to the new person. A trainee should know who is second in command, who has what authority, whom to turn to if help is needed and you aren't present. Make sure the more senior employee becomes an older sister or brother, there in the event of emergency and not "big brother" hovering in the background.

Although rules (if they exist) about dress codes, smoking, whatever, should be explained the very first thing to a new employee, take the opportunity while training in specifics to restress these and other pieces of general information (such as how the staff conveys the store's image, how each individual's personal contribution enhances the stated goals of the store, or how the entire staff has as part of its responsibility store security and guarding against pilferage or shoplifting, both external and internal). It can't be repeated too often that each member of the staff, whether they be two or twenty, is part of a single team working together for success.

The more imbued a staff member is with the concept of service to the community, of helping customers, of making the bookstore an efficient as well as pleasant place to be, the more attention he or she will pay to the mechanics that make it all function smoothly.

Instruction in mechanics depends upon the job the new person is to fill, but it is always a plus for everyone in a small business to know how to do everybody else's job, to know how all stages of the operation work. The salesperson is more professional if he or she knows how to open a carton of books and how to check them off a packing slip, for price and quantity, noting any damage at the same time, and then how to check the invoice or packing slip against the order. This not only instructs on what happens to the books before they reach the sales floor but is the best way to learn stock. The person who can handle books without absorbing some information about them, without retaining some memory of what they looked like and where they are, isn't right for a bookstore. Sales staff should shelve books, set up displays, read catalogs, do all that is necessary to make themselves aware of titles, current and upcoming, past and even out of print.

Similarly, staff hired to work in the office are far better able to cope with invoices and statements and accounts receivable if they have some basic knowledge of how books are ordered and then processed through the store from receiving room to final sale at the cash register. Nor does it hurt the salesperson to know the problems the accounting staff face each day.

The most logical first step, then, would seem to be the receiving operations, with an explanation of how all that is accomplished, and then how books are categorized and arranged on the shelves, with an in-depth tour of the placement of categories within the store. An explanation of the store's stock control system and why it is used takes place in the receiving area. This leads inevitably to a discussion of backlist titles and their enduring importance to the store as compared with the constantly shifting new titles. It is a good idea at this juncture to give the new employee a copy of the *ABA Basic Book List* to study at home, as a way of becoming familiar with steadily selling titles. Allow plenty of time during this phase of training for the new person to become familiar with the system and, even more important, begin to feel easy with the multitude of titles that comprise a bookstore's stock.

During this period, introduce the trainee to the many tools of the trade, *Books in Print, Forthcoming Books, ABA Newswire, PW, American Bookseller,* and publishers' catalogs. As you explain the purpose and use of each, give the new person some problems to solve using the tools, such as finding the title of a not-yet-published book or seeking out the first work of an author still in print, whatever will give the newcomer hands-on experience with these tools.

Meanwhile, the trainee should be working the books on the shelves. At first, this can take the form of taking each book off the shelf and dusting it, noting what each title is and where. Perhaps the employee can check to make sure the books are in alphabetical order on the shelf, or that all the bread books are together in the cookbook section if that is how you shelve in your store, or that a psychology book hasn't strayed into the history section. If you have a card file for each book on the shelves, the trainee might "card the shelves," meaning check the cards against the actual books. The purpose of all this, of course, is to build a knowledge of what is on the shelves.

Before the trainee is ready to approach a customer to offer assistance (even if they have been taught what to say and what not to say and they know where things are), he or she has to understand completely the technical aspects of consummating a sale. Booksellers are notoriously independent souls, and this makes for the richness of the profession, but when it comes to handling money, to ringing up sales on the cash register, giving credit slips, writing up credit card purchases, or handling exchanges, independence must give way to rigid adherence to the rules. There is no room for creativity here. Procedures must be followed unless you are willing to risk unpleasant future consequences. All security advisers tell retailers to devise rigid rules and step-by-step procedures in the handling of money and sales. Devise these rules before beginning the business, and then make sure each and every person in the store, including yourself, follows them.

Explain carefully and slowly each intricacy, whether it be ringing a regular sale, how to handle a no-tax sale or a service charge, figuring a postage charge, giving a refund or a merchandise credit, or what to do when handed a gift certificate. Anticipate everything that might arise at the cashier's desk, know what your procedure is for it, and instruct the new employee in that procedure. Because there will very likely be a gap between the time of your instruction and the actual occurrence of some of these examples, this is the perfect place for the buddy system to operate if there are other, more senior employees. If there aren't, have written instructions for each operation someplace near the cash register so the new employee can refer to them when needed.

Along about now, both the trainer and the trainee will have had it with the whole process. The one wants to stop instructing, the other to have done with being told what to do. Yet still to be dealt with is the most difficult and most important aspect of the job—bookselling. Because the neophyte may consider this the easiest of all, it is well to build a foundation of reference information, in which the new person can place herself or himself. It is hoped the new person has by now become familiar with the reference tools mentioned above and knows how to use them. Using them creatively with customers to make sales is the step beyond mere familiarity.

The customer asks, "What is the name of the new book by ____?" or, "Who is the author of ____?" What the book*seller* does is say to the customer with a known interest in a certain author, "Do you know about the new book by ____?" or, "Have you read the earlier books he wrote? They are..." The bookstore employee knows, having read *PW* and *American Bookseller*, that a new book is coming on a certain subject that is of public interest—or special interest. The employee performs a service for the customer as well as making a sale for the store by letting people know about this book that is coming.

Selling is sometimes considered an annoyance, but good selling is so subtle it never annoys. It only assists. It has been going on in bookstores since their inception. One of the best places the fledgling bookseller can begin to learn about this old and respected profession is in this volume, in the preface where Bob Hale answers the question, "Why does one become a bookseller?" Couple his answers with your own background, why *you* are a bookseller, what being a bookseller really means to you and to your community. Share with your employees your personal style of conducting business and dealing with customers. Set your standards for them, but let them know that although you want them to meet those standards and the goals you have set for your store, you still want to encourage them to find their own individual place in bookselling and its history.

Be grateful if your employees never stop asking questions. If they know it all and have nothing more to ask, your training program has not been a total success, because in bookselling, nobody ever understands everything. Let your staff know that they need never be embarrassed to ask a question or ashamed if they don't know something. The reason bookselling is ever-challenging is because you continue to learn each day, no matter how many days or years you are at it.

Chapter 11

Promoting the New Store

STEPHEN COGIL

You have selected a site, signed a lease, designed a floor plan, laid out fixtures, purchased an opening inventory, hired a staff. Your lifelong dream is about to come true. Now what needs your urgent attention is promotion of the new bookstore. Actually, that promotion began way back when you decided on the image you wanted to project to the buying public. Image, mood, atmosphere are all established by everything you do to sell books in the space you have created. What you need to do is establish that ambiance in the public's mind and then with a symbol be able to call it up to the public whenever the symbol is seen.

This symbol is a logo, a specific design that is unique to your store, or a tag line, a motto that instantly says who you are and what you are about in that bookstore. This logo or line can and should be used everywhere possible, on your store's sign, all of your advertising, your stationery, bookmarks, all bags and paper supplies. Because the logo or tag line should be a part of the bookstore from the very beginning, and come to be a major part of its recognition in the eyes of the public, much care should be given to its design. It will probably be with you for as long as the store exists—logos being considered assets when businesses are sold—so do whatever is necessary to make it right. You may have the idea but need a professional artist to create the design. Or you may be artistic enough to do it yourself. However, this is not the place to skimp on investment. If it is a tag line you are choosing as a logo, try it out on lots of people for their reaction to make sure it carries the message you want to convey. Also make sure it is either original with you or at least in the public domain so you are not in legal difficulty for taking over someone else's tag.

Word of mouth is an unsurpassed form of advertising for the

new store as well as for a new book. Nothing excites people more about a product or a place than hearing it talked about informally. You can build this excitement and get people talking by clever signs on the front of your store during the construction/setting-up phase. Let the world know what is going to be there. This is the first place to use your logo—prominently—with progress reports. "Three weeks from now, Such and Such will open on the Date." "The shelves are up. Books are coming in. Only __ more days till opening!"

On Fifth Avenue in New York City, where everyone is supposed to be jaded, Barnes & Noble created incredible enthusiasm when they were building a new store, by erecting an enormous sign on the front of the building at the outset of construction: "Wouldn't it be nice if a Barnes & Noble bookstore opened here?" By the time it opened everybody thought it would be nice. That sign had everyone talking about the store before it existed. Any bookseller can do the same thing by clever use of progress reports on the front of the store. Using the logo in those reports begins to establish its recognition factor so that when the public sees it in newspaper ads they'll know at once it is the new bookstore at whatever location.

To promote the new store to those who do not walk past every day, print advertising and perhaps radio (and possibly even television if the budget allows) must be scheduled. Whatever amount it takes to do a credible job should be considered as part of the start-up expenses that are estimated separately from the budget planned for the first period of operations. In an annual budget, 2 percent of gross sales is frequently allocated to advertising. However, because there are no annual sales at the time of opening, and because the 2 percent of projected sales will be needed during the year for regular advertising, an amount based on local costs of advertising must be figured in along with the expenses of fixturing, initial inventory, and so forth.

Print media varies in every locale. Everything that is available should be analyzed for effectiveness. Talking to established retail merchants in the neighborhood may serve as a guide to the selection of newspapers or shoppers, though the bookseller must in every case consider whether that particular outlet is read and used by book buyers. Because there are never as many advertising dollars as are needed, you must spend what you have where it will do the most good.

Teaser ads, similar to those progress reports on the storefront, are good for building interest in your new store. Telling potential customers what is going to be can make them look forward to coming in as soon as you are open for business. Don't forget to use that logo in all teasers.

The same sort of thing can be done effectively on radio advertising. Here the tag line is the important thing to establish, along with location. If the listener only remembers two things—the line that describes your store and its location—then the money is well spent.

As you are paying for this advertising, try to get as much free space in newspapers and as much free time on radio or television as possible. Free space and time are available. They come from contacting the local media sources and telling them of your plans. The launching of a new business is local news, and the opening of a new bookstore seems to have special appeal. Be enthusiastic in approaching these people. Share the aspirations that led to the decision to open a bookstore. Because a bookstore retails ideas as well as physical objects, it lends itself to public discussion—and support or rejection. Make use of this asset.

Frequently, free space and time go hand in hand with paid space and time. That's fine, as long as the new bookseller makes both work to the store's advantage.

As the grand opening approaches, a step-up in advertising and promotion is necessary. This might be the time to have flyers ready to be passed out door to door or put in the windows of cars in the parking lot of a shopping center if that is your location. Make sure to check all rules regarding such flyers before proceeding, and make them effective advertising tools, not just litter basket candidates. Advertising in print and on the air might be increased with either more small ads or larger ads. On the storefront itself, make the progress reports into banners that nobody can miss. Make opening day so important that people can barely wait.

And be prepared for opening day.

Promotion for the new store isn't just going on outside the store. It should be going on inside as well. Everything that is being done should be done with promotion in mind. You planned the layout to sell books. You stocked the shelves with books you think will sell. You set up displays to catch the eye and build sales. You planned the checkout area not only for efficient sales transactions, but to make impulse sales as well. All of this is preparation and should be ready for the grand opening. The goal on that first day is to have customers say, "It's as if you have always been here." What you don't want is, "I'll come back when you're ready for business."

Grand openings aren't usually one day long; more frequently, they last a week. Whatever the length of the festivity, it should be a time to establish firmly in the minds of customers that this is a business with people in charge who know what they are doing and are capable of doing it. If it is a time of confusion or excessive experimentation, those who come in to look over the new bookstore will receive a very negative image. Some new retailers let a few people trickle in before the grand opening, putting it off until there have been a couple of weeks of "dry run." This extra time allows the kinks to be worked out and may make those few trickles feel they have been backstage, which is a plus. The minus might be kinks that turn customers into cranks.

All of the promotion toward the grand opening must establish what kind of bookstore this new business is to be. There are many kinds of bookstores, and different people go to different stores. If it's to be a sports bookstore, let that be known, and advertise in the places where you will encounter buyers of sports books or whatever other specialization you are featuring. If it's to be a general bookstore, there will inevitably be some emphasis—the finest in fiction and nonfiction, or whatever. Emphasize the emphasis in the preliminary advertising so as to attract the customers for whom you have built an inventory.

And then, as part of the grand opening promotion, do whatever will appeal to those customers. If you think price will get them, have some opening-day bargains—being careful not to set a precedent for bargain books if that isn't to be part of your operation. If it's literature, try to have as guests some literary types, authors or reviewers or anybody else who would appeal to the literati. Whatever the goal, attempt to have special lures for those opening festivities to launch the business in the direction you want to go.

Make the opening a party if you want. Serve food and drink if that fits your image. But remember, you want people to see books they will want to buy—if not that day, then later. The books and the services are more important than the entertainment. While everyone is having a good time, so good they will want to come back, make sure they are getting the impression that this is a good bookstore, one to be remembered when they want to buy a book.

"Hit the ground running!" is a favorite phrase of managerial types. Make it part of your opening plan.

II
Operations
and
Management

Chapter 12

Basic Record Keeping

STEPHEN COGIL and DAVID COLEN

The purpose of this chapter is to acquaint the reader with basic retail record keeping procedures. You may do your own bookkeeping, or hire a bookkeeper if the budget allows, but no matter who keeps the accounts, it is essential for the owner/manager of the bookstore to understand the figures so that decisions can be made based upon what they represent.

Your record keeping should begin long before the doors open for business. As soon as you begin to have expenses of any variety having to do with the planning or setting up of your store, you should keep track of those expenses. It is sad but true that there will be many expenses before there is any income from sales. All of the expenses incurred in the planning stage will figure eventually in your initial investment and so have a bearing on your return-on-investment figure and your first year's profit or loss.

It isn't just the large amounts that need to be recorded, such as inventory, fixtures, and whatever was required to make the space leased suitable for a bookstore, but all of the other amounts as well, from consultants' fees to postage and telephone calls. Record them systematically, and use them when it comes time to report what you have put into your business.

There are many reasons why it is a good idea to set up a separate bank account for the new business early on. How much you put into that account depends upon how far along you are in the planning, what your immediate needs will be, and what your immediate access to money is. Whether borrowed or simply transferred from your own savings account, having a bookstore account from the very beginning gives you a start on efficiently recording those expenses you pay by check. Cash expenditures should also be recorded.

You will want to set up expense accounts in a journal that can be as simple as a loose-leaf notebook in which you have put columned accounting paper. This allows you to keep on one page all the costs having to do with leasing the store site, on another page all the expenses of professional advice, on another all those resulting from setting up an office, including the cost of that notebook and the paper. There is not enough space in this chapter to offer a complete bookkeeping course, but any basic book on the subject would give you a chart of accounts that might be adapted to your purpose and much good advice on how to keep those accounts.

It is essential, of course, to record all the costs of accumulating inventory as it is purchased and received, including all the freight costs of getting whatever you plan to sell into your store. Do this systematically because these figures all have a direct bearing on your cost of goods sold, which decides the gross profit on those sales, and it is from that profit that you will pay running costs.

All of the preceding is record keeping prior to actually becoming a bookseller. It is preparation and set-up expense. Once the doors open for business, the record keeping of sales begins. All sales must be recorded. Although there are those who still prefer to keep their cash in a cigar box or drawer, noting their sales on slips of paper, a cash register is much more efficient and provides records that are invaluable. The amount of time it saves pays for the investment, because in a business that is paper and detail intensive, any saving of time is the equivalent of a saving in dollars. The price of cash registers has dropped drastically in recent years (ironically as they have become more complex), so even the smallest retail business can probably afford one.

All types of cash registers should be investigated, but the simplest register for a bookstore would have the capability of recording sales in several categories, should distinguish between cash and charge sales, and should further be able to distinguish between cash (including checks) and credit card sales if that is important for your record keeping, although it is common practice to consider bank credit card sales as cash inasmuch as the sales slips will be banked with the deposit into the bookstore account. Non-bank credit card sales (such as American Express), which must be billed back to the credit card company for redemption, can be rung as charge sales, inasmuch as the retailer does not have the money for those sales until the credit card company makes reimbursement. These could be considered part of accounts receivable. Even if you do not plan to have in-house charge accounts for your customers, it is a good idea to have charge account capability on your register.

Your cash register should also record sales tax where applicable. Many registers compute the sales tax automatically as the sale is rung, with the possibility for nontaxed items to be added to the total transaction simply by pressing a tax deletion key.

At the end of the day, the register will be "rung out," giving you what is usually called a "Z" tape. This tape will have the totals for all your categories separately, such as books, magazines, cassettes, cards, or whatever categories you have designated. It will also give you the total sales tax and the totals in cash sales, charge sales, and whatever other breakdowns you have built into your system. If you do have in-house charge accounts and take payments at the cash register, you would show a total of payments on accounts receivable taken in that day. In other words, you will have a final record by total of all that day's transactions. There is a second tape in the machine that is called the detail tape. On this tape is a duplicate of every single transaction rung into that register that day.

Now you have your Z tape with all the totals. What do you do with it? You have to "balance" the register, meaning you have to count all of the money, cash, checks, charges, whatever, in the register, deduct the amount of cash you started with at the beginning of the day, and come up with the correct amount for deposit. This is an essential and vital daily chore for each cash register in the store. If you decide not to have a cash register, you must add up all of the transactions, getting the same figures the Z tape would give you, and then use those to do your balancing.

Let's take a moment to explain that amount of cash you started with at the opening of the day. Because it is necessary to make change, starting with the first transaction of the day, you must have in the register, ready to do business, a quantity of pennies, nickels, dimes, and quarters, as well as some single-dollar bills, probably a few fives, and maybe a ten or two depending upon the volume of business. This specific amount of money ("specific" meaning you should decide what you need and then start each day with the same amount) is called a "bank." It should be sufficient to meet your needs but not tie up more money than is necessary.

For a very small store, the bank consists of the contents of the register at the opening of a business day. For a larger store, the bank might consist of what is kept in the register plus a reserve fund of rolled coins and perhaps some singles in the safe to replenish the register if the need arises. If the register runs out of quarters and there is a roll of quarters in that reserve fund in the safe, it should be "purchased," meaning a ten-dollar bill should be taken from the register and put into the reserve fund when the quarters are taken out to be put into the register. The point is simply to maintain the level of the bank in the register so that one has that as a constant when beginning to balance the day's receipts at the end of the day.

There are numerous ways to do the balancing. You can start

with your total sales, or you can start with your bank. If you start with the sales, add up the checks you have taken in during the day (including credit card slips if you count them as cash sales), deduct this total from the deposit figure shown on the cash register tape, and you get a difference that should be the actual cash you took in during the day. Remove that amount of cash from the drawer and put it to one side with the checks. Then count what remains in the drawer, and if you are in balance, what remains is the amount of money you started with at the beginning of the day, or your "bank." If you do not end up with the correct amount, find out if the charge slips you have written total the amount shown on the Z tape for total charge sales. If not, you may have rung a charge sale as cash or vice versa. Make the proper adjustments, and then proceed to look for other errors if your cash is still not in balance. It is common for minor mistakes to be made in the process of making change, so a few cents over or under is not unusual, though not to be accepted as a matter of course (those few cents can indicate larger problems).

There is another method of balancing the cash: first, remove from the register drawer as much of the coin as possible, plus whatever bills are needed to come up with the bank, which is, remember, the amount of money you started the day with before there were any sales. What is left in the drawer in cash, checks, credit card slips, or whatever should equal the totals of the day's transactions. If it does not, check the charge slips against the total shown on the tape, and so on, exactly as described above, until you find your errors and know why your cash is not in balance.

It is obvious why having cash register tapes is most efficient. If one has to add up, even on an adding machine, all the day's sales broken down by cash, charge, or whatever and also broken down by categories for later recording, the balancing performance and the record keeping become increasingly burdensome and subject to error.

Balancing the register is only the beginning of what is required to record sales. All that has been done to this point is to account for the money. Now the accounting of the figures begins. Part of the process includes those amounts that had to do with balancing, especially if anyone other than the owner or manager did the balancing. Having a form for this purpose can be very useful. Those shown in tables 12-1 and 12-2 are merely examples that might be adapted to whatever system you choose.

Daily sales should be entered in a sales journal. Again, this can be as simple as sheets of columned accounting paper in a loose-leaf notebook or regular ledgers.

Standard procedure is to put the dates down the left-hand side

TABLE 12-1

1.	Deposit figure from Z tape			_____ *
2.	Checks taken in	+ _____		
3.	Bank credit card slips	+ _____		
4.	Total of lines 2 & 3		= _____	
5.	Difference is cash needed for deposit		_____	
6.	Remaining cash in register:			
	20s		_____	
	10s		_____	
	5s		_____	
	1s		_____	
	quarters		_____	
	dimes		_____	
	nickels		_____	
	pennies		_____	
	Total		_____	
7.	Cash at beginning of day	− _____		
8.	Difference (over or under)		= _____	
	(Added or deducted from deposit)			
9.	Actual deposit		_____	

*After adjustments:
    Voids
    Cash refunds not rung as paid-outs
    Gift certificates redeemed

TABLE 12-2

1.	Cash in drawer:			
	20s	_____		
	10s	_____		
	5s	_____		
	1s	_____		
	quarters	_____		
	dimes	_____		
	nickels	_____		
	pennies	_____		
	Total	_____		
2.	Less starting bank	− _____		
3.	Remaining cash		+ _____	
4.	Checks		+ _____	
5.	Bank credit card slips		+ _____	
6.	Deposit (actual)			= _____
7.	Net cash sales	+ _____	+ _____	
8.	Net charge sales	+ _____		
9.	Total sales	= _____		
10.	Payment Accounts Receivable		+ _____	
11.	Paid-outs		− _____	
12.	Deposit			= _____
13.	Difference between lines 6 & 13 (over or under)		_____	

Adjustments:

of the page, having a cross column for each day of the month even if one isn't planning to be open for business each day. If you wish to do subtotals of sales as you go along, perhaps at the end of each week, leave an extra cross column between each of the weeks of the month. The categories of sales are put across the top of the page, such as Books, Cards, Records, or whatever categories on which you want to keep separate records. These will obviously be the same categories that have been put into your cash register system or that you keep track of manually. In each of the examples so far, we have simply stated "books." Some booksellers want to distinguish paperback sales from hardback sales or mass-market paperback sales from trade. If this information is useful to you, record it at the time of sale and utilize it. Your records are to be tools for you as well as accounts for tax and other purposes, so set them up to suit your needs as well as those of possible auditors.

The example in table 12-3 shows a store that sells Books, Cards, Cassettes, and Other, which is all the other nonbook merchandise the store carries. There are columns for each of those categories, then a column for sales tax on those sales, and then a column that shows total transactions, which is the sales plus the sales tax.

The next columns to the right show how those sales were paid for by the customers. The first one is Cash, which means both cash and checks. The next, Bank Card, is the total for the day of credit card sales. Then comes a charge column, this bookstore having an in-house charge account capability, which means that the bookstore allows its customers to charge and then bills them each month. The final column in this group is Other, and here "other" would mean other means of paying, with a gift certificate, for instance, or a merchandise credit. The figures of columns two through six in total must equal the figure in the Total Transactions column. And the figures in columns eight through eleven must also equal that transactions column.

At the end of the month, all of the category columns can be added, to arrive at the total sales for each category during that particular month. And the sales tax column can be totaled to see what is owed to the city or state. Then the totals of the categories plus the total of the sales tax are put together to equal the total of the transaction total column for the month. In other words, the totals across in columns two through six must balance to column seven each day and at the end of the month. And that same total of column seven must equal the totals of columns eight and eleven.

So far in our sales journal, we have shown the details of our sales, where the money we took in came from. The next step, where

TABLE 12-3

1. Date	2. Sales Books	3. Sales Cards	4. Sales Cassettes	5. Sales Other	6. Sales Tax	7. Total Trans.	8. Cash	9. Bank Card	10. Charge	11. Other	12. Sales Dep.	13. Over Under	14. Acc. Rec.	15. Pd. Out	16. Gr. Dep.	17. CC Fee	18. Net Deposit

the money went, is frequently recorded alongside the sales information.

Column twelve, Sales Deposit, is the total of the cash equivalent and bank credit card columns. The next column, Over/Under, is for overages or shortages. Column fourteen is Accounts Receivable, assuming this store has in-house charge accounts and takes payments on those accounts at the cash register. The next column, fifteen, is money that was paid out at the register for any purpose, be it a cash refund or COD or freight charge, or whatever. More about paid-outs in a moment. Column twelve, plus or minus column thirteen, plus column fourteen, less column fifteen equals column sixteen, which we call the gross deposit.

The final deposit will consist of cash or equivalent as shown in column eight plus bank credit card amounts, which can be deposited as well, as shown in column nine. However, a fee has to be paid to the bank for processing these credit card sales. The CC fee, in this case 4 percent, is shown in column seventeen. The net deposit in column eighteen, therefore, is the total of column sixteen less column seventeen.

In this example we have shown the source of each day's income, for example, sales by category, and put them into a journal of sales accompanied by a deposit log that shows the disposition of that income, what was paid out and what was banked. The charges, whether they be in-house or credit card charges that have to be billed to the credit card company rather than deposited in a bank, are dealt with in column ten. Thus we have totals of each day's transactions on a page or a two-page spread that covers a month.

Now that word about paid-outs. Whether a petty cash box is maintained in which an amount of money is kept for paying incidental expenses or the money is paid out directly from the cash register, a complete paid-out record must be kept. Some accountants prefer a petty cash box with a receipted slip for each paid-out and then a recording of those slips each time the cash in the box is replenished by check (in which case the recording of where the money went would be in the check disbursement journal). Others prefer to have the money taken from the register and rung out each time, with the validating receipt being attached to the register slip, and then have these paid-outs recorded in a paid-out journal each day. Whichever is preferred, do keep track of exactly what those paid-outs are so they become part of the total disbursement record.

In our example we showed charge account capability for this bookstore. Obviously charge sales have to be recorded in such a way that the money can be retrieved through periodic billing, whether the accounts be in-house or nonbank credit cards.

If one has a cash register, the customer's sales slip that pops out of the register when the transaction is completed is sufficient for the customer's purposes of receipt, and the store's need for a record of that sale is satisfied because the details will appear as part of the totals on the Z tape when the register is rung out at the end of the day. (If you do not have a cash register, every transaction must be written in duplicate with a receipt copy for the customer and a record copy for the store, from which details will be taken for balancing at the end of the day.)

However, the cash register slip isn't sufficient for a charge sale. A charge sales slip has to be written with customer information and details of the transaction on it, so this information can be transferred later to the customer's charge record. Each charge customer should have an account card on which is recorded all of that person's charge and payment transactions. It is from these account cards, supported by the charge sales slip documents, that monthly billings will be prepared. These records should be kept up-to-date on a daily basis. They are valuable because they represent money and should be as carefully maintained as your checkbook.

Obviously if you have a computerized system, the details above will differ, but the principle is the same—to record information for later retrieval.

Disbursements are the next phase of record keeping. Obviously we don't just mean the petty amounts mentioned above, but all the disbursements of all the store's monies. Much of it will go to pay for new merchandise, and much will go for overhead and operating expenses. Some, we hope, will eventually go to the investor, but wherever it goes, a record of it has to be kept. "I don't know where the money goes" isn't an allowable lament in the retail business. We aren't talking about budgets in this chapter. Budgets will guide your expenditures, but whether you are on budget or not, you must record exactly what happens to all the money that comes in. It is of interest not only to you, but to accountants from all levels of a tax-collecting government.

In the sales journal we show in detail where the money comes from and what we did with it. We banked it, or most of it, having already paid out small amounts in cash. Now we are going to record where we spent the money so happily deposited.

Just as with cash receipts or sales, it is necessary to have a journal in which disbursements are recorded. It is possible to purchase checking account systems that have the capability of indicating with carboned checks and an underlying columned sheet not only to whom each check was written, but to which expense account it is charged. Whether you do it this way, enter each disbursement separately in a journal, or have a computerized system that does it automatically, records must be kept of all monies paid out.

A first step is to decide which categories of expense you want to establish. An acountant's advice is invaluable here, especially if that accountant will help with filing tax reports later. You should keep together the costs of space, such as rent, tax adjustments if any, utilities, and so forth and, in other categories, advertising, office expenses, supplies, staff (very accurate records have to be kept of wages paid, income tax and FICA—Social Security—withheld), and so on. And of course it is essential to keep track of all the costs having to do with merchandise purchased for resale, the cost of the goods themselves as well as the freight costs to get them into the store, and the costs of returning books to the publishers.

The disbursements journal can be set up along the same lines as the sales journal, with categories of expense across the top of the sheet or sheets if a double-page spread is needed, and a date column down the left-hand side. In this journal, however, because there may be many disbursements on the same day, the date is written in only when the disbursement is recorded. Thus an entry might show on line 1, dated April 1, check #501 to John Bent for $127.00, and then across the sheet in the supplies column, $127.00 again because the check was to pay for bags bought from Bent. Line 2, dated April 1 again, check #502 to Harper & Row for $1,018.43, and then across the sheet in the books purchased column, $1,000.43 and in the freight column $18.00. Line 3, still dated April 1, shows "cash" in the column where the check numbers are above and PC (petty cash) #367 in the payee column; the amount is $24.00, then across the page there is $12.00 under postage and $12.00 under supplies. This transaction #367 covers two paid-outs, one to the post office for stamps and another to the grocery store for paper towels, the receipts of which are stapled together with a cover slip showing the number #367 and filed away sequentially (table 12-4).

Some disbursement journals are sufficiently detailed so that they are complete within themselves, having all of the withholding information on wages paid, for instance, and everything else. Other disbursement journals show the actual amounts paid out, with the detail of how that amount was arrived at indicated in supporting journals of individual accounts, in which each category has its own pages for more complete information.

As with the sales journal, the disbursement journal must be balanced. In this case, the "Amount" column has to equal the total of all the columns showing the categories of expense.

A bookstore's major disbursements will be paying for merchan-

TABLE 12-4

Date	Check #	Amount	To	For Adv.	Postage	Supplies	Books	Cards		Freight
Apr. 1	501	127.00	John Bent			127.00				
Apr. 1	502	1,018.43	Harper & Row				1,000.43			18.00
Apr. 1	cash	24.00	PC #367		12.00	12.00				

dise purchased for resale. Small stores may simply keep their unpaid invoices for merchandise received in an "open file" until paid, after which they are filed by publisher in the paid file. While one pays invoices and not statements, it is especially important in this basic system to attach to the vendor's invoices that vendor's statement showing exactly which were paid, by what check, and on which date. In essence, these statements become individual vendor account journals.

The limitation of such a simple system is that you have no instant access to the bookstore's total record of purchases and payments with an individual vendor; neither is there a running figure of accounts payable. If a purchase journal is kept with supporting file records for each publisher, total information is always accessible. The bookseller has to decide which system is most useful and affordable.

All record keeping takes time, so keep only those records that are essential for tax purposes and for you own use in managing the business. However, without exception, records must be kept of what you sell, what you buy for resale, and what you spend to keep the business operating.

Because of stiff legal requirements for accurate reporting of payroll information, even the smallest store should keep that information in a separate payroll journal. This can be set up in two parts, the first on a period basis, however one pays help (by week or month), to show the detail of wages paid during that period, and the second part by employee so that each member of the staff has a separate page in the journal on which all the details of that person's wages, withholding, and the like, are recorded.

With all income, receivables, disbursements, and payables properly entered in their journals, the next step in keeping financial records is "posting" the total figures from these journals to the ledger. A ledger is a summary of accounts that shows increases and decreases. It is where all the information about each of the accounts is brought together.

The ledger will have a page for each account of both income and disbursement, as well as asset and liability accounts. All these figures provide the information for the trial balance and the financial statement, balance sheet, tax reports, and any other report that is required based on the flow of money through the business.

We are now getting to bookkeeping, which is a step beyond simple record keeping. While it is not impossible for a nonprofessional to do his/her own bookkeeping, it is impossible to provide an adequate bookkeeping course within this manual. This is where the bookseller has to exercise one of several options: study a book on retail accounting, attend an accounting course, or hire a book-keeper.

Earlier in this chapter, it was suggested that an accountant set up the bookkeeping system for the store, establishing proper accounts, working out the forms to be used, and so on. With such a system established, and some instruction from the accountant, any intelligent bookseller could probably do all of the steps in record keeping, bookkeeping, and even preparing tax reports as well as financial statements. However, bookkeeping can get to be an almost full-time job if it is combined with office correspondence, bill paying, order processing, and all the other paperwork that is involved. So the question must be asked, Do I want to be a bookseller so I can be a bookkeeper? Or do I want to be a bookseller so I can meet the public and sell books, so I can do displays and plan advertising, so I can buy those books I know my customers will want? Although it is essential for the owner or manager of a bookstore to know what the figures are, where they came from, and what they indicate, it is frequently a misdirection of energy for the bookstore's creator to be tied to journals and ledgers. If the bookseller is more interested in the business of the business than in anything else, then of course that is where the bookseller should spend time, hiring someone creative to do the other things.

The point is that a bookkeeper trained but not as exalted as an accountant can easily keep the books for a bookstore, providing that bookkeeper does not feel drowned by detail. The paperwork is daunting. Whatever the decision—to do it yourself or to hire a bookkeeper—it is wise to have a regular accountant do an annual check of the accounts. This can be a full audit or merely an unaudited inspection to make sure you stay on the right track. Accountants can sometimes spot problems that are not as apparent to the person who is working with the figures each day.

We conclude as we began by urging the bookseller to be aware of the figures. The best hired bookkeeper is a keeper of books, a recorder of facts and figures. The bookseller is the one who will make decisions based on those facts and figures and so must know what those figures are and how they came to be.

Chapter 13

Reading, Understanding, and Using Financial Statements

G. ROYSCE SMITH

Whether or not you do your own bookkeeping and accounting, you must be able to comprehend the two main documents that are the end product of all this ado about figures: the balance sheet and the profit and loss statement. The balance sheet is like a still photograph: it shows your financial position at a specific time. The profit and loss statement is a movie: it shows your financial activity. Together they constitute the financial statement of a business. The balance sheet tells you at a glance whether your financial news is good or bad. The P & L statement tells you what *you* must do, as a good director, to make the news better.

Although it is true that we can pay someone else to do everything we need done for us, including interpreting a financial statement, it is you who will make the final decisions on what steps must be taken to improve your financial position. There is seldom complete objectivity when it comes to interpreting financial statements. Numbers may not lie, but the ways in which they can be interpreted are various.

It behooves every store owner to develop a degree of proficiency in understanding financial statements. You must comprehend what financial advisers are saying and be able to assess whether it is in line with your ultimate goals. Decisions made with purely financial logic may not be the best decisions in the long run. Financial (and legal) advice is only that: advice. The buck (on business decisions) stops with *you*.

The Balance Sheet

A balance sheet consists of three main parts: assets, liabilities, and owner's equity. A balance sheet is given its name because, quite simply, it is a sheet on which everything must balance. The sum of the assets must be equal to the sum of the liabilities plus the owner's equity.

ASSETS = LIABILITIES + OWNER'S EQUITY

Examples of what assets, liabilities, and owner's equity consist of can be found in table 13-1.

TABLE 13-1

SAMPLE BALANCE SHEET ACCOUNTS (1–500)

ASSETS (1–300)

	Account No.
Cash (1–50)	
Petty Cash (Cash on Hand)	11
Cash in Bank—General (Regular Bank Account)	21
Cash in Bank—Payroll (Payroll Bank Account)	31
Receivables from Others (51–100)	
Accounts Receivable—Customers	51
Accounts Receivable—Others	81
Inventories (101–150)	
Inventory—Goods for Sale	101
Inventory—Supplies	121
Prepaid Expenses (151–200)	
Prepaid Advertising	151
Prepaid Insurance	161
Prepaid Interest	171
Prepaid Rent	181
Property and Equipment (201–250)	
Land	201
Buildings	211
Buildings—Allowance for Depreciation	212
Automobiles and Trucks	216
Automobiles and Trucks—Allowance for Depreciation	217
Furniture and Office Equipment	221
Furniture and Office Equipment—Allowance for Depreciation	222
Leasehold Improvements—Rented Property Improvements	246
Leasehold Improvements—Allowance for Amortization	247
Miscellaneous Assets (251–300)	
Business Starting Costs	251
Deposits (Advance Payments)	261

LIABILITIES (301–500)

Notes and Amounts Payable to Others (301–350)

Notes Payable—Short-term	301
Accounts Payable (Bills Payable)	311
Sales Tax Payable	321
FICA Tax Withheld	331
Federal Income Taxes Withheld	332
State Income Taxes Withheld	333

Expenses Owed to Others (351–400)

Accrued Wages (Wages Owed)	351
Accrued Federal Unemployment Taxes (Owed)	371
Accrued State Unemployment Taxes (Owed)	372
Accrued Real Estate Taxes (Owed)	381
Accrued Inventory Taxes (Owed)	382
Accrued Federal Income Taxes (Owed)	391
Accrued State Income Taxes (Owed)	392

Long-term Obligations (401–450)

Notes Payable—Long-term	401
Mortgages Payable	411

Owner's Equity (451–500)

Capital Investment (Investment in Business)*	451
Capital Stock (Stock Issued)†	461
Drawings (Cash Used Personally)*	481
Retained Earnings (Profit Not Spent)	491

*Sole owners and partners only.
†Corporations only.

The first three categories—cash, receivables, and inventories—are the most important because they are the most volatile and the most controllable. Cash on hand, for example: no more should be kept than is needed for the day-to-day transaction of cash business, such as the amount of bills and change you begin the day with in the cash register, plus a small amount of backup change and small bills to replenish the supply when necessary. A petty cash box out of which are paid such incidentals as stamps, small delivery fees, and the like is frequently maintained with a low fund balance. It is possible to pay for these incidentals out of the cash register if the "paid out" information is kept accurately and later recorded in the proper expense categories.

Receivables seriously affect cash flow. Receivables are the amounts of money owed to the store by charge customers on in-house accounts as opposed to bank credit card accounts, which are collected upon deposit. If your customers pay you promptly, they give you good cash flow. If a disproportionate number of them, however, pay after sixty days or more, you may have a difficult time paying your creditors. If you have to borrow money to pay your bills because your customers are not paying you, not only is your cash flow in trouble, but you have the added expense of interest on loans.

Booksellers with slow-paying customers should consider the possibility of using bank credit cards exclusively rather than in-house charge accounts, even if such a change would mean the loss of a few of those slow-paying customers.

Inventories that are abnormally high in relation to turnover also result in adverse cash flow. Moreover, whenever interest rates are high, either on loans or on savings (and especially when on both), turnover is more important than net profit. Turnover is the number of times the average inventory for a given period is sold. Because it is so important, this chapter will study turnover at some length.

The most volatile health signs under liabilities on a balance sheet are notes payable (short-term), accounts payable, and, to a lesser degree only because they are less flexible once they have been arranged, notes payable (long-term). All these items are controllable by merchandise budgeting and cash-flow projections. Merchandise budgeting is the subject of the next chapter, so let's turn our attention to cash-flow projections.

Even if you have never run a business, you must have run up against a time when you were short of cash. Although this is traumatic for an individual, it can be disastrous for a business. Even profitable businesses have been forced to close their doors as a result of cash shortages. Inability to pay bills and replace fast-selling stock can be reversed through proper cash-flow projections, which are estimates of how much cash you'll be receiving and spending during a particular period.

If you are just starting in business, a crucial time at best, these estimates are difficult to make with any degree of accuracy. Though you have no real experience with actual expenses, it is critical that you make an attempt at estimating income rather than fly totally blind. If you have been in business for more than a year, you should be able to make such projections more easily.

Here is the formula for projecting cash flow:

BEGINNING CASH ON HAND + SALES INCOME − EXPENSES = ENDING CASH ON HAND

Example: Cash-flow projections should be done on a weekly basis for new businesses or whenever cash is tight, but monthly estimates should be sufficient for a going business. In the former case, you will need to know the weeks when fixed expenses such as rent and loans are due. You must also time your payments for inventory (for example, during weeks when demands on cash are less severe). Generally, cash-flow projections should cover periods of three or six months if they are to be useful. Projecting ahead a week at a time will give you little, if any, help. And don't forget to revise your plan when reality causes inevitable deviations and detours.

Why go to this trouble? To avoid bigger troubles and sleepless nights. As with the cash-flow projection's handmaiden, merchandise budgeting, the purpose here is to keep you from being shocked out of your peace of mind, which is essential to creative merchandising. Neither cash-flow projections nor merchandise budgeting will eliminate your problems, but they *will* warn you in advance when a problem is coming and what it will be, thereby allowing you to plan strategies for minimizing the problem or avoiding it altogether. You may decide to plan a sale to generate additional sales income, postpone a payment that is not absolutely or immediately required, or go to the bank for a short-term loan, which you'll be more likely to get if you have a cash-flow projection in hand. It reassures your banker that you know what you are doing.

Now, having looked at how we may use the first two elements of the balance sheet, we must return to our discussion of the third element, owner's equity, which is the difference between assets and liabilities.

Owner's equity is more than just a figure that tells you the net worth of your business. It is a factor in determining one of the most important figures that your financial statement can generate, your return on investment (ROI). ROI is the amount of money your investment is producing. There are many ways that money can be invested and return in excess of 10 percent. Therefore, it is expected that retail businesses should return 12 to 15 percent. Otherwise the owners, if they are in retailing for the purpose of making money, would be well advised to put their cash in a safer, higher-yielding investment. From these remarks, it should be obvious that even a high percentage of net profit is not a true sign that a business is "profitable." In ROI terms, profit is measured on monies invested, not on sales. Here is the formula for determining ROI:

$$\text{NET PROFIT} - \text{OWNER'S EQUITY} = \text{ROI}$$

The Profit and Loss Statement

"How's your P & L?" the business doctor may ask. You're being asked about your profit and loss statement. I hope you are able to say, "Very well, thank you."

The P & L (table 13-2) is also divided into three major parts—sales, cost of goods sold, and expenses. The difference between the first two—sales and cost of goods sold—gives you your gross profit. When you subtract expenses from gross profit, you get net profit or loss.

TABLE 13-2

PROFIT OR LOSS STATEMENT ACCOUNTS (501–800)

Sales and Other Income (501–550)	Account No.
Sales of Merchandise	501
Sales Returns and Allowances	502
Cash Discounts Allowed (Customer Discounts)	503
Service Charges	511
Rental Library Income	521
Miscellaneous Income	541
Cost of Goods Sold (551–600)	
Cost of Merchandise Sold	551
Freight on Purchases	561
Operating Expense Accounts (601–799)	
Wages and Salaries	601
Rentals	611
Advertising	621
Taxes (Except Federal Income Taxes)	631
Interest	641
Supplies	651
Dues and Subscriptions	661
Repairs	671
Travel and Entertainment	691
Outgoing Postage to Customers	701
Outgoing Postage—Returns to Publishers	702
Telephone and Telegraph	703
Group Insurance	711
Workers' Compensation Insurance	712
Bad Debts	721
Heat, Light, and Power	731
Depreciation	741
Professional Services	751
Miscellaneous Expense	761
Federal Income Tax	800

The elements in determining cost of goods sold are as follows:

Beginning inventory, at cost
Purchases
Inbound shipping charges
Inventory markdowns
Known shrinkage

These are added together, and from them are deducted:

Cash discounts on purchases
Ending inventory, at cost

The resulting figure is cost of goods sold.

Obviously, anything that affects sales, cost of goods sold, or expenses affects the bottom line, net profit. But they are not the only factors affecting net profit. Turnover also plays a part here, just as it affects the total profitability picture and the bookseller's return on investment.

Turnover is the number of times the average inventory for a given period is replaced to produce sales for the period. It is computed by dividing the gross sales for a given period by the average inventory at retail for the same period. Turnover may be computed for any desired period of time. Normally it is computed for periods of one year or any fraction of a year. Computing turnover for longer periods of time would not seem to have much practical value.

To compute the turnover for any specific quarter of a year, we total sales for the period (table 13-3).

TABLE 13-3

Total Sales

(First Quarter)

January	$3,000
February	2,500
March	3,000
	$8,500

We then compute the average inventory for the period. First, add the beginning inventory on January 1 to the ending inventories on January 31, February 28, and March 31 (table 13-4).

TABLE 13-4

Total Inventory

(First Quarter)

January 1	$12,000
January 31	10,000
February 28	12,000
March 31	12,000
	$46,000

We divide the sum of these figures by 4 to obtain the average inventory for the period. (Although the period covered is three months, we are entering four figures into our sum. Thus, we must divide by 4.)

$$\$46,000 \div 4 = \$11,500 \text{ } average \text{ } inventory$$

Now we divide total sales by average inventory.

$$\$8,500 \div \$11,500 = .74 \; turns$$

If we maintain the same ratio between sales and stock throughout the year, we may project that the annual turnover rate will be 4
times .74, or 2.96. In other words, we multiply the turnover rate for
the period by the number of times the period occurs in the year.

*Always remember that in these computations we must use only
figures of the same kind.* If we work with sales figures at retail,
inventory figures must also be at retail. If either figure is at cost, the
other figure must be at cost.

Turnover has been called the best yardstick for measuring the
success of a business. Some booksellers, who think they are in
business only for aesthetic considerations, ignore turnover and wonder why they never show a profit. Attention to turnover can be
taken to extremes, but viewed realistically, it can be a tool by which
a retailer may gauge performance.

Assume that a store is doing an annual volume of $100,000 at
retail and shows a net profit after expenses (*including salaries*) of
$3,500, or 3.5 percent. Turnover, even without any change in sales,
can seriously affect the health of this operation. This $100,000 store
operating on an average inventory of $50,000 retail is getting only
two turns a year. The investment in a $50,000 inventory, assuming a
clear 40 percent discount for purposes of illustration, would be
$30,000 at cost. The net profit of $3,500 represents an 11.7 percent
return on the $30,000 investment. But if the store were to do the
same $100,000 volume on a $25,000 retail inventory ($15,000 cost),
the return of $3,500 on the investment would be 23.3 percent.

On the decreased inventory the store would be operating with
fresh, current stock. Profits should increase because the owner
would not constantly have to borrow money on which he must pay
interest; his inventory taxes would be lower; he would need to have
less stockroom space and could give more space to the selling area;
he would spend less money on markdowns because his stock would
not stay around long enough to get shopworn; he would be able to
control his smaller inventory more easily, and pilferage should
decrease; and most important, he would find a new sense of
confidence and well-being, which would allow him to think more
about making sales than disposing of dead stock.

On the other hand, demanding too high a rate of turnover can
create serious stock problems. Basic titles will not always be on
hand; new, fast-moving titles will be in short supply; and the store
will not have a representative stock within the fields it has chosen to
cover. Consequently the buyer who goes too far in trying to increase

turnover will find he is producing a negative effect. It is necessary to have the right amount and kind of stock to generate the desired sales. Too low an inventory results in lost sales, and customers who are repeatedly disappointed go to other booksellers.

The "right" turnover varies in every business. The right turnover for floor coverings is considered to be two turns a year; for millinery, eight to ten. The consensus is that bookstores should aim for between three and five turns a year (paperback stores should aim for the higher figure). The lower the price of the item being sold, the higher the turnover should be. Scholarly bookstores will usually have to be content with the lower figure. But any store whose turns fall below two will be in serious trouble.

How can you spot the causes for bad turnover in your store? One reason might be a low outgoing-postage figure. This suggests that no returns have been made. The buyer has been unwilling to face up to correcting the mistakes that have created his abnormally high inventory either by making returns where possible or by taking markdowns where necessary.

Where should he look for the stock that is not moving, which must be returned or marked down? First and most obvious are last season's new books that did not catch on or didn't sell as well as expected. Returning these titles should have begun the day after Christmas. Some of these books can be sold at 50 percent off in the store, and that is less costly than making returns.

Aside from new titles, we should look at other categories of books. Perhaps the western Americana section has slowed down. Maybe there has been a shift in emphasis in the cookbook section. Are there too many kinds of Bibles? Are customers favoring paperback children's books over your extensive selection of cloth?

Do you really know how many copies of a title you need to have on hand? A two-month supply when two weeks' worth will do can sabotage turnover. Or are you not carrying enough of a fast-moving title? Turnover is controlling fast- as well as slow-moving titles. Inventory controls will keep stocks down and sales and turnover up.

Peak selling seasons require properly timed buying. Turnover will nosedive if you bring Christmas merchandise in on September 1. On the other hand, if you don't get it in until December 1, you will not have books on hand for the beginning of the selling season. If merchandise arrives too late for any promotion through the fault of the shipper, it should be returned promptly.

How can you use a budget to improve turnover? Any budget at all will help accomplish this. A very simple budgeting rule will help: *If you want to get four turns a year, the stock you have on hand at the beginning of any month should not exceed the sales you plan to make during the next three months.*

Turnover can be improved by the wise buying of new titles. Nothing is easier to say or harder to accomplish. If you do not think you have a customer for a book, don't buy it. We all know that far too many books are being published. The editor of a publishing house has reasons for each title selected for publication. You must have your own reasons for stocking each title. Even so, do not buy an inordinate amount, particularly if you are within range of a good wholesaler. Certainly you should not buy on your initial purchase the entire amount you expect to sell. Sales reps, if you have them, will disagree with this statement because that is their job. Your job is to manage your resources so that you will remain in business. Following are some questions to ask yourself if you want to improve turnover:

1. Do I give valuable space to slow sellers or merchandise past selling peak?
2. Am I slow to take my medicine on a dog, by either return or markdown?
3. Will I buy more of an item than I really need in a reasonable length of time to take advantage of a price concession or higher discount?
4. Do I fail to get books to the selling floor within twenty-four hours of receipt?
5. Do I find it easy to ignore the fact that overstocks reduce turnover and increase markdowns and shopworn merchandise?
6. Do I buy up to the hilt so that there is no cash in the bank for sleepers?
7. Do I buy with my total season's sale in mind rather than the first month's?
8. Do I keep an old sideline or gift-book line when I take on a new one?
9. Do I buy merchandise that I think just *might* sell?
10. Do I spread myself too thin by offering too many titles in too many subject classifications?
11. Do I buy for the best discount and poor turnover from publishers rather than for a fair discount and excellent turnover?
12. Do I reorder basic stock on past rather than current performance?
13. Do I think I can be everything to everybody?
14. Do I buy from publishers equally rather than concentrate on those who give the best terms and service?
15. Do I take in merchandise after the cancellation date that I have put on my order?
16. Do I mark an item or line down without first trying it in a different location or with a different display?

17. Do I often buy books that are outside the price lines that sell best in my store?
18. Do I guess at how long a book has been in stock rather than age it at the time of receipt?
19. Do I think that fast-turning items will take care of themselves?
20. Do I think all the classifications in my store should have the same rate of turnover?
21. Do I carry an extensive array of titles purely for prestige?
22. Do I carry duplicate items by carrying competing lines?
23. Do I take seasonal merchandise in too far ahead of the selling season without extended dating for payment?
24. Do I keep promotional merchandise (such as remainders) too long after the promotion has passed?
25. Do I work without a buying plan?
26. Do I think it would be good to have a better system for following up on orders but find that I don't have time to work on it?
27. Do I accept the publisher's representatives' stock counts and suggested orders without question?
28. Do I think that turnover is in itself a sought-after objective?
29. Do I stock up from the publisher to take advantage of a discount break or an advertising allowance when I would be saving money by relying on my jobber?

The correct answer for all these questions is "No."

Turnover is not all science. There are subjective decisions that affect it, and one of these is what a store stocks. When a store is just opening, it analyzes its community. Then it tries to get together a stock that is representative for that community.

Beginning booksellers (and some who have been in the business long enough to know better) are inclined to think that there ought to be one single list that will make them and all other booksellers instantly successful. There is no such list.

The only person who can tell you what a truly representative stock will be for your bookstore is you.

A representative stock on Nantucket will certainly not be representative in Salt Lake City, just as what may be representative in a store down the block may not be representative for you, even though it may have common elements. A representative stock reflects the personality of a community as it is filtered through the personality and sensibility of the bookstore buyer.

All buyers, being human, bring to their work some degree of subjectivity and an even greater degree of subtlety as well. The best buyers are the ones who recognize and allow for the differences between their own personalities and those of their communities and realize that the personalities of both are constantly changing.

When we keep sales records by title or record lost sales or analyze our special orders, we are looking for the ways in which we may respond to such changes.

Stock with good turnover is flexible stock. A flexible buyer can respond to these changes as they occur, and a flexible stock will result. There is a scientific tool to help the buyer do that. It is called "merchandise budget" and will be considered in the next chapter.

You may think we have strayed from the subject of this chapter by spending so much time and space discussing inventory turnover. We have not. We are showing you how to use the information apparent in the financial statement figures. You want to increase your sales while reducing the level of your inventory, which will increase the rate of your turnover and improve your cash flow. These improvements will also increase your profit and your return on investment.

You will also use your financial statement, especially at year-end to compare percentages of expenses with national averages and to make other comparisons, with your own previous year-end statements, for instance. How are you doing? Are your increases where they should be—in sales? Are you reducing your percentage of cost of goods sold? A series of financial statements could be considered a chronological report card. If you are becoming a better business-person, those statements will give you better grades each year, and better grades mean greater return.

Chapter 14

Budgeting

ELIOT LEONARD

This chapter explains the importance of budgeting for both new and experienced booksellers, as well as how to make, monitor, and modify budgets. Budgets are among the most important tools of retail store management, and all booksellers should make ongoing use of them to attain success. Essentially, budgeting is planning: in simple terms, a budget is a number of carefully considered figures that the bookseller can use to set reasonable financial and merchandise goals. As results come in, the bookseller monitors them against the budgets for discrepancies that demand a change in certain management actions and/or the modification of some budget figures. That procedure—making, monitoring, and modifying a budget—is what can keep a business on a profitable course.

There are successful bookshops built without such careful planning by entrepreneurial-type owner/managers. More often, however, businesses fail because their owners needed, but did not employ, tools such as those offered.

Profit and Loss Budget

This is the major budget for a new or established bookstore, with which a bookseller can set profit objectives for his or her whole operation. If you use this tool, you will consciously reason out the cost of goods sold and each operating expense, rather than work in a vacuum. To be effective, the annual budget plan should be divided into twelve sales months so that you can compare actual performance with your budget each month. This way you'll notice danger signals early, and problems will not grow to catastrophic dimensions. Early detection allows for easier correction.

Table 14-1 is a sample profit and loss budget in which a bookseller plans for an increase in sales from $132,000 in the prior year to $150,000 in the upcoming year. The figures contained within the chart are not important, although they are reasonable and realistic for a store of this size. We will use table 14-1 to show how a budget is made. For a new store, there are no previous-year numbers, so the new bookseller needs to use educated guesses. To increase the accuracy of such guesswork, the new bookseller should use the most recent ABA financial survey plus other industry figures and should seek the advice of experienced booksellers. Whether new or experienced, a bookseller should include the following items in a profit and loss budget.

1. *Sales.* This is the first and most important element in a P & L plan. Sales pay for all merchandise costs and all operating expenses, which in turn must fall within acceptable parameters when expressed as percentages of sales. As you think about what your sales goal should be, go over all the reasons for volume increases and decreases and how they might affect your bookstore in the coming year. In table 14-1, our bookseller budgeted a 13.6 percent increase ($18,000), 10 percent because sales have been trending up and the merchandising continues to get better, plus 3.6 percent for inflation. There can be many other causes for volume changes.

2. *Cost of Sales.* The following five factors are involved here:

   Actual Cost of Merchandise Sold. Buying will be more efficient because our bookseller has gained experience in the market and is able to buy at greater savings. Thus, in table 14-1, the discounts average 41 percent, as compared with 40 percent the prior year.

   Transportation. Our bookseller will save 0.1 percent over the previous year by combining small orders and special orders with larger stock orders, thus cutting down on total transportation costs.

   Markdowns. Our bookseller plans to buy more efficiently and to watch publishers' returns policies more closely, resulting in fewer markdowns. Markdowns are budgeted with a 0.2 percent saving over the previous year.

   Shortage. Security is still a problem, so shortage, which covers pilferage, breakage, and all other shrinkage, is budgeted at 1.5 percent of sales, the same as in the prior year.

TABLE 14-1

Profit & Loss Statement

	Upcoming Year		Previous Year	
	Dollars	*Percentage*	*Dollars*	*Percentage*
Sales	$150,000	100.0	$132,000	100.0
Cost of Sales				
Cost of merchandise	88,500	59.0	79,200	60.0
Transportation	4,200	2.8	3,828	2.9
Markdowns	1,500	1.0	1,584	1.2
Shortage	2,250	1.5	1,980	1.5
Cash discounts (+)	(450)	(0.3)	(396)	(0.3)
Total cost of sales	96,000	64.0	86,196	65.3
Gross Margin	54,000	36.0	45,804	34.7
Operating Expenses				
Salary & Wages				
Owner (12,000)				
Staff (10,950)	22,950	15.3	21,516	16.3
Payroll taxes	1,350	0.9	1,188	0.9
Rent/occupancy	12,000	8.0	10,956	8.3
Advertising	2,700	1.8	2,640	2.0
Supplies	750	0.5	924	0.7
Utilities	1,500	1.0	1,452	1.1
Telephone	750	0.5	660	0.5
Insurance	900	0.6	792	0.6
Postage	1,050	0.7	792	0.6
Depreciation	1,200	0.8	1,188	0.9
Taxes & licenses	750	0.5	660	0.5
Miscellaneous*	2,550	1.7	2,244	1.7
Total operating expenses	48,450	32.3	45,012	34.1
Net Profit	5,550	3.7	792	0.6

*Includes repairs, maintenance, bad debts, cash over/short, travel, fees, donations, benefits, professional services.

Cash Discounts. This is a credit factor. Our bookseller earns a special discount for paying bills on time. It will remain at 0.3 percent of sales.

3. *Gross Margin.* The bookseller in our example predicts he will be much better at providing merchandise in the upcoming year and will reduce the cost of goods sold from 65.3 to 64.0 percent

of sales. Therefore, the gross margin will increase from 34.7 to 36.0 percent. We have indicated only one or two reasons for each change, but there could be many. We have stated percentages rather than dollars to stress the relationship of every store's cost to sales and the importance of keeping costs in a reasonable proportion to sales. This is the way to think about the future operation.

4. *Operating Expenses.* In bookselling, one of the main reasons for little or no profit, or even store failure, is the lack of efficient expense control. A bookseller who does not examine and question each expenditure is likely to overspend. When you consciously budget—when you study prior payouts, then think of how some might have cost less—you will find savings and be able to lower the budget on those items. It is not fatal if one or two expenses are out of line occasionally, but three or four out of line too often indicate bad management.

The section of the profit and loss budget devoted to operating expenses should include the following items, among others:

5. *Payroll.* This is the largest and most controllable operating expense in retailing, the first element one should consider altering to attain more profit and one of the first expenditures to get out of line when sales do not come up to budget. Salary and wages at 16.3 percent of sales last year are only a little above average, but our bookseller recognizes that the staff should be more efficient and productive as sales volume builds. Therefore, he plans the payroll at 15.3 percent of sales, 1 percent lower than in the previous year. If sales increase as projected, he will be paying out more dollars in payroll even though the percentage is less.

6. *Advertising.* This expense is budgeted too high in too many stores. The 2 percent spent last year is not too high for a bookshop that does productive direct mail, book fairs, or author parties, but our bookseller is not sure the results justify the money he's spent. He is willing to spend about the same dollars, but that expenditure reduces the budget by 0.2 percent, to 1.8 percent, in the expectation of increased sales.

7. *Supplies.* This is another area for potential savings in many bookstores, if management would examine how supplies are purchased and how they are used. A new store needs to spend

extra dollars on beginning supplies, but a mature store should spend under 0.7 percent of sales. To save dollars next year, our bookseller will buy supplies at variety and discount stores instead of from commercial stationers. He will also seek bids on major items such as merchandise bags and gift papers. He will keep supplies under better control in the stockroom. These actions should save 0.2 percent of sales, so that supplies are budgeted at 0.5 percent of sales. This is the way all expenses should be analyzed when a new budget is made. Sometimes you will plan to spend more on one or two items; in table 14-1, for instance, the postage expense increases from 0.6 to 0.7 percent of sales. But in most cases you should look for ways to reduce expenses.

8. *Utilities.* Although there is an anticipated increase in dollars for utilities, because of the anticipated increase in sales, the percentage for this expense will drop.

9. *Telephone.* Telephone expense remains much the same, though undoubtedly with greater attention to the use of publishers' WATS lines and to increased economies in regular-usage telephone, expense could be decreased as a percentage of sales.

10. *Insurance.* Some of the increased dollars here reflect a somewhat increased inventory plus the ordinary boosts in insurance premiums.

11. *Postage.* This item is going to go up. Not much we can do about that.

12. *Depreciation.* This item is controlled by purchases of equipment or fixtures that are depreciated over a number of years. There is such a small increase in dollars that the whole as a percentage of sales decreases.

13. *Taxes.* Taxes will remain the same as a percentage of sales.

14. *Miscellaneous.* The same is true for miscellaneous even though a few more dollars are budgeted for this catch-all account.

15. *Total Operating Expense.* In the sample P & L budget, our bookseller plans to spend 1.8 percent less on total operating expenses than he did the prior year.

16. *Net Profit.* When that 1.8 percent saving is added to the budgeted 1.3 percent reduction in cost of sales, the bookseller has an improvement in net profit of 3.1 percent of sales. With net profit itself budgeted at 3.7 percent of sales, the improvement is highly significant.

But this is only the making of the budget. How does a bookseller ensure that his store keep to its plan as closely as possible? By comparing the budget with actual results as they come in and determining which items are off course. These are danger signals that alert the bookseller to possible problem areas, to the potential need to change operating and/or merchandising procedures, and to the definite need to modify budgets for future months to reflect current actual results.

Examine sales, the prime element in retailing, closely each month. If they are higher than budget, great; you have only to make sure that you restock titles that are selling and have enough help to sustain the increased sales. But if sales are behind plan, you have to monitor and adjust expense items on your P & L statement.

Analyze why sales are behind plan. Think of all the controllable and uncontrollable factors that might affect sales, and correct what you can. It's very important that you also analyze what happens to cost of sales and operating expenses when sales fall short. Sales being under budget for just a month or two may not be too bad; small adjustments will take care of the problem. But if there are large declines or three to four months of sales under predictions, you should take strong action.

For example, if you planned January and February sales at $10,000 each month and attained only $9,000, or 10 percent under budget, look first at controllable expenses, because they rise as a percentage of sales when sales are under plan, reducing net profit even further. Decide which controllable expenses you must re-budget. For each expense, the actual dollar figure must be reduced so that the original percentage of sales figure is restored. Reduce book buying, and be even more efficient if possible. With spending curbed, your percentage of net profit may continue close to your original plan.

If payroll was budgeted at 15 percent of sales for the months of January and February, and sales come in at $9,000 instead of $10,000 each month, then a monthly payroll of $1,500 becomes 16.7 percent of sales. To bring the business back on course, you must reduce payroll dollars. Advertising, utilities, telephone, and all the rest rise as percentages of sales when sales decline, so you must look for ways to reduce them and to tighten budgets. Monitoring and modifying a profit and loss budget is the only way to retain as much as possible of the profit you originally planned. You might not attain it completely, but you must not just sit and wait for sales to improve. The more you put on paper in planning, the better chance you give yourself to succeed and grow according to the original plan.

Merchandise Plan

Budgeting money is important, but so is budgeting merchandise. Planning the flow of books and other items into and out of the bookshop is one way to avoid another big reason for retail store failure—not having the right amount of merchandise at the right time. A merchandise plan helps control the flow of merchandise by relating inventory and purchases to sales.

Table 14-2 is a sample merchandise plan. Here's how to make, monitor, and modify it.

Step 1. Divide a columned sheet into three sections that run vertically on the page: purchases, sales, and end-of-month inventory. Divide each section into three columns: previous year actual results, current year planned results, and current year actual results. Merchandise plans usually cover six-month periods; list the six months to be budgeted along the left-hand edge of the sheet.

Step 2. Fill in the previous year's purchasing, sales, and inventory figures in the appropriate columns; you'll include six figures in each column, one for each month, as well as a beginning inventory figure at the head of the end-of-month inventory section. The latter figure is actually the ending inventory for the month prior to the plan's beginning. All the figures should be available from your accounting records.

Sales

Step 3. Now make the new budget. Start by planning sales, the ruling figure on which all other budgeting depends. Use the previous year as a starting point (booksellers whose stores are new will have to estimate), then try to think of every factor that will increase or decrease sales this year. There are dozens of reasons for different sales figures: Have your business hours changed? Is there more or less competition? Will you be doing a special summer or school-opening promotion this year? Did you have more book fairs last year than you plan this year?

In table 14-2, our sample bookseller plans an increase in sales each month because positive factors outweigh the negative. Also, because this is the bookseller's third year in business, his accumulated experience helps to continue building volume. Therefore, he plans a total sales budget for the period of $91,000, versus the $83,000 of the previous year.

Step 4. Now plan your end-of-month inventories. Your main guides are your prior-year figures and the turnover you want to

TABLE 14-2

Merchandise Plan

July 1, 1984 to December 31, 1984

Month	Purchases			Sales			E.O.M. Inventory		
	1983 Actual	1984 Plan	1984 Actual	1983 Actual	1984 Plan	1984 Actual	1983 Actual	1984 Plan	1984 Actual
Beginning of Period							40,000	41,000	42,000
July	10,500	11,000	11,000	8,500	9,000	9,000	42,000	43,000	44,000
August	11,000	13,000 (12,000)	13,000	9,000	10,000	11,000	44,000	46,000	46,000
September	13,000	16,000	15,000	11,000	12,000	12,000	46,000	50,000	49,000
October	13,000	16,500 (17,500)	17,500	11,000	12,500	12,500	48,000	54,000	54,000
November	16,500	17,000	18,500	12,500	13,500	13,500	52,000	58,000	59,000
December	29,000	34,000 (33,000)	34,000	31,000	34,000	35,000	50,000	58,000	58,000
Totals	93,000	108,000	109,000	83,000	91,000	93,000	46,000	50,000	50,285
Monthly Average									

This merchandise plan might fit a $150,000-annual-volume, 1,200-square-foot store doing about 60 percent of its sales in the second half of the year and about 40 percent in the first half.

All figures are at retail. Turnover is about 1.8 for this period, figured as follows: Turnover = sales/average inventory = 91,000/50,000 = 1.82.

achieve. In addition, estimate when your sales will be highest and when they will be lowest, and anticipate these periods by buying heavily just prior to peak months and lightly just prior to valley months.

Beginning of Period Inventory

In table 14-2, our bookseller begins by entering the inventory—$41,000—for the beginning of his budget period—July 1, 1984—under "1984 Plan." This is actually the ending inventory from the budget for the previous period, which ended June 30, 1984; since the new budget was prepared before that date was reached, the bookseller uses the budget, rather than the actual, figure. He then fills in an inventory figure for each of the six months. He adjusts them a little to achieve a turnover goal of about 1.8 for the half year (the seven inventory numbers average $50,000, and divided into planned sales of $91,000, they give a budgeted turnover of 1.8).

Purchases

Step 5. Now you budget the one area left—purchases. You do so by simple arithmetic; no guessing is involved. For example, in table 14-2 our bookseller plans to start July with $41,000 worth of inventory and to sell $9,000 worth in the course of the month. If he does, he will have $32,000 of inventory on July 31. But he budgets an end-of-month inventory of $43,000 on that date and so must bring $11,000 worth of merchandise into inventory during July. This is not necessarily a buying or ordering figure, but rather the value of the inventory that passes through the bookkeeping system during the month. Some of the merchandise that arrives could have been ordered two months before, and some orders written during the month might not arrive for another three months. But the experienced bookseller has an idea of when his purchases can be expected or will keep and refer to a running ballpark figure.

In the same way, by simple arithmetic, compute purchases for the remaining months. You know what you plan to start each month with (the inventory for the previous month), what you plan to sell each month, and the planned end-of-month inventory and so can easily figure the purchase plan. Do not expect to hit planned figures on the nose. Even if inexact, the figures are still useful as guides to future buying, as you will see in the next step, monitoring the budget.

Step 6. The six-month budget is made. As results come in each month, register them in the three current-year actual results columns. Total sales should be available in a day or two, but a week or two may pass before a month's purchases and end-of-month inventory totals are available. When they are, monitor them; look for variances from the budget that might be warning signs. This is the main reason for making the merchandise budget.

For example, our bookseller planned an ending inventory for July at $43,000, but he actually ended at $44,000. How did this happen? It turns out he ended the previous six months with $1,000 more inventory than he planned, thus starting the July 1 budget with $1,000 too much. Sales and purchases in July came in as planned, so there was no other effect on the inventory. However, monitoring has uncovered the $1,000 variance, which must not be ignored. The bookseller had planned to bring $13,000 worth of inventory into his store in August, but he reduces the amount to $12,000, as shown under the "Purchases—1984 Plan" column in table 14-2. The July figures might become known too late for the bookseller to have much effect on the store's August performance, but his alteration will gradually bring the plan back on course.

Our bookseller ended September with $1,000 less inventory than planned and marked October purchases $1,000 higher, at $17,500 instead of $16,500, in compensation. In November the bookseller purchased $1,000 too much but sold $1,000 more than planned in December and so wiped out the surplus. The store ended December 31 on the budgeted figure of $58,000.

If sales and/or purchases are way out of line for a couple of months, affecting planned inventory badly, you should modify all the remaining months on the budget. Too much inventory too often could lead to excessive returns and markdowns, extra investment of capital, and cluttered shelves that lose sales because bad books hide good books. Too little inventory too often could mean lost sales and clientele; you won't get the full potential of your market. The bigger you are, the more important it is to have a tool like the merchandise budget. If you have a computer, you can make, monitor, and modify your plan more easily.

Cash Flow Projection

This third and relatively simple budget shows how money will flow during the budget period—six or twelve months—and projects cash on hand for the end of each month. It is particularly useful for a new or experienced bookseller applying for a loan because it provides information the prospective lender wants to see. But is use is broader: all merchants should have a clear idea of how much money will be available in each period to pay for merchandise, operating expenses, and possible capital improvements such as a new register, safe, or fixtures.

Table 14-3 is a sample six-month cash flow projection. Here's how to make and use it.

Step 1. List the months included in the budget period—in our example, July through December—at the heads of six vertical columns. Along the left, at the heads of seven horizontal columns, project the two types of income, cash sales and accounts receivable; the three types of payments, operating expenses, accounts payable (merchandise purchased for resale), and capital expenditures; and finally, monthly total and end-of-month cash on hand.

Step 2. In the upper-left corner, indicate how much cash is on hand at the beginning of the budget period—in our example, $1,000. In the appropriate spaces, fill in your predictions of income and payments for each month.

Step 3. For the first month, add the income figures, then subtract the expense figures from the sum to arrive at the monthly total. Then add or subtract the monthly total from the original cash-on-hand figure to arrive at the end-of-month cash-on-hand figure. Then perform the same calculations chronologically for each month, in each case using the ending cash-on-hand figure for one month as the beginning cash-on-hand figure for the next.

In table 14-3, for instance, our bookseller plans that $50 more will come into the store than go out. When he adds the starting $1,000, the bookseller has $1,050 as his end-of-month cash-on-hand figure; this number then becomes the beginning cash-on-hand figure for August.

Even if done less formally than the way illustrated here, budgeting is an essential element in bookstore success.

TABLE 14-3

Six-Month Cash-flow Projection

Cash on hand	July 1st	August 1st	September 1st	October 1st	November 1st	December 1st	Total
	$1,000	$1,050	$ 610	$ 810	$1,110	$ 1,365	
Cash sales (+)	6,000	6,000	6,500	6,500	7,500	13,000	45,000
Accounts receivable cash in (+)	1,500	1,000	1,500	2,000	2,000	5,000	13,000
Operating expenses paid out (−)	2,500	2,450	2,600	2,675	2,950	3,500	16,675
Accounts payable paid out (−)	4,950	4,690	5,200	5,525	6,175	11,485	38,025
Capital expenditures paid out (−)	—	300	—	—	100	—	400
Monthly total (=)	+ 50	− 440	= 200	+ 300	+ 275	+ 3,015	+ 3,400
End-of-month cash on hand	1,050	610	810	1,110	1,385	4,400	4,400

Cash flow is the actual movement of available cash into and out of the business, resulting in a cash-on-hand amount at all times.

Chapter 15

Inventory Management

MICHAEL ALAN FOX

Inventory is the merchandise stocked for resale to customers and is typically a bookstore's largest single financial asset. It is essential to a shop's well-being that the inventory be controlled; the owner must know at any given time what is in stock and out of stock. He must also know what is or is not selling, what has or has not been reordered, and, finally, what the inventory is worth in dollars.

There are two complementary aspects of inventory control. *Dollar controls* chart the aggregate financial results of buying for stock, of customer sales, returns, or markdowns. The use of good dollar controls assures a healthy relationship between the planned inventory level, the anticipated sales, and the other financial aspects of bookstore operations. Dollar controls, or merchandise budgeting, are discussed in depth in chapter 14, "Budgeting."

This chapter will concern itself with *unit controls*. Here the concentration is on specific titles and specific quantities, whether in stock, out of stock, or on order. The focus is also on the sales history or lack of it and on information leading to the decision to return or mark down. The point of all this is to have the right book at the right time for the right customer. A customer comes into a store with money to spend on a copy of *Lord Jim* and will give it to the bookseller in exchange for the book if it is in stock. He will not part with his dollars if *Moby Dick* is in stock, but *Lord Jim* is not . . . unless the bookseller is extraordinarily persuasive and the customer is unusually compliant.

In the broadest view, unit controls are of two types: *perpetual* or *periodic*. A perpetual inventory-control system provides a bookseller with ever-current information about the stock status of each title carried. When books arrive and are ready for shelving, that title's additon to inventory is noted; when those books are sold, sales are subtracted as they occur from the on-hand inventory count. Providing this level of title-by-title information requires systematic discipline and considerable record keeping. Some booksellers do not find it worthwhile to make records of sales as they occur, feeling that the paperwork involved makes demands on their time that outweigh benefits received.

Periodic unit controls are less rigorous but provide less timely information than perpetual unit controls. Where perpetual systems count *sales* by recording them as they take place (a *positive* approach), periodic systems count *unsold* books on an X-number-of-times-per-year schedule (a *negative* approach). With a periodic system, inventory counts can be put off to those times during the year when selling books makes fewer demands on the bookseller's time or when it is appropriate to cull dead titles out of the inventory.

It is not possible to recommend one system exlusively over the other. There are successful bookstores using each, and some stores use both. The bookseller should understand the advantages and disadvantages of both systems, consider some of the methods that can be employed for recording the information and yielding the desired results, and then adopt, and adapt, one of the systems in a workable form. The system chosen should be one on which the bookseller doesn't resent spending time, whether for temperamental reasons, cost reasons, or benefits derived.

When considering all available options for stock control, the bookseller should be mindful of the following factors: (1) Books that sell must be kept in stock; (2) books that don't sell should be identified and either returned to the publisher or marked down; (3) the system should be adaptable enough to yield up-to-date information in a time frame that is useful to the bookseller; (4) the system should be simple, yielding its results as easily as possible; and (5) the system should operate as inexpensively as possible.

The chosen system will always be supplemented by the most primitive of all control systems available: visual awareness of stock. This is frequently referred to as the eyeball method. Some stores, particularly small ones, use this to the exclusion of any formal system. The great virtue of eyeballing is that it encourages direct awareness by the bookseller of the books in stock. Authors and titles are far more easily remembered by association with the physical entity of each book: its bulk, color, location, and jacket art. A great drawback to this method is that while a well-trained memory may recall many thousands of titles, it is virtually impossible to remember accurately each book's rate of sale—particularly if the title isn't selling well or if it is a title that historically sells slowly but consistently. The eyeball method can simplify and supplement other systems to the bookseller's great benefit, but those who rely on it exclusively are likely to find that many titles will be overstocked while others are out of stock too frequently.

Still, this extreme is probably preferable to exclusive reliance on a system, no matter how good. Systems seem to encourage dependence, and they freqently lull their users into an utterly unwarranted belief that things are under control when in fact a bit of alert common sense could be doing things much better. For example, sales history might suggest in early 1986 that books on Halley's comet be reordered; but common sense might better suggest that since there would probably be more appealing titles available when interest reawakens in 2062, the books reordered in 1986 might not answer the need.

A less extreme example, one that occurs hundreds of times each year: a dazzling sales history for a hardcover becomes meaningless when the paperback is about to appear. Direct awareness of the rhythms of publishing and bookselling can provide a needed supplement to the numbers that a system furnishes.

Perpetual Systems

The most common perpetual inventory system requires the bookseller to write down the title of each book as it is sold. This sales information is subsequently posted to a master card for each title that will record orders, reorders, and sales. This card provides the greatest benefit of a perpetual system: it gives the bookseller a sales (or nonsales) history for each of the titles carried. In the case of staple backlist books, this sales history furnishes an excellent, though not infallable, guide to future orders and stock levels. Even with books having a short shelf life, the recorded information can be very useful.

In some cases an individual title may never be reordered, yet its sales history can be applied by analogy to similar titles that the bookseller anticipates would appeal to a similar market. And with a master card file, the store has a convenient record of what is usually kept in stock.

The means of recording sales efficiently are various. Some booksellers like the simplicity of the daily list on a yellow legal pad at the register. Others maintain that writing each title on a small slip of paper is more flexible, since after sales are posted to the master card, the slips can be sorted according to publisher and used for writing orders. If the only purpose is to alert for reorder, either system is workable. However, if one is keeping separate title cards with full purchase and sales records, the flexibility of sorting stock slips by title or by publisher is preferable.

Periodic Systems

Perpetual systems record sales. Periodic systems record non-sales. The essence of perodic systems is regular stocktaking. As with perpetual systems, different methods can be employed to obtain the desired results. One common and inexpensive method is to use publishers' order forms and count on-hand quantities for each title. This has the advantage of being cheap for the store since publishers' order forms cost nothing; the disadvantage is that the order forms rarely coincide with the way a store displays its stock, and taking inventories is therefore time-consuming. The cheapest method—it's free—is to rely on publishers' reps to make stock counts of the lines they carry when they visit the store to present new titles. Although it is painful to turn down a free service, most booksellers should not rely exclusively on reps. Most booksellers will see a rep only twice a year, if that, and therefore may be out of a title for months before its absence is noted. Alternatively, stock levels may have to be set too high to carry the store through until the rep's next visit. Other stores keep cards in shelf order, so that counting stock is rapid, but creating the cards involves an expenditure of time.

A periodic system has one inherent advantage over a perpetual one: since its essence is to count books still on hand, books that have not been sold, it necessarily identifies books that should be considered for return. In itself, a perpetual system will not do this since it calls attention only to books sold.

That benefit may make a periodic system seem more desirable, but a reasonable criterion for an efficient system should be that it devotes attention to a title in proportion to its importance. A periodic system does not do this; titles within a subject category or titles listed on any publisher's checklist are counted whether they have sold one hundred, ten, or no copies. And any bookstore will show enormous ranges in rates of sale among the titles it stocks. If stock counts are done frequently enough to keep up with very active titles, the bookseller will spend an inordinate amount of time counting titles that do not require much attention. If inventories are taken less often, it is probable that active titles—those with which the bookseller should be most concerned—will not be kept continuously in stock. This is asking for lower sales.

Conscientious eyeballing—checking important titles outside the usual inventory procedures—should supplement any kind of system and make it work in a more timely way. Some bookstores keep what they call a hot list, twenty-five or so titles that the bookseller always wants to have in stock, no matter what else is happening. This list might be checked every morning to ascertain which of the hot titles should be reordered that day from a wholesaler to maintain their in-stock position. Titles on the list may change constantly, depending on what's new and selling fast or what selling season it happens to be. Paperback dictionaries will appear on the list as long as school is in session; the new best-selling romance may appear for three weeks and then be replaced by a new spy thriller or a TV tie-in; one or two basic cookbooks may be listed because you never want to be out of them at any time; and so on.

Some stores affix stick-on dots of different colors to the spines of books as they come into stock, using a different color for each month or season and thus identifying books that have remained unsold in stock too long. Other stores lightly pencil in the month of arrival somewhere inside the book. These supplemental devices illustrate that no one method in itself is ideal. Inventory control is above all a practical art, and a composite system is likely to be more practical in terms of results and costs than an elaborate system that takes too much time to maintain. It is a temptation to want to design a rigorous, aesthetically satisfying system, but it is probably best to resist the temptation. Experienced booksellers are unanimous in their use of some kind of formal system and are nearly of one mind in their view of systems as a means to an end.

This chapter was originally written in the years when computer inventory-control systems, although widely available, were sufficiently expensive that they were not necessarily a wise investment for small booksellers and perhaps, in retrospect, not even for large ones. As of this writing, the costs for both hardware and software have fallen dramatically, and there are systems available to suit even quite small stores. Such systems are discussed in chapter 16.

An even bigger change, however, is in the availability of personal computers and database programs of surprising power at truly bargain-basement rates. These can be used very effectively as timesaving aids to a manual system. For example, a publisher's list entered into a computer with appropriate detail can subsequently be sorted by subject and author (for stock checks), by month of publication or receipt (for pulling returns), by order activity (to generate best-seller lists), or other ways that may strike the fancy of the user.

An advantage of this kind of manual/computer hybrid is that it does not require the kind of system and procedural discipline tht a fully computerized system entails. A computer in this instance is used strictly as a more flexible typewriter and adding machine.

Even though such a primitive system has obvious limitations, it does afford the bookseller some mechanical aid, while not imposing a fixed way of doing things. A more formal system requires set procedures, and many booksellers are just not comfortable with that kind of rigor. Additionally, as stated before, systems—and not just computerized systems—can lead to some bad bookselling practices.

In the last analysis, almost any system can be made to yield acceptable results. But maintaining a perpetual system does not require much more time than maintaining a periodic system, and being able to spot a title as soon as it starts selling is a benefit that makes worthwhile the time spent, since sales are the principal object of running a bookstore.

Supplementing the perpetual system with a periodic review of master cards identifies nonselling titles for return or markdown. Not all booksellers will agree with my conclusion. It has been my experience in talking with many booksellers over the years that we tend to be even more vehement and opinionated on the subject of inventory controls than we are about our favorite books. High passions, indeed.

Chapter 16

Computers in the Bookstore

WARREN CASSELL

I sympathize with booksellers who are frightened of committing themselves to a large cash outlay for computer equipment. I would like to help alleviate this fear by sharing my firsthand observations on how the computer can substantially improve profit margin, help minimize and organize the overwhelming burden of paperwork that is indigenous to the retail book business—and cut your normal work load down from the usual sixteen hours per day to no more than twelve and a half (give or take fifteen minutes in December).

Admittedly, not all of the computer applications that I find so useful or profitable will be germane to all booksellers. On the other hand, there is a phenomenal number of untapped uses for the personal computer yet to be discovered. Some of the financial savings resulting in increased profit margins are clear cut, quite visible, and easily measured; other benefits are not directly related to immediate cost savings. Rather, there is a great high that comes with making a dumb machine help bring to fruition your latest creative ideas in many areas of retail organization, marketing, advertising, and record keeping.

These benefits apply to practically every bookstore with a gross of $100,000 and up. Although stores on the low end ($100,000 to $250,000 per year) will have some difficulty in justifying the cost outlay for a computer system, I hope that this article will help to convince them of the virtues of these electronic marvels. My system has much more than paid for itself since it's been in operation for the last three years.

Accounts Receivable

My major initial need for a computer was accounts receivable. Like most independents, I run a personal charge account system. Unlike most retailers, I do not accept any credit cards, and consequently I send out anywhere from four hundred to six hundred statements a month. During the stone age of billing at Just Books, a charge was recorded by hand on a customer statement card with the following information: date, title, price, tax, postage and handling if applicable, total sale, and account balance. Whether a customer bought ten books (not an unusual event) or one book, all of the information had to be noted—by hand. At the end of the month the statements were photocopied by some poor soul standing over a hot, in-store copying machine all day. The next day these bills were folded and stuffed into envelopes, sealed, and sent off.

Shazam! Enter the age of computers. I found, after a six-month search, a new cost- and time-efficient way to do my monthly bills electronically. Using an off-the-shelf program (as opposed to a program designed specifically for my needs), I managed to duplicate my old form, which had previously gone the photocopier route. However, there were some differences as a result of the computer. First, I had to enter the date only once for all of the day's charges rather than on each individual transaction. If one hundred books were charged in one day, that alone would indicate a savings in time. After the initial entry of date, the only other information to be recorded was title, price, and postage and handling where applicable. The program does the math, enters and computes the tax, and keeps a running total of all of a customer's charges automatically.

What do I save? On an off-the-cuff estimate of two thousand transactions a month at a nickel per transaction (for the old-fashioned manual entry system, replete with human errors), that equals $1,200 per year in labor costs. My billing process now takes less than one full day rather than all of two. But equally important, instead of someone feeding the photocopier statement forms all day, I now feed the computer information storage disks with all of my accounts receivable data, press a few buttons on my awesome Apple, and presto, my statements start rolling out of the printer—untouched by human hands—leaving my help and me more hours and energy for the fun part of this business, selling books. By using a computer I have consolidated the time needed for reproducing statements at the end of the month, and I estimate I save an additional thousand dollars a year on labor costs. In other words, I can recover the cost of a modest computer system in one year even if I use it only to bill my customers.

If you bill at least one hundred customers a month by hand, that's enough to cost-justify computerization because there are still a heck of a lot of applications out there. Let's take a look at some others.

Accounts Payable and General Ledger

Like all retailers, I need to maintain a general ledger and to pay inevitable bills. I initiated several bookkeeping programs which, if they didn't take the pain away, at least made paying easier, faster, and more efficient. In my old precomputer life, the daily invoices arriving with the mail or accompanying incoming orders were filed in an ever-burgeoning accordion folder. At the end of the month I would take the folder home and fine-tune the filing so that all invoices from the same publisher were grouped together. I would then examine each publisher's invoices for dates and amounts and make a list of those to be paid on the thirtieth of the month and those to be discounted and paid on the tenth. In addition, there was always that miscellaneous batch awaiting credits, or dated bills, or those in dispute that went back into the folder to be held over. . . and frequently overlooked. In drawing up the list to be paid, I would generally make use of a calculator or pencil and scratch paper to determine total amounts, credits, and discounts. The results of all these efforts would then be brought to the store the next day, and my assistant would take my lists, write out the checks, address envelopes, note check numbers, date, and amount of payment on the invoices, and eventually enter the checks in the general ledger.

Unless the operation is large enough to afford a full-time bookkeeper, the owner takes on this burden; paying out money is serious business, and most owners want to keep close tabs on that aspect of their bookkeeping. By computerizing these functions, I keep a more watchful eye on money being spent and do it in a less costly, less time-consuming fashion. In addition, I generate a whole bunch of financial reports I never knew I needed but am finding quite useful. How does all this happen? Well, those invoices that once went into that famous accordion folder now get entered into the computer every few days. (And this includes the legendary miscellaneous "hold" batch that usually went back into the accordion folder because I didn't know what else to do with it.) Each regular supplier is given a code number so that calling up a publisher from the computer's storage files is a simple operation.

Once the supplier's name appears on the screen, a series of questions is asked about the invoice—date, number, payment date, amount due, and payment disposition. The entire process takes about thirty seconds per invoice or credit to be entered and digested by the computer. Several times a month I ask the accounts payable program to give me an "aging report." The computer takes all the information about what I owe to whom and when it is due and then lines it up in several neat columns. More specifically, the aging report tells me exactly how much I owe each supplier on the tenth and thirtieth of the current month and the tenth of the next month as well as future dated obligations. In addition, the report gives a grand total of the amount due for all invoices on the various dates.

When it comes to that awful time of the month when payments are to be made, I simply load the program into my computer and print a report showing who is getting paid how much and for which invoices, as well as the date and check number. I then load special checks into the printer, push a few buttons, and let it roll. Within a few minutes, fifty to seventy-five checks are printed, complete with invoice information for the payee's benefit. They are ready to be slipped into window envelopes because the supplier's address is printed on the checks. After this, a check register is printed for the permanent record.

At the end of the month, any other checks that had to be written by hand during the previous thirty days are noted in the computer accounts payable program. I then transfer all of the accounts payable information to the general ledger program by hitting a few buttons. Some other data related to the month's gross sales, charge and cash sales, bank deposits, and sales taxes are then fed into the ledger program. All of this input takes but a few minutes. Then I'm ready to print my ledger and profit and loss statement for the month. This means making sure paper is in the printer and pushing a few more buttons. I'm getting very expert at pushing those buttons by now. But what's more important is to be able to push them and then walk away from the dumb machine while it does its work of figuring, reporting, and printing.

Now the bottom line question: How much do I save in time and dollars having a computerized accounts payable and general ledger? I don't know yet. I do know that when my accountant gets a neatly printed profit and loss statement for each month of the fiscal year, his number-crunching efforts will be minimal . . . and so, too, his fee for my end-of-the-year P & L. What I've saved in time is already immeasurable . . . and I'm using that time for the more creative efforts of selling books.

Word Processing

Speaking of creative efforts, let's take a look at one way an independent can sell books with a really personal flair. I am referring to a monthly newsletter that I send to my 2,500-name mailing list of cash and charge customers. This is a chatty, informative selling piece that raises my customers' consciousness about where to purchase books... and does so on a regular basis, month after month. There are four basic costs associated with this endeavor: typing, labels, printing, and postage. I haven't been able to reduce my expenditures on the last two items. However, the typing, which used to run two hundred dollars a year, with the same amount spent on labels, is now a thing of the past. I currently maintain my own mailing list in one of the software programs, and my computer printer does such a fine job that I don't need to have a professional typist do a final copy for the offset printer to work with. In addition, I saved over a thousand dollars more this year in typesetting costs for several other promotional mailings. What does all this have to do with "word processing"? Well, for me that's just a fancy name for using the computer as a typewriter. I used it to write this article, and I use the computer cum typewriter for my correspondence with customers and suppliers. In any event, I reduce my costs of sales and sales promotions considerably and, conversely, increase my profit margin.

There is much untapped potential for additional sales using a word-processing program and customer interest lists filed in the computer's memory. One example: Let's say you have a hundred Ludlum fanatics identified as such in your mailing list. Knowing that new Ludlum thriller is in the works for release next month, you write a low-key sales letter to each of the fanatics and have the computer address it to them individually. One hundred (thousand? more?) personalized letters is again simply a matter of pressing a few buttons. If your printer is good enough, the letters will look completely individualized, and your customers will be thankful for your personalized service and attention to their literary needs.

Miscellaneous

Many people, when making a connection between a retail store and a computer, almost instantaneously come up with the concept of inventory control. For my operation this would be counterproductive in terms of time and effort. I sell very little backlist, and although I do a considerable volume in less than six hundred square feet of selling space, I manage to keep most of the inventory in my head. Where I do find it useful to track stock is in the area of fall purchases. Starting with orders placed at the ABA Convention and continuing with salespeople's orders throughout the summer, all of the fall purchases are entered into a database. A database is simply an electronic filing system in which the information can be manipulated in many ways with a great deal of facility. Each title purchased is entered into the database with the following information: publisher, price, subject category, promotional possibility, quantity purchased, and expected month of delivery. At some point in September when most of my purchases have been made, I ask the computer to sort the information several ways. First, I ask for an alphabetical listing of all titles I have on order. This list comes in very handy when customers ask for a new book that hasn't hit the market yet. I simply check my alphabetical list, and if it's there, I can tell my customers that it is on order and I'll call them when the publisher ships the books. I also sort my purchases by categories, so that when the fifth rep shows up with a great seventy-five-dollar coffee table book on aardvarks, I can consult my list and let the rep know that I have my full quota of aardvark books. This function comes in particularly handy when buying calendars. I tend to go overboard on calendar purchases, and the computerized list helps me restrain my ordering. Finally, I sort my purchases by publisher, and this along with the category grouping helps me in selecting books for my December holiday catalog. The key factor here is co-op reimbursement, and since publishers' policies are so dissimilar, the lists give plenty of basic data to help me decide what to include and what to omit from my catalog.

These are just a few of the ways I have made my life as a bookseller easier by using a computer. By now I trust you are ready to head for your nearest computer store, plunk down hard-earned cash, and enter the computer age. *Don't.* At least not until you've done a bit of preparation. The best investment you can make now is the purchase and thorough reading of a book with the unlikely title *Computer Wimp: 166 Things I Wish I Had Known Before I Bought My First Computer,* by John Bear, published by Ten Speed Press. Probably one of the most important questions will be, "What needs do I want to meet in buying a computer?" When you have resolved that easy dilemma, you should then decide what software will meet those needs. Only after those questions are settled should you select a computer system.

The ins and outs of my first system purchase are too tragic to recall here and could possibly make the subject of a long-running soap opera. While everything that I have described above concerning my present computer use is an accurate reflection of a fairly smooth-running system, it wasn't always so. Many of the troubles came from my own inexperience and lack of knowledge, the poor salesmanship and meager support at local computer stores, and too little money to invest initially. For the tyro starting out, I would strongly suggest the following:

1. Buy more memory than you think you will need.
2. Don't scrimp on the quality of the printer you purchase.
3. Don't try to work too many applications in at one time. That blinking green screen can be quite infectious.
4. Do not trust a computer salesperson's knowledge of your business. S/he doesn't have any.

III
Ordering and Receiving

Chapter 17

Stock Selection

CHARLES ROBINSON

With at least forty thousand books being published each year for the trade and more than seven hundred thousand in print, it is obvious that any one store cannot hope to carry every available title. A store of approximately three thousand square feet, for example, might carry somewhat less than twenty thousand titles. Selection of stock is a crucial issue and a major undertaking. There are two factors that determine selection. They are philosophical and pragmatic. Philosophical factors include:

The kinds of books you like. This is an area in which booksellers must be cautious. Carrying only the books we like can severely limit sales. On the other hand, enthusiasm is a major force in selling, so if the market is there, you might easily sell a great many of the books you like.

The kinds of books you don't like. This is another area in which a bookseller must exercise caution. However, every bookseller makes buying decisions that are based somewhat on moral or philosophical judgments. For instance, a bookseller may not want to stock books that are blatantly sexist or racist or advocate a cause with which he or she disagrees. These considerations are fine when ordering stock for the shelves if tempered with reason but should not restrict the bookseller from obtaining any book a customer wants to special order.

The kinds of books you have chosen to emphasize as a specialty. This is both a philosophical and pragmatic decision. The philosophical aspect is linked to the previous two. You most likely will select to specialize in books that appeal to you. It becomes pragmatic when you select specializations that are determined by your market; this will be discussed momentarily.

The overall image you wish to project. Let's assume you wish to project the image of a scholarly bookstore, and that it fits your market. You would not likely select romance novels for your basic stock. Perhaps you are located near a beach and want to attract passers-by with books that are good for "beach reading"; in such a case, you might not go heavy on university press titles, at least in the window display. Decide on the image you want to project to fit the market you hope to acquire, then select books to match that market. Image is influenced by pragmatic factors, but most often it is a philosophical decision.

Pragmatic factors in determining book selection distinguish the romantic from the business side of bookselling and dramatically affect a bookstore's chances for success. These factors include:

Who your customers are or will be. This is without doubt the most important aspect of choosing books for a bookstore. The market research you conduct to determine location should yield much information on which you will later base selection decisions. Such things as education level, occupations, income levels, and special interests of potential customers will have great bearing on the types of books to be carried in the store. Is the market family-oriented, single or business and professional; is yours a college community or a resort area? Other retail businesses in the area are a good barometer for understanding your potential customers. What are they selling, and to whom? The public library is also a good market indicator. Library patrons are also book buyers. What kinds of books are they borrowing in your local library?

Sales history can be a most useful guide in selecting books for your customers. However, inasmuch as there is no history when a store is just opening, you have to depend upon external factors in the beginning; but be prepared to adapt your selections as you do capture sales history. As you see some types of books moving faster than others, adjust your buying to strengthen those areas in the future.

Ideally one has a specific customer in mind for each book purchased for a bookstore's stock. In practice that is impossible. However, the closer one can come to the ideal by thinking in types (if not always in individuals), the more successful the store will be.

The available space. If the space to display books is limited, selection is affected because more than ever each book has to be considered carefully for the space it is to take. Space means you have to be very selective and carry fewer copies of titles than you think you'd like in order to have room for more titles. This can be very good for turnover, but it requires vigilance in inventory control.

The available money. As with space, money is a prime factor in book selection. If it is unlimited, you can buy as much as you want, but if it isn't—which is more likely to be the case—then you have to select wisely as well as economically. You may decide you have a better chance of selling three medium-priced hardcovers or a dozen paperbacks than a single copy of a fifty-dollar art book. On the other hand, you may want that single expensive book to highlight a group of books that will sell if they are noticed.

The season of the year. Christmas and Hanukkah holiday seasons have a most dramatic effect on book selection. They bring people into bookstores who do not ordinarily frequent such places. And books are sold then that would not sell at any other time. Books are bought for gift giving, and the bookstore's selection must be ready for that. Other seasons can also have an impact on sales and thus on selection: special festivals, sports or tourist attractions, and so on.

The bookseller's interests and expertise. Philosophical aspects were touched on earlier, but practically speaking, it is easiest to sell books that one knows or cares about. Areas of specialization within a bookstore should reflect this. If, for example, you never read mysteries, specializing in mysteries regardless of the market may not be the wisest decision. On the other hand, if you are a cookbook connoisseur and have the market, chances are you could develop a very successful specialization in cookbooks in your store.

Tools to Aid Selection

There are a number of tools that can be useful in selecting inventory for a bookstore. It is imperative a caveat be offered here. Tools cannot build a house. A carpenter carefully using those tools builds the house. Similarly, the tools that follow can aid the bookseller in selecting books for the store, but in the final analysis the decision is yours. You must select from the choices suggested by the tools.

Basic Book List. Published by the American Booksellers Association, this list is put together periodically by booksellers who agree that the titles compiled therein might be considered basic. "Basic" in this case means within the context of the category in which it is listed. No bookstore would stock all of the titles on the *Basic Book*

List, but a store specializing in cookbooks, for instance, might well stock most of the titles in the cookbook section of the *BBL.*

Trade Publications. American Bookseller, Publishers Weekly (particularly the seasonal announcement issues), and *ABA Newswire* are very helpful in book selection because of publishers' advertisements and the editorial material that is offered on titles: Pick of the Lists in *American Bookseller,* for instance, and Forecasts in *Publishers Weekly.* The *Horn Book* is of great use to booksellers specializing in children's books. There are periodicals covering almost every specialty, and most of them contain news of books. Reviews and book news in general publications should also be scanned regularly.

Publishers' Catalogs. Although this is the best source of prepublication information about a book, it is well to remember that catalog copy is written to sell. Learn to read between the lines. Do use the publishers' catalogs, however, especially their full "in print" catalogs, for help in establishing a backlist stock.

Publishers' Representatives. Many new and smaller stores may not see publishers' reps. For those lucky enough to be called upon, a good "rep" becomes a strong liaison between the bookseller and the publisher. They often have information about books that did not make the catalog or additional information about those titles that are listed, such as early reviewer response, promotion plans, and so forth. As reliable reps get to know a bookstore they are invaluable in making stock suggestions, and not just of their own titles.

Book Exhibits. The annual ABA Convention, held in late May, is the largest exhibition of books in North America. Almost all the trade book publishers publishing English-language books use this convention as their introduction of the major fall titles. Also, they are increasingly exhibiting books recently published as well as basic backlist titles. There are much smaller but very useful regional association trade shows, these usually held in the fall. A prime value of these shows is the display of regional books that the bookseller might not see at the ABA Convention but would need to have in a good bookstore.

ROSI. This stands for recommended opening store inventory. It is a computerized list offered by Ingram Book Company, a national wholesaler in Nashville, Tennessee. A bookseller gives Ingram information on the opening inventory budget, with emphasis on categories that will be specializations. The wholesaler then puts together a suggested opening stock list based on that information along with its own best-selling titles list. Although this program is extremely useful to the complete neophyte, caution must be observed as always in buying. The bookseller must select those titles that he or she thinks will sell in his or her store—regardless of how well or how badly they are selling elsewhere. In addition, no matter how excellent this ROSI might be for a particular store opening, initial inventory dollars should always be held back for special titles that are necessary but not in the wholesaler's stock.

Regional Wholesalers. Some regional wholesalers have less sophisticated but still helpful basic stock lists, and local best-seller lists, which should be used. If possible, examine titles in a wholesaler's warehouse; this is an excellent way to become familiar with what is available (there, at least) and what might fit into the bookstore's inventory.

Other Bookstores. Studying the stock in other established bookstores is always helpful in putting together lists of books to be stocked in one's own store. Longtime booksellers do this all the time. No matter how long they have been at it, and how much they know, it is seldom that they don't see something they think they should have and didn't know about until they paid a visit to another bookseller.

Stock selection for a bookstore is a cumulative process that obviously goes on for as long as the bookseller is in business. It can never be reduced to a formula. It is always a gamble, but with constant refinement and ever-increasing sensitivity to the needs of one's customers as well as to trends and developments within the world of books, one can reduce the risk—though never to such a point that the business of buying for a bookstore loses its stimulating fascination.

Chapter 18

The Mechanics of Ordering

ALLAN MARSHALL

Ordering must be orderly. That may sound like a play on words, but it is not. Stop for a moment to consider how many publishers you might deal with in a year and the number of orders you might have outstanding at any given time to each publisher. How many orders are being prepared for wholesalers? How many STOP orders are you waiting for? How many orders have been only partially filled? How many telephone orders do you place in a week, a month, a year? How many orders are placed with sales reps on their order forms; how many orders are placed on your own order form? Then also think about the number of requests for titles that you're holding that have not yet become part of an order, research yet to be done on customer requests, and on and on. You will quickly begin to see that your ordering procedures, indeed, must be organized in an orderly fashion.

Modern technology, in the form of computers, offers a way to create, transmit, and file orders easily with a minimum of human contact that can often translate into human error. The long-standing aversion to computers in the minds of many booksellers seems to be disappearing, because computers offer many advantages over the manual ordering process.

Where do the books come from? Books for your store can be purchased from publishers, wholesalers, individuals, maybe even from your customers if you choose to deal in used books. Other chapters point out the advantages and disadvantages of each source, so that you can decide for yourself which holds the most promise. Most booksellers use them all at one time or another, depending on their needs, the availability of stock, and how they are set up to do business. Use each source to achieve the best results for your store.

Now let's address the business of ordering. For the sake of brevity, we will assume you already know what it is you want to order. Every order must be written down in a form that will later furnish you with all the details of what you ordered, from whom, when, and under what terms. This is true even of a telephone order. Without a written copy of each order, follow-up becomes impossible, and control is lost. A completely written system—though it will seem a pain in the neck at the time you're doing it—will also provide necessary details for receiving, accounts payable, inventory control, merchandise budgeting, returns decisions, and customer notification that the book they ordered is now in stock.

The forms used to record each order will vary. If you are dealing with sales reps, they will have the publisher's order form and will prefer that it be used. Fine. All that has to be filled in are the quantity, any special terms of purchase or discount, the ship-to and bill-to addresses for your store, and your purchase order number. Be sure to get a complete copy of the filled-in order form before the rep leaves your store. Make sure that all points covered on the original form are also covered on the copy you keep for your files.

The Purchase Order Form

Having your own purchase order form is an absolute necessity. You can design your own, if you are so inclined, or you may purchase the camera-ready artwork for a form from the ABA at a nominal price. For our purposes here, references will be made to the ABA form (see figure 18-1). Whatever form you use, be sure that it is legible. Type it or print it, so that it can be read by anyone.

1. In the space where it says "Bill To:" enter the name and billing address of your store. Also enter the SAN (Standard Address Number) assigned to you when you joined the ABA. The SAN is a seven-digit number assigned only to your store. If you have branch stores, entirely different numbers will be assigned to each location.
2. In the space labeled "Ship To:" enter the name, address, and SAN if the location where the shipment is to be made is different from the "Bill To:" location. If it is the same, write "SAME" in the space provided.
3. Enter the purchase order number where it says "No." This should be a sequential number that is different on each successive order to be issued. The numbers can be preprinted, typed,

PURCHASE ORDER

③ No. 00004
This number must appear on **all** invoices, packages, & correspondence.

THESE ITEMS ARE FOR RESALE   ACCT. NO.   ④ Date 4/15/86

Bill To: **SAN** 123-4567   Ship To: **SAN**

① Urban Plaza Bookstore, Inc.   ② SAME
798 Center Plaza
Big Town, USA   12345

Vendor: **SAN**

⑤ Big Time Book Co., Inc.
456 Far Out Rd.
Little Town, USA   67890

⑥ **SHIPPING INSTRUCTIONS**
Ship via: 4th Class Book Rate -- Special Handling
Ship (XX) at once   Cancel all shorts except
⑦ ( ) on_____19____   NYPs. Cancel NYPs
Do NOT ship fewer   if not shipped
than _____ books.   ⑧ within _30_ days.
( ) Do ⑨ (X) Do NOT insure at our expense.

If this order requires   Name ⑩   Phone No.
FOLD clarification, contact: A. Person (222)999-9999

Please furnish __2__ ⑪ invoice copies

⑫ ISBN	⑬ Quantity	⑭ Author	⑮ Title or Description	⑯	⑰	⑱
0-123-12345-X	5	Dromedary, A.	Demise of Two-Humped Camels	5.95	Paper	29.75
0-123-67890-5	3	Foote, F.T.	Roads I Have Run	4.95	Paper	14.85
0-123-24680-8	2	Eatter, B.	Waistlines Big and Small	6.95	Paper	13.90

FOLD

| | ⑲ 10 | | | | | |

⑳

㉑ Aloise Person
Authorized Signature   Aloise Person

Fig. 18-1. A standard purchase order.

handwritten, or applied with a hand numbering machine. The numbering sequence can start at any number (even the number one) so long as there is no repetition over a two- to three-year span of use. After that, the sequence can go back again if you wish and start at the beginning.

4. On the line marked "Date," enter the date on which you are submitting the order. The date could also be used as the purchase order number; however, you might wish to use a subscript number for the first, second, and third orders on a given date, so that the purchase order number might then appear as 4/1/88-1, 4/1/88-2, 4/1/88-3, and so on.

5. In the box labeled "Vendor," enter the publisher's or wholesaler's name and address. To be sure you are using the correct address, look up the publisher's listing in the *ABA Book Buyer's Handbook* and use the address listed next to "Address for Orders."

6. In the box labeled "Shipping Instructions," there are several decisions to be made and noted. First, at the line printed "Ship via," the choice is up to you: U.S. Post—Fourth Class; UPS; Special Handling; First Class—Rush; Truck; Cheapest; Interoffice truck—call me for pickup; Parcel Post; and so on. There is no problem about shipping when you are ordering mass-market paperbacks; the publisher always pays. There is no problem on hardcovers or trade paperbacks when the publisher has made a free shipping offer. But when the choice is up to you and you are paying freight, it is to your advantage to stop, look, and think. You will not always be right, particularly if your order gets shipped in many small lots, but with experience you'll come to have a better handle on the situation.

7. Decide, and mark the appropriate box, whether you want the order shipped at once or on a specific date.

8. Indicate whether you want back orders canceled "at once" if not available or canceled "within __ number days" if not available.

9. Indicate whether you do or do not wish to pay for shipping insurance.

10. Indicate the name of the person in your store to contact if there is a problem about the order. Be sure to enter the person's telephone number with area code.

11. If your bookkeeping system requires a certain number of invoice copies, enter that number in the space provided.

12. Now we get to the part of the purchase order that has to do with books. In the column headed "ISBN," enter the International Standard Book Number for each *title* being ordered. The ISBN consists of four parts. The first part is a group identifier, which

for English-speaking nations is always a zero (0). The next portion is the publisher identifier and ranges from two digits for a publisher with a large output to seven digits for publishers with small output. The third portion of the ISBN is the title identifier and is assigned to a particular edition of a title by the publisher. The final portion of the ISBN is a one-position computer check digit. If the order being written is to a wholesaler, they may have their own numbering system or require that books be ordered simply by title. A quick call to your wholesaler(s) will confirm which approach is preferred.

13. In the column headed "Quantity," mark in the number of copies you wish to receive of the desired title.

14. In the column labeled "Author," write in at least the author's last name and first initial. If there happens to be more than one author, write the first author's last name and the words "et al." (example: "Smith et al."), which is Latin for "and others." If the translator's or editor's name is more important, write in that name (example: "Smith, trans.," or "Smith, ed.").

15. In the column headed "Title or Description," write in the title of the book you are ordering. To save space, initial definite and indefinite articles can be omitted. If the title is particularly long, a judicious shortening or abbreviating is permissible, just as long as the title is still discernible. This is also the place to indicate a particular edition of the book, a special binding, or the fact that it is a particular volume in a series or is a boxed set. Even with the use of the ISBN, there is nothing as descriptive of what it is you want as a clear and concise English-language description!

16. The next column on the form is not headed, but you may choose to enter here the retail price of the book as listed in the publisher's catalog or in *Books in Print* or whatever your reference source for the book being ordered.

17. This column is not headed either. You may choose to use it for any number of purposes, such as to indicate whether the title being ordered is hardcover or paperback. Though it is optional, you might indicate the discount in this space.

18. This column, like the two before it, is not labeled—its use is up to you. You may choose, after the order has been sent to the publisher, to use this space to extend the value of the title being ordered for use in your merchandise budget when checking in the order upon receipt or for some other purpose of your own devising.

19. This space can be used to indicate the total number of books being ordered.

20. This space should be left blank for the publisher's or wholesaler's use.
21. This purchase order is really a contract and requires a signature to make it official. The authorized signature may belong to someone other than the person placing the order (as indicated in space 10): the head buyer, the manager, or the owner. In a small operation, we all know that person may be one and the same. If the signature is a particularly fancy one, it is advisable to type or clearly print the name below the line where the signature appears.

Be sure to make at least one copy of the purchase order for your files to use to check against the shipping slip when the shipment finally arrives on your doorstep. It is also necessary that you have this copy of the order if there is to be any further contact made by you with the publisher or wholesaler concerning nonreceipt of the order or portions of it or about any errors in filling your order. Don't trust your memory; keep a copy of every order. Some stores require that a numerical file and/or a date file of all purchase orders be kept, separate from the vendor file. Such procedures are entirely up to you.

One other point worthy of note: The ABA purchase order form has notations at two places along the left-hand side indicating where to fold the form, so that the vendor's or publisher's name and address will appear in a standard window envelope, which, if used, will save you the trouble of having to write the vendor's name on an envelope.

Next comes the problem of filing orders pending receipt at your store. There are many valid ways from the publisher to file orders. The simplest is alphabetically by publisher's name, and if there happens to be more than one order outstanding to a publisher at one time, I suggest putting them in ascending date order, so that the oldest is on top. These all may be placed in an alphabetical file and/ or in separate folders for each publisher, whichever you prefer.

If a particular order has on it one or more titles being ordered for a particular customer, it is also advisable to note on either the face or the reverse side of the order which title(s) it is and who the customer is, so that when the books are received, you will be able to cross-reference the book in your hand with the customer information in your special-order file. The customer, when inquiring about the order, will rarely remember the publisher's name but will, of course, remember his or her own name, and it is on that piece of information that you should be able to research his or her request.

When you place telephone orders, it is a good idea to request that a written confirmation be sent to you, although I have often found that the confirmation arrived long after the order was shipped ... or not at all. I always wrote out a copy of the order and filed it along with the others. It is helpful to have what I called my number book. In an inexpensive spiral notebook (I used only one such book in ten years), I kept a handwritten record of each purchase order number I used and what I used it for: the date, the publisher's name, whether by telephone or mail, a general note on what was ordered, the method of shipment requested (if pertinent), and any special notations that might later be helpful, such as the name of the order clerk. When I called to find out why the order had not been received or if there was a special promotion being planned by the publisher for a title in the order, it was easy to locate the relevant information. This book also allowed me to quickly check which orders were overdue without combing through the entire purchase order file.

There are many ways to write out a purchase order. There are even more ways to file them and handle them (or handle them too much) in the course of doing business. There are probably as many filing techniques as there are booksellers. As in all things, IBM's old acronym is always a good rule to follow in this situation: KISS (Keep It Simple, Stupid). And remember *my* old acronym: WED (Write Everything Down).

The Single Title Order Plan

The Single Title Order Plan is the result of cooperative efforts of the American Booksellers Association and the Association of American Publishers. The form is now called STOP instead of its original name SCOP (Single *Copy* Order Plan). With the new form it is possible to order more than one copy of a given title.

The purpose of the STOP form is to facilitate delivery of special orders at the lowest cost and greatest ease to both bookseller and publisher and to speed the book to the customer before the need for it has passed. A majority of publishers do not care how many copies they ship of a single title as long as cash accompanies the order. It is recommended that booksellers send checks with the amount open rather than filled in. This accommodates price increases and postage charge changes.

This form (see figure 18-2) is designed to be as simple but as adaptable to today's conditions as possible. Please note that this form is printed on NCR paper. It is not necessary to use carbons to produce copies. Use either a ballpoint pen or a typewriter. The instructions below set forth the recommended use and alternative use. Do not order more than one title on this form, but you may order more than one copy of the title from most publishers.

SINGLE
TITLE
ORDER
PLAN

DO NOT BACK ORDER

PACKING LIST

DATE _____

LIST PRICE EACH $ _____

TOTAL LIST PRICE $ _____

DISCOUNT _____ %

NET PRICE $ _____

POSTAGE $ _____

TOTAL $_____

FROM | PUBLISHER

SHIPPING LABEL

ORDER NO._____

SPECIAL FOURTH CLASS RATE - BOOKS

TO | BOOKSELLER   SAN # _____

QTY	ISBN	AUTHOR	TITLE

INSTRUCTION TO PUBLISHERS:

1. Complete information in upper right hand corner and on check, if necessary. Price information is essential and urgent.

2. Use shipping label above and enclose packing list at top of form.

3. If book cannot be shipped, check reason below. Return this entire form with check to bookseller.

☐ Out of stock until _____   ☐ Price increase to $ _____   ☐ Not our publication

☐ Out of print   ☐ Value of check too low   ☐ Not yet published

Other _____

© Copyright American Booksellers Association, Inc. 1975

Fig. 18-2. American Booksellers Association STOP (single title) order form.

Recommended Use

1. Enter the date in the upper right-hand corner.
2. Enter the discount expected from the STOP booklet or from the *ABA Book Buyer's Handbook.*
3. Enter the publisher's name and address in the box provided.
4. Enter your name and address in the box provided. Above your name and address enter your standard address number (SAN). If you use a rubber stamp, be sure to stamp the second copy.

5. Enter your order number (may be the same as your check number), quantity desired, ISBN (if known), author, and title in the spaces provided.
6. Complete your check, leaving the amount spaces open. (So that you may keep your regular checking account properly balanced while using an open check, it is recommended that you establish a separate checking account for STOP. Advise your banker to inform you when the balance in the account reaches a minimum level so that you may replenish funds.) You may write on the check or have a rubber stamp made reading "NOT VALID FOR OVER $____." or you may have that statement printed above the signature space by your bank. Enter the maximum dollar amount, including postage, which you will pay for the book.
7. Remove the top strip that holds the form together.
8. Retain the green copy for your files.
9. Fold the white and yellow copies so that the top and bottom edges meet. Attach check and insert in a standard No. 6¼ or No. 6¾ window envelope so that the publisher's name appears in the window.

Alternate Use

When you do not want the book if the price is higher than the most recent information you have (*Publishers' Trade List Annual/ PTLA, PW*, or publisher's catalog are preferred; *Books in Print* is the least reliable source), follow these steps, which correspond to "Recommended Use":

1. Same as above.
2. In addition to discount percent, complete all price information. If you do not know the weight of the book, use the following chart as a guide in computing postage, using current U.S. Postal Service rates:

Retail value	Weight of book, packed
Under $5	2 lbs.
$ 5–$10	3 lbs.
$10–$20	4 lbs.
Over $20	6 lbs.

When you order more than one copy, multiply postage by the number of copies.
3, 4, 5. Same as above.
6. Complete the check, including the amount spaces.
7, 8, 9. Same as above.

Drop Shipments

Since fewer than 10 percent of STOP orders are for drop shipments (books sent directly to customers), provision for such shipments has been eliminated from the form, which simplifies it vastly. In order to use the form for drop shipments, simply strike out the words "shipping label," "from," and "to" on the form. Attach your own shipping label to the lower half of the form. Insert the words "USE ATTACHED SHIPPING LABEL: RETURN THIS COPY TO BOOKSELLER" between the words "SINGLE TITLE ORDER PLAN" and the price information on the upper portion. If you use most of your forms for drop shipment, you might have a rubber stamp made rather than write the instructions in each time. STOP forms may be obtained by any retail bookseller from the American Booksellers Association.

Chapter 19

Buying Directly from Publishers

JEAN B. WILSON

One day a person stopped in The Book Shop to chat with one of the staff at the checkout desk. He gestured at the store with a wide sweep of his arm and asked, "Why do you stock all of this in Boise, Idaho? Why don't you just carry the five hundred best-selling titles and forget the rest?" He went on, "Where is your microfiche? I don't see a computer. How can you run a store without a computer? Your inventory is too high." And so on and so forth, ad nauseam.

While he was bombarding the person at the desk, another member of the staff was quietly helping a customer select books from a shopping list, showing the customer related books that had just come in that weren't on the list. When the customer had selected those she wanted, there were eight to be rung up and bagged rather than the four she had come in seeking. None of the eight were on the top five hundred titles of any existing list.

Fortunately, the bombarding efficiency expert was still at the checkout. He was surprised at the total sale being rung up. He stopped commenting and listened to a satisfied customer. After she left, both the person he had been lecturing and the staff member who had made the sale said to him, in unison, "That's why we do it the way we do it!" It was suggested the nonbook efficiency expert look at titles instead of just books and see the spectrum of choice in the store. A perfect ending would be that *he* bought eight books instead of none. Maybe next time.

This lengthy introduction serves to illustrate why it is necessary to buy from publishers if you want a store that doesn't just churn out the same old titles with none of the excitement of "selling" a book or finding a special title a customer hasn't been able to find anywhere else, "even in San Francisco." Buying directly from publishers opens the entire gamut of what has been and is being published to the bookseller. Choosing from those thousands of titles gives the bookseller an awareness of what is available even if it isn't carried in the store. It is accumulated book knowledge that can be used to sell. It is knowledge that customers could not find in stores that only stocked the top five hundred titles.

In the past few years other reasons have arisen to buy from publishers rather than just acquiring this knowledge and accumulating a complete stock. These reasons reflect in the bottom line. *FPT* or *freight pass-through* from many publishers has had a dramatic effect on the profitability of bookstores. Although FPT schedules vary, the rule of thumb is that a bookseller realizes fifty cents to a dollar on each book sold (from a participating publisher), and this helps offset the costs of getting books into the store. Unfortunately not all publishers have an FPT program. Those who do have found great support from booksellers.

Dating plans from major publishers are another plus for the bookstore buying directly. Buying in January and paying in May, or buying in the summer and paying in January, is good business practice. Dating plans help publishers reduce their backlist inventory, while helping the bookstores replenish their stock. There are also increased discounts to consider. Most publishers give a larger discount on stock dating plans. Some charge a nominal 5 percent payment per month prior to the date of the final payment, with each of the cash payments being deducted from the total. These plans build dollar profits for booksellers.

Publishers have been forced to tighten their credit policies as money has become more expensive to borrow. "Thirty days net" is a common term, though some offer early payment cash discounts. With careful planning these terms can be met. And at certain seasons of the year publishers may offer ninety-day to one-hundred-twenty-day extensions or an option of extra discount. These options are usually part of sizable stock offers. Your account must be in good credit standing to take advantage of the offer. If possible, these can also add to the profitability of a bookstore.

Publisher's sales representatives are a special bonus for booksellers. They can help establish an account with their house if the bookseller doesn't already have one. They are calling on bookstores to make sales, of course. If they do not make those sales, they will not continue to call. Seeing a sales rep can be time-consuming, but the information learned is of great benefit. While catalog copy glows, it is the sales rep who has been to sales conference and knows ad budgets and print runs for titles, who can report on the sales force's reaction to a title as well as the reaction of other booksellers.

Bookstores are in the information business. The more a bookseller knows and can share and sell, the more successful he or she will be.

Sales representatives also assist in obtaining cooperative advertising where this is feasible for a bookstore. They are especially helpful with regional books and/or authors. Author appearances can be a great promotion for a bookstore. Most of them begin with discussions between the sales rep and the bookseller.

Special orders are a lucrative part of many bookstore operations, especially those that have moved beyond the one- or two-copy special orders to special orders for ten, twenty, or perhaps one hundred copies of a title. These orders come from schools, book clubs, businesses. Combining these orders with the bookstore's own backlist order can boost the quantity into a higher discount bracket. Having an account with a publisher is essential for this type of ordering. Usually a publisher is the only source for a sizable quantity of a title. To make it easier for booksellers to order from them directly, most publishers have 800 numbers (listed in the *ABA Book Buyer's Handbook*) that cost the bookseller nothing to use and speed up delivery.

Returns are an expensive but essential part of running a bookstore. Books can usually be returned to publishers with fewer penalties than to wholesalers, providing, of course, all the conditions of returns terms are met. No matter who is getting the returns, the bookseller plays the freight; this is part of the expense of doing business.

No publisher, bookseller, or sales representative is ever going to be completely accurate in forecasting sales success. This is the main reason why the returns privilege exists. It is inevitable that some stock purchased in good faith will have to be returned. While the system is far from perfect, it does allow the bookstore to stock a wide variety of titles. It should be considered a kind of partnership between publisher and bookseller to expose as many books as possible to the public.

Buying directly from mass-market paperback publishers is not as simple as buying directly from regular trade publishers. Mass-market houses are inflexible in requiring minimum quantities for opening accounts and for each successive order. This may make the retailer feel direct accounts with these houses are not worth the trouble. Not so. Mass-market paperback publishers ship freight free, which is a definite bottom-line consideration. Most mass-market houses have a direct telephone sales force that speeds up delivery time. These telephone sales representatives keep in constant contact with accounts, giving the bookseller advance information on movie tie-in titles, television tie-ins, and many other promotions. Having these books when the public wants them is important not only for sales, but for the bookseller's credibility.

Small press titles can add luster and depth to a bookstore. Considered a salvation by some and an impossibility by others, small presses are worth the trouble it takes to be in touch with them and to stock their titles where it is pertinent. Discounts will not be as high as those of major houses and many other terms are not as commerce-oriented, but knowing their specializations and handling those that fit the image of your store builds your reputation.

The same can be said for university presses. Wholesalers do not usually stock many university press titles, so buying directly becomes a necessity. University press terms are the most difficult in the business to decipher because of their scholarly/trade/text crossovers. Careful ordering is a must. If done properly, good discounts are possible and returns can be minimal.

Paperwork is the greatest disadvantage in buying directly from publishers. The amount of it is staggering. Reconciling invoices and statements takes time and so costs money, but it is absolutely necessary. Attention to myriad details is part of the process. Writing stacks of checks for a month's supply of books is also expensive and time-consuming. Customer-service departments at publishing houses are not always responsive. Correcting an error, theirs or yours, can take weeks. Getting a dust jacket to replace the one that disintegrated in shipping can be a major undertaking. In all such instances, it is best to contact a person at the publishing house rather than a department. The *ABA Book Buyer's Handbook* has names and telephone numbers. If a credit problem arises, contact the head of the credit department. If it's sales, go to sales, and so on. Publishers are as interested in solving problems as are booksellers, but it takes time.

As does everything in running a bookstore. It takes time to select the right books to stock and to unpack and shelve them. It takes more time to go to a section with a customer to show books and discuss them than to just point a finger, but it also sells more books. Time spent productively is time invested. That efficiency expert standing in our store, telling us how to run it as a business, was not a bookseller. He did not understand what he was criticizing. We believe all that extra time we spend on ordering and on selling, and all those books we have on our shelves that we could only get by ordering directly, and all the time we spend on paperwork and details are the reasons we enjoy hearing customers say, "You have it! We couldn't find it anywhere else, not even in San Francisco!"

Chapter 20

Buying from Wholesalers

ROBERT D. HALE with STEPHEN COGIL
and A. DAVID SCHWARTZ

Wholesalers who have instituted the most efficient order-fulfillment and delivery systems, and who have expanded their inventories to anticipate the bookseller's most urgent needs for current titles, have over the past decade become the independent bookseller's best friends. They have become an integral part of the business of bookselling. Their services have made it possible for hundreds of small stores to become successful. No full-service bookstore can depend solely on wholesalers for its inventory, but no full-service bookstore can survive without them.

The practice of buying forthcoming titles cautiously from the publisher's rep, planning to reorder as needed from the wholesaler, was a way many experienced booksellers did business for a great many years. It was, and is, sound. However, as the wholesalers moved forward, growing to national proportions and developing systems that were vastly more efficient than those of the publishers, some booksellers stopped looking to publishers for their stock and began using the wholesalers exclusively—which meant their inventory was automatically limited by the wholesalers' inventories. They in effect became outlets for portions of their suppliers' selections. This is not the best way to build a business, unless the tastes of one's customers (and one's own tastes) totally reflect that of the wholesaler.

The purpose of this chapter is to enumerate the reasons for and the ways to use a wholesaler. They are many, but they do not mean the bookseller should not also purchase books from publishers. The successful bookseller, now as always, buys wisely from both.

When considering inventory needs it is important to remember that the greatest success factor is having what the customer wants when he wants it. A bookstore's reputation for availability of titles surpasses all others as a drawing card. Because no bookstore can stock all books at all times, ways have to be found to get those wanted books that are not in stock as rapidly as possible. This means not only the individual special order that the customer may not have expected the bookstore to have, but the title that has suddenly "taken off" because the author was on television or the cover of *Time* magazine or for some other reason. Customers want that book "now!" not three weeks from now. Unfortunately that's probably what it would take to get it from a publisher. If the wholesaler has it in stock, delivery can take two or three days, depending upon how they ship their orders.

This speed of availability is a wholesaler's major selling point, though there are others that we'll get to in a moment. Many wholesalers have systems the bookseller can use to give the customer a yes or no answer instantly. These are as simple as a microfiche of the wholesaler's weekly inventory or as technical as on-line communications. This instant information continues with most wholesalers when the order is placed; the order taker, if the order is telephoned in, responds to each title either with an "in stock" or "out of stock" answer. Knowing what to tell your customer builds your credibility and professional appearance.

Wholesalers are a solid selling tool if used properly. They are also savers of time, which is money. The bookseller should understand as much as possible the time consumed in bookkeeping for individual publishers' orders, invoices, statements, and payments, plus processing individual damaged and/or incorrect title returns. Every piece of paper handled is an item of expense, even if the bookseller didn't have to pay directly for the paper. The ideal would be for a bookseller to be able to place a single order for all books needed, process a single shipment, and pay a single bill. That can't be, but it is possible to drastically cut paperwork by combining orders and statements and payments for a portion of the business.

Using the information supplied by the wholesaler, whether it be by reading the microfiche or going over printed stock lists or telecommunications, the bookseller can order books in modest quantities per title from a variety of publishers all at one time. These titles might include several special orders, those books that have begun moving and an assortment of others that are needed to fill out the basic stock before a regular stock order can be placed with a publisher. Publishers' stock offers, with dating as well as increased discounts, are too good to miss, but there are times when titles have to be replenished in between these offers.

The bookseller should investigate all potential wholesalers and know all their terms, discounts, quantities, freight charges, delivery schedules, and the like—and their types of inventory—before proceeding with orders. The terms vary, and so does the stock carried. The national wholesalers tend to be generalists, carrying a selection of current titles and some basic backlist—or what they consider basic. Regional wholesalers might be just that, stocking books of regional interest. Local wholesalers can be anything from full service to strictly mass-market paperbacks and periodicals. There are also specialist wholesalers, who offer everything from small press to genre. The bookseller will need to know which are most useful to his or her particular requirements.

Wholesalers' terms have improved greatly in recent years; now they are competitive with publishers in many instances, especially those who offer extra discount for prompt payment. This discount is usually available for full payment of the previous month's invoices by the tenth of the following month. A savvy bookseller might consider this and buy accordingly, doing the heavy wholesaler orders early in the month and tapering off toward the end to build the necessary cash reserve for prompt payment from the sales of the books acquired from that source.

No part of the bookseller's turnover will be greater—if the buying is done carefully—than that of merchandise acquired from the wholesaler, simply because it is the fast-moving titles that are thus purchased. The stock turn from wholesaler-acquired inventory might be twice that of the more basic and/or risk titles purchased directly from publishers. This does *not* mean that total inventory if purchased from wholesalers would turn at that rate. It is the combination of sources that is most successful. This increased rate of turn from the fast-moving merchandise (wherever acquired) when averaged with the slower moving is, of course, what gives a store its overall turnover rate, and as explained in chapter 13, anything that helps that rate increase is worth considering.

Although discounts must always be considered, the specific discount on a specific title is not the definitive answer. Acquiring a $10.00 book when it is needed and making a sale even though the discount from the source was only 38 percent, for instance, rather than 40 percent that might be possible from the prime source, is $3.80 gross profit in hand now, rather than a maybe $4.00 somewhere down the line. Used properly, the wholesaler adds actual dollars to the bookseller's gross profit in availability, reduction of paperwork, and increased turnover.

Wholesalers aren't the whole answer, however, for several reasons. They do not have all the titles a bookseller will need, any more than a bookseller has all the titles the customers want. Thus they certainly cannot be the sole source for special needs. Nor, for the reasons mentioned earlier, should they be the sole source for new titles and/or backlist. A bookstore acquires a reputation for its inventory, for what it has and does not have in stock. It is a prime responsibility of the bookseller to build an inventory that not only fulfills his market's needs, but anticipates and expands them. This cannot be done with predigested selections made by someone else somewhere far away.

The penny-wise bookseller takes advantage of every opportunity to increase gross margins, and there is no way any wholesaler can compete with publishers' periodic stock offers, nor with most publishers' large-quantity discounts. These are as essential to an overall buying program as are those other good things mentioned earlier (such as availability).

Although many wholesalers have moved into the business of supplying information as well as books, and do an excellent job of alerting booksellers to publicity about titles, special promotions, and the like, direct contact with publishers is vital for a successful bookseller. Publishers' representatives call not only to sell, but to pass on all kinds of news about their books that can help the bookseller sell as well as buy. Even if a bookstore is too small to be worth the publisher's expense sending a rep, having a direct account entitles the store to receive lots of printed information, the most important of which are catalogs.

Booksellers from the smallest to the largest can from time to time use publishers' cooperative advertising money. Even though some wholesalers accumulate sales figures on which such funds are usually based, it is still the publishers who allocate the money. Direct contact with them for this purpose is essential. (For full information on cooperative advertising see chapters 48, 49, 50, and 55.)

Both the publisher and the wholesaler have advantages and disadvantages for the book retailer. Timing and planning are keys to success in the business. A bookstore must have the titles currently in demand in constant supply and must also have the basic stock upon which all the other sales are built. Use the wholesaler and the publisher at the right times and in the right ways, and what might at first appear to be a perplexing problem can become a winning combination.

Chapter 21

Receiving Procedures

JOAN RIPLEY

In chapter 18, we covered the mechanics of ordering. Now all those books are going to arrive at your store. It is worth the time and effort to make certain that what the suppliers say they shipped is exactly what you receive.

The first thing to remember about receiving is, do *not* sign for any trucked-in shipment before making sure that the number of cartons received matches the number shown on the bill of lading, that all cartons in the shipment are addressed to your store, and that no cartons are damaged. Your signature on a shipping receipt implies acceptance of the quantity and condition of the merchandise. It is difficult to claim that you didn't receive all the cartons, that some of them had been damaged or previously opened, or that you didn't want the books anyway after you've signed for them.

It's fairly simple to match the number of cartons with the number shown on the shipper's document. It's also immediately obvious whether they are in good condition. If the condition is questionable—and you won't really know until you have unpacked and inspected them—have the person making the delivery note this on his document and on a memo for your files. Because most publishers indicate your purchase order number someplace on the shipping label, it is easy to quickly pull that purchase order number out of your file and assure yourself you have not canceled the order. If for any reason an order has been canceled, it should be refused immediately. The delivery person will put it back on the truck and return it to the publisher at no expense to the bookseller. If a canceled order is accepted and then later returned, both incoming and outgoing freight charges are the responsibility of the bookseller.

If you do not accept the shipment or any part of it, write up a memo with full particulars for future communication with the publisher. You will undoubtedly be billed for the shipment on the next statement from the publisher; you want as much documentation as possible to explain why you aren't paying.

In a normal shipment, all cartons will arrive as listed with no problems and be accepted with eagerness.

When your initial checking is accomplished and the shipper's document is signed, the next step is to open the cartons—with caution. A cutter knife swept across the top of a carton can slash right through the jackets of the entire top layer of books. If you cause this damage, the problem is yours; getting dust jacket replacements is more difficult than getting new books. If you cut deeply enough to slash the books, they are a total loss.

The best way to open a carton is to carefully cut the tape binding the top sides, loosening the cover flaps enough so they can be raised an inch or two. This allows the tape along the center of the top to be sliced far enough above the contents so the blade does not touch them.

What you need now is a packing slip or an invoice for the shipment. It can be anywhere—on the outside of one of the boxes, in the bottom of a carton, tucked inside a book—or it may even be missing. There is no standard location for either the invoice or the packing slip.

The difference between a packing slip and an invoice is simple. The packing slip lists quantities and titles included in the shipment, sometimes with the retail prices, sometimes not, but packing slips seldom are extended—the quantity of each book times the price is not listed, nor are discounts or shipping charges shown. The invoice has complete information, including the total cost of the shipment with the publisher's payment terms.

Some publishers enclose packing slips with their shipments and send the invoice by mail. Others include both invoice and packing slip in the shipment. If the invoice arrives separately before the shipment, it should be filed in the receiving room in an "Awaiting Receipt" file. If it comes after the shipment, it will be necessary to match it with the filed packing slip against which the shipment was checked in.

The shipment has to be checked in. You must make sure the titles shown on the packing slip and/or invoice match the books you are taking out of the box. Check the exact quantity, title, and price. Note if the books are cloth or paperback. If the price is not shown on the packing slip and you do not yet have the invoice, write the prices of the books on the packing slip as you check them in to make sure jacket prices agree with invoiced prices. (A side note: We always use a clipboard as backing for checking packing slips so there is no danger of doing it on top of a stack of books and thus marking the glossy dust jackets. We also use a red pencil to contrast with the pen or print color of the publisher's marks.) If there are any discrepancies—different quantities, wrong titles, or whatever—note on the packing slip exactly what you have received. Always document as you go along; you will be better able to state your case to the publisher when seeking adjustment.

A number of publishers offer "freight pass-through," which invoices the books at an amount less than the retail price printed on the book jacket. Some publishers print both the retail price and the freight pass-through price on their invoices, and others don't. Most publishers who use freight pass-through code the retail price at the top of the dust jacket with FPT. Many will also code the FPT price (the invoiced price) either at the inside bottom of the dust jacket or on the back of the dust jacket. For instance, on a Holt title the suggested retail price print at the top of the inside of the dust jacket reads "FPT > $13.95." On the back of the dust jacket at the bottom it reads "Ret:1087:001345:50." Translated, this means the book was published in October 1987; the freight pass-through price is $13.45; and it is fifty cents lower than the suggested retail price. As a general rule of thumb, the FPT price is usually fifty cents lower for a hardback and twenty-five cents lower for a regular-size trade paperback. As is standard in the publishing industry, there is no standardization. You'll have to train your staff about FPT for both receiving and returning procedures. Soon they will become familiar with each publisher's system for FPT.

If everything is correct and the contents agree with the documents, the next step is to check the packing slip against the original purchase order, noting in some fashion on the order the books that have arrived. Because of rapidly changing prices, it is a good idea also to check the price shown on the purchase order against the price on the packing slip or invoice. Increases can affect your merchandise budget—be aware of them.

Always check the terms of sale, such as discount, delayed payment date, or any other special terms—shown on the purchase order against those on the invoice. If you purchased the books on an added discount or any other kind of special offer, make sure the invoice shows this because you will be paying from the invoice.

Also check the actual amount of postage or other shipping charges listed on the cartons against the freight charge on the invoice. If there is a difference, remove the postage meter tape from the carton and staple it to the invoice. Once again, it's documentation for future negotiation.

If the shipment is only part of the original order, look over the invoice or packing slip to see if there is information on when you might expect the titles that were not shipped. They may be listed as out of print or out of stock. If your original purchase order stated "Do not back order" or "Cancel all shorts," you should consider the order complete even if all the books did not come. You will have to order the unshipped books from another source. If the shipment is part of a salesperson's order covering an entire season's list, it will obviously not be complete; the books received should be checked off on the order and the order put back in the file box until all the books listed on it have arrived.

If an order is complete, many booksellers pull the order, staple the checked packing list and/or invoice to it, and put the papers on the bookkeeper's desk for entry and payment. If there isn't a book-keeper and the system is basic, just put the papers in the ready-to-be-paid file.

Do not be afraid to make whatever notes are necessary on all these documents. If there are errors, show them boldly. If there are no problems, indicate it with an OK or some symbol of approval, and sign and date the form. You will want to know the actual date the shipment was received and checked.

Some stores use a simple receiving form that has spaces for date of receipt, date of invoice, total retail value, total amount due on invoice (including freight, and the like), and cash discount, if any, for early payment. This form is attached to the invoice and all other documentation as an aid to easy payment.

Many stores have receiving logs, which are ongoing records of shipments received. Each shipment is given a number that is put on all the documents. Opposite that number in the log (which can simply be a loose-leaf notebook), the date of receipt and the name of the vendor, publisher, or other are recorded.

If there are problems with the shipment—defective books, incorrect titles, and so forth—document the problems and proceed as soon as possible with corrective measures. Defective books should be packed up and returned immediately in a box marked "DEFEC-TIVES." Note this on the packing slip and invoice, and deduct the defectives so you will not have to pay for them. When the publisher replaces them, you will be billed on a new invoice—do not pay for them twice. You also do not want to pay freight in and out on defective books, so include freight costs both ways on your charge-back document. (See chapter 22 on returns.)

Incorrect titles might be handled in the same way, but because returning wrong titles without prior permission seems to confuse publishers' receiving rooms, most booksellers send off a memo telling the publisher of the errors, asking for the right titles to be sent and for permission to return the wrong ones. Once again, make sure you aren't charged freight on publishers' mistakes.

You will also have to notify publishers of errors in quantities shipped and/or billed, if hardbound was sent and paperbound was ordered, and so on. Because all this correspondence is incredibly time-consuming, it helps if you can devise a simple form on which various common errors are listed, so that you can merely make a few checkmarks, fill in a couple of purchase order and invoice numbers, and so on, and thus convey the information in a clear fashion without resorting to lengthy formal letters.

Make sure in all cases that whoever is paying the bills or doing the correspondence knows exactly what is happening. If the receiver is also the check writer, the problem is simpler, though the time between the first and the second act may be long enough to allow a memory lapse. Documentation is essential.

Simple discrepancies can be taken care of when a book is received. The most common is that a different price is shown on the book from that on the invoice. If the book is a hardcover with a dust jacket, clip the dust jacket price and pencil in the invoice price. This does *not* apply to FPT titles. If the price problem occurs with paperbacks, you can argue with the publisher about lowering the invoice price to match that shown on the books, or you can hold the books in your receiving room until the publisher sends you new price stickers to apply over the old price. Both solutions are maddening.

Once everything is checked in and all the mistakes are noted, the next part of receiving is to do whatever is necessary to comply with the bookstore's inventory-control system. This might mean simply jotting a date code in each book or entering facts and figures on file cards or into a computer. We won't go into that here but refer you to chapter 15.

The books are checked in and priced. They are now ready to go into stock, preferably straight onto the sales floor. Getting them from the delivery truck to the sales floor may seem a long and overly complicated procedure, but by taking time and attending to all the dtails now, you can save a lot of grief later on. Receiving is one of the most important aspects of bookselling—it is worth doing properly.

Chapter 22

Processing Returns

JOAN RIPLEY

January and July usually prove to be the best months for booksellers to assess inventory and make returns. During these two periods of "ruthlessness," you must—if you never do it at any other time—evaluate every book in stock. You must question seriously not only the salability of each title, but also *when* you think you'll be able to sell it. Sentimental favorites have to come under the same conscientious scrutiny as least favorites.

If you have an inventory-control system that indicates how many copies you have sold of a given title and when they were sold, the decision is immeasurably easier. A general rule of thumb is that if a book hasn't sold in six months, it's probably best to return it. Exceptions would be seasonal titles or titles that might sell at a book fair or other special event you may be staging in the near future. You should know when you first received a book and what its rate of sale is in order to make a valid decision. There are a variety of methods for controlling or aging a title, but in order to ensure a clean, viable stock, this information must be available.

Once the decision has been reached that a book must be removed, the question then is, what is the best method for disposing of it? Returns or markdowns are the principal methods for cleaning up an inventory. Careful thought must be given to each title, whether you can sell it at a reduced price or whether you should return it to the publisher or wholesaler from whom you bought it.

An age-old argument exists as to whether it is better to mark down or return. For years, markdowns won. Then returns had a strong advantage for the next decade. Now, with postal charges escalating, it is time to rethink the whole problem. There are four reasons for marking down a book: The book is eligible for return, but it is too shopworn to be acceptable to the publisher. The book was once considered basic stock, but sales have dropped off and it is no longer eligible for return. The book, in pristine condition, is eligible for return, but it is cheaper to mark it down than to return it because of the publisher's return policy or because you do not have the proper information to receive full credit. Finally, the book was bought on a nonreturnable basis and must be kept.

When is it cheaper to mark a book down than to return it? When you can sell it for 12 percent less than the credit you would receive from the publisher. This figure used to be 5 percent, but postal considerations now force the percentage two to three times higher. The current percentage reflects only the higher cost of postal charges and *not* today's higher dollar cost of processing the return.

If you must look up invoice numbers or else accept a flat 46 percent, or some other penalty discount, on the return, it is cheaper to sell the book at half price. This is especially true if you must write for permission to return in addition to the expense of packing and shipping, even if you get credit for full purchase price.

For example: a $10.00 book, on which you received a 40 percent discount plus freight-in of $.89, costs you $6.89:

Cost	$6.89
Permission letter	.22 (postage only)
Freight back	.89
Subtotal	$8.00
Credit received	$6.00
Net loss	$2.00

On that same $10.00 book, marked down to $5.98, the net loss is $.91 (or the cost price, $6.89, less the sale price, $5.98).

If the book were marked down to $4.98, your net loss would be $1.91 or $.09 less than that incurred by returning the book—not counting the time and materials involved. The key word is sell. Can you *sell* that book you mark down? Dead fiction, for instance, usually can't be *given* away. A novel that didn't sell at $10.00 probably won't sell at $5.98 or $4.98 either.

Once you have decided that a title must be removed from prime shelf space, several factors must be considered in the decision to return or to mark down. For instance, a lot of old books looking a bit shopworn could detract from your store's image. On the other hand, you may *want* your store to be thought of as a bargain hunter's paradise.

Space is a consideration. Small stores need the room and are forced to get rid of marginal books more quickly than a markdown sale would accomplish.

Examine your current credit situation with the publisher involved. If you owe that publisher a lot of money, it might just be best to erase some of your debt with a return.

Consider the type of book—big gift book, children's book, cookbook, and so on. What types of promotional books do your customers usually buy? Would the book you are considering marking down fit into this special-value promotion pattern?

Here is a suggested markdown schedule:

Original Price	Markdown Price
$16.96–$18.95	$9.98
$14.96–$16.95	$8.98
$12.96–$14.95	$7.98
$10.96–$12.95	$6.98
$8.96–$10.95	$5.98
$7.96–$8.95	$4.98
$6.01–$7.95	$3.98
$4.01–$6.00	$2.49

Of course, these books will have to be reduced even further if they do not sell at the original markdown. Age your markdowns as you do your new books, so you know when to reduce them again or promote them differently. Many books you will want to return.

When you are set to make your returns, be sure you are in the right frame of mind. Don't think of returns as gigantic mistakes—unless you're planning to return 20 percent of your inventory. Returns are a normal part of the business. It is rare for any bookstore to sell absolutely every book purchased. If that happens, a bookseller should think about the fact that he or she is probably losing additional sales on additional titles by purchasing only completely proven sellers. As stressed earlier, try not to be sentimental. There are a few books you're bound to keep because you must have them in stock, but think of the bottom line—and *pull*.

Sort the books by publisher. Add to these stacks the books that you've been accumulating for returns during the past few months—books that were damaged or definitely not selling or ones that the publishers' reps pulled for you. Never miss the opportunity to have the reps pull returns when they come to call. They will spot some titles that you might miss, or they may have information about why certain titles should go back. If you have to seek publisher permission to make a return, do not pull those books from the shelves until permission is received. Merely list those titles with all pertinent information and send off your request. Some of the books may sell between requesting and receiving permission.

If you have a large number of books from a single publisher, you are probably better off returning than marking down. But if you have ones and twos from a variety of publishers, it might be more advantageous to mark such books down—*if* they will be sure sellers at the reduced price. Another possibility would be to return the ones and twos to the jobber if you have purchased them from him. Many times you will have purchased the same title from both publisher and jobber. If this is the case, it is certainly easier to make one return to one location rather than packing up several small boxes.

Make certain you are following the publisher's return policies as stated in the *ABA Book Buyer's Handbook*. If you need permission first, write for it immediately. In some instances, time can be saved by asking your publisher's rep directly for a return label when he or she is in your store to sell the next season's list. Some will have the authority to give you labels themselves if you show them what you are planning to return. Mass-market publishers' reps almost always have labels with them and will supply you with one if you ask for it.

If your stock-control system is a good one, you will not have to search through invoices for return information. It should be readily available, and you should lose no time in writing up your charge-back form, remembering to include all information that the publisher's return policy requires. A copy of the charge-back should be filed with your records and a copy enclosed in every carton. Remember, when you are returning freight pass-through titles, the price you should enter on your charge-back is the FPT price, *not* the suggested retail price. You were invoiced at the FPT price, and that is the same price that must be used when returning.

Don't forget to include your account number on all correspondence, and if more than three months goes by without receiving your credit, call or write to the customer-service department and find out why you haven't received it. This is especially important if you have a blanket postal insurance policy that sets a time limit on coverage for lost shipments.

Returns aren't much fun, but most books have a certain life-span. It is up to the buyer to determine when that lifetime is over. Every day a dead book stays on your shelves, it is costing you a little bit more. If you are conscientious about reviewing your stock, you can maintain a clean, viable inventory that may mean the difference between a profit and a loss in your store's operation.

IV
Merchandising

Chapter 23

Selling Books

SUZANNE HASLAM HINST

You can be blessed with a beautiful store in the best-possible location, a superb stock, an inventory system that works perfectly, a front-page story in the local newspaper about the store, and yet all you really have is an expensive hobby until sales are made.

Rule #1—Selling is fun. It means assisting people in their selection.

Everyone who opens a bookstore believes rule #1. If we didn't, we'd be operating out of a warehouse with a mail-order catalog. We want to be with people. So, the front door opens and people stroll in. Immediately you are faced with "salesmanship." Nothing to it, you think. But as the days, weeks, and months go by, you notice you have very little repeat business; those people who strolled in once do not seem to stroll in again, and the sales record on the cash register tape isn't as great as you had envisioned. Maybe you aren't as good at selling as you thought you were.

Relax. Salesmanship is not automatic, but it can be learned. Just study the rules and practice them. The results may not be instantaneous. It won't happen overnight, but it will work. Practice can result in sales, and then selling really is fun.

Rule # 2—Customers do not come in the front door. People come in the front door. They are potential customers.

Keep rule #2 in mind as you read the rest of this chapter.

There are three simple steps to good salesmanship: realization, skill, and practice.

Realization. It doesn't matter if one is the owner, manager, janitor, or bookkeeper; when that person comes into personal contact with a potential customer, he or she must realize, "I am a salesperson!" (for better or worse). When you make that personal contact, you represent the store. In fact, to the potential customer, you *are* the store.

The first thing a potential customer notices about you on first contact is your appearance. Appearance isn't just a matter of clothing, though one's attire should fit the overall image of the store. Appearance is also grooming. If you've gotten dirty unpacking cartons, wash your hands before you wait on customers. Appearance also has to do with one's bearing. Always present yourself in a discreet professional manner, speaking calmly and with confidence.

Realize that the potential customer expects you to know the books you are trying to sell. It is unfortunately all too common in retail stores to have a bored or surly clerk say something such as "Everything we have is on display. If you can't find it, I guess we don't have it." Realize that it isn't the potential customer's job to find it. That is the job of the salesperson. Think how, as a customer, you react positively to a salesperson who knows the store's stock and knows how to get an item for you that isn't currently in stock.

Realize that the only way to learn inventory is to work with it. There is no magic formula. A properly stocked store will carry the best titles in its categories. Physically handling the books, picking them up and scanning the information on the dust jacket or on the back cover of paperbacks, will go a long way toward enhancing your knowledge of titles and authors. It is also a good way to develop an awareness of publishers who consistently produce quality books as well as those who do not.

Realize that part of selling is knowing where to find information. Master the use of trade reference tools and catalogs so that you'll be able to track down and obtain books customers want that are not currently in stock.

Realize pride in knowing the stock.

Skill. Remember all those people coming into the store are potential customers. Each one is unique. Yet there are some common denominators. Let's think about them by imagining yourself as a potential customer in different kinds of specialty stores.

Your first stop is a sporting goods store. You've just started dating somebody who is crazy about racquetball, and you are determined to take up the sport. You must buy a racket. With no idea of what they cost, you're hoping to find one for under ten dollars, but it was love at first sight, so you're ready to drain your savings account if necessary. Instantly you discover the el-cheapo racket in Day-Glo pink is $14.98 and the deluxe graphite model a mere $250.00. However, an alert salesperson understands your quandary and helps you select a perfectly respectable racket for $29.98—while also giving you a few tips on the game.

The next stop isn't really on your agenda, but you're in no great hurry, and as you're going past your favorite clothing store, you decide to stop in just to see what is new. The salesperson knows you so you just smile and say hello as you wander off to browse. It isn't long before something strikes your fancy, and miraculously that salesperson is right nearby to help you make the purchase.

Last stop is a hardware store. You are in a hurry now, having spent too much time in the clothing store, but you have to buy a power saw for your uncle. You borrowed the one he had and broke it. You have written down the exact brand and model you want to replace. An intelligent salesperson takes you directly to the power saw display, finds the model you want, explains the warranty, and helps you make the purchase quickly. You are in the store only twelve minutes, and you leave pleased with the purchase you have made.

In each of these examples, you were a different type of customer. At the sporting goods store you were determined to buy something though you needed expert assistance. At the clothing store you were not intent on buying and wanted to be left to browse. At the hardware store you were eager to buy if they had exactly what you wanted.

Each salesperson handled your buying moods in a most professional way, ensuring the best-possible chance for a sale and a satisfied customer. Each of them knew how to approach different types of customers, sensing, as good salespeople do, the two sets of conditions that inevitably exist.

Some people are in a hurry. Some people are not in a hurry.

Most people are on a budget. Some people are not on a budget.

A bookstore is a specialty store and as such probably appears perplexing to most people. People coming into a bookstore usually need some kind of assistance. Frequently they have only the vaguest notion of what they want. The classic "I don't know the title or author, but it was on television and has a red cover" is a puzzle that can be solved with a few gentle questions. Always put the potential customer at ease. Always assure the person that the two of you can come up with the answer, the title and author, by working together.

Bookstores appeal to all kinds of people, even those who only buy a book once or twice a year. Some buy three or four books a week. Others wander into a bookstore every day and seldom leave without making a purchase. Many people have never read an entire book outside of school, but they will buy books for others. Be especially considerate of those who are uncomfortable in a bookstore for whatever reason. Remember how you feel when you go into a store and how you return to those stores where you feel comfortable, where the salespeople are friendly and helpful.

Never pass judgment on a potential customer's literary knowledge. Not everyone knows how to pronounce all the names, and this includes those who are booksellers. Never judge potential customers by their appearance, even though they may be judging you by yours. The bearded kid in dungarees may just be the foremost authority on oceanography. Booksellers provide a gateway to knowledge and understanding, inspiration and entertainment. Everything they do must keep the gates open with the welcome mat out for those who would come in.

Combining the knowledge you have about the stock you carry and the reference tools that tell you how to get what you do not have with a genuine desire to be of assistance to the person who comes into your store develops selling skill.

Rule #3—Greet all potential customers, preferably with a smile.

A smile makes a person feel welcome. Again, think how pleased you are when you walk into a store and the salesperson seems visibly happy to see you.

After the smile, it doesn't matter much what polite greeting you use as long as you avoid anything that denotes high-pressure techniques. A simple "hello" is perfect. A fine next phrase is, "Please let me know if I can be of any assistance." "If you need me, I'm right here" or "If you can't find what you want, let me know" does not press the person but does imply that you're ready to do whatever it is he or she wants you to do, including being left alone to browse. This gives the potential customer breathing room not to feel rushed or pressured to buy. Avoid, "May I help you?" because that almost inevitably gets a "No." And it seems to say to a potential customer, "May I sell you something?"

The determined-to-buy customer has already decided to purchase a book in your store and will, barring a major error on your part. This person usually has a particular subject in mind, but not a specific title. She might ask for the pet section (what she really wants is a book about Dalmatians). Or she might ask to see your cookbooks (she wants a Chinese cookbook for her sister). Or perhaps she mumbles something about fiction (she wants a new Agatha Christie mystery, even though she knows there isn't one).

As you take her to the section, ask, "Did you have anything particular in mind?" This may result in clues that will help you point out a specific book or several books that would fulfill the need. If no useful answer is forthcoming, leave her to look for herself, but don't go too far away because it is likely she will need further assistance shortly. Don't hover! Do something such as straighten a shelf or rearrange it, so you don't seem to be waiting for her obvious need. Perhaps she isn't finding anything, or there may be so many choices she can't decide. Timing is important. Learn by dealing with people how to offer help when it is needed and neither before nor after.

While helping a potential customer, be serious. You can kill what would have been a sure sale with an offhand remark. Sense the direction the person is going and go in that direction, too. Avoid voicing personal opinions that might offend. Everyone has a different idea about what is fun to read, or enlightening or inspiring. Allow individuals to choose their own torrid romance or volume of Proust or Norman Vincent Peale without mentioning your personal objections if you have them. Confirming their taste with your own affirmation is fine if it's sincere. Shared enthusiasms bring customers back.

So, discover the needs of the determined potential customer and remember timing. Present the books and point out features that fulfill the need, remembering budget. Offer alternatives if necessary, such as suggesting a contemporary writer similar to Agatha Christie. Provide the customer with a good reason to buy, perhaps using one of the favorite selling sentences that follow later in this chapter.

"Just browsing" is probably the most oft repeated comment made in any and all bookstores. Happily, many people delight in visiting bookstores. They love books and have an avid interest in what is new on the shelves. They have no prejudice about buying if they decide a book is irresistible even though they may not have known the book existed before they saw it on the shelf. They are almost always impulse buyers, and they usually sell themselves more books than any salesperson could.

The best response to "Just browsing" is, "Wonderful, we're happy to see you." You've identified yourself as a salesperson, so you can now leave this customer alone until help is asked for. Do make sure you're easy to locate if needed. If this browser is a regular and you know what his interests are, it doesn't hurt—in fact, it's considered a favor—to remark in passing, "There's a new (whatever it is) on the shelf—you might like to look at it." Or, "The new (whoever) just came in. I've put them on the new arrival table." What you are doing is feeding the browser's ego by letting him know you remember the books that interest him and planting a seed that may sprout into a sale.

The "open to buy if you have a specific book" potential customer can be the easiest or the most difficult. This person usually has written down a title and sometimes the author, publisher, price, and so on. You are a winner if you can walk to the proper shelf, take down the book, and hand it over. Unfortunately, what the person has written down as "exact" information is too often incomplete or inaccurate. It isn't unusual for this person to give you the title of the review rather than the title of the book reviewed. It is a time for tactful communication.

Remember that most people have no idea how the book business operates. They have a vague notion that all the books in existence lie in a warehouse on the outskirts of town and you have a list of them right there in front of you. They have no realization of the hundreds of thousands of titles that are in print, the tens of thousands that come into print each year, and the additional tens of thousands that go out of print. Trade, text, scholarly, hardbound, paperback are terms that mean little except for the last two, and frequently customers have those mixed up.

Although it isn't up to you to educate the public, you do have to (very tactfully and gently) determine the true needs of the potential customer who knows exactly what book he specifically wants. Having gotten the information through a combination of bits provided by the potential customer, reference tools, and your own knowledge, you finally come up with the title and the author, and you know where to find it if it's in the store, or where you can get it if it isn't. This includes offering to advertise for it if it is out of print. It's also smart to give the person an alternative if one exists and then let him decide whether to go for a substitute or wait for the special order or search service.

Whatever the decision—and one hopes it will result in an accomplished sale—the effort expended in attempting to fill that person's specific need is worth every second it took because he will return when he needs a book to the store that tried to help him.

Presenting books to potential customers is a minor art that can easily be attained by anyone willing to think about it. Books should be handled with care but without fear, with obvious appreciation of their worth but without affectation. Some people do not know how to hold a book, especially a large-format book, without doing it damage. The salesperson who handles books easily sets a good example for potential customers.

When presenting a book to a customer, point out its major features—its contents, obviously, and its quality, the fine photographs if there are photographs, the clean, clear typeface, the binding, paper quality, best-seller status, the author's reputation, whatever positive things that can be said about that particular book. Do not remark on the quality of paper if the paper is poor, nor point out illustrations if they are inferior. Concentrate on the book's best features, and comment on them.

Place the book being considered into the potential buyer's hands as soon as possible. This directs attention to the suggested selection and permits the person to really examine it, to see what you have pointed out.

When presenting several choices, mention the advantages of each without being negative about any, so that although differences are readily apparent, no book is made to seem inferior. Again, be aware of how the potential customer seems to be leaning, and do not upset a sale by putting down the book the person may prefer. Remember, each book has its own audience, its own appeal and merit. If it doesn't, it should not be in your store. Your purpose as a salesperson is to help facilitate a decision that will satisfy and please the buyer. As each person is unique, so is each book.

Selling up is a fun part of the business. It simply means adding a sale to one that is already made, such as selling another book to the person who came in determined to buy and found the one wanted and bought it as the first purchase. Or it means selling to the browser who hadn't intended to buy at all. Or selling to that specific title seeker another book as well.

Here are some suggestions that can create extra sales:

"This book is brand new, just came in, you're the first to see it."

"This is the Joe Author book. Did you see him on TV last night?"

"While you're here, don't miss the display of Mother's Day (or any other gift-giving day) gift ideas."

"I just read that they're making a movie (or TV miniseries) of this book."

"There are some great buys on that bargain table."

"Do you have a thesaurus to go with this dictionary you're buying?"

"All of the books on this display have been autographed by the authors."

These are only a few of many things that can be suggested to a potential customer in passing without making any big deal of it, but with the possibility of adding sales. People are interested in "inside information," and you have focused their attention on something they might have missed. Suggestions can be made by clever signs as well as by spoken comments, especially if they are conversational in tone and not aggressive.

Practice. As you repeatedly use these skills, they become second nature and increase your professionalism; you will discover that they work *and* that there are exceptions to every rule. Every bookstore has its own group of customers that reflect the bookstore itself, its stock, and its staff. Because personality is an integral ingredient in salesmanship, it can be considered an art practiced in whatever way the situation demands. Where subtle suggestion may work for almost everybody, another type of salesperson might do better with strong personal recommendation. Adapting the art and practice to the need is key to success.

Even the best salespeople encounter buying resistance. No salesperson has a one hundred percent record. There is only so much one can and should do to complete a transaction. A potential customer may have a genuine change of heart and would feel better giving Aunt Clara a necklace rather than a book. Be gracious when a person decides not to buy. Remember that you want that person to come back again. Showing your disappointment over a lost sale or using high-pressure tactics are not conducive to repeat business. Remember the importance of making potential customers feel comfortable in your store.

If the potential customer is looking for a reason to decide to buy, and wants to buy but needs justification, then it is okay to offer reasons that might result in the sale. Be ever alert to the potential customer's true mood and intent.

Here are some favorite selling sentences:

"If this book is a gift, there's no reason you can't carefully read it first before giving it away." (You've suggested a way to double the customer's money's worth.)

"Which one did you choose?" (This is for the potential customer who hasn't been able to make up his mind. You're positively asking his reasons for choosing one.)

"That's a fine choice." (This for the customer still mulling but obviously leaning toward one title. You are complimenting her ability to make a wise selection.)

"Books are among the least expensive and most enduring passions in today's market." (This is true. Compare them with outside entertainment.)

"This book is on the best-seller lists" or "Did you read the rave reviews this book got?" (You are telling the customer that other people think the book under consideration is good.)

"I'm not sure which of those two books is best, but I do know this one sells better." (Be truthful because you are using other buyers' unspoken recommendation.)

"This car repair book will probably more than pay for itself the first time you use it." (A statement that can be made about any of the practical how-to books.)

Good salesmanship results in prosperity for the well-run bookstore. And good salesmanship is the result if you remember that selling is fun because it is assisting people; customers do not come in the door, the people who come in are potential customers; the best way to greet a potential customer is with a smile and a welcome.

In conclusion: Books are what you sell, goodwill is what you give away for free. A good salesperson does both.

Chapter 24

Hardcover Bookselling

**ROBERT D. HALE with FRANK LOWE
and JEAN B. WILSON**

"Hardbacks are the dinosaurs of the book trade" and "Nobody buys hardcover books anymore" are the comments of cynics with more arrogance than awareness. Tens of thousands of titles are available only in hardcover, old titles as well as new. Only a fraction of the new titles published each year will be reprinted later in paperback editions. Hardcover book sales are a major part of the total trade book business and will continue to be.

Many readers prefer hardbound books—books that are bound to last. This isn't just because they look more impressive on the home library shelf, though that is a factor. Most hardcover books are easier on the eyes than paperbacks, though of course there are exceptions in both. The quality of the paper as well as the print is usually better in a hardcover. The stiff price of a hardcover isn't so rough to take when compared with the stiff price of a quality paperback and the potential shelf life of both.

Hardbound books are not purchased just by "older" people who were reading before the paperback explosion. Serious readers of all ages purchase hardcovers as well as paperbacks. The ever-increasing numbers of copies of top best-selling hardcover titles that are sold indicate that millions of people not only don't want to wait for it to "appear in paper," they acknowledge that hardcover book prices are still reasonable when compared with other forms of entertainment.

Various studies have indicated that a large percentage of hardcover book sales represent gifts, and this is probably true. There is something a bit grander about a wrapped hardcover than a wrapped paperback, even for those weaned on paperbacks. Frequently the receiver of the gift and the giver are one and the same. "It's a gift I'm giving myself—I've wanted it for such a long time" is a comment often made by customers as they approach the cashier with an exceptionally expensive book.

Book collecting is probably more widespread today then ever before, and people collect all types of books—from comic books to limited editions. Young people are great book collectors, and they look forward eagerly to new books coming along in their area of interest. They are as avid for first editions and "clean copies" as any bearded elder.

Reference, business, and technical books, even when they are available in paperback editions, are often preferred in a cloth binding for its durability. Cookbooks in paper are popular for cookbook readers, but cooks who use cookbooks prefer hardcovers because they are so much easier to use. There are, as always, exceptions to this, but in general, when given a choice, those who plan to use the cookbook choose the hardcover for practical reasons.

Hardcover editions can bring school and library business into a bookstore, even though schools and libraries also use paperbacks. For "permanent" collections or for titles that are in constant circulation, hardcovers are usually preferred because of their durability and consequently greater economy.

For the bookseller there is great excitement in carrying the latest, hottest books that are making news or hitting the top of the lists. Even for the bookseller who does not depend on "best-sellers," having those titles displayed says to customers that this bookseller is aware of what is going on in the book world. "Do you have . . . ?" "Indeed I do, and I also have . . ." is selling books.

The bookseller has to consider dollars as well as the everyday delights of being in a bookstore, and hardcover sales bring in more dollars more quickly than paperback sales. Now, a rack of paperbacks in an airport or on a busy downtown corner is going to ring up sales rapidly—if the rack is stocked with books people want. But most bookstores aren't in a situation where thousands of people flock through the premises every day. It is essential to secure as many sales from as many people who do come in as is possible, and it is good business to make each sale as large as possible.

The person behind the cash register is probably going to be paid the same hourly rate no matter what is rung up. It doesn't take one bit more energy to ring up $17.95 than it does to ring up $7.95, and the time to make change and bag the book is the same. The major difference is $10 in sales of which at least 40 percent or $4 goes into gross profit.

Hardcover professional books are usually very expensive, and they are sold to bookstores by publishers at a reduced discount as a rule. The immediate reaction is, "I can't survive on twenty percent" (or whatever that professional publisher's discount is), and certainly everyone wants as large a percentage as possible. But the dealer in professional books ringing up high-priced books is making more actual dollars per transaction (in spite of the short discount) than those selling less expensive books with a greater margin.

All full-service bookstores have to carry both hardcover and paperback books. The mix will depend upon each store's special circumstances—market, traffic, overhead, and so on. A mix is really the ideal because it allows a bookseller to appeal to a much wider clientele—those who only want paperbacks and those who want a particular book, no matter what its binding. The combination gives a store a total look that is rarely present in either a totally hardcover or totally paperback bookstore.

Price resistance isn't the only reason people buy paperbacks. There are those who honestly prefer them, as there are those who want clothbound. However, for those to whom price is an overriding factor, hardcover reprints and remainders are an entrée to the other side of the book world. Sometimes these customers await the bookstore's own markdowns. Money is not always plentiful for book buyers. Anything that helps them acquire books they desire is an investment in the health of the business.

Specialists have to have hardcover books if they are to be taken seriously, unless their specialization is paperback science fiction or something similar. The true science-fiction aficionado, however, is going to seek out old out-of-print titles that probably never made it to paper. Children's book specialists have to have hardcover classics as well as the new books that come along with each list. Regional specialists have to carry privately printed materials frequently as well as the trade published items. Many of these are in hardcover.

Obviously, hardcover books are an integral part of bookselling. Publishers spend hundreds of thousands of dollars each year hyping their newest hardcover titles. The authors of hundreds of these books tour the country, appear on television and radio shows, are interviewed by newspapers and magazines. If the author is a celebrity or a statesman, s/he will probably make the covers of magazines and the front pages of newspapers, and her/his books will become "news." The hardcover bookseller is on the fringes of this excitement and one of the beneficiaries of the business that is generated by it.

No bookseller can afford any longer to be snobbish about carrying paperbacks. Nor can any real bookseller shut out hardcover books, considering them relics from the past. If they were relics, publishers would stop printing them, and they would not be selling as well as they are to all segments of the population. The theater has been described for thousands of years as an invalid near death, and yet it goes on. Printed books, especially hardcover books, are almost equally blessed by doomsayers, and yet they go on, as they will continue to go on. They are the essence of bookselling.

Chapter 25

Paperbacks in the Bookstore

ROBERT D. HALE with CHRISTINE HUFFMAN and STEPHEN COGIL

There is no question that paperback books are popular with consumers. Price is not the only reason for this, though certainly the generally lower price of a paperback has appeal to a vast audience. Many readers prefer paperbacks because they are lighter to hold, more flexible to handle, and, with mass-market editions, at least, more disposable. As people live in more restricted space, shelves for home libraries become less common, and for many people throwing away a paperback book is no more traumatic than throwing away magazines and newspapers. There are others who regard paperbacks, mass market as well as trade, the equal of any hardbound book. Those people will find space for their collection of paperback books. For them, buying paperbacks is an aesthetic as well as an economic choice.

Publishers have moved from doing paperbacks only as reprints of books already published in hardback to doing simultaneous publication (hardback and paperback at the same time) or to publishing titles only in paperback. This is true of mass-market as well as trade paperback publishing. Thus, if readers want those books—and enough of them do to make this a viable market—they must purchase them in paperback.

The paperback market is not confined to any age or to any socioeconomic group. Everyone who buys books buys paperbacks with varying degrees of frequency. Only a store of unbelievably esoteric specialization would not carry some paperbacks in stock and still be able to adequately serve its clientele. Paperbacks generate traffic. They are an exciting and vital part of the merchandise mix in a first-rate bookstore.

Trade paperbacks are generally published by regular full-line hardbound book publishers. They are usually sold on the same terms as hardbound books, with similar discount schedules and returns privileges. The production of trade paperbacks is similar in most ways to hardbound books, except for the binding, obviously. Frequently the paper used, the typeface, and so forth are all very close to the same title in hardbound. For a number of years these were referred to as "quality" paperbacks, indicating the physical aspects of the book and not the contents.

Mass-market paperbacks are produced (as the name implies) for a mass audience. In the beginning they were produced by publishers who did only inexpensive reprints of already successful hardbound books, distributing them through magazine wholesalers to nontraditional book outlets, such as magazine and cigar stores, airport and bus station stands, and the like. Now mass-market paperbacks are in all (or most) bookshops as well as being in all of those other nonregular book outlets. And thousands of new titles never previously published are brought out in mass-market editions each year. To add another wrinkle, a number of major mass-market publishers have begun to successfully publish hardbound books, reversing the historic process.

Whereas mass-market paperbacks are basically the same size (trim, 4 inches by 6¾ inches), trade paperbacks come in all sizes and shapes, which has made them much more difficult to display. Very early on, mass-market paperback publishers designed racks for installation in their outlets that would display their books, mostly face out, and were very simple to service. Mass-market merchandising requires a fast turnover of titles. Customers want the latest as soon as it is available, and they don't want to see what was hot six weeks ago still in the same rack space today. What they want there now is today's top title. To accomplish this efficiently, both the racks and the book sizes were standardized, and with a few exceptions they have been maintained. This makes setting up the mass-market paperback department relatively easy—*if* only mass-market paperbacks are to be displayed in that area.

Displaying trade paperbacks can be considered a challenge or a pain. Although many of them are produced in formats that are comparable to hardbound books, and so can be similarly shelved, housing is not the same as displaying. Hardbounds stand up on shelves. They can be displayed spine out and still have all the pertinent information—author, title, and publisher—visible to the customer. Some trade paperbacks have very narrow spines; they require some support if they are not to buckle. Trade paperbacks have also become a kind of art form in themselves. They are produced in formats ranging from fanciful to ridiculous. Large poster books, for example, are very exciting to behold but impossible to shelve—either in a store or in one's home library.

Because there is no standardization in format, booksellers have to be innovative in finding ways to properly display and merchandise these very exciting kinds of books. Adapting magazine racks or greeting card racks is only one suggestion. Trade paperbacks are often shelved in bookstores along with hardbound books, in which case the oversized books have to be put on top shelves. Putting the books in their proper category with hardbound books is standard procedure, though all new titles, whether in hardcover or soft, should have their time in the sun of a "new arrivals" display at the front of the store.

There are differences in acquiring trade and mass-market paperbacks. Here trade paperbacks are easier than mass-market, at least in the beginning, simply because their sources are the hardbound publishers, whose terms take into account the very small bookseller. Mass-market paperback publishers by their very nature have to deal in larger numbers. They are producing a relatively inexpensive item that has to sell in vast quantities before anybody makes any money on it. It costs money to service retail accounts, and for this reason mass-market publishers frequently are not interested in opening new small accounts. They urge the new bookseller to use the local wholesaler instead.

Wholesalers are an essential part of a bookseller's success. In general, it makes much better sense for booksellers to buy mass-market books from a wholesaler, after shopping around to see which wholesaler will give the best terms and provide the best service, than to attempt to buy in the quantities required by a publisher. When volume reaches a point where regular orders to the mass-market house are feasible for the bookseller and worthwhile for the publisher, then that is the route to go, using the wholesaler for reorders and filling in as is necessary.

It is wise to open accounts with as many publishers as one thinks will be regular suppliers of books right in the beginning of the business, even if wholesalers are to be heavily used for a while. Inevitably there will be titles needed that aren't available from the wholesaler. It is easier to have the account open and ready to use when the need arises rather than have to go through all the paperwork when you want an order filled promptly.

When the bookstore account is considered worth regular attention by the mass-market publisher, then the purchasing of new titles and restocking of backlist titles become as routine as the acquiring of hardbound and trade paperback stock, except that movement in mass-market books is usually much faster. Turnover has to be much greater in mass-market titles if they are to bring in the dollars that fewer sales of more expensive books would provide. This means constant attention to what is selling, what is coming out, what people want or might pick up on impulse.

To keep booksellers alerted to what is coming, most mass-market publishers field large sales forces and deluge the bookseller with mailed materials heralding what is to be published three or four months hence. These announcements always include stock checking forms for easy reorder of basic and current selections. Using these materials for advance orders as well as to maintain a base inventory is an excellent way to keep on top of this frequently frenetic part of the book business. To keep one's own balance, a schedule of rotated stock checks by publisher—either by the bookseller or the publisher's rep—is a sound practice.

Dead paperback stock must be returned exactly the same as dead hardbound stock. There is sometimes the tendency to think it isn't worth the time to go through those "inexpensive" paperbacks, but they represent dollars on the shelves just as do the most expensive art books. Keep the inventory clean. Return. Become familiar with the returns requirements of all the publishers you use. Trade paperbacks are generally treated as trade hardbounds, with full book return required after a certain period in the store. Mass-market paperbacks also have schedules, but instead of returning the entire book, most publishers accept return of just the front cover. This is certainly much easier and more economical than having to pack up and return the books themselves.

However, one then has to dispose of the coverless (now referred to as "stripped") paperbacks. By dispose, we mean destroy. Although the body of the book remains with the bookseller, when the publisher gives the bookseller credit—upon receipt of the cover from that book—ownership of that book has theoretically reverted to the publisher. Any disposition of it that isn't decreed by the publisher is illegal. Selling "pirated" stripped paperbacks is a heinous practice that undermines the business of bookselling. Don't be a party to it.

Paperbacks are as much a part of bookselling as are hardbound books. In many instances they compete with each other, but in more cases they complement. When they began to appear in quantity in bookstores, they were usually segregated to a "paperback department." It is more common now to see books of a genre or category displayed within the same area, if not on the same shelves. This makes good selling sense. The customer interested in the poetry of Robert Frost might come in looking for a paperback and then see a more expensive edition that can't be resisted. Few customers know or care about the industry differences between "trade" and "mass market" paperbacks. They want to buy a book, and for whatever reason they want it in paper. The customer who just wants something to read about a certain subject has a wider choice if there are titles available in several types of binding. Paperbacks aren't putting hardbound books out of business. Paperbacks are enhancing bookselling by widening the market. They are a vital part of every bookstore.

Chapter 26

Bargain Books Basics

LYNNE JACOBS

Who can resist a bargain? What customer isn't delighted by a sale? Which book lover couldn't find something to love from a selection of beautiful art books, collected works, histories and novels, cookbooks or children's books? Hardly anyone. But bargain books mean more to customers than just a good buy. The range of titles available in excellent editions assures that everyone will be able to find something that suits their interests, and *that* is something very special indeed.

An active and well-maintained bargain book program is not just excellent customer service, however. It will build a customer base and can account for 20 to 30 percent of a store's sales. Very few stores are so specialized or so small that they can afford to overlook bargain books.

Most bargain books fall into four basic categories: *remainders* (publishers' excess inventory, as a result of overprinting, a newer or paperback edition coming out, and so on), *special imports* (books printed in other countries for the world English-language market), *reprints and original publications* (new editions of previously published titles; classics, collected works, translations, blank books, and the like), and *hurts* (books slightly shopworn or stickered, not defective).

The reps from remainder houses, as well as the promotion people in their home offices, will be eager to work with you on your bargain book program. Also, many full-line wholesalers (both national and regional) can provide you with selected titles. Hurts, however, are generally obtained directly from the publishers and are usually available only by skid or carton. Some are all one title, and some are an assortment. There is usually a maximum per title in such assortments. A fourth source of bargain books is a lot closer to home—your own stock. In those many instances where it is simply not profitable (because of time, postage, paperwork, small quantities, and so forth) to return a title to a publisher, or in those instances where you feel that a book has good sales potential at a lower price, you might decide to mark it down. This self-remaindering is a necessary step with any inventory bought on a nonreturnable basis and should be done regularly.

There are three basic approaches to a successful bargain books program, although many stores combine aspects of all three.

The Event. This is a special sale for which you have ordered particular titles. It is held once or twice a year (maybe in conjunction with other promotions—preholiday, Presidents Day, Mother's Day, Spring Cleaning, Sidewalk Days, and so on) and should be advertised strongly in your local media. Most promotional houses have good advertising allowances and offer other promotional support as well (art, copy, signs, whatever). Contact them two to three months in advance to work out your title selection and promotional details. Your own in-store signs (such as a copy of your newspaper ad) and customer mailing will help make this an eagerly anticipated event and maximize your sales. The sale titles can be general in scope, or you might want to specialize with children's books, cookbooks, books for the home, and so on. Some booksellers report amazing success with sales as specialized as textbooks and hardcover novels.

The Sale Table(s). An integral part of almost all successful retail operations, the sale table is a good place to start your own bargain book program. The conventional wisdom here is to have stacks of books pyramided for maximum display, with as much face-out as possible. However, unconventional methods, if approached thoughtfully, can also be effective. Books can be displayed spine out for browsers if grouped by price point or by subject matter. You should be able to display at least thirty titles on one table, and store signs are essential. Some good ones: "Buy One, Get One Free"; "Books for Less"; "Books for Browsers; Only $4.98!"; "Books and Change for Your $10 Bill"; "Famous Authors/Low Prices"; "Fiction for Less"; "$1, $2, $3 Books" (for children's books); "Fancy Food at Bargain Prices." The three most important things to remember about your sale table are to locate it in a high-traffic area, highlight it with lots of signs and display material that contribute to the books' *perceived value* ("Was $20, Now $4.98!"), and maintain it assiduously lest it look like a messy pile of rejects.

Mixed in with Stock. This approach is one way to add depth and character to your regular sections and works particularly well in such areas as history, biography, mystery, fiction, regional or Americana, cooking, hobbies, and art. The trick here is to still indicate the books' "special value" to the customer. Some stores do this by stickering the spine ("a red dot = $5," "a blue dot = $4," and so on), or you can use store signs ("Everyday Bargains").

Now a word about discounts and freight. Take advantage of publishers' 50 percent nonreturnable discount whenever possible, since absorbing freight costs on returns can nearly eliminate profits. Order in smaller quantities on a nonreturnable basis for regular sale tables and stock and in larger quantities on a returnable basis for special events. Caution: Check to see if co-op allowances are available on titles bought at 50 percent; sometimes they're not.

The world of bargain books is large, diverse, and exciting. If your store could benefit from an increase of at least 25 percent in sales and a six- to eight-yearly turnover on books displayed in a relatively small, well-maintained area, then it's time to take your business in your own hands with a well-planned bargain books program. After all, value and beauty are in the eye of the beholder.

Chapter 27

Specialization

ROBERT D. HALE

Most booksellers would like their stores to have every book any customer might want. Ideal but impossible. Most booksellers would also like their "share" of the market: to have enough customers so they can thrive in their less-than-ideal but the-best-that-can-be-afforded location. They certainly desire loyal customers who will happily walk past all those other bookstores to get to theirs to buy best-sellers, paperbacks, cookbooks, or whatever. Getting one's share of the market is difficult, and holding on to it is even harder. Loyal customers are not as plentiful as they might be.

Personal service is the old tried-and-true lure, but when something more dramatic is needed to attract customers, many booksellers turn to specialization. They begin with a growing collection of books on a favorite subject or especially successful category, and display these books, as a labeled unit, in the midst of their general inventory. Promotion is the key to successful specialization, so as soon as the word has been gotten out that this strong collection of books on a certain subject exists at Such and Such Bookstore, local book buyers seeking that kind of book will bypass the other bookstores and make an extra effort to get to Such and Such. They know they will find there not only the greatest selection of books in their category, but knowledgeable assistance as well. As word goes beyond the immediate area, through advertising as well as word of mouth, the bookstore's market is expanded—by customers coming from greater distances and orders coming through the mail.

Specialization implies, correctly, special attention. No truly successful specialized department or specialized store just happens. You can't call up a publisher or wholesaler and say, "I want to specialize in children's books. Please send me a starter kit." There are basic lists available in all kinds of categories, from the ABA and other sources, but they are only the beginning, a base. If you are to become a specialist, you have to learn about your specialty.

Specialization takes not only time but space—you have to display the books in the specialized area so that everyone who walks into your bookstore will know without question that you have a fine collection of books on travel, drama, or cooking. If a travel section is to become your crown jewel, set it up that way. Don't stick it off under the stairs. It needs prime space if it is to produce premium income.

The specialized area also needs an investment in inventory that might not turn as fast in the beginning as the rest of the store's merchandise. If you are going to have the supreme collection of automobile books, you must search through all the publishers' lists for automobile books and keep those that look like standards past the normal returns period. You must have the books from the current season's publications and from the past seasons as well. You may even get into out-of-print books in your special area. That says you are truly a specialist, and that's when the world beyond your street corner begins to pay attention.

All this extra investment of effort, time, space, and money has to pay off in dollars, or it's a failure. It should also pay off in pleasure and satisfaction. Do not choose a specialty that bores you or, worse, one that is of interest only to you. If you are already selling books, you must know that certain kinds of books excite you more than others, and you wouldn't mind giving them added attention. Expand these books into a specialization, but not before you do some market research to find out if there are enough customers around for that kind of book to make it a paying proposition. You might also approach it the other way around. Examine the market to find out what particular kind of book has the greatest potential for specialization in your store. If you think you could live with that category, proceed. A natural might be for a great collection of computer sciences books if your store is surrounded by electronics or data-processing firms: scientific and technical books may work in an area packed with research centers. Experiment a little, and test the market.

Almost every bookstore should have a strong section on regional books. It goes beyond mere strength when the stock contains old as well as new titles. Women's liberation and gay liberation are two categories of books often given prime space in general bookstores. Now there are whole bookstores devoted to one or the other of these movements. Any and all categories of books can be considered for specialization and in-depth promotion.

Once you have chosen your category, proceed cautiously but firmly. Use all the reference tools you can find to compile basic lists of books on the subject. Ask publishers and distributors for suggestions, and visit other bookstores to see what they stock in that category—and don't be afraid to ask which titles sell steadily. Also ask your customers. Those who are interested in your specialized choice will have their own favorites. They will know about the "classics" and tell you about titles that are "impossible to find."

Shelve your choices prominently and proudly. Sign the department attractively. Position the display where it might be expanded, where the displays on either side can be moved away to make room if necessary. It's fairly important for the special department to stay put within a store and be where the regulars can find it. That permanence says you are serious about what you are doing—this is not just another in-and-out promotion; it's going to grow and become a haven for those who want that particular category of book.

Let the world outside your store know about your specialization. Advertise where it will attract customers who want that kind of book. If you're specializing in pet books, advertise in the classified pages of your newspaper in the "Pets for Sale" column; if it's travel books, advertise in the travel section. If you have a fine collection of books on music, advertise on the classical radio station and in concert programs; if you're into books on film, advertise on screen, if possible, at the best local cinema.

Plan your promotion as carefully as you planned the selection of your specialization and the collecting of the books. Advertise and promote. When you are ready, try to attract regional and then perhaps national customers. Advertise in magazines, either in their classified sections or in small space ads, but make sure you are special enough to attract attention. Don't pull in people from far away, in person, by telephone, or through the mails, unless you've got something to give them when they get there.

You should do some personal promotion by going out to speak to organizations that would be interested in your specialty. Better yet, take displays of your books to sell at the meetings of those organizations—a garden book display and/or talk at a garden club meeting, wine books for the gourmet club. Sell yourself as a specialist and your store as *the* place to get books on that subject.

You do not have to specialize in only a single subject. For example, you can be the only store in town to have books in fine bindings for special gift occasions, to have miniatures, limited editions, first editions, and autographed first editions! Your specialization can be esoteric or wildly vulgar, but whatever it is, it cannot be common. If it's available everywhere else, in every other bookstore and on every newsstand, there's no reason for anybody to come down your alley. Offer what other booksellers do not.

Specialization can be a cure for crushing competition if the market exists and can be expanded, if the time, energy, and investment are given, and if the expertise of the specialist grows as the department develops. It is almost impossible not to learn from your customers in a specialized situation. Let them know you seek their advice and want to learn; it flatters and brings them back. They will also tell others about you. Booksellers in your area will refer customers to you for your kind of book. Word of mouth can become your most successful—and least expensive—form of advertising.

If you have put your specialization together properly and given it loving care and attention, you will have snared your share of the market and developed a loyal, growing group of customers. No bookseller could ask for more.

Chapter 28

Children's Books

BARBARA THOMAS

There are a number of positive and especially nice things about working with children's books, a field of such abundance and variety it allows for a wide range of choices in quality literature and fine artwork. Those who buy children's books for children are very pleasant people. People who buy children's books for themselves are usually even more pleasant and even more enthusiastic. Both groups make selling children's books a joy. Another added benefit of this specialization is that once a children's book becomes a best-seller, it is very likely to remain a best-seller—even fifty years later. If you have read a great deal as a child, or if you have been a teacher, a librarian, or a parent, you probably have a knowledge of children's books. If not, if you need your memory refreshed, or if you are new to this field, you will find the following useful:

Selection Tools

Children and Books (Zena Sutherland and May Hill Arbuthnot). This is one of the best books for acquiring a historical perspective of children's literature. It lists specific titles that will be of importance to back stock in many subject areas.

Children's Books: Awards & Prizes (Children's Book Council). In addition to the Newbery Award and Caldecott Medal, this book lists chronologically the winners of all sorts of awards given to children's books.

The following four volumes will aid in selection of current titles. They are especially strong on fiction and include a brief annotation with recommended age levels. Many parents like to have these books in their home library, so you might want to consider stocking them for resale in your store.

Choosing Books for Children: A Commonsense Guide (Betsy Hearne)

Babies Need Books (Dorothy Butler)

The Read-Aloud Handbook (Jim Trelease)

Parent's Guide to Children's Reading (Nancy Larrick)

The Children's Catalog and *Subject Guide to Children's Books in Print.* These two books are valuable for their listing of nonfiction titles. They are most useful for supplementing certain subject areas, as they list nonfiction books by categories. *The Children's Catalog* is arranged by the Dewey decimal system and will give a short annotation of each entry. You will need to check availability from the publishers. It also lists fiction books by author. *The Subject Guide to Children's Books in Print* does not have annotations but is updated annually and lists categories for both fiction and nonfiction books.

ABA Basic Book List. This list includes a children's section with titles arranged by publisher. If you are just beginning, it is a good checklist for contacting publishers and for acquiring a core of backlist titles.

Periodicals

The following three periodicals review new children's books and also have articles on authors and illustrators. Although publishers present many of these books before the review has a chance to come out, do use the reviews as a checklist and an evaluation of the newest titles.

Book List

Horn Book

Publishers Weekly

Other Tools

Anyone associated with children's books should be well acquainted with the Children's Book Council, Inc. This nonprofit organization, which promotes children's literature, provides lots of information on books and promotional materials. For a one-time fee you will be included on their mailing list and receive their newsletter, *The Calendar*, which will inform you of other publications.

Book Selection Standards

As you order your children's books, do consider the market in your area. Will you be selling mostly to children, to parents, or to teachers, to collectors or to institutions? Or maybe to various combinations? You may discover that two-thirds of your needs will be books for infants to children six years old. You may need to order three paperbacks for each hardback. Or you may realize high demand for hardbacks in picture books, the classics, and award-winning books. For the age range of seven to twelve years, most booksellers carry more paperbacks than hardbound. Track sales as you progress so you know when to increase or decrease a category. The size of a selling area can fluctuate greatly in the number of titles stocked depending on the time of year.

Within each section of the store, or children's department, try to achieve variety and balance. In selecting stock there are a number of criteria:

1. Consider hardback versus paperback—do you need both? more of one kind? Is the price difference substantial enough to matter?
2. Consider different editions of the same title—is one illustrator more popular than another? Do you need to offer an inexpensive edition, a medium-priced edition, a deluxe edition? Customers usually want hardback editions of the classics, as gifts or for their own personal library.
3. Consider the levels of reading. For instance, you might consider an easy-to-read edition of fables for the beginning readers, a nicely illustrated version as a gift item, and a complete collection superbly illustrated for the collector.
4. Consider the size of each section in your store. Do you need two dozen different dinosaur books, or would a well-chosen selection of six be just as marketable? If biographies are much more popular than sports books, increase or decrease each section accordingly. Careful control of the inventory, not only how many but which books are selling, will result in increased sales.
5. Consider censorship—the censorship pendulum swings with great regularity, and yet we need to offer quality selections even if a particular group does not approve. In a children's store, the sex-education section is always under fire. One solution is to locate these books on a shelf about five feet high with no stepstool

in sight. The theory is, if the child is tall enough to reach the book, then he or she is probably old enough to read it. Do read all books to which parents voice objections so that you can understand the nature of the complaint and defend the book's merits if need be.

6. Consider quality—children's literature is enjoying a wonderful period. There is much to choose from in text and illustration. In fact, there is such abundance that one should choose only the very best. In a time when every retail outlet carries some type of book, bookstores should certainly lead the way in selecting quality books and providing them for children. Good children's literature has the same qualities as good adult literature. It is the finest prose or poetry or artwork, and it is timeless and lasting.

Stocking the Store

Stock should be arranged in a simple, easy-to-comprehend fashion. Fiction for babies to school age children should be shelved in consecutive order on one side of the store or department, with nonfiction grouped by subject matter with mixed reading levels.

Within the fiction section, have several categories arranged without rigid boundaries because these sections tend to flow together, which allows for different reading and interest levels. Primarily, there are groupings for:

1. *Babies.* Cloth, vinyl, and board books make up most of this section. Cloth books need to be selected carefully to ensure good text and to have clear colors and clean printing. Cloth books are difficult, but many customers request them. Parents like to put them in the crib so an infant may enjoy the colors. One picture per page helps begin vocabulary development. Vinyl or light plastic books can pose some of the same problems as cloth books, but the colors are usually more vibrant, and after all, both are cleanable and chewable.

Board books are a mainstay. They are durable, brightly colored, and can be educational for even the youngest of children. A child who can sit up can begin to handle these, and many come in small sizes for little hands. Suggested board books for babies include the one-word-one-picture-per-page type moving into the brief-story-and-vocabulary-enrichment types. Board books should not be dull. Many have sprightly stories and lots of information. Be choosy.

Mother Goose rhymes are also recommended for babies. No, they can't chew or read it, but parents can read and should. It is the sound of the parent's voice and the rhythm of the language that are important to an infant. Stock a varied selection with a good choice of illustrations and a wide price range. Have a few old-fashioned ones, as many customers have fond memories of their own Mother Goose editions. Encourage parents to buy the edition that appeals most to them, for they need to enjoy this book that they will be sharing with their child.

2. *Toddlers (Ones and Twos).* Next to the baby section—indeed, overlapping quite a bit—is the toddler section. Mother Goose and board books are still excellent for this age. Now is the time to introduce board books about the community, vehicles, animals, books with longer stories. Concept books such as alphabet, counting, seasons, and opposites are very popular. Good artwork and clarity in text are the standards to look for here. Toddlers are ready for paged books of brief stories, for picture books. Arrange them by author or illustrator, and whenever possible, display these books face out to show the artwork. Attention spans begin to develop at varying rates about age two, and some children can enjoy longer stories at an earlier age than others. So the picture books for toddlers are combined with the ones for the next group.

3. *Preschoolers (Threes and Fours).* Although this age can still use the concept book and picture books, include the shorter folk tales as well. Preschoolers particularly like lots of repetition such as is in "The Gingerbread Man" and "The Little Red Hen." Tales with threes such as "The Three Bears," "The Three Little Pigs," and "The Three Billy Goats Gruff" are perennial favorites. Also compatible with this age are large books about the everyday world such as the Richard Scarry books and the easy-to-comprehend nonfiction books that will begin to answer "why" questions. A child at this stage will love to be read to from books with fewer pictures such as the Beatrix Potter series. Many of the Caldecott Medal books have fine stories for the preschooler.

4. *Beginning Readers (Fives and Sixes).* Some preschoolers can read and so flow naturally into this section. Other first-graders may not be ready to read and still want only picture books. However, the beginning-to-read section does stress controlled vocabulary and should be arranged from easiest to read to hardest. Include some short chapter books here and some jokes and riddles. Controlled vocabulary does not have to mean instant boredom. Choose books with a strong storyline, a humorous vein, or informational text. Most children don't remain at this stage for very long, and if you want to keep them as reading customers, it's worth keeping them interested while they are learning to read.

5. *Readers (Seven to Twelve).* Once a child has begun to read, there is no holding back. Often the challenge is not what can they read, but what is suitable for them to read. Fiction for these ages should be arranged library style, by author, shelving hardbacks and paperbacks together. Because paperbacks are so popular for these readers, you should stock more paperbacks than hardbacks in their section. Knowing your stock is particularly important for this area, as many customers come to depend on your expertise in recommendations. Certain authors become favorites with children, but not all authors write books for only one age group. Reading some of the more controversial titles and knowing which books are appropriate for which ages can keep both adults and young readers happy. Some publishers print a suggested interest level and an estimated reading level on the back cover. The codes will appear as such: RL 3.8—IL 7–12. RL is reading level third grade, eighth month. A child needs to read at least that well to comprehend this book. Interest level is seven to twelve years. Children between those ages would be interested in the subject matter of this book. In addition, a seven-year-old who reads quite well could enjoy this book as well as a twelve-year-old who did not read as well. Like all assessments of this kind, some people agree with them and some don't. At least one is given a "ballpark" figure with which to work.

Although there are many ways to group nonfiction books, arranging them by category is most workable (for example, all of the dinosaur books, whether for a six-year-old or a twelve-year-old shelved side by side). Many a parent will buy one for his child's reading level and a more difficult one to use as a family reference. Signs that clearly mark each category are essential in the nonfiction section both to highlight the extent of this section and to guide customers to their area of interest. Subjects to be considered for the nonfiction area are astronomy, foreign language, fine arts, cooking, science projects and experiments, health, history and biography, natural sciences, hobbies, and sports. One of the most requested sections (and one that is probably peculiar to children's booksellers) is problem-solving. Categories within this group include books dealing with handicaps, death, divorce and separation, stepfamilies, sibling rivalry, moving, losing teeth, and visiting the doctor and dentist. Here do combine both fiction and nonfiction books for the convenience of parents and teachers.

Obviously, the arrangement of your store will depend on the space available and your own preferences. Once a decision has been made, it needn't be ironclad. Often rearranging stock can result in immediate sales of books that have never been noticed. Live dangerously—rearrange at will, but be liberal with signs to avoid confusion.

Displaying Children's Books

The artwork in children's picture books is usually of such excellent quality that these books can literally sell themselves—*if* the customers can see them. Display them face out as much as possible. Slanted shelves designed for the purpose do an especially good selling job. These shelves can be easily made by using shelf holders that are slanted at a forty-five-degree angle. By adding a lip to the shelf itself, books will remain on the shelf and not slide off. These shelves can also be made into a free-standing display to highlight special books such as the Caldecott Medal winners. A flat board can then be nailed across the top to allow for merchandising of books and related nonbook items together.

Besides shelves and regular bookcases, you can also use tables for displays and milk crates, which lend themselves well to stacking. You can also tier books on a shelf or on a pyramid in the middle of the floor. If some type of large cube can't be located, they are fairly easy to construct. Boxes and cubes are so versatile that they are worth some effort. Children's books come in such assorted sizes that creative shelving is necessary and can be as attractive as your imagination envisions.

Since a children's product is being sold, the atmosphere of a children's department or bookstore should be colorful, clean, and comfortable. Brightly painted walls make an excellent backdrop for the artistic quality of most children's books, and carpeting on the floor will invite children to sit or lie down with a book. This eliminates the necessity for a play area that takes up selling space. However, many stores do find a children's area with toys and books supplied to be a help in controlling and occupying little ones while parents are browsing.

A table with comfortable chairs for both adults and children can be very successful. One strong point for this is that it lends an air of peace and quiet in the midst of the brilliance of colors and activity in the store. Second, it provides an oasis for the parent and/or the child to sit and review a stack of books being considered for purchase. Such an arrangement conveys to the customer, You are welcome; sit down and spend some time with us.

In the arrangement of the displays, always consider traffic flow. Children's bookstores and departments see a great many baby strollers. Aisles need to be wide enough to accommodate them easily. It is to your benefit to keep displays low enough to spot browsing customers and to leave some wide spaces between bottom shelves so that small children can be easily retrieved by parents. Because there are so many young ones, all furniture and displays need to be sturdy and well anchored to keep them from toppling over. A workable arrangement of your store should be achieved with clever planning to avoid having to put up negative signs. Because you are selling children's books, you obviously have to be prepared to handle some children. The goal should be to make children welcome, to put them at ease while keeping the store easy to maintain, with displays set up to attract buying customers.

Selling Children's Books

Having chosen the best-possible editions and set up the most inviting displays, you are now ready for the main purpose of a bookstore—selling books. In order to sell a children's book, you need to read the book or at least to have read about the book. Some books do sell themselves, but most of these are by popular authors, the proven classics, fabulous picture books or award winners. But to sell a new, unknown book, you must be able to relate the story or the main points. In addition, knowing which astronomy book is suitable for a six-year-old and which for a ten-year-old requires a familiarity with the books themselves. Knowing your stock will be your biggest asset as a children's bookseller.

Once you have become familiar with your stock, there are a number of ways to increase traffic in your store:

1. *Free Publicity.* Try to get as much as possible. If you have a story time, cooking classes, or an author coming, write your local newspaper and media stations well ahead of time. Keep a file of their addresses, phone numbers, contact persons, and especially their deadlines and copy specifications. When you are having a store event, go through the file and contact those you think will be interested. Also, don't forget community newsletters.

2. *Store Mailers.* These can be your best return in advertising. Take customers' names from their checks and have a sign-up box for those interested in being on your mailing list. Sending out a mailer is a good way to announce new publications or in-store events and to provide reading lists for parents to clip and save.

3. *Store Events.* Consider having in-store events. Many stores report boosted sales by having autograph parties, book talks, creative writing classes for children, cooking classes by the author of a new cooking book, story time, and puppet shows.

4. *Out-of-Store Events.* One of the best ways to reach new customers is to be invited to speak outside the store. Book talks and book fairs can be very beneficial.

5. *Store Promotions.* Many parents like reading checklists of recommended titles. Annotate your lists and give suggested age groups if possible. The most popular lists will be seasonal and award winners. Many customers will use them as a reading guide for their children and will eventually purchase the entire list.

It is very handy to keep a stack of promotional bookmarks at the checkout counter available to customers. Your store's bookmark should have your logo, name, address, phone, store hours, a map, and a brief description about the type of books you offer. Pass these out at book talks and book fairs and give your customers extras to give to their friends.

Having a children's bookstore or a children's book department doesn't mean you have to go around scrubbing peanut butter and jelly—or worse—off the walls; it doesn't mean you can never read a best-seller again; and it doesn't mean you always have to dress up like a clown or a large yellow bird to tell a story. All of these are possibilities, but it doesn't have to be like that every day. Selling children's books does mean you can influence young minds to the joys of reading, and it does mean you can reap the satisfaction of helping adults choose meaningful lifetime gifts for children of all ages.

Chapter 29

Regional Books

JEAN B. WILSON

It has been my pleasure to be associated with a bookstore for almost twenty-five years that was built on selling regional books. The store has expanded many times in its one hundred years of business, but the heart and soul of our business remains the regional section. More dollars have been invested in books, more time has been spent in display, and more dollars have been realized from this one section than was ever imagined when it all began.

The advantages of selling regional books are many and varied, but uniqueness has to be at the top of the list. Competition is keen for the book dollar, and the bookstore that has those special books in demand that no one else in the area has gets the sale. If your store is in a tourist area, tourist dollars will be spent there if you have books about your region. More people are traveling than ever before, and they are eager to find information on the places they visit. This includes not only local history, but the flora and fauna, the good restaurants, inns, museums, cultural events, gossipy personal memoirs, and picture books. If you are in a tourist area—and all areas are visited by tourists in varying degrees—design a logo to stress your region. We use the outline of our state on all of our bookmarks, ads, tote bags, in-store T-shirts, and business cards, and though we have a very common name for a bookstore, the logo leaves no doubt where we are and where our interest is focused.

When best-seller sales slow down, as they sometimes do in certain areas at certain times of the year, promotion of a local title can bring zest and excitement into your store. This promotion is especially effective in late winter. This is when regional titles from small presses come into their own. Their scarcity in most bookstores adds to the unique quality of the store that features them. These regional titles from small presses are great gifts for people who want to give, or get, books from a place they love.

Building a worthwhile regional section is hard work. The bookseller must really understand the region and constantly gather information on all its aspects. Some titles are going to be fairly scholarly, and the bookseller may not feel qualified to judge it or may want to depend on reviews and book jacket blurbs. Local historians will usually provide opinions at no charge. Historical societies are pleasant to work with; they are cooperative because of their own enthusiasm and mutual interest. Don't forget—they also publish books and need outlets other than their own museum.

If you are from a state like New Mexico, for instance, you have an extra plus in the New Mexico Book League and all the libraries that are organized sources of aid. Libraries in other regions are just as cooperative but sometimes do not have the same resources. Most state libraries attempt to keep a bibliography of authors of the state, and this is a valuable aid you should use.

Enormous help can come from your local newspaper and your customers. Writers and readers love to pass along local information. The bookseller interested in the region may have to listen when they could be spending that time elsewhere, but remember—to build the regional section, a large investment of time is required. Local authors are an excellent source of information. If they have written a personal memoir, the bibliography might be small, but if they have written a study of the area, they have done a body of research. Take advantage of this and check their sources. Reading bibliographies is not too exciting, but you may find a title or two to add to your shelves.

Don't forget to check remainder lists for regional titles. Some of the best buys can be found in these "bargain" lists. Many times a book you have been searching for will suddenly appear. If you have a very strong regional section and merchandise effectively, some remainder houses will publish a pictorial for your region. These are usually marginal on text but perfect for a memento.

Sales representatives are an important source for regional information. All the major houses do not include biographical information on authors, but an alert sales representative can supply this information. *Sylvia Beach and the Lost Generation* does not sound like a regional title for Idaho, but it was written by a woman born and raised in Idaho, and by noting that in our newsletter and the media, we sold thirty copies instead of the three we might otherwise have sold. Sales representatives can also turn into book scouts for your store. We have built our Vardis Fisher collection just this way, through sales reps who found Fisher books in other stores and either brought them to us or alerted us.

Earlier, I mentioned filling the selling season gap with regional titles; autographing is a "must" part of that promotion. Do it on a consistent basis, and your store will soon be known as the one that gives area authors the most support. Support works both ways. The fun of regional autograph parties is in the attendance. You need not fear, you will have a crowd—if all the author's friends and family have been sent invitations. The media will usually help promote a local event. Terms may not always be generous when it comes to discount, especially if the book is from a small press, but an autograph party where the author's family pays postage on the invitations, co-ops the ad, contacts the media, buys the book, and then thanks the bookseller is a good investment of time, effort, and expense.

Display your regional titles in a setting that reflects the region. It doesn't have to be artsy-cutesy, but it should utilize some imagination. Signs set the theme so customers quickly identify with the special section. It should be the most prominent section in your store. If you have a window, use it for pictorials and recreation titles. These are the books that have the most appealing jackets and can be tied together in one theme.

In our store we are fortunate to have a large children's section. We have made a permanent display there for a regional children's section and find this has worked well. Librarians especially appreciate this repeat of our major specialization.

You can expand your regional book market by carrying out-of-print titles. Here is an area where time is well spent. For a comparatively small investment you can acquire out-of-print titles that can be marked according to a used-book guide. Sometimes, depending upon availability, you can even price them higher. You should buy a whole publisher's closing inventory when your bank account allows. Exclusive dealership is nice once in a while. You can also expand regional clout by publishing your own books, which has been done successfully by Robert Dike Blair of Vermont Bookstore and Sam Weller of Sam Weller's Zion Bookstore.

A newsletter is a must for a bookstore stressing regional titles. It doesn't have to be typeset and printed on elegant paper. You are providing information, and a simple format is all that is required. Send it to all the libraries of your particluar region, regular customers who have indicated an interest, leaders in the community, newspapers or a favorite reporter, colleges and schools in your area. We started with a postcard with three titles, and now our newsletter is six to eight pages, includes thirty-five to forty titles, and is illustrated. It has taken us ten years to evolve from cards to pages.

Sales derived from the newsletter can be the basis for a mail-order business. The person who does our out-of-print search service handles all of our mail orders from the newsletter. She has established a rapport with the recipients over the years and has kept detailed records. This staff member is also in charge of all mail orders from our regional titles ads. By putting someone in charge, we keep an accurate pulse on this target market.

The media—television, radio, and print—can be of invaluable aid to the regional bookseller. Very rarely does a regional book get ignored. It may not get the best reviews in the world, but it does get mentioned. Book-and-author-combined articles are common in local papers. One year in Boise a book on a local hotel was published by a leading local author. It garnered a full page in the feature section of the newspaper, and three TV stations came to our autographing. The bookstore was featured as much as the author. Advertising is fine—good publicity is priceless.

There are instances where regional bookselling requires out-of-store appearances. Every year someone on the staff attends library and school conferences. We set up a display of regional titles right beside the exhibiting publishers and computer and audiovisual people. We get the most attention. One year, as a result of these appearances, the Idaho Library Association invited me to be the banquet speaker. The publicity was great for the bookstore.

Selling regional books is more than just selling local history and local authors' books. It's all the peripheral materials. In the West, "regional" connotes railroads, mining, exploration, geology, nature, wilderness survival, river running, backpacking, mountains, and progress—fiction and nonfiction! Nor is it just books—it's calendars, pamphlets, posters, and cards as well.

"Regional" is all that *has* happened in your area, all that *is* happening, and how to enjoy it. Knowledge and a constant flow of information are essential for the regional bookseller. The excitement of discovery is as much fun for you as for the customer, and the possibilities for expansion are tremendous. Regional bookselling is a way to be considered special, which reflects your appreciation of where you live and your service to your community. It also rings up sales.

Chapter 30

Selling Religious Books in a General Trade Store

ELIZABETH HASLAM

Should you put a section of religious books in your store? Who would buy them? Is this a practical idea? Yes, it is definitely practical. You will be appealing to a market that is constantly growing: at least 18 percent of all sales by religious publishers are with trade bookstores. It provides one more service to your customers while adding sales that would otherwise be going elsewhere.

When a person leaves your store, one of three things should have happened. He or she has purchased the book needed, you have special ordered it, or you have helped to solve the problem by sending the person to another bookstore. Why send a prospective customer to another store? Why not answer the need yourself? Even if you are in an area where there are good religious bookstores, you should be keeping some of that business for yourself.

Books that sell by the hundreds of thousands each year should be on your shelves. I am not referring to denominational material, but to standard reference works, inspirational titles, and a selection of Bibles. Consider this: There are more that forty religious titles that over the last ten years have sold well over three million copies: *Halley's Bible Handbook, Cruden's Concordance, Josephus, Imitation of Christ, Foxes Book of Martyrs, Power of Positive Thinking, Why Am I Afraid to Tell You Who I Am?* and *Streams in the Desert* are just a few. The Bible is the best-seller of all time.

Who is the market?

The person you were going to send somewhere else. Many people are more comfortable shopping in a general store than a religious store. A Gallup poll showed that 59 percent of the people who buy books need to buy a religious book at least once during the year. For every two Bibles sold in a religious bookstore, one was sold in a general bookstore. One college student in four considers himself or herself very religious. People need to purchase a large-print Bible for a great-aunt, a graduation, birthday, or Christmas gift for a serious Bible student, or a book of Bible stories for a young child. Parents, grandparents, and teachers are all good prospects for religious book sales.

How do I become informed?

You may not be interested in religion personally, but do not let this deter you. There are many sources of information to help you decide what to stock and how to promote these books. Begin with those your customers have been asking for. What have you been special ordering for them? Then read the *ABA Basic Book List*. It has a section of recommended religious titles. Check the best-selling religious booklist on the fiches put out by Baker and Taylor, Ingram, and other wholesalers. Watch for the religious issues of the *American Bookseller* magazine and *PW*. Read the monthly religious section in *PW* conducted by William Griffin. Shop your competition. Check the catalogs of wholesalers of religious books and Bibles. (Riverside-World and Spring Arbor are only two good sources.) Work closely with the reps from publishing houses with religious departments. Become familiar with the best-selling religious authors.

How do I determine my basic stock?

Choose from the religious best-seller lists two copies of each of some of the hardbacks and three each of the paperbacks. Try for a balanced selection: some reference works and study guides, a few inspirational titles, and several different translations of the Bible. Represent the books of local authors. Your selection should include Bible handbooks, dictionaries, concordances, atlases, and commentaries.

As you enlarge the section, include some of these additional suggestions: *Your God Is Too Small*, Phillips (Macmillan), *Diary of Private Prayer*, Baille (Scribner), paperback works of C. S. Lewis, Thomas Merton, Paul Tournier, Paul Tillich, and Pierre Teilhard de Chardin. Add some of the best-selling titles from the Doubleday Image series of paperbacks. The works of Emmet Fox (Harper) and the New Testament commentaries of William Barkley (Westminster) are popular. *A Shepherd Looks at the Psalms*, Keller (Zondervan), and *The Road Less Traveled*, Peck (Simon & Schuster), are often requested.

Set up the section next to Bibles or gift books. (Because the purchase and selling of Bibles is covered in another chapter, we will not discuss that in this article.) It is a good idea to have one staff member become informed and be chiefly responsible for the section, even when only two people run the store. Having books on the occult and Eastern religions shelved in a separate place seems to work better than mixing them with the other religious materials.

To introduce religious titles into your children's section, you could begin with just one shelf of books; one or two each of hardbacks and two or three each of the paperback. Older publications that have stood the test of time in regard to the quality and accuracy of storytelling and illustrations remain popular and are often asked for by name. For the entire family there are several Bible storybooks designed to be read to children when they are small and then reread by the children themselves when they are about ten years old. Usually these have a continuous narrative of the Bible from Genesis to Revelation done in large clear type with many illustrations.

Among the best-sellers in this category are *Hurlbut's Story of the Bible* (Zondervan), *Egermeir's Bible Story Book* (Warner Press), and *The Children's Bible* (Golden Press). The editorial advisers for *The Children's Bible* include a Catholic, a Protestant, and a Jewish scholar, and the format is like that of the Bible, in double columns. *The Tall Book of Bible Stories* (Harper) is a simple retelling of stories from both the Old Testament and the New Testament.

Two delightful books for the younger people are Caldecott winners—*Prayer for a Small Child*, Field (Macmillan), and Peter Spier's *Noah's Ark* (Doubleday). Rand McNally has several good picture books for younger children, and Concordia Press publishes a devotional for families entitled *Little Visits with God* that is well done. *The Golden Bible Atlas* (Western) is such a great book that it can be sold to adults as well as children. It contains full-color maps, archaeological material, and very interesting text. *A Picture Book of Jewish Holidays* (Holiday House) gives basic facts about the year's festivities. *The Power of Light* by Isaac Bashevis Singer is available in both cloth and paper and contains eight excellent stories for Hanukkah.

How do I promote?

You promote these books like everything else in your store. Put the top best-seller in with your other best-sellers. Have special displays for Easter, National Bible Week (which is in November), Hanukkah, and Christmas. Contact the editor of the religious page at the newspaper and offer to loan books for them to review; send letters to all churches in the area requesting they put a note in their church bulletin that you can provide the books they need. Offer to take or send a display of books to church training sessions and retreats. Be alert to special authors who will be speaking locally and offer to provide a table of books at the function.

Once you have assembled some titles, make a special display of them so your customers will be conscious of this new department in your store. Adding religious books will expand your market and provide real service to your community. Just think, if you add only two new customers each week by putting in this new section of books, you will gain one hundred new customers over the period of a year. This means that one hundred people will tell others in their Bible class that you have the books they need, or they will think of you when they listen to a religious author promote his book on TV and check to see if you have it in stock. They will look to you for help with other books, also. Adding a religious book section in a time of expanding religious awareness can expand your business.

Chapter 31

Bibles in the General Bookstore

J. RHETT JACKSON

There seems to be some reluctance and fear on the part of some bookstore owners to set up a really good Bible department. By really good, I mean one that compares favorably with sections on medicine, history, travel, or any other section the store takes pride in. As a result, most of the Bible business goes to the religious or denominational stores in the area. This is a strategic error for the owner of a general bookstore because a good working knowledge of the various translations of the Bible can be a real service to the community, and Bible sales can ring the cash register frequently and with significant dollar amounts.

There are so many translations and so much variation in price and quality that one can easily get anxious about buying and stocking Bibles. As a first step, I recommend asking a couple of sales reps from leading Bible publishers to sit down and give you an education on translations, bindings, covers, paper, type, and the reasons for price variations. If your time is limited, at least talk with the Oxford and Nelson reps. Nelson represents good, medium-priced Bibles, with good price value. Oxford has a great selection of the medium-priced to the higher-quality leather-bound Bibles. Time spent with reps from these two publishers will give you confidence to begin making selections for your stock. Ask them to make out a suggested starting order for you to study. Go over the order carefully and study the catalogs along with it. You and your staff should become familiar enough with the purpose and history of each translation to talk comfortably with your customers.

One good source for information on translation is a useful booklet published by Oxford University Press, *The Oxford Bible Handbook*. The following information about the differences in the translations is extracted from this booklet. (For a free copy, write to the Bible Department, Oxford University Press, 200 Madison Ave., New York, NY 10016.)

Major Translations

King James Version (1611). A translation based on Hebrew and Greek texts and on earlier English translations, it was the work of more than fifty scholars appointed by King James I of England. The most widely known and used Bible in the English language, the KJV has had enormus influence on the whole of the English language and literature. It has been the basic text for a number of later versions and editions. It is published in various styles and bindings by almost all major Bible publishers.

The New English Bible (New Testament, 1961; complete Bible, 1970). Sponsored by most of the major churches and the Bible Societies of Great Britain, it was carried out under the direction of an ecumenical committee of fifty scholars. They produced a version in contemporary language, based on the most widely accepted Greek, Hebrew, and Aramaic texts. Literary quality as well as accuracy were major considerations. A continuing committee, which includes representatives of the Roman Catholic church, works on revision and improvement of the text. Published by Oxford, Cambridge.

Revised Standard Version (New Testament, first edition 1946, second edition 1971; Old Testament, 1952; Apocrypha, 1957). A revision of the American Standard Version of 1901, using more recent Hebrew and Greek texts, this version was prepared by an ecumenical committee of scholars for the National Council of Churches of Christ in the U.S.A. Their aim was clarity of language, suitability for public and private worship, and preservation of the best qualities of the King James. Published by Oxford, Collins-World, Holman, Nelson, Zondervan.

The Living Bible (paraphrased, 1971). A paraphrase by Kenneth N. Taylor, in consultation with others, and based initially on the American Standard Version (1901), the Living Bible has strong evangelical emphasis. Separate parts have been published as *Living Letters, Living Prophecies*, and so on. There are also illustrated editions, including *The Way*. Published by Tyndale House, Holman, Our Sunday Visitor (Roman Catholic edition).

The New International Version (New Testament, 1973). Sponsored by the New York Bible Society International, it was prepared by a "transdenominational" and international group of evangelical scholars, whose goals were accuracy, clarity, contemporary idiom, and dignity. Published by Zondervan.

Today's English Version (Good News for Modern Man; New Testament, 1966, 1970, 1971; the Psalms, 1970). Sponsored by the American Bible Society, this version aims to communicate the Bible message in very simple terms—primarily to non-Christians and to those with limited English vocabulary. Published by the American Bible Society, Holman, Nelson.

The Jerusalem Bible (1966, 1967, 1968). Translated by Roman Catholic scholars from ancient texts in the light of up-to-date biblical knowledge, The Jerusalem Bible follows the interpretations of L'Ecole Biblique in its *Bible de Jerusalem.* This translation is recognized for its literary quality. Published by Doubleday.

The New American Bible (1969, 1970). Sponsored by the Confraternity of Christian Doctrine, this translation was prepared by members of the Catholic Biblical Association of America from the oldest-available texts of the Scriptures. It is the first official Catholic Bible to depart from the Latin Vulgate text. Published by Benziger, Catholic Book, Catholic Press, Collins-World, Daughters of St. Paul, Ferguson, Nelson, Royal.

Other Well-Known Translations

American Standard Version (1901). This is an American version of the English Revised Version of 1881–1885, which was a revision of the King James Version. Published by Logos International, Nelson.

New American Standard Bible (New Testament, 1963; Old Testament, 1971). A revision of the American Standard Version (see above), it was sponsored by the Lockman Foundation of California. Published by Collins-World, Creation House, Gospel Light, Moody Press.

The New Testament in Modern English (J. B. Phillips, 1958, 1973). This very popular paraphrase in contemporary language was done by the Reverend J. B. Phillips. Published by Macmillan.

Jewish Holy Scriptures. A new translation is replacing an older English-language edition from the Masoretic text. Already published: Isaiah and Psalms, 1973; Jeremiah, 1974. Published by Jewish Publication Society.

In Addition

The Scofield Reference Bible: King James Version (1909, 1917). Edited by the Reverend C. I. Scofield, who provided references, footnotes, and interpretations, this study edition is a favorite with evangelicals. Other features include introductions, concordance, and maps. Published by Oxford.

The New Scofield Reference Bible: King James Version (1967).
A committee of leading evangelical scholars, headed by E. Schuyler
English, completely reedited the Scofield Reference Bible for today's
reader. The many reading and study helps include a revised introduction to each book of the Bible, a new index to annotations, a new
concise concordance, and the New Oxford Bible maps. The marginal entries (cross-references and subject chain references), the
footnotes, and the subheadings have been greatly expanded. Obsolete and archaic words in the KJV text have been updated for clarity.
Available in both black- and red-letter editions. Published by Oxford.

The Pilgrim Bible: King James Version (1948). Edited by E.
Schuyler English, with the assistance of thirty-seven evangelical
scholars, this edition has been especially prepared for young people
and beginning Bible students. Study helps include simplified notes,
introductions, cross-references, special articles, and maps. Published by Oxford.

*The Shorter Oxford Bible (1951; edited by G. W. Briggs, G. W.
Caird, and Nathaniel Micklem).* These selections from the King
James Version are set in prose form. For daily reading and school
use. Published by Oxford.

*The New Oxford Annotated Bible: Revised Standard Version.
(The Oxford Annotated Bible, 1962; The Oxford Annotated Apocrypha, 1965; The Oxford Annotated Bible with the Apocrypha,
1965; The New Oxford Annotated Bible with the Apocrypha, 1973.)*
Edited by Herbert G. May and Bruce M. Metzger, this Bible
combines a modern translation with outstanding study features,
including introductions, page-for-page annotations, cross-
references, supplementary articles, and the New Oxford Bible maps.
Published by Oxford.

The Common Bible: Revised Standard Version (1973). In this
Bible the Apocrypha books are placed in the order more familiar to
Roman Catholics. Published by Collins-World, Nelson.

After you have learned something about the various translations, studied various formats, selected several price ranges, placed
your order, received the Bibles, and displayed them in your store,
you still may not have made a sale! At this point this fine inventory
has only added to your negative cash flow, and you want to hear
that cash register start ringing to get your money back with profit.

So, let's sell a Bible. When a customer comes in and asks for the
location of your Bible section, you should avoid "sending" her.
Instead, you need to accompany the customer. As you reach the

Bibles, you need to start asking questions so that you can help the customer make an intelligent selection. What is the Bible for—travel, wedding, gift, study course? Does she prefer a particular translation? The customer might ask which one is best and why. Is it for a college student? (You should know which translations are used by the religion departments of the local colleges.) Does she need large-size or large print? If it is for an older person, he or she usually wants a King James Version in large print. Does she know the difference between a translation and a paraphrase? The Living Bible is not a translation; it is a paraphrase. Does she want good quality at a reasonable price or a genuine leather cover with fine India paper? Does she need special features like study maps or annotated study notes? Of course you should be prepared to deal with these questions with knowledgeable answers.

Some Bible customers will ask you why we now have so many translations and why each year brings new ones. You can explain easily that the twentieth century has witnessed many advances in biblical scholarship. Important discoveries in the fields of linguistics, textual criticism, and archaeology have provided scholars with a wealth of information that was not known to the translators of the King James Version (published in 1611). Nor were these discoveries made before many of the later revisions. As scholars continue to study new evidence and anthropologists continue to make new discoveries, the need becomes apparent for new translations. Also, over the ages, people have expressed the need for a Bible written and presented in clear and contemporary English. Scholars are continually challenged by this call.

It is also possible to find out which translations are used in your area by the various denominations, communions, or religious groups. This kind of knowledge is invaluable in putting the right Bible into a customer's hands. The more liberal or ecumenical your customers are, the more likely they will be to want the newest translations. If you arm yourself with the kind of knowledge mentioned in this article, you will be well prepared to sell Bibles. Don't forget that special days sell a lot of extra Bibles. Easter and Christmas are peak times for Bible sales, with Mother's Day and Father's Day coming close. You will want to increase your inventory of Bibles during these times of the year. Selling Bibles is not difficult. Order catalogs and information booklets from all of the Bible publishers, study them carefully, learn from the reps, and you will soon have enough confidence for a Bible department that produces substantial sales.

Chapter 32

Technical–Professional Books

MARY KATHRYN HASSETT

Selling technical and professional books in the general bookstore is now widely accepted as a good idea. But between idea and the act falls the same old shadow—a nameless fear peculiar to booksellers alone. This fear is, of course, activated by any book in which the flow of words is interrupted by the unsavory presence of numbers, graphs, charts, and formulas. The fear blossoms into outright phobia when confronted with low discounts, large price tags, specialized markets, and other dreary notions attached to the aura of technical books. This article is about overcoming the fear, about replacing it with a devotion to profit.

The profit will derive from what, at first, seems a negative factor—the expensive price tag. Remember that you have to sell ten $3.50 paperbacks to make the same profit you would on the sale of one $40.00 engineering book. Some advantages, however, are more subtle—for example, the nonseasonal nature of technical book sales. This feature can smooth out the fluctuations of the highly seasonal trade book business and solve some of its attendant cash-flow problems.

Let's assume, however, that the readers of this article are already convinced about the advantages of selling technical books and know that the market has expanded dramatically in the last few years. Let us turn immediately to the question of how to discover a share of this expanding market and then how to buy, merchandise, and promote technical and professional books for that market.

First, some definitions. This discussion of professional books will exclude law and medicine, which are most frequently sold in exclusive outlets. It will also virtually exclude textbooks and books in the pure sciences and emphasize books pertaining to applied fields: engineering, computer science, architecture, investments, real estate, and business management. Computer books will be discussed more fully since, for many stores, they have provided a recent and profitable entry into the field of technical book sales. Reference books will be discussed only briefly since their role in inventory is well known to most booksellers.

Technical and professional books as discussed in this article will be defined by their application; that is, they are books primarily used in earning a livelihood in a particular trade or occupation. They are thus distinguished from the how-to categories (automotive repair, photography, do-it-yourself plumbing, and the like) that are a familiar presence in most bookstores. Often professional books are described as "short discount" books, but referring to their application is more useful since many technical books, especially in business and computer fields, are available at long discount.

Discovering Your Market for Technical and Professional Books

Location is, of course, the key determinant in what you can sell. Remember that in selling technical and professional books, however, you can draw from a much larger area, sometimes city-wide or regionwide. People are willing to drive much farther to purchase a hard-to-find technical book than a standard best-seller. Thus stores not yet located that plan a major technical focus can settle for a less-than-prime location. A fringe area or warehouse area, a place not given to high rent, high traffic, might possibly serve. This kind of location can be realistic considering that telephone sales can be greater than walk-in sales in the technical business. In fact, stores just setting up a technical department should consider adding personnel to cover additional phone service, special ordering, shipping, and possibly billing operations.

With this expanded draw factor in mind, a market analysis can be conducted in a quite simple, inexpensive way. If you are not familiar with the local economy, a study of the Yellow Pages and business directories available from the Chamber of Commerce or local library can provide a sufficient overview. It is, of course, fairly easy to determine the dominant industries, but anticipating their book needs is more difficult. A personal call or even a telephone call to the purchasing agent or, in some cases, the corporate librarian can be both a powerful selling tool and a way of soliciting information about the kinds of books the company uses and how they are currently acquired. This information can be helpful in selecting inventory and in developing future promotional plans.

If some businesses in your area are not large enough to maintain separate purchasing operations or in-house libraries, the executive secretary is often a good source of information. Remember that hardly anyone is immune to the flattery implicit in being asked his or her opinion about what books you ought to carry.

Professional societies and associations are another important source of market information. Many of them, particularly engineering and architectural groups, are actively involved in providing their membership with books. Checking with them on sources of supply and on materials needed for various licensing examinations can be very enlightening. Finally, for the already operating bookstore, customers can be a gold mine of information.

Whatever fields define your market emphasis—manufacturing, electronics, aviation, agriculture, petroleum—there is one field that cuts across all of them and is applicable in almost all locations. You've already guessed: computers and data processing. Most stores, of course, have already accepted a section for home computers and hobbyists as essential. Higher-level professional computer books, however, fall within that shadowy area where fear still prevails. But a well-stocked, well-selected professional computer section can be a reasonable way to enter the technical book market. Another universal and even more familiar entrée would involve upgrading your general business section with more specialized and higher-level books.

Buying Technical Books

The key issue in technical book buying is discount structures. Obviously, the standard 20 percent discount that prevails in many categories of technical books is not acceptable. It is especially frightening to booksellers who have long considered a 40 percent trade discount absolutely minimal. To overcome the discount problem, stocking technical books usually means a commitment to the agency plans offered by most major publishers. Typically, the plans are initiated by ordering a selection of backstock titles and signing an agreement to have the new titles in certain categories shipped automatically. The store, of course, makes the choice of categories and, in some cases, can preselect the new titles, often by reviewing the choices of the publisher's representative. The plans vary a great deal in their requirements, but almost all of them raise the discount from 20 percent to a higher figure—typically 32 percent. If possible, smaller stores and stores just initiating a technical section might be advised to preselect titles rather than have them shipped automatically. This method enables a store to have better control over the quantity and types of books in stock.

The recent trend in the technical book business is that some technical publishers, Springer-Verlag and Elsevier, for example, offer a given number of certain popular titles at a trade discount.

Even better, Prentice-Hall has been designating many titles as trade that would once have been short discount. This change is especially true in the computer science categories.

In addition to making discount structures more favorable to retailers, agency-plan publishers can offer other support services. Addison-Wesley, for example, provides a quarterly computerized report on the performance of their titles in your store, obviously a great aid to inventory control. Most significant, publishers can provide a knowledgeable rep. If the rep grows familiar with your store, your budget, and your market, his or her advice can become invaluable. In most cases, however, even a dedicated rep cannot be expected to understand which of the vast number of new titles in his line can meet the specifics of your market. In other words, you will be much more on your own and can expect less help from technical publishers than from their trade counterparts.

As an aside, you can learn to turn this "aloneness" to your advantage. Just as you will have no choice but to develop buying skills on your own, so, too, will you have to develop on your own a creative and aggressive marketing plan. Technical publishers will give you less help than trade publishers, but at least you will not be the clone or captive of the media campaigns of those trade publishing giants who love to feature their latest "exercise guru" or "positive-thinking messiah." The retreat from "show biz" bookselling can be, at the very least, a relief.

Once you have established your agency plans and know the categories of books to stock, how to select from the overwhelming number of available volumes is still a mystery. Many of the techniques used in buying trade books are transferable. There are basic stock items in each technical field. The list of important titles developed by Lyman Newlin and available from the Professional and Scholarly Division of the American Association of Publishers (AAP) is a starting point.

Even more than in trade publishing, each publisher has developed a strength in certain specialized fields. June Kapitan's list from the previous edition of this book is a helpful guide to these strengths and is reproduced in figure 32-1 in slightly revised form. Although I have focused on publishers known for their technical lines, most trade publishers, notably Macmillan and Harper & Row, produce books geared for the general business market, which, with their larger discounts, can enhance the profitability of a professional business section. University presses should not be ignored as a source of professional titles that can add distinction and interest.

Additionally, there is a group of publishers and special imprints, most of them relatively new, that have developed specifically to meet ever-increasing demand for computer books. In many cases these are producers of computer hardware and/or software who have established their own publishing arms. Many of them address both the business and personal computer markets. The following list is partial:

Anaheim	Matrix
Arcsoft	Mike Murak
Ashton Tate	Osborne McGraw
William C. Brown	Que Corporation
Computer Science	Sybex
Datamost	Yourdon Press
dilithium	

Finally, stores that have developed specialized technical markets may want to investigate the publications of various professional societies. Generally the discounts available are quite small, but providing these titles for the convenience of your customers can add credibility and even enhance profitability in the overall picture, if not on the basis of each individual sale. *The Manual of Steel Construction* from the American Institute of Steel Construction is a good example of a professional publication that can add credibility and, in this case, even specific profit, to a store with a construction/ engineering focus.

More specific knowledge of basic technical backlist can also be derived from visits to important technical stores in other areas. What would be unacceptable "spying" in other industries can be, in the book business, a source of profitable camaraderie. Contact with universities and colleges in the area can provide valuable clues about what should be stocked since most professors keep up with current publishing in their fields. Unless you serve a university community, beware of being lured into stocking textbooks since most of them are available at only a very short discount.

Merchandising Technical and Professional Books

One of the hidden advantages of stocking technical books is the surprisingly small space required. Very few technical titles really need to be faced out. This treatment can be reserved for emphasizing important new titles. Customers are content to root library-fashion through a section placed in an obscure corner of the store. Among technical customers there is a minimal amount of impulse buying, but they are likely to be impressed by a wide selection of

Fig. 32-1. MAJOR TECHNICAL PUBLISHERS AND SPECIALTIES

*ACADEMIC PRESS	Physical Science, Math, Computer Science, Engineering
ADDISON-WESLEY	Psychology, Computer Science, Management
AMACOM	Management
CBI	Business, Restaurant & Hotel Management
DOVER PUBLICATIONS	Math, Physics, Architecture (historically important reprints)
*ELSEVIER–NORTH HOLLAND	Computer Science, Management
JOHN M. FREEMAN COMPANY	Astronomy, Biology, Psychology
GULF PUBLISHING COMPANY	Petroleum
**HAYDEN BOOK COMPANY	Electronics, Computer Science
RICHARD D. IRWIN	Investment, Management
INDUSTRIAL PRESS	Industrial Engineering, Machine Tools
McGRAW-HILL BOOK COMPANY	Engineering, Architecture, Handbooks Computer Science, Management
*PERGAMON PUBLISHING	Physics, Chemistry
*PLENUM PUBLISHING	Physics, Chemistry
PRENTICE-HALL	Computer Science, Engineering, Management, Real Estate
**HOWARD SAMS & COMPANY	Electronics, Computer Science
*SPRINGER-VERLAG	Math, Computer Science
**TAB BOOKS	Electronics, Computer Science
VAN NOSTRAND REINHOLD	Computer Science, Architecture, Management
WADSWORTH, INC.	Computer Science, Engineering, Mathematics, Health Science
JOHN WILEY & SONS	Engineering, Business Management, Architecture, Computer Science

One asterisk (*) indicates publishers of high-level, research-oriented books, some with an applied emphasis.

Double asterisk (**) indicates specialized publishers with professional/technical titles at trade discounts.

Remaining names, in most cases, are comprehensive publishers with multilevel trade and technical lines.

titles. To some extent the inventory can function as advertising. You may not have the exact title needed, but your wide selection encourages a customer to come back, to consider special ordering, and to pass on the word that you are a credible resource for technical and professional books. In short, breadth rather than depth is the key to a good technical book inventory. With a good reorder system, well over half the titles you stock can be single copies. And another hidden advantage—you won't have to listen to salespeople say, "But if you only take one, you'll never know. . . ." One is quite enough in many cases since the technical book business is not so trendy and the shelf life of most titles is predictably longer.

The importance of good signs as a merchandising tool is too obvious to require more than this one-sentence reminder. An external sign with a name or tag that signifies you are in the professional and technical book business is worth considering. Don't expect much help from publishers in the merchandising area: no dumps, no posters, very little pizzazz. Happily, however, some publishers have recently come up with better jackets and book designs. Their books no longer look as if the design contract had been awarded to prisoners in solitary confinement for the last thirty years.

Many booksellers find that the most perplexing merchandising problem now is how to arrange an inventory whose subject matter is a mystery. I have seen computer sections, for example, arranged alphabetically by author and by title, in both cases more for the convenience of clerks than customers. For customers, subject categories seem to work best. Within large subject categories, authors might be arranged alphabetically. A reasonable breakdown for computer books, for example, might be: General Introductions, Buying Guides, Specific Languages, Machine-Specific Books, Operating Systems, Data Processing, Computer Logic, Computer Security, Artificial Intelligence, Computer Software, Computer Games, and Computers and Children.

Too much agonizing over the arrangement of inventory is a waste. Instead, spot those customers who have a rage for order. They are usually happy to help you arrange books around their knowledge of a field. After all, it's a rare opportunity to demonstrate considerable knowledge in a very short time. Few can pass up the opportunity.

Some of the crossover merchandising opportunities between trade and technical stock will be surprising and profitable. Computer customers, for example, often like science fiction; placing it strategically in their path can pay off. Without planned distractions they are likely to head straight to their section as if with blinders on. Engineers are rarely distracted by history; instead try a section of math and logic puzzles near their area. Lawyers can easily be lured into a good mystery section; businesspeople frequently pause if a travel section is nearby. The possibilities of crossover merchandising are endless and limited only by the bookseller's imagination and budget.

Promoting Technical and Professional Books

If you could only do one thing to promote the sale of technical and professional books in your store, what would it be? The answer is given only for those counterparts of Rip Van Winkle who have had the possibly enviable pleasure of sleeping through the last several decades. For everyone else, "advertise in the Yellow Pages" is the obvious answer; the only question concerns the size and arrangement of the ad. Given the expense of this kind of advertising, those just initiating a small technical department might consider expanding their regular column listing to a trademark ad rather than financing a display ad. Another possibility is listing the names of the technical publishers they carry in stock and seeking to recover some of the cost through publishers' co-op ad programs. Unlike the convention in trade books, publishers are quite flexible in responding to co-op ads for professional and technical books. Be creative and aggressive in this area.

For stores with a full technical section, advertising in trade journals has the obvious advantage of a targeted market. The rates, especially when compared with those of large metropolitan dailies, are often surprisingly reasonable. Sometimes local or regional chapters of national trade associations publish newsletters that are worth investigating.

For many small stores, conventional advertising channels may be prohibitive in cost; innovation and personalized promotion must be used instead. Direct calls on companies, mentioned earlier in the article, can be very productive. One bookseller reports a 20 percent success rate in opening new accounts through cold calls over the telephone. Often the person you're contacting on the phone has a friend in another company who also needs to order books. The possibilities are endless. When soliciting business for technical fields, don't forget to mention your ability to supply dictionaries and other general reference aids for the support staff; multiple sales in this area can balance some short discount sales. The advantage of ordering books from a single source is immediately obvious to the purchasing agent who has been juggling purchase orders or prepayment requests for fifteen different publishers. One purchase order, one monthly statement—what a relief!

Some localities have chapters of special library associations that meet regularly. Often they are looking for program speakers. Offer to tell them about new books coming in their fields or about your book supply services. Some publishers—Academic, for example—will provide you with very generous assistance in setting up a technical book fair for their publications within a corporate or academic setting. Where high-level research is taking place, this can be an appropriate and profitable venture.

Some small promotional efforts can have elaborate results. Never let a technical book leave the store without a small sticker applied at the time of sale which records the name, address, and telephone number of the store. This "message in the bottle" approach can bring in orders from far distant places. Your tale about the order from Hong Kong or Nairobi could outshine all others when stories are swapped at your next ABA Convention.

Finally, any discussion about promoting technical and professional books must take into account the publisher's own promotional programs, including direct mail and book club campaigns directed at established professional markets. Do not be frightened by this kind of direct competition from major publishers. For one thing, there is plenty of room in the marketplace for different approaches. For another, the publishers' programs can often dovetail with your own. Some customers call their local bookseller when the publisher's brochure arrives in the mail. They don't like various features of the book club approach; they've had bad experiences with shipping problems; in the best example, they appreciate the services provided by their booksellers. A number of reasons have been advanced to show that direct sales by publishers will not destroy the promotional efforts of a well-organized and aggressive bookseller who has found his market.

This aspect of promotion really brings up the larger question of bookseller/publisher relations. On a hopeful note, some publishers are recognizing the need to support the local retail booksellers. If they do not, in the long run they will be left without a showcase where a wide selection of their titles can be seen by a diverse and often unknown group of consumers. There are many technical book buyers unknown to publishers and not reachable through their conventional direct-mail marketing programs. Professional book publishers need retail stores as much as retail stores need them. Fortunately, some publishers realize this and have chosen to expand their market by supporting retailers rather than competing with them. One of their most useful efforts is to supply the retailer with new book announcements imprinted with the store name. An even more useful effort involves referring corporate and business customers to local retail sources. From my obviously subjective view-point, the most far-sighted publishers view this kind of cooperation not as loss of potential revenue, but as realistic long-range market planning.

Financing a Line of Technical and Professional Books

I sense in the skeptical reader one last question: What about financing this effort? Of course, much has been discussed about finances in other sections of this book, but a word here about the outlay necessary for the initial inventory might be in order. Will it console anybody to know the initial investment made by Ted Brown, former owner of Brown's Book Shop in Houston, Texas? Everyone has heard of his legendary efforts in pioneering technical book sales in the Southwest, but it's surprising to hear what his first step cost. He tells us himself: "Less than $2,500 . . ." ("Technical Booklist," *American Bookseller*, January-February 1978, pp. 11–13.) Even multiplied for our inflationary times, one can see that a small initial inventory is a manageable expense and is no barrier to future success in the field.

The most cautious approach of all would be to add professional titles only from those companies with whom you have established accounts. Dictionaries in chemistry, various branches of engineering, computer science, business, and economics would be good additions to the reference section and are often available from trade publishers. Some of the standard handbooks from McGraw-Hill would also fit well in reference. They are available at 40 percent discount to agency plan members in quantities of five, to nonmembers in quantities of twenty-five.

Generally, the profitability of technical book sales is dependent on the special-order factor mentioned earlier. The large proportion of special orders, including multiple-copy orders for training programs and the like, enables you to maintain a turn rate for your inventory equal to or better than that for trade books. Some book-sellers report a turn rate of five times a year in certain technical sections. Because so many books are presold before ordering, you can afford to keep certain titles on the shelf for six, even eight months, waiting for them to find a market. Of course, an effective reorder system on accepted titles is mandatory to maintain both your turn rate and your reputation.

Whatever approach one selects, selling technical and professional books can be a bridge between the old and the new in bookselling. The subject matter may be high tech and futuristic, but the sales approach is decidedly old-fashioned. Special attention, personal service, customized inventory—these requirements are the province of the traditional bookseller. An operation geared to mass marketing, discounting, and self-service is not well adapted to the sale of professional and technical books. Consequently, selling professional and technical books, like other kinds of specialization, can be a very effective way to meet the inevitable competition in the modern marketplace.

Chapter 33

Computer Books, Magazines, and Software

DAVID CIOFFI

A tremendous world of opportunity awaits booksellers willing to explore the market for computer books, software, and magazines. Whether you do or do not appreciate the influence of computers on our society, you must face reality—computers are here to stay. Booksellers should buckle up their seat belts and steer cautiously but confidently into this fascinating world. There are three avenues of opportunity, and this chapter will explore each: (1) computer books, (2) computer software, (3) computer magazines. (The market in all things having to do with computers is so volatile that many of the titles cited here will surely be revised or replaced by others by the time you read this chapter. They are mentioned here only to illustrate points made in the text.)

Selling Computer Books

If your bookstore is not selling computer books, you are missing a phenomenal opportunity to capture sales and improve your bottom line. As was once stated in *Software Merchandising* magazine, "The thirst for computer knowledge has grown and is expected to continue growing at an astronomical rate. New books hit the market daily as more and more consumers purchase a computer for home or business, and the need for books is expected to go unabated. Without a doubt, books have become a necessary accessory."

Obviously there is money to be made selling computer books, and bookstores should be making it. However, if you continue to procrastinate, your local computer dealer or department store will capture the market.

Bookstores that have stocked computer books have witnessed unbelievable growth in a very short period of time. Back in 1982 it was simply the dearth of books that restricted sales. Potential customers were out there hunting fruitlessly for nonexistent books. It didn't take aggressive publishers long to pick up the scent. Today there is a tremendous outpouring of computer books from scores of enlightened publishers. We are rapidly approaching market saturation. Some publishers pop out books just to get them on the shelves. Their content is frivolous. Publishers like dilithium and Sybex, however, who were pioneers in the computer book generation, continue to publish high-quality, informative, and "user friendly" books. Likewise, publishers such as McGraw-Hill, Wiley, Prentice-Hall, Addison-Wesley, and Springer-Verlag, whose textbook publishing experience help them deal with the complexity of computer technology. Bookstores that stocked these books in the beginning devoted little shelf space to them. Today these leaders in the bookstore industry have expanded and expanded until their computer book areas are among the largest in the store. And they do indeed pay their freight!

How can booksellers capitalize on this market? You must first identify your potential market and then proceed intelligently. There are five distinct levels that must be considered.

1. *The Curious Market.* Computers are permeating our society. It is difficult to escape them. People are sensing a need to become computer literate before they are left too far behind to ever understand what is going on. Even those who don't plan to purchase a computer want to learn about them. Others who are planning to purchase a computer (or another computer!) want to be sure they make an educated decision before spending hundreds or even thousands of dollars. Local libraries see a need to stock books that might assist patrons in understanding about computers. People who already own a computer and have no plans for a newer one wish to keep abreast of changing technology. All these people buy books such as:

> *The Personal Computer Book* (Ballantine/Prelude)
>
> *The Random House Book of Computer Literacy* (Vintage)
>
> *Computer Wimp* (Ten Speed)
>
> *Webster's New World Dictionary of Computer Terms* (Simon & Schuster)

These books explain essentials to people before they buy computers. They also offer information for those who are curious but never plan to live with a computer. Rapid advance in computer technology assures that new books are mandatory to keep pace with new developments. For booksellers this means steady sales.

2. *The Novice Market.* As computer prices tumble and computers become commonplace in homes, this introductory level holds the most promise for booksellers. Novice computerists soon master owner manuals, even when these manuals are difficult to comprehend. If the manual does its job of teaching the basics of operation, the novice will then come to a bookstore for more information. Books such as these launch novices on their way:

> *The Elementary Vic 20* (Datamost)
>
> *I Speak Basic to My Commodore 64* (Hayden)
>
> *Atari Fun and Games* (TAB)

These customers soon wish to know more about the potential of their new computers. And, as new computers appear, so will new elementary books about them, and you should stock them. This is a dimension of the business that will be repeated over and over again as modern technology creates smarter computers and advertising campaigns convince ever more consumers that they can't live without a resident machine or can't live without a better or another computer, perhaps one for the kids so parents can also have their own computer time.

3. *Intermediate Market.* When computerists reach this level of sophistication, they suddenly develop an insatiable appetite for more information. They leave space between themselves and computer neophytes. If they live near your bookstore, they will be constantly perusing your shelves for books that test their aptitude on the keyboard. At this stage they have become proficient in programming and thus are beyond game playing, although they do still play. They have become discerning buyers, and after flipping through a book they will tell you whether or not the book should be on your shelf. These people are quick to share acquired expertise. You can get valuable information from them. They tend to purchase books such as:

> *Inside the IBM PC* (Brady)
>
> *Apple Works* (Hayden)
>
> *The Addison-Wesley Book of Apple Software* (Addison-Wesley)
>
> *Amiga Programmer's Handbook* (Sybex)

They will also consume books on programming, and this will be covered later in the chapter. People at the intermediate level are knowledgeable, their ranks are swelling, and bookstores must move beyond the ilk of books noted under "The Curious Market" to secure their valuable patronage. Because many computerists never move beyond this middle stage, you will find this market to be nearly as lucrative as "The Curious Market." Those stores that were early entering the computer book market often find this intermediate level to be the backbone of their business. These customers often have a special area of interest, such as graphics, programming games, or maximizing the potential of their computers for home accounting and management.

4. *Professional Market.* This is no market to dive into until you have succeeded with the preceding markets. Depending on your location, however, it can be cultivated. If your store is in a small town, you may not have the market. If you are located in a college town, Silicon Valley or a clone of it, or have computer service businesses around you, then there is potential. If you have any doubts, wait until you are doing well in the other levels before you pour money into books for professionals. Once you determine that you have potential in this top market, go after it. Computers are a part of the working-day life of these people, and it is imperative that they stay abreast of developments in their field. They crave exciting books:

> *The 8086/8088 Primer* (Hayden)
>
> *User Guide to the UNIX System* (McGraw)
>
> *Compiler Construction* (Springer-Verlag)
>
> *Digital Image Processing of Remotely Sensed Data* (Academic)

Prices have little bearing on buying decisions for these customers. Often purchases are charged to company accounts. Bookstores enjoying the most success in this particular market usually belong to computer book agency plans. Here you must rely on the expertise of sales representatives from technical publishers such as McGraw-Hill, Addison-Wesley, Wiley, Prentice-Hall, Springer-Verlag, Van Nostrand, Academic, and others. Turnover is slower here, but prices can be astronomical, which means two or three sales yield excellent dividends. By joining agency plans you can receive higher discounts (28–33 percent) on these highly technical books, including textbooks. It is imperative you have a functioning inventory-control system so you can cull outdated deadwood regularly. Few bookstores stock these professional books, so if you build a reputation with them, the word will spread and your market expand. With the higher discounts from agency plans you will appreciate special orders.

These customers never mind waiting because they understand it is impossible to have in stock all the very special books they need.

5. *Business Market.* Treat this as a distinct market. Customers in this genre span a wide spectrum—from the one-dentist office to a three-hundred- to four-hundred-employee corporation. It has endless possibilities. As in the professional market, prices are little impediment to sales. Now that there are affordable computers for small businesses, shrewd business owners are tapping into their potential. It was a market that started slowly but is now leaping forward. Benefits reaped by small businesses that own computers justify a reasonable budget for purchasing computer books such as:

> *Microcomputer Communications in Business* (Chilton)
>
> *Does Your Small Business Need a Computer?* (TAB)
>
> *Using 1-2-3* (QUE)
>
> *Execucomp* (Wiley)

Note there are two categories of books under this heading. One category is books that discuss hardware (such as a business computer buyer's guide). The other deals with software (a book explaining how to use Lotus 1-2-3) or even a book with business software programs within. Businesses that recognize the value of computerization also recognize that computer books are tools, computer accessories, to help them maximize their potential use of the computer. Books are a piddling expense considering the outlay for a computer and the necessary software, although software is not as expensive as it used to be. Once the cost of software was beyond the budgets of small businesses, and this impeded business computer sales. Not so today—and businesses have been quick to grasp this new technology.

Once you have decided to go after one or more of the previously mentioned markets, how do you set about organizing a computer book department? Certainly it should be arranged so that customers can easily find books they want. Stores that successfully sell computer books have an organized way of shelving them. They are not all exactly the same, but there is considerable common ground. Customers appreciate a system the puts them into quick contact with books they might like to own. The following is just one method of organizing books. Depending on how many books you eventually stock, some of these categories can be combined to make a very effective display. To simplify things, we will start at the fundamental level.

Fig. 33-1. Computer software and accessories (blank disks, disk files, etc.) have a home at The Dartmouth Bookstore, and bring profit to the bottom line. (Photograph by Dexter M. Pierce)

1. *General Information.* These books are meant to explain computers to people who know little or nothing but are developing an interest in them. People who have already purchased a computer also purchase these books. They would include titles such as:

> *Random House Book of Computer Literacy* (Vintage)
>
> *What a Computer Can Do for You* (Widl/Video-Scribner)
>
> *The Personal Computer Book* (Ballantine/Prelude Press)

Often, after reading these books, a vibrant chord is struck, and some people decide to buy a computer after all.

2. *Buyer's Guides.* The marketplace is cluttered with new computers, and all this competition has put computer prices within the budget of average citizens. Books can sort out the features of all these computers and make valid comparisons of which ordinary individuals are not capable. It is easy to buy a computer with features you might never use. A few dollars invested in a

book can save hundreds of dollars on a purchase. People about to buy their first computer and those trading up to a spiffier model appreciate books such as:

1985 Personal Computer Digest (DBI Books, Inc.)

Everyone's Guide to Personal Computers (Ballantine)

You can expect a steady stream of new computers with jazzier features and lower prices, so these books will continue to warrant revisions. There will always be a steady stream of sales for bookstores that update their basic selections.

3. *Computer Models.* Books on specific computers are the heart of a computer book department. In the beginning of the computer revolution came new computers, and then came books about them. But that's not so today—bookstores were receiving books on the IBM PC Jr. and Coleco Adam before these models were available in their area. Owner guides accompanying new computers barely whet the appetite of hungry computer jockeys. For a while the computer distribution channels restricted sales possibilities. However, these channels are now being flooded, and that's great for sales. In our case an Apple dealer opened up in town, which prompted Apple computer book sales. When IBM PC and Commodore 64 computers came to town, we couldn't stock books about them fast enough.

A bookstore should assess its market before an initial computer book order. It is senseless to stock books on the Kaypro or Acorn if they aren't being sold in the vicinity.

Within each computer group there are various potential markets. The novice who is poised to move beyond the owner's manual purchases books such as *Compute's First Book of Atari* (Compute! Books). And then when books of this range are mastered, it's on to an intermediate stage, and *Compute's Second Book of Atari* (Compute! Books) presents challenges. It is at this stage computerists begin to use their computers for the purposes of home accounting and home organization. It's time to challenge the limits of the computer, and a book such as *Commodore 64 Programmer's Reference Guide* (SAMS) can help. This is about the time word processing comes into play, and we will touch on that soon. The hard-core computerists find uses beyond the home and start applying the potential of the computer to their work or business. Some computers are better than others for these applications. For example, if one invests in an IBM PC, more than likely the purchase was planned for future professional use. A Vic 20 or Texas Instruments 99/4A has more limited capabilities. Bookstore stock should be balanced accordingly, less books on running a business with a Vic 20 and more books on running a business with an IBM PC. Reading computer magazines and conversing with customers for signals will help you stock accordingly. As this chapter is being written, the Texas Instruments 99/4A has been abandoned by its company. The price was reduced drastically to unload them in the $75–$85 range. The customers who purchased them are beating down doors for applications books. They realize the marketplace will soon have no books for them. They are right, because books about that computer have been canceled from publisher catalogs.

4. *Computer Languages.* Books on computer languages also do very well, particularly books about languages for specific computers: *I Speak Basic to My Commodore 64* (Hayden) or *Basic Exercises for the Apple* (Sybex). Language books not dealing with a specific computer also do quite well and are worth stocking, including *Basic Programming* (Wiley) or *UCSD Pascal—A Beginners + Guide to Programming Microcomputers* (Reward). BASIC has been the language producing the most sales, but other languages are also becoming popular. BASIC is being revised by its authors—John Kemeny and Thomas Kurtz at Dartmouth—and once this is accomplished it might again leave other languages far behind as it did early on in the computer generation. Their "cleaned up" BASIC will be named "true BASIC."

Pascal is another language that is supposedly easier to learn and in some schools is the first programming language taught. LOGO, a language designed for teaching children how to use the computer, is getting much use in schools, and books about it are doing well. "C" language, like LOGO, is also enjoying growing popularity.

Other languages a solid computer book department should represent include FORTH, FORTRAN, COBOL, ADA, LIST, and Assembly language. Undoubtedly more languages will surface. Along with languages bookstores should also stock books on operating systems. An operating system is a collection of system programs controlling the overall operation of a computer system, whereas a language is the set of words, and rules governing their use, employed in constructing a program. Books covering "CPM," "D-BASE II," and "UNIX" are most popular. Watch for other operating systems to crop up.

5. *Game Books.* These can be stocked in two locations. They do very well, as both novice and intermediate computerists scoop them up. A book such as *70 Games for the Timex/Sinclair 1000 and 1500* can be stocked with other Timex/Sinclair books and in

the "Games" section. *Basic Computer Games* (Workman) and *Create Your Own Games Computer Play* (Digital) belong only in the "Games" section. As a computer disappears from production, so too does software for it, and this can work miracles for game book sales. History often repeats itself, so be aware of computers discontinued and be aggressive to garner sales others are running away from—don't hit the panic button if your sales for that particular computer have been steady. And game books appear to be the most sought after, since game software disappears fast.

6. *Kids and Computers.* These books are a must in any store selling computer books. Some stores stock them with their children's books. Others insist on shelving them with their computer books. We have tried both but feel we do sell more books when they are shelved with the computer books. Here we pick up plus sales to older computer beginners who might never encounter them in our children's department. These books are great for any age because they assume absolutely no prior knowledge and explain everything in simple language. On the other hand, parents looking for computer books for children tend to ask for them, so we don't think many sales are lost by placing them with computer books.

Datamost Inc. has published marvelous books for children geared toward specific computers (such as *Kids and the IBM PC*). There are plenty of salable books for children, and you should encounter no problem building this area. These books truly do teach.

You can go one step further here and follow up the "Kids and Computers" section with a "Computers in Education" display. Computers are destined to be used more and more as a teaching tool in the classroom. They offer a unique approach to one-on-one teaching, particularly since software is being upgraded with teaching in mind. Teachers need guidance since the computer is a new piece of furniture in the classroom. They need ideas that come from a sharing of knowledge by others who have had success with the computer as a teaching tool. *Practical Guide to Computers in Education* (Addison-Wesley), *Mindstorms* (Harper), and *Using a Computer in the Classroom* (Prentice-Hall) are perfect examples of the nucleus of such a section. Parents will also be customers here. Look for more of these books in the future as experience is gained and shared by educators.

7. *Word Processing.* Even people who have treated the advent of the computer with disdain cannot argue the benefits of word processing—particularly typists who have suffered bleeding ulcers

over the possibility of mistakes in the last paragraph at the bottom of the page. Businesspeople and professionals were quick to discover the glories of word processing. Now even families find word-processing equipment an affordable and valuable aid in the home, a worthwhile investment for homework and correspondence. Books about word processing are fast movers. *Questions and Answers on Word Processing* (Prelude), *Writing with a Word Processor* (Harper), and *Practical Wordstar Uses* (Sybex) illustrate what sells. Word processors have demonstrated their value, and they are here to stay. There will be no end to books that supplement word-processing software. Any bookstore that is striving for an above-average computer book section should have these books.

8. *Computers in Business.* Earlier in the chapter we mentioned that this market appears limitless. Computers have been the salvation for inventory control and financial analysis. Creative business software like VisiCalc and Lotus 1-2-3 can do for a computer-run business in a jiffy what would have taken a legion of accountants weeks in days gone by! Word processing and data file bases save innumerable hours, so businesses can now spend more time with customers. Books offer a supplement to software and a convenient source of information for training employees. A small library of computer books can save dollars on the payroll and at the same time incite interest and appreciation for a business computer system. Best of all, these books can be purchased on company purchase orders and written off as a business expense.

Computer books for business can be divided into two classifications:

1. *Books on Hardware.* Hardware is the computer and equipment accessories, disk drives, monitors, and printers. The business computer market already appears glutted. How does a business select a system that matches its needs? By reading about what is available in books such as *The Small Computer in Small Business* (Stephen Greene Press) and *Handbook of Computer Applications for the Small or Medium-Sized Business* (Chilton). Before investing a few thousand dollars in hardware, it can't hurt to be knowledgeable, and the price of a book is nothing in relation to the price of a computer system. No sense paying for whistles and bells you might never use. Good books can steer a business in the right direction.

2. *Business Software Books.* Software is what controls the operations of a computer. Understanding how to maximize the capability of a business computer is a must. Business software is abundant. Books can first help make proper software pur-

chase decisions and then explain in detail how the software works. They can also illustrate new applications for software that an owner's manual never considered. *Financial Analysis with Lotus 1-2-3* (Brady), *Computers and Business Information Processing* (Addison-Wesley), and *Handbook of Data Processing, Administration, Operations, and Procedure* (American Management) are typical examples of salable books. If you can find out what business software your local computer stores are pushing (such as Lotus 1-2-3 versus Multiplan), you can target your market. Most businesses will purchase word processing, a database, and a spreadsheet software package when they purchase computers, so order books with that in focus. Computerized businesses soon learn that an in-house library of informative books is a valuable resource.

Programming and Software Books

It is usually more productive to put books about programming and software for a specific computer with the books for that computer—such as *Graphics Programs for the IBM PC* (TAB) or *Teach Yourself Computer Programming/Commodore 64* (David McKay). If you have space, it can't hurt to put a book in two locations—one with the specific computer books and one in the programming/software department.

Books that surely belong here are those that discuss programming and software in general terms. Examples include Schaum's *Computers and Programming* (McGraw), *Software Tools* (Addison-Wesley), *1984 Programmers Market* (Writers Digest), and the classic series *Art of Computer Programming* (Addison-Wesley). Here you are wandering into quite technical territory, so move cautiously. These books are expensive and turnover is slower, but they do sell and yield worthwhile profits. It should be emphasized that programming and software books speaking to specific computers belong first with books about that computer. These move very fast, and bookstores will have no trouble selling them.

If you want to go after the professional market, read on. If not, go to "Instant Computer Book Department" later in this chapter. When you decide to fish in these waters you must show solid sales in all the other categories. The professionals have probably purchased other computer books from you in the past when they were just learning and when computer books were difficult to find. These customers browse computer departments so they can stay informed. They may have stopped buying books from you because you don't have technical computer books. But they can be won back.

Agency plans can provide the nucleus of sales in this arena. Simply stated, if you have enlisted in a computer book agency plan with a publisher, you have committed yourself to buying a minimum number of copies of each newly published title in this discipline. Generally you can choose not to accept books above a certain price (such as $40). Agency plans deliver you into the hands of a publisher. It is a rare bookseller who understands these books. Publishers with agency plans have expertise and common sense. They will do their utmost to make it worthwhile for both parties. Occasionally you can't even pronounce some of the words in the title, but believe it or not, you can sell these books if you have computer professionals in your market. Classic textbook publishers such as Wiley, Prentice-Hall, Addison-Wesley, Academic, Springer-Verlag, and others offer good deals for bookstores. On an agency plan you get 28–33 percent discounts on books you are likely special ordering and for which you are getting only 20–25 percent. Obviously there is a market for these books, or they wouldn't be published. Someone should be selling them, and it might as well be you. If you choose to chase this market, here is one method of sorting them out and organizing them so they are easy to find. These cutomers don't enjoy wasting time wading through books in which they have no interest. They appreciate an organized computer book department.

Microcomputers and microprocessors. Microcomputers are those small computers you now find in homes and small businesses. Their memory size ranges from around 4K of memory to 64K of memory at this time. A microprocessor is the chip within a microcomputer that determines the limit of what a microcomputer can do. It has both logic and memory capabilities. Books shelved here go well beyond explaining how to use a computer. They get inside a computer and discuss internal mechanisms. Sexy titles such as *Z-80 User's Manual* (Reward), *6502 Systems Programming* (Little, Brown), and *Microprocessor Interfacing* (TAB) are published for this market. Code names like "Z-80," "6502," "8086," or "8088" (these are all chips) signal a book not intended for the average computer user.

Computer electronics. This is a science in itself. There really are customers out there who will buy books about the flow of electrons through the guts of a computer! Not just professors and computer science majors, either—serious computer hobbyists crave books such as *Fundamentals Handbook of Electrical and Computer Engineering* (Wiley) and *Structured Digital Design* (Prentice-Hall). You can laugh all the way to the bank when you register sales of $40,

$50 per book and more. The rapid pace of new developments in this field means revisions of old books and new books explaining new theories. Agency plans are truly a necessity here. Even sales representatives are baffled by these books.

Data communication. The rapid and accurate transfer of information from point A to point B has been enhanced since the advent of computers. Whether the data must flow from a cash register on the main floor to a computer upstairs or from the East Coast to the West Coast, it is a complicated procedure. *Data Communications Networks and Distributed Processing* (Reston), *The Local Network Handbook* (McGraw), and *Telecomunications and the Computer* (Prentice-Hall) are all salable books, and this area is growing.

Other categories that can be created with these professional books include "Computer Math/Algorithms," "Artificial Intelligence," and "Data Security." There is no point in getting into specifics; enough examples have been given. In the future, new areas will need to be encompassed within your computer books for professionals. Be open-minded and cautious as you move deeper into these books. Don't expect instant miracles, but do expect a steady increase as the word spreads that your bookstore stocks computer books not stocked by anyone else. Computer professionals communicate with one another and advise novices and intermediate users. If this market exists in your area, you definitely should cultivate it.

Finally, a computer book department needs a "Miscellaneous Computer Books" section. This becomes a home for all books that don't fit neatly into one of the preceding sections. Watch this area closely because it has a habit of getting out of hand. It will grow and grow if you don't prune it regularly. When you have five or six books in a given category, pull them out and put them together in a section by themselves. It will generate sales as well as look impressive.

Instant computer book department. Booksellers who have zero IQ when it comes to computer books shouldn't stay out of the pool. There is a way for you to have an instant computer book department. Some wholesalers are very knowledgeable and can put you in business in no time. Ingram Book Company is particularly adept at this. They publish a computer book directory and a weekly microfiche inventory of computer books on hand. They can ship you an opening inventory based on their sales with other bookstores. It's a sensible way to enter this market.

Publisher's representatives are also becoming tuned in to the computer book department. Not all of them—but the ones you have always had confidence in can steer you in the right direction. Some publishers have very organized computer book sections within their seasonal catalogs. They are informative, and it makes it easy to find books on a given topic (such as BASIC). Once you commence selling computer books, a sound inventory management system will keep you on course. You will learn quickly, stack your book selection where the sales are and refrain from topics you are not selling. Don't let the absence of sales in one area (Pascal, for example) discourage you completely. Within six months you should have a handle on your potential. But do advertise to let people know you have the books. Don't expect huge success if you merely order in the books, shelve them, and tell nobody about them.

Computer Magazines

Bookstores that sell computer books have a built-in market for computer magazines. To computer hobbyists these magazines are the equivalent of drugs to an addict: they truly have to have them. You will recognize that as soon as you start carrying them, and the monthly issue of *Byte* or *PC World* is a few days late. The turnover on most computer magazines places them among the best-sellers on a magazine rack.

Innumerable magazines are available for computer users, and their numbers are destined to multiply as they offer the best up-to-date information available for computer jockeys to stay informed. Don't worry about subscriptions eroding your sales because computer users "window shop" until they find one or two that have articles they must read. Computerists do subscribe to magazines for owners of specific computers. Despite this you will find that these types of magazines also do very well. Apparently, a number of computer owners prefer not to subscribe so that if a given issue has information they don't need, they are not committed to buy. General-interest magazines—*Personal Computing, Byte,* and *Compute*—will usually sell better than computer-specific magazines. But that is not an absolute.

Computer magazines offer the same discount as other magazines, 20–30 percent, depending on your magazine supplier's policy or the publisher's policy if you order direct. Most local distributors deliver to your door, so there is no 3–5 percent freight charge. Some have generous retail display agreements available (you promise to allow a magazine full cover display on your magazine rack). If you accept, you can generate an additional 5–10 percent margin. Computer magazines will bring in potential book customers on a regular basis, so displaying them near your computer books has advantages. When your magazine rack is away from the computer books, you have a tough decision—to give up or not give up the impulse sales available on the magazine rack to generate book sales. Of course, if you have space to burn, you can stock them in two place.

If you don't carry computer magazines now, contact your local magazine distributor. Most will happily cater to your needs and do a good job putting you into business pronto. Don't expect a distributor to manage your sales after the start-up. You must determine if they are shipping you enough, or too many, of a given issue. It's simple to change your allotment. Returns are also no problem because you exchange old issues for new issues. Don't let an enterprising wholesaler talk you into stocking old issues. Rarely is this worthwhile.

Computer magazines can lend an interesting new dimension to your store that can make money for you. Too many bookstores look for sidelines offering a 50 percent profit margin that have very slow turnover. Don't turn your back on magazines because of the lower profit margin. By all means give them a shot if you have space or if you have a dying sideline that can be removed without significant loss to your bottom line. Remember, bookstores are watering holes for information seekers, and computer magazines offer the very latest in computer technology. Your customers deserve and will appreciate this service. And, at the same time, it can help your computer book sales.

Computer Software

Wait! Don't bypass this section without some study. Computer software offers bookstores the best opportunity we have had since the inception of paperback books. It is a wide-open market offering incredibly lucrative sales. In 1984 software came into its own in New Orleans with the SOFTCON convention. Put this new opportunity into perspective before you close the door.

What makes the software publishing business so alluring is its explosive growth rate, not its present size. From virtual invisibility a few years ago, software has become one of the fastest-moving segments of the computer industry, with an annual growth rate of at least 50 percent. Bookstores should not sit idly by and watch other retailers capture this market. You better believe that all these new computer buyers are not computer experts capable of writing their own computer programs. They are consumers with disposable income looking for the latest software that need only be plugged into their computers for easy use.

What is software? *Webster's New World Dictionary of Computer Terms* describes software as "programs, languages, and/or routines that control the operations of a computer in solving a given problem." Software currently comes in three forms:

1. *Cartridge.* This plugs into many home computers and requires no additonal equipment. Home computers like the Commodore 64 and Atari use them.

2. *Cassette.* To use a cassette software program you need an expensive ($75–$100) accessory—a program recorder. They look like your average recorder but require a special cable to interface with a computer. A cassette, like the cartridge, is used primarily with a home computer and not with personal computers.

3. *Disk.* A disk for a home or personal computer is around 5¼ inches in diameter and looks like a small record. To use software on disk you do need a very expensive ($250–$500) accessory—a disk drive. Generally they are used on personal computers, but some home computers (such as the Commodore 64) also have a disk drive.

Do all these formats present a problem? Not really—with discretion you can represent them all. When you ascertain which format sells best in your store, you can adjust purchases accordingly. Disks seem to be the most popular of the three.

Software can be categorized for an organized department arrangement. Here is one method:

1. *Recreational Software.* For a while recreational software was all there was in the marketplace. This is not the case today, but you can still expect the majority of your sales to come from game software (35–50 percent).

    Arcade games were first on the scene; they are the typical games you find in the game rooms of shopping centers and bars. They can best be described as "shoot 'em up" games (Star Trek, Zaxxon). Eye-and-hand coordination are essential to play these games.

    Adventure or fantasy games are for thinking people—Zork (Infocom), Wizardry (Sir-Tech). People who read books enjoy these games. You can move at your own pace, figuring out solutions as the game moves along. The action is slower. Astute publishers like Infocom created this facet of the business and are nursing it along. Dungeons and Dragons players support these games and anxiously await newer, more challenging puzzles to appear and challenge their wits.

2. *Educational Software.* The computer is proving to be an excellent teaching tool. It offers a one-on-one approach, and when the software is good the results are very encouraging. Educational

software for preschool and elementary-age children has a massive potential market. One company (Spinnaker) has set the pace with games that are instructional as well as fun to play. Children who could care less about learning are intrigued, and simply by playing they learn. They never realized schoolwork could be such fun! When they play games like Fraction Fever and Facemaker, they don't consider it burdensome schoolwork.

Educational software is gradually being introduced for the older age groups. Topics include spelling, math, reading, science, and even preparation tests for the SAT and GRE. This will be an interesting segment of the market to watch and cultivate in bookstores.

3. *Home Productivity.* Homeowners can find helpful software for managing their home and its finances—*Home Accountant* (Continental) and *Home Inventory* (Creative). Checkbook accounting programs have done well, and so have investment analysis programs. Homeowners with computers will try anything on the computer even when it is obviously quicker to use a pen and paper.

4. *Tutorial Software.* There is a thin line between tutorial and educational software. Many stores consider programs that teach you how to operate your computer or how to operate with a program or language as tutorial, such as *CDEX Training for the IBM Personal Computer* (CDEX) and *64 Forth* (Hesware); likewise a program that teaches you how to type on a computer. This segment of a software department is dependent on the computers being sold in your area. It will do very well once you find your market.

5. *Business Software.* This is a part of the software market you should nudge into. Software is very expensive, but prices are crashing as new companies find better and cheaper designs. Visicorp, for instance, was first with a comprehensive spreadsheet for financial analysis (VisiCalc), and it originally sold for $400–$500. Soon spreadsheets like this will sell for less than $100. It will probably be better for bookstores to refrain from stocking high-priced business software. However, you can sell to small businesses when prices are under $100—*Accounts Payable and Check Writing* (Commodore). You don't have to demonstrate to this market. It would be advisable to stay away from this at first; then, after you have had calls to special order some business software, try stocking some. When you have a good supplier you can special order and receive the product within a week.

Word Processing

This function alone can make a computer a worthwhile investment for both homeowner and business. Children can do homework assignments, and secretaries can type without fear of ruining a page with a typographical error in the last paragraph.

As with business software, stocking word-processing software above $100 is very risky. Most large businesses buy their word-processing software when they buy their computer. But word processing under $100 is of little risk. *Bank Street Writer* (Broderbund) and *Word Writer* (Timeworks) have both done well in the home and small-business market. People who own computers tend to add accessories, and at some point a printer is acquired. The printer is useless without a word-processing program, so this phase of the market is earmarked to grow, and word-processing software is a must in any good software department.

Other types of software will appear and should be absorbed into your software stock. It's an industry that more and more is resembling the workings of the book industry—particularly with games that are best-sellers today and dust catchers tomorrow. Monthly best-seller lists now appear in computer publications and on wholesaler-supplied point-of-sale posters. There are now sales records for understanding trends. More publishers are moving into this segment of the software market. It is predicted that by 1987 educational software sales will catapult to nearly $1 billion.

So what does all this mean for bookstores? Is there help out there so you can enter this market with confidence and not with haphazard guessing? Yes, there is. Capable wholesalers exist (such as Ingram Book and Softsel Co.), and they offer well-thought-out stocking options. They maintain a vast assortment of software that represents the best available. Their expert buyers have weeded out publishers' lists, and this is an invaluable asset for greenhorn booksellers. Returns policies are similar to book return policies (not quite as liberal—for instance, you may have only 90 or 120 days to exchange deadwood). It is necessary to have a functioning inventory-control system. If you decide to get into software overnight, you will probably have around ninety days to try everything you receive in your initial shipment. There would be no returns limit on your initial shipment within this period.

Book publishers are now into the software market. They are offering the same returns policies on software that they offer on books. You can choose to buy direct from them on new titles and then reorder from a wholesaler. It will be a while before most book representatives can offer the advice available from good wholesalers. After you have been in the software market for five or six months, you should be capable of selecting salable software. Publishers like Sybex, Prentice-Hall, Wiley, and Addison-Wesley have been marketing software for a while and have proven that publishers can and should sell software. They are working hard to convince bookstores to get on the bandwagon.

Software Competition

Besides a handful of bookstores, there are other outlets gloating over software sales. Computer store franchises (Computerland), deparment stores like K mart, and local independent computer stores are all aware of the potential. In fact, some have even started to stock computer books. These stores are merely dabbling; they haven't committed themselves to doing the thorough job bookstores can if they approach software as they have books. They sell these along with the computers. Department stores operate at the other end of the spectrum. They concentrate on low-end recreational software and a very limited educational selection. Mail-order houses that advertise in computer magazines are aggressive and offer 25–35 percent discounts from suggested retail prices. But again, the selection is limited. Moreover, a customer has to deal from long distance, pay freight, get no advice during the process of selection, and order a fairly hefty minimum amount. And when the software is defective or not up to par, it is complicated to correct the problem.

Bookstores can move comfortably into a secure position in the software market. We can position ourselves in the middle—between computer stores and discount suppliers. To do it we must offer a comprehensive selection, become somewhat knowledgeable, maintain a friendly returns policy, and advertise.

Be aware that software packaging can be deplorable. Some are impossible to display. Some software publishers do a terrible job explaining on the outside of the package what is actually in the package. Be prepared to break open the shrink wrap so interested customers can study the owner guides to determine if the software will do what they think it will do. A $300–$400 investment in a shrink-wrap machine will prove to be worthwhile. This is a service you can offer your customers that they won't get in most competitive stores.

Computers and the accompanying software are here to stay. Software offers bookstores a splendid opportunity. We have been chipping away at publishers, asking them to help us with better discounts, better returns policies, and cheaper freight charges so we can improve our bottom line. Many publishers are now coming forth with software that belongs in a bookstore and fits the bookstore image. Their software discounts and policies are fair, and the bottom line can only improve if bookstores respond. Time is running out for bookstores to be considered the place to go for software. Publishers are truly baffled by our faint response to their offerings. Perhaps this chapter will inspire you to jump into the software market and reap the rich harvest available. Software and books are indeed compatible. In fact, they live together in some books. Booksellers should open their doors and let software move in! There is money to be made in the software industry, and bookstores might as well be raking it in.

We have explored a vast territory in this chapter—computer books, computer software, and computer magazines. No doubt it is foreign territory for most booksellers. The potential is astounding. It could be the retail opportunity of the twentieth century. In software, particularly, there will be a shakeout of publishers, but booksellers need not worry—providing they don't put all their eggs in one basket. Soon computers will be as commonplace in homes as are televisions and refrigerators. Bookstores can become centers for computer information and software just as they are centers for printed-word information. We must act now to gain this image because computer stores and mass merchandisers are targeting this market. They are doing it in a piecemeal fashion, and few of them are approaching it with wide vision. For instance, mass merchandisers look for inexpensive bargains—often software that is being discontinued. Computer stores carry few books and only expensive software. Bookstores have cultivated an image these stores will never have—we have always offered personal service and customer satisfaction. We don't need to be computer experts in this market. Software publishers offer technical support for customer inquiries. Most have a direct telephone number for customers to call if they need help in operating a software program. Demonstrating software is not a necessity (if you are a computer jockey, by all means demonstrate), particularly if you stay away from high-priced packages.

Publishers are having a difficult time convincing bookstores to stock computer books and software, even though each offers 35–45 percent margins and a future diet of steady sales. If booksellers don't respond to publishers' overtures soon, those millions of computer users will have to go elsewhere for their needs. We have an opportunity now to build the image that portrays a bookstore as the place to go for computer books and software. For booksellers who get on the bandwagon, it promises to be an exciting and rewarding trip.

Chapter 34

Small Press and Self-Published Books in the Bookstore

ANDY ROSS

Small press titles are an essential component of a full-range bookstore. Many of these books are as profitable and as fast-moving as books by large commercial publishers. Their inclusion adds range and depth to a store that helps distinguish it from the homogeneous merchandising that increasingly characterizes the chains.

Small press titles are not necessarily obscure literary endeavors or slender volumes of verse. They include such subjects as metaphysics, women's studies, gay subjects, health, travel, and local or regional topics. These kinds of books have tremendous sales potential if ordered with each bookseller's unique clientele in mind.

Small press books such as *The People's Guide to Mexico* and *How to Keep Your Volkswagen Alive* have been backlist best-sellers for years. In our store, regional books like *Above San Francisco* and *How to Do Your Own Divorce in California* consistently outsell the so-called best-sellers on the national lists. The instances of national best-sellers originating with small presses are legion. Rita Mae Brown's *Rubyfruit Jungle*, Ernest Callenbach's *Ecotopia*, and *The Whole Earth Catalogue* all began as successful small press publications before they were picked up by major publishers. Do not stock these titles simply out of a sense of noblesse oblige. They are an intrinsic part of basic backlist, which is the bread and butter of our business.

Small presses present several buying and merchandising problems that must be surmounted in order for such titles to be profitable for booksellers. Since small publishers have limited resources, small press books are not likely to receive the same amount of promotional support as books from large commercial houses. Reviewers in the national media frequently ignore small press books. Consequently the audiences for these titles tend to be limited, and they often have to be sold mostly by word of mouth. It is especially critical with small press books that you, the bookseller, be aware of the diverse audience that makes up your clientele. You cannot rely on mass merchandising formulas, rather you must be sensitive to the unique and heterogeneous needs of your particular community. You must be willing to reach out and respond to these needs through imaginative display and salesmanship.

It's only fair to warn you that logistical problems in dealing with small presses can be something of a nightmare. Because the small publisher has only a limited number of titles, the bookseller has to deal with time-consuming inefficiencies of very small shipments and the burden of increased paperwork caused by a multitude of small invoices. The value of returns is problematic, since, as a practical matter, you may never get around to returning such a small quantity of books. Or if such a return is made, you will be issued a credit by a publisher from whom you may never order again. Since many small presses are one-man operations, the bookseller is also likely to encounter inconsistent and unprofessional billing and shipping systems causing additional delays and hassles.

Fortunately, there are ways of minimizing these problems, so that you can order a wide range of small press titles without massive paperwork and unprofitable returns. As much as possible, you should order small press titles from distributors who specialize in selling such books. Bookpeople in Berkeley, California, is the largest and oldest of these enterprises. It has since been joined by such companies as Bookslinger, in St. Paul, Minnesota; Inland Book Co., in East Haven, Connecticut; the distributors, in South Bend, Indiana; and other distributors who are more regional or specialized.

By dealing with distributors who stock numerous titles from myriad small presses, the bookseller can order these books as if they were from one large publisher and avoid the costly diseconomies of small orders, small shipments, small invoices, and small returns. Additionally, these distributing companies can provide expert marketing advice on selecting a range of titles that will be appropriate for a select clientele.

Cody's has for years relied on Bookpeople as the major source of our small press books. Bookpeople stocks over six thousand small press titles. They publish an annotated catalog by subject, which makes ordering simple. They combine all of the books into large shipments with computerized invoices and clear monthly statements. If we did not consolidate our orders through such a company, our receiving department would grind to a halt from processing so many small shipments, and our office would drown in a sea of invoices. By ordering as many small press titles as possible from a single distributor, we are able to treat these titles as if they belonged to one large publisher. The efficiency of scale gained from this consolidation allows these titles to become an extremely profitable part of our business.

There are some additional small press titles we choose to carry that cannot be purchased from distributors. Most of these are self-published books by local authors. Although these books rarely prove profitable to us, we feel we have a responsibility to nourish the literary life of our community by helping to display works that might otherwise have no retail outlet. Berkeley is a particularly fertile ground for self-published poets and novelists. Many of these books are printed unprofessionally, sometimes even without bindings. Their audience is limited or nonexistent, and the books are extremely difficult to display. Dealing with these writer-publishers can be exasperating. They are often inexperienced in business, and they have unreasonable expectations about the marketability of their books. These expectations often manifest themselves in outrageous behavior toward the bookseller.

I do not wish to recall all the times I have been accused of crass philistinism by irate poets who felt that Cody's did not give their masterpieces sufficient attention. My predecessor, Fred Cody, was once being interviewed over the radio; in a particularly expansive moment, he said that he would carry at least one copy of any small press book submitted to him. The store was subsequently overwhelmed with a tidal wave of paper (one hesitates to call the commodities books). Many of the publications were Xeroxed or even mimeographed and stapled together. After this experience, Cody's became considerably more selective in acquiring self-published titles.

Now our policy regarding self-published books is to scrutinize each title to determine if there is at least some intrinsic merit or potential interest to our clientele. If we choose to carry the books, we purchase them on consignment. We take the book for ninety days. At the end of this period, we pay for whatever books have been sold. The author is responsible for picking up unsold copies. Since we have had problems in the past with authors coming in after two years demanding payment for their books, we have our own consignment forms, which clearly state that we will not be responsible for books that have been left longer than ninety days. We clear out the titles regularly so that they don't fill up the shelves, and we dispose of them after a decent interval. We will not deal with consignments by mail, since it entails too much time and labor for us. By creating these standards, we are able to save a tremendous number of hassles with the self-published writer. In addition we cut our expenses to a minimum in dealing with these kinds of books.

I do not wish to discourage booksellers from carrying self-published books. Although many of them are only marginally salable, we have had notable successes as well. And in spite of the difficulty in dealing with some authors, we have built up tremendous goodwill as a store that is committed not just to making money, but to fostering the cultural environment of the community. This kind of intangible goodwill has paid off in dividends to us many times over.

During the last ten years, the chains have become the dominant force in bookselling in America. They have done so by heavy emphasis on best-sellers and highly commercial titles at the expense of backlist and small press selections. The result is that retail bookstores are becoming increasingly uniform by appealing to the lowest common denominator of the public's taste. It is very difficult for the independent bookseller to compete for this segment of the book market. We must take a different route, emphasizing a diverse selection of backlist and small press titles. Experience indicates that the book-buying public is sophisticated and understands the importance of a store that is responsive to the values of the community it serves. Careful attention to stocking small press books is an essential part of a strategy that will give the independent bookseller distinction, depth, and a stature that would otherwise be lacking.

Chapter 35

Foreign Books for the American Bookseller

KAY VAIL-HAYDEN

Most American booksellers view selling foreign books as indicative of galloping lunacy and an open invitation to disaster. This attitude, while regrettable, is easy to understand. It is difficult enough for a bookseller to wade through the output of American publishers without compounding problems by adding still more publishers and titles from other countries in languages that may be recognized but are not understood. But wait! There are those who can not only identify these mysterious writings, but actually revel in every curly letter or umlaut. The foreign books audience is out there, and the enterprising bookseller will find it worthwhile to address it.

If it is important for a buyer to know the market when ordering regular books, it is twice as vital when stocking foreign ones. There is much to consider—which titles, which languages, which editions—and tremendous nightmare potential if it is not done correctly. Imagine the distress, for example, if after loading up on Japanese haiku you discover the ethnic community you were aiming at turns out to be Norwegian. Of course, there may be Japanese-speaking Scandinavians, but you might want to hedge your bets for them with some Ibsen in the original. Know your customer base, your potential customers, before you place your orders.

If your store is happily situated in an area where there are first- and second-generation immigrant Americans speaking the language of their country of origin or nationality, a number of things bear checking. Do the members of this community in fact want to read in their native language? Older persons may be satisfied with periodicals, so carrying these is worth thinking about. Younger readers frequently have only a speaking knowledge of their parents' native language; their reading is limited to English. Still, in any ethnic community there are some book readers, and once word gets around that you stock or order foreign books, you will be surprised at how many customers turn up. Get to know them. Initially the shock of spotting non-English books in your store may render these people temporarily unable to communicate. However, as a rule, when calmness returns, so does their English. These people are valuable sources for titles, authors, and word-of-mouth advertising.

If you are in an area with varied ethnic communities, get in touch with the different social organizations and churches and ask for suggestions. As well as information, you may get instant customers since these groups frequently offer courses, lectures, or study sessions on particular aspects of their native culture. We once sold a staggering number of Greek Old Testaments to a group industriously working their way through a church-sponsored seminar in ancient Greek.

Another market for foreign-language books is composed of those whose native language is not that of the book they are buying. These are English speakers who have learned a foreign language at school or while traveling. They may be trying to improve or retain their knowledge of that language, or they may be students wishing to read more works by an author than is required for a class. Still others may be interested in reading the original of a book enjoyed in translation. For all these buyers, perusal of a college reading list can suggest appropriate stock, as can faculty members in foreign-language departments. (If yours is a college bookstore or one located near a university, a periodic foreign-language book sale, adequately advertised, will receive astonishing support.) Visitors from abroad are also potential customers. As recent arrivals, they are in closer touch with the home country than the aforementioned readers and may not only be more interested in books in their native language, but may also offer excellent suggestions for contemporary titles to consider stocking.

Finally, do not forget the children, or rather, parents who want their offspring to be acquainted with another cultural and ethnic background and see foreign-language books as a positive way to begin. The English-speaking parent who seeks to expose his child to a second language as early as possible is a likely candidate for the attractive and colorful children's foreign books, as is the parent who has perhaps been stationed overseas and wants his bilingual or trilingual child to develop skills.

Once your market has been defined, you must next decide what to stock and where to get it. To a degree, the former will determine the latter, but consider this basic guideline: Foreign authors who constitute your backstock in English translations are the writers who will sell in the original. You know many of them—Camus, Gide, Cervantes, Garcia Marquez, Tolstoy.... Two points: First, literary works—classics—are the most reliable sellers, though there are, of course, exceptions. (You may find it difficult to keep Simenon mysteries in stock, for example.) The most important literary works written in the Romance, Scandinavian, and German languages are available in comparatively inexpensive paperback editions. Second, avoid hardbacks, especially gift editions and art books, because their prices are usually very high. Requests for gift ideas may be best answered by suggesting bound collections of classics, which are less expensive.

As you develop your list of titles, you wonder where in the world you will get them. You have two choices—to order directly from publishers or wholesalers overseas or to use an importer based in the United States. There are advantages and disadvantages to both. In going direct you are working with many different sources as opposed to only one or two importers, and you are faced with a variety of currencies, depending on how the billing is done. Shipments from overseas can take three months or longer, and you may not have returns privileges. You will, however, have the advantage of lower prices, vast selection, and the promise of some truly inspired correspondence in fractured versions of each other's languages. (Conversely, you may also endure long periods of silence, which allows you to brood over what has caused the problem this time— your incorrect order, the mail, revolution?) It is worth requesting, and possibly even receiving, overseas catalogs. If you can't read them, your potential customers can. Sources for names and addresses of foreign publishers and wholesalers include the *International Literary Market Place*, the *ABA Book Buyer's Handbook*, and a recently updated list available from the National Association of College Stores in Oberlin, Ohio. If you attend the ABA or NACS conventions, you will find foreign publisher representatives and exhibits that will provide you with invaluable opportunities to discuss your problems or possible success with the people directly involved on the other end. In addition, you should make every effort to seek out other booksellers involved in the foreign book wars to exchange ideas.

If you decide to use importers, consult the same lists mentioned above. Also, even if yours is not a college bookstore, communicate with a textbook buyer at a nearby university that offers foreign-language courses. This person is under constant pressure to get books in time for classes and therefore can give experienced advice on those sources that are most reliable. Importers may specialize in only one or two languages or in several. Although they offer discounts between 20 percent and 40 percent, their suggested retail prices are considerably higher than those in the country where the books were published. There are no list retail prices for imported books. You should price them as fairly as possible, given your costs in obtaining them. Sometimes books arrive prepriced in the currency of the country, as do our mass-market paperbacks. It goes without saying that some customer fortuitously armed with the latest *New York Times* containing today's exchange rate will grab the book and demand that you explain your pricing. Spare yourself this grief and sticker over the original and no longer pertinent foreign prices.

Finally, in dealing with an importer, realistically expect delivery of regular stock items in somewhere between three and five weeks. Many of the importer's other customers will also want standard titles and will always be out of some you have ordered. He will either cancel or offer to import the books he does not carry on a regular basis. Consider this option carefully. Find out his expected due date if you choose to import, as you may find it to your benefit to order directly rather than wait the extra time. Also, though importers usually have a returns privilege not unlike those of most American publishers, it may not apply to books specially imported for you.

To be perfectly honest, trying to get foreign books once you have committed yourself to them can drive you crazy no matter where you order. If you go direct, it seems like families are born and raised before any books show up, and when they finally do the shipment is accompanied by fragile bits of paper with incomprehensible notations billing you in who-knows-what currency. Sometimes all that arrives is the fragile bit of paper, and instead of obscure numbers it is covered with anguished apologies housed in fantastic, baroque sentence structures. Do not torture yourself; recognize that you cannot decipher these messages, so just relax and enjoy all the people you will meet trying to get these "invoices" translated.

On the other hand, if you use an importer, everything becomes much more predictable. The invoice will be in English, which will help you very little as you note the prices are undoubtedly higher than the last time you ordered. Part of your order will be out of stock (the part you really wanted) but importable in ten or twelve weeks, maybe, and the two special orders you took will turn out to be titles no one can identify. Finding an importer from whom you can accept all this without becoming suicidal, knowing he has done his best for you, is pretty much a trial-and-error undertaking. Be persistent. Your special partner in this endeavor does exist, and once you have succeeded in locating this paragon, cling tenaciously.

Many booksellers might wonder how important it is to have a knowledge of any foreign language to be able to run a foreign book department. Obviously, it can make things easier, but it is not essential. You may not *want* to know what those fragile bits of paper say. Your regular customers can help you out in many ways as you get to know them, and they enjoy becoming a part of your effort to please them. Far more important than language knowledge are patience, enthusiasm, and above all, a sense of humor. You have never seen packing material until you unwrap a box from Mexico!

Chapter 36

Trade Books on Campus

BETTY E. MUNGER

The trade book department of a college store offers its manager an opportunity for both financial success and a lively role in the academic process. Students turn to the trade department for exploration, delight, and recreation. The books in the trade department are not required so are viewed with much greater enthusiasm than those in the "rear" department. Trade books enhance and expand the importance of any college store.

Fewer than half the enrolled students will continue their formal education beyond college. After graduation their only approach to intellectual pursuit is through libraries and bookstores. In their adult life, unless they are seeking a particular book, they are more apt to enter bookstores than libraries. Managers of their college bookstores can create an enthusiasm for future browsing and buying and can hook young people on books for life.

The college bookstore frequently serves the whole community. Obviously the personal book needs of the faculty can best be filled through their immediate store on campus. Less obvious is the fact that townspeople come to the college or university store in search of special books not found elsewhere. Good service and attention will bring them back. The college bookstore trade department can and should be the intellectual crossroads of the college. What angle of vision should its managers maintain? Of paramount importance are an enthusiasm for a knowledge of books. The best pusher is an addict! The manager must also be able to master systems. Paperwork (whether we do it ourselves or have competent aides) should be as simple as possible within the limits set by college administrators. Purchases and returns, inventory control, special-order fulfillment, and budget management can be time-consuming, even chaotic. As in all bookstores, tight organization in the office permits the manager to be out in the store among the customers and the books.

Book Selection

Our clientele is comparatively uniform and, while seemingly constant, changes completely every four years with each succeeding generation of students. Our inventory should reflect both the constancy and the changes. It has to include a large number of backlist titles, old but golden, mostly in paperback. Academic communities are one of the largest markets for paperbacks. Although we may carry some lovely best-selling trash on our shelves, we must never let our store become an airport booknook or a supermarket stand. We are dealing with diversity in ideas in a high quality of language, so we watch for the unusual books, including those from small presses and local publications. The faculty expects attention and honor for all their publications. Scholarly books for use as supplemental reading and material for term papers should be stocked. We also offer variety—cookbooks, quality children's books, art books, books on travel and many other interests. As the fall season moves along, the store should begin to bulge with books for Christmas giving— there are no better gifts than books. Remainders and reprints are well worth a section in the college trade department. An occasional special promotion of those bargains is good merchandising, but a permanent display of remainder books, chosen with a careful eye to our particular market, is a constant source of speedy business. Particular mention should be made of one section of the college bookstore—the reference section, which ought to be well stocked with a multitude of dictionaries, style manuals, guides for scoring high on board examinations, and many other essential tools for education.

The silicon revolution has brought an exciting and expansive dimension to the college bookstore. Computer courses are multiplying like rabbits, and an increasing number of students are bringing personal computers to college. Books for and about computers have become a most essential ingredient in the store's mix. We must keep up with the deluge of books now being published while staying acutely alert to our own store's particular demands and needs. In such a rapidly changing field, this is far from easy. But it is increasingly evident that an ever-larger percentage of our sales and requests will be computer-related. There is no doubt that this area will be the fastest-growing section of our store, no matter what size or kind of school we serve.

Granted that such a program of book selection requires casting at least a quick glance at every piece of promotional material that appears on our desk with the morning mail, we must always be looking for books that will expand the horizons of the many people who pass through our store. We must listen for the changing interests and enthusiasms of the college population and be ready to meet them wisely.

Selling and Promotion

Although we practice the good bookselling procedures common to all well-managed bookstores, there are responsibilities that are unique to us. Good planning is essential, for in addition to observing the usual calendar events, such as Christmas and Valentine's Day, there is the college calendar to be noted and acted upon. Alumni weekends, parents' weekends, and many other special occasions offer us the opportunity for displays and lively promotions.

Many speakers who appear on campus have written books. By developing a close rapport with the student and faculty speaker committees, we can have their books on display before the lecturer arrives. When there is available time, an in-store coffee and conversation session pleases both the visiting author, who happily autographs books, and students, who get a chance to meet the famous person. If there is a writer in residence for an extended period, the bookstore might present readings of his work in progress with a discussion afterward.

The overall ambiance of a college trade department should be not only welcoming but intriguing. Students must want to stop often to see what is happening in the department. Promotion in widows, on display tables, and near the checkout counters must be eye-catching and foot-stopping. It should be witty and informative, but never tacky. This does not mean that a large chunk of budget has to go toward display. Signs that are bright and neat will do the trick. For instance, a simple sign saying "In Their Own Write" on a table of faculty publications is sure to attract browsers and buyers. There is time for a "Bare Bones" sale at Halloween with some cardboard skeletons dangling from the lighting fixtures. Keep a list of your displays because four years from now you can use them all again!

What about a regular column of thoughts and book notes in the student newspaper? Or a campus newsletter titled *Words from the Bookstore?* Many college stores are not allowed to advertise beyond the campus limits, but the student radio station might welcome a regular book chat program. Ideas come from all sorts of events and people. The National Association of College Stores, for instance, keeps a continuous stream of promotional ideas coming our way. Membership in the NACS and the American Booksellers Association is invaluable not only for helpful hints, but for professional guidance in all phases of bookstore management.

Unlike many independently owned bookstores, college stores have general managers, business officers, and administrators to whom we are responsible. Open communication is essential for successful cooperation because others set the overall policy and parameters of our operation. Areas of responsibility must be clearly defined and understood. Mutual respect and trust should be developed through regular discussions of budgeting, major problems, and plans. Moments of crisis are no time to establish a smooth working relationship.

Managing a trade book department in a college store requires efficient organization, awareness of books coming off the publishers' presses, and an internal radar that is finely tuned toward all phases of campus life. It is no sinecure. On the other hand, there is laughter, nonsense, and warmth. Life in a college bookstore is never dull.

Chapter 37

Used Books for Fun and Profit

MICHAEL POWELL

Most booksellers have similar goals for their businesses. All want to make a reasonable income and be proud of their stores. If you are in the book trade for the glitz, what follows is probably not for you. Only the avaricious and adventurous should proceed.

The reasons why there is so little profit in what we do are depressingly well known. Discounts and discounters head the list. Paperwork, returns, freight, special services, and bad judgment calls all run up the tab. The pressure to stock best-sellers, count turns, and look like B. Dalton is enormous. The oft-repeated advice is to give the customer more service. More service! Any more service and we would be reading the books for them.

So what to do? More cards, maps, bric-a-brac? That was not what you had in mind when you dreamed of being a book person. It is not that these lack profit or charm, but ultimately they are irrelevant to your mission, to find and sell books.

There is someone in your community who has known an answer to this dilemma for quite some time, your not-so-friendly neighborhood used-book dealer. You know the place. It's dirty, actually dusty. It's disorganized, with stacks of books, boxes of books, piles of books to the ceiling. The place reeks of disdain for everything that smacks of business. Scheduling is based on the "if the door's open, then we're open" policy. I've seen used-book store owners eject customers because they didn't like the tone of a question. Independent, you bet. Mad, almost certainly, but clever mad.

Look closer. A couple of important lessons can be noted. Our used-book man is having a lot of fun. And as important (at least for this article), he* is probably making more money than you are.

*It is a curious fact that almost all general used-book stores are owned by men.

That claim may require a little proof. Make a list of the longest continuously operating bookstores in your area. I'll bet the majority of stores on your list will be used-book stores. It's four out of five in my city. Of course it helps that used-book men seem to live forever, in itself not a bad fringe benefit.

So there they are, abusing yet rewarding their customers, leading disorderly (only sometimes drunken) lives, loving their books and their ubiquitous cats. Think what they have to do without— paying freight, checking invoices, special ordering, inventory systems, returns, employees to do the above, buying unproven titles, paying 59 percent of list. What our used-book seller has going for him is equally interesting. He selects his books from a title list that goes back to Gutenberg. He offers bargains to his customers ("1987 Books at 1957 Prices"). He provides the public with a place to sell unwanted volumes, something for which they are very grateful. People hate to throw away books. It is important to them that the books be recycled. A new home for their books is often more important than the amount of money involved. And our bookman has a profit margin of at least three times his investment.

The point can be illustrated by the purchase and sale of a book that was priced at $10 new. Typically it would be bought used for $2 (20 percent of original list) and sold for $6, three times the original investment, for a $4 gross profit. In comparison a new book sold at $6.00 would make $2.45 before all related overhead, such as freight-in handling costs. If the same book, new and used, is available in your bookstore, the new at $10 and the used at $6, the same gross profit of $4 would be made on each, but the investment in and costs of selling the new are greater. A customer will frequently buy the used copy and thank you for the bargain. Everyone profits.

Why ignore a whole world of wonderful books—most of them "out of print"—with their wonderful profits and happy buyers? If you have an image problem—the lack of glamour in the concept "used books," consider a 1937 Rolls-Royce. Would you think of it as a "used car"? Age enhances more things than wine. Once you're over this hurdle, how do you proceed?

Stocking

Shelve your used books where they belong, fully integrated into your stock. Don't put them in a wheelbarrow, on a table, or anywhere cute. They have earned their place in history, they will be all right on your shelves. Reflect on where paperbacks were ten years ago. Now is your chance to be a pioneer. And it won't hurt a bit.

Where do you find these great books? Lots of places. The very best source is your own store. Emphasize whatever subject areas you are concentrating on already. Post notices and distribute flyers announcing your new service. Something on the order of "Cash for good used books" or "Wanted! Unwanted books. Top value paid." Do not mention a specific price. Use your mailing list. Most important, place a good-sized ad in the Yellow Pages. Make use of all your promotional skills, and remember, your customers provide free freight.

Then there are thrift shops, library sales, house sales, and charity sales. The latter are not for the faint of heart. Move quickly, make stacks, find out why you have elbows. There is plenty of time after you have creamed the offerings to have second thoughts and return mistakes to the tables. Don't be disappointed by what you accomplish compared with the more experienced used-book dealers and books scouts. It's an acquired skill.

When you know what you want, visit other used-book stores. Offer to trade them titles. On a cash basis expect a 10–20 percent discount. Travel around and have some fun scouting. Remember, business trips are tax-deductible. It is remarkable how so many of the places you have always wanted to visit turn out to be just the spot to look for books.

How to Buy

Carefully. Buy to your strengths. Start with whichever categories you are most comfortable with in new books. Buy with the same critical standards you would apply to an offering by a rep. Don't buy (or at least keep) large mixed lots. Be selective!

It's been my experience that the following categories are the safest: cookbooks, children's books, classics, good literature, science fiction (paper), mysteries (paper), westerns (paper), regional titles, military, arts and crafts, automobile, hunting and fishing, history (pre-nineteenth century), occult, theology, technical, gardening, music books. Titles in these categories do not become dated. An early edition of the *Settlement Cook Book* is always in greater demand than a new edition. Also, the more specific the title, the better; a repair manual on a 1950 Ford pickup is worth more than a general manual on 1950 autos.

Buy paperbacks. Good paperbacks will be hard to keep in stock.

There are some areas of particular danger. These include hardback literature, travel guides, popular biography, religion, best-sellers, bookclub books, last year's fads, sets, encyclopedias, any damaged books, old books, collectibles, current events, Americana (outside a local area), ex-library books, anthologies. These titles tend to date or are too common to be desirable. The only encyclopedias that have proved durable are the eleventh to thirteenth editions of the *Encyclopaedia Britannica* ($200–$1,000 retail) and the post-1972 *E.B.* ($200–$600). Recent (post-1970) *World Book* and *Americana* sets also have an audience. Most sets are valuable only for decoration. The very famous names of literature—Dickens, Lamb, Shakespeare—can be sold, but only in attractive and well-printed editions.

Trust your instincts. If you have hesitated, there's probably a reason. You do not owe it to anyone to buy or keep a book you don't want. You will hear every story. Just say politely, "I'm sorry, we already have too many of these titles." Keep a list of alternative places they can be taken, such as nursing homes, libraries, and the like.

Do not keep free books; you can drown in them. Do not trade books with customers. Trading is the quickest way to prove bad goods will drive out good. You can offer customer/sellers some small improvement over cash by giving credit against future purchases. Offer a credit slip; a lot of them will never come back.

What to Pay—What Price?

This can be the tricky part. Generally books should be bought at 20 percent list. This applies equally to paperbacks and cloth. Naturally this will vary depending on local circumstances. Don't be too eager. Most people have already decided to sell the books before you offer anything. A few will not be satisfied, but only a very few.

Make your offer as a statement, not a question. Do not bargain, you are not running a flea market. You are providing a needed and valuable service. Quietly separate good titles from bad and make a bulk offer. Do not offer unnecessary explanations; after all, you are now the arbiter of Western civilization!

You are not yet a rare-book dealer. It is better to buy one hundred books for $1 each than one book for $100. Rare books are just that, and they require skills and customers that you do not yet have. Do keep a few price guides and bibliographies handy. Those stories of great discoveries do happen.

Pricing your purchases demands patience and forbearance. The greatest danger is to overvalue your finds. You know what is a reasonable profit, and your customers know a reasonable price.

Use *Books in Print* to determine current value. Price at about 60 percent of list. Demand, scarcity, and condition are the variables to be considered. Out-of-print titles present the greatest challenge. Consider what it would cost if it were in print and apply the same criteria. In the long run, your average o.p. price should be in the $7–$9 range. Similar practices apply to paperbacks. In all cases, be certain to remove older prices. Use a black felt pen on paperbacks to cover up original prices, but do not do this to any of your collectibles.

Remainders can now become an important element in your strategy. Those interesting white-sale titles can go into inventory, augmenting your new and used selections. I like labeling them "New Special." They can be bought in small quantities and can often fill in for a much more expensive lookalike.

Customers will love having the chance to find a bargain, and if the bargain is not to be had, they will often buy the higher-priced option. You are now in their eyes different from all other bookstores. Your selection is more current than a used-book store, but broader and more interesting than your new-book rivals. You are unique and uniquely profitable.

A note about the fun of the hunt. There are pleasures here for the most jaded bookseller. You might find a nice title for a quarter or, while going through a box of *Reader's Digest* books, find a county history. That house call could reveal a wonderful library. Then there is the satisfaction of rescuing an important volume from oblivion and putting it back in the cultural mainstream. Few of us will die rich, but I wouldn't trade places with anyone.

Chapter 38

Antiquarian Bookselling in America

JACOB L. CHERNOFSKY

For those of us whose memories reach back to the years before the Second World War, when used-book shops cluttered New York's Fourth Avenue and there was a "Bookseller's Row" in each large city, feelings of nostalgia for a world that is no more are rather common. The changes that came about in urban centers as well as in smaller towns in the postwar years certainly included the disappearance of a way of life for many who enjoyed spending their free time browsing among dusty shelves.

American social habits have changed for a variety of reasons, and bookstores in general do not play the same role they did half a century ago. In spite of these changes, readers can still find ample opportunities to browse among books, but they will have to look a little harder to find a used-book shop.

Actually, the antiquarian book trade is alive and well, but it has undergone changes even more drastic than the new-book business. There are today as many booksellers as there were earlier in the century who deal in rare, used, or out-of-print books, but most of them do not have walk-in shops. Mail-order dealers have, in fact, increased the volume of business above and beyond the loss of trade due to the declining number of used-book stores. In addition to the increase in mail-order business, many other changes have affected the antiquarian book trade in the last half century.

From a historical perspective, changes have not been uncommon in any form of the book trade. For centuries after the development of printing with movable type, the roles of printers, publishers, and booksellers overlapped. Printer and publisher evolved into bookseller when he traded items on his "list" for items of other printers or publishers. The beginnings of antiquarian bookselling as a distinct specialty are obscure.

Even before the advent of printing, the dealer in manuscripts distributed the products of scriptoria as well as previously owned handwritten books, which were necessarily quite valuable. Even after Gutenberg's invention made books more accessible to a greater number of people, used books were still more reasonably priced, and it became evident to the bookseller quite early on that there was more profit to be had in the antiquarian trade.

In actual practice, booksellers had long been dealing in both new books and antiquarian or used books. Although there were a few booksellers in the nineteenth century who specialized in old books, it was not until this century that the specialty of antiquarian bookselling was widely accepted.

Against this background, the antiquarian book trade in the United States today has developed a distinct structure in response to the varying needs of its customers. Who are the customers they serve, and why do they want the books?

There are, of course, those who simply want reading copies of the books. They go to the antiquarian dealer or to the out-of-print market either because the books are o.p. and there are no reprints or because they want cheaper copies. In addition to individuals, customers for antiquarian books may include libraries that need them for replacement of new titles or place orders for titles they don't have.

Also figuring prominently among the customers of antiquarian booksellers are other dealers. It is in the nature of the antiquarian book trade that dealers buy extensively from each other since each may have a clientele of its own.

The other major category of customer is the collector. The collector's need for a book may start with a reading interest—and I would like to believe that most collectors either read or intend to read the books they buy—but primarily, collectors buy books for the possession of the physical object. This is an entirely different kind of customer from the one who wants a reading copy. The latter might be satisfied with a photocopy of a book; the collector will not.

Before listing the various types of dealers that make up the structure of the antiquarian book trade, it might be helpful to note that they may usually be described as either general or specialist booksellers. The general dealer will usually serve more customers seeking reading copies than collectors. Such customers, however, may sometimes find it more practical to go to the specialist dealer if the book sought is clearly in a definite subject specialty, but the general dealer can search for books in any specialty as well.

The specialist antiquarian dealer limits his stock and transactions to one or more subject specialties that he gets to know rather intimately. A good proportion of his customers will usually be collectors because most collectors specialize in particular fields. Many serious collectors, in the course of time, acquire reputations of being knowledgeable in their fields—so knowledgeable, in fact, that they may know more about their specialty than most dealers. Wise dealers learn to respect the expertise of their collecting customers.

At this point it might be helpful to define my own use of the word "antiquarian" as applied to books. Antiquarian books are either old, rare, used, or out of print. My own extended definition also covers fine press or limited-edition books that may be new and in print. All these are the stock in trade of antiquarian dealers.

Whether generalist or specialist, the antiquarian bookseller may be further described according to the way he does business; in all cases there is considerable overlap among the various categories.

At one end of the spectrum is the *rare-book dealer*. His product will usually be more expensive than those of booksellers in other categories. He may deal in his shop, at his home, by mail, or by catalog. Shops are generally open to the public during specified business hours or by appointment at other times. Dealers working in their homes usually see customers only by appointment. The shop, of course, need not necessarily be a traditional store; many rare-book dealers conduct their business in offices.

While rare-book dealers usually do business by means of face-to-face meetings with customers who can examine the books, quite a few limit their business to mail-order or catalog transactions. In such cases, the customer usually has the right to return the book within a reasonable period of time.

The main characteristic of the rare-book dealer (without going into concepts of rarity as a factor in price) is his stock of expensive books. A customer can usually walk into the shop of H. P. Kraus in New York City and walk out with a single purchase amounting to a quarter of a million dollars or more.

When the bookseller's stock includes a high proportion of less expensive and not particularly rare books, he is simply described as an *antiquarian dealer*. (Less expensive books can carry price tags from $20 to $100.) Unlike rare-book dealers, antiquarian dealers might also include some new books in their stock, particularly if they are specialist dealers. The antiquarian dealer may also do business in a shop, from his home, by mail, or by catalog.

The next category is the *used-book dealer*. He has the traditional type of shop (or loft or barn) where the customer can browse among dusty (or clean) shelves. The books are generally inexpensive. While the rare-book dealer and the antiquarian dealer will serve mostly collectors as customers, the customers in a used-book shop will include a high proportion of those interested simply in reading copies.

In another category belong the *mail-order* or *out-of-print* dealer and the *search service*. They all deal by mail, selling to both collectors and reading-copy customers (mostly the latter). Many of the newer or younger dealers in this category have gone into this business either part-time or full-time from jobs in academic life or the professions.

One member of the antiquarian book trade who is not as well known as the dealers in the previous categories is the *book scout*. At one time known as "runners" in England, the book scout usually does not stock books for an extensive period of time, and he usually transacts his business entirely within the trade, buying from one dealer or thrift shop and selling to another dealer. He usually knows what his dealer customers need and searches for suitable items wherever he can find them. In effect, he performs the leg work for which a dealer has little time.

A variation of the scout is the *quoter*, who looks for books wanted by dealers, generally builds a stock of items he anticipates dealers will want, and quotes books to dealers by mail in response to their specific or general wants. These quoters make an efficient search service possible.

Those in the last three categories mentioned require little capital to get started in business and operate on a very low overhead; their number has increased substantially in the past few years.

The last category of actual bookseller is the *new-book dealer*, who conducts a search service for his customers and, in a few but growing number of cases, actually stocks some used books. This category has also increased in number in recent years—particularly at a time of declining retail profit and problems with publishers. Many new-book dealers, however, will provide o.p. search services largely for customer goodwill rather than profit.

Although not strictly classified as a bookseller, there is one further category in the antiquarian book trade—the *auction house*. Book auction houses accept consignments of books—usually the more expensive items, although groups of cheaper books may be "lotted"—and conduct sales regularly or periodically. Among the consignors may be private individuals, estates, or antiquarian dealers. Auction houses have increased in number on both sides of the Atlantic in recent years, a development over which many dealers have not been ecstatic, contending that it deprives them of business.

There is one national trade association for antiquarian book dealers—the Antiquarian Booksellers Association of America, Inc. The association attempts to set standards for the trade, deals with such tradewide problems as theft, and conducts book fairs. A directory of the ABAA membership that lists dealers' names, addresses, telephone numbers, specialties, and so on may be obtained by writing to the association at 50 Rockefeller Plaza, New York, NY 10020.

With the substantial increase in business by mail in many of the dealer categories during the past few years, there has developed in the antiquarian book trade a need for some sort of forum that would provide opportunity for face-to-face meeting between bookseller and customer. That need has largely been filled by the enormous growth and popularity of antiquarian book fairs.

Ten years ago there were two or three large book fairs a year sponsored by the ABAA in major cities and a few institution-sponsored dealer fairs. Today, there are half a dozen large international fairs sponsored by the association each year, along with fifty or sixty smaller events.

Although the mournful refrain by booksellers that "all the good books have disappeared" has been heard down through the ages, the antiquarian book trade has managed to survive and prosper in a variety of forms; its prospects for the future seem bright indeed.

Chapter 39

Discount Bookselling

ELIOT LEONARD

The only big surprise about the explosion of the sale of books at deep and varying discounts is that it did not happen sooner. There has always been some form of price cutting of trade books by individual booksellers, by variety and discount merchants, and occasionally by department stores and others. But now, with the burgeoning of discount stores and promotional advertising, more and more smaller "list price" booksellers are being affected. Some claim to be losing "many" sales, others say a "few," and a couple say they have not lost any customers to this new generation of stores. Other booksellers expect the roof to cave in and believe they will be forced out of business.

There is no doubt that the growth of the number of discount stores and the spread of the discount image created in customers' eyes is serious and cannot be ignored. A few trade bookstores in discount areas have recently closed, but it is not known if the new competition was the major factor or if it was the final straw, added to other fiscal and operational difficulties. Therefore we do not yet know if discounting is as serious a threat to the conventional general bookstore as the wringing of hands implies. A definite answer is not yet in.

But one element is evident—fear. Many booksellers are now becoming very conservative in their merchandising actions and are operating on fear rather than paying attention to the details of keeping their bookstores healthy. But sitting back and believing that the end is near is not productive.

The important question these booksellers should ask themselves is how to adjust their philosophy, procedures, and methods to offset the attraction of sale pricing in other stores. Low-price merchandising prevails in almost all categories of goods sold in stores, and "loyal" customers shop all kinds of retailers. Everyone loves a bargain, and since the demise of fair trade, almost all "discounting" is legal. It is not going to go away, and other booksellers must learn to live with it. If affirmative actions replace negative thinking, the majority of booksellers will survive the discount trend.

A few facts have emerged in the latest cycle of discounting:

1. The potential loss of customer traffic and volume is directly related to the distance between competing stores.
2. The potential loss is also directly related to the amount of continual advertising and promotion of price comparisons and, to a lesser degree, to the percentage of cut-price titles in stock versus total titles stocked.
3. Full-list-price bookstores retrieve some of the lost traffic after the newness and novelty of the discount store fades.

A bookstore in the same market area with a discounter has some options open to try and retain customer traffic. No one action will overcome the competition fully, but there are a number of sound retail measures that should alleviate the situation. The following ideas might be useful.

1. Try to convey as much bargain and discount image as you can, while keeping to your basic merchandising philosophy. Display and highlight savings continually; promote your remainders, reprints, and specials with flat display, window display, good signs, an exciting banner, price comparisons, and any other means to catch the attention of potential customers. Let them know that you have bargains, too.

   If you stock just a few bargain titles now, you should consider expanding this section or department and keep trying to change the face of it with new items. Remember that 50–75 percent of the stock of most discount stores is made up of these kinds of books. Use the help of the bargain book companies. The trade discounts are good, with returns privileges in most cases and even allowance for a bit of co-op money for advertising. You, too, can promote the cut-price image.
2. The greatest factor attracting customers to some bookstores rather than to others in the region is "availability"—having the best selection around. You must not retreat to the trenches and become more conservative when competition arrives. You should

take the offensive and merchandise even better than before. Add to your inventory the ones and twos that build your categories with the extra basic backstock and extraordinary titles, the kind that attract the real book readers and buyers. The broad selection encourages browsing, which creates impulse sales. Many discount operators do not have that kind of selection because cutting the prices of slower movers is not profitable. Your customers who might buy from the discounter will wander back to your store if you offer them "availability."

3. Sell your services—this is where the smaller bookstore can really shine. Personal customer help can build store loyalty. Many people want more than self-service, and the personal bookshop is in the position to offer it. Management on the scene can provide complete, quick, accommodating answers to customers' inquiries. Two of the best services that book customers look for are the taking and filling of special orders quickly and a reasonable return and exchange policy. Stores offering these benefits do gain customers. Courteous, efficient telephone service, gift wrapping and mailing of packages, check cashing, charge/credit card privileges, and so on all help offset the possible savings in another store. One store just put a sign-in book on a stand where customers can enter their name, address, and two mail subject interests—they will then receive a note about new arrivals in those subjects. How many of these services does your competition offer?

4. Check the discounter's weak points and try to capitalize on them. You might have to adjust your philosophy and ways of doing business or even your mix of merchandise. Are there sidelines— magazines, calendars, or adult games—that could help retain customer traffic? Can you offer better "open-for-business" hours or a local delivery service? Can you find out-of-print books? What about building one of your sections into a specialty such as the best juvenile or technical book department around? Because the discounter's main emphasis is on new hardbound titles, it might be best to expand the paperback inventory while reducing the hardbound selection gradually. This has been and will be the direction that the trade is going anyway, and it is not unreasonable for the average smaller bookstore to have 80 percent or more of its inventory in paperbacks. There is less discount appeal and smaller price savings in these items.

5. Try to improve the display and merchandising of all books in the store. Highlight your best titles in each category in flat display, impulse spots, even on shelves. Feature radio, TV, and movie tie-

ins. One of the best traffic builders is a good, large selection of regional books that includes local authors, books about the area (especially picture books), and those on the history of the city, state, and region. Small autographing parties a few times a year build a little volume, but more important, they publicize the store. Create signs that attract people and encourage them to examine a display. In-store book fairs are sometimes good traffic builders. Many of these kinds of actions are not done by the competition and could encourage visits to your store.

6. Many customers who go into general bookstores question the prices and compare them with discount books they have seen advertised. How do you answer them? You should take this opportunity to give immediate, honest answers. Explain why you cannot cut prices on a few best-sellers or on all titles:

   a. Tell them about the extra services you provide.
   b. Tell them about the extra help you employ to provide service.
   c. Tell them about the extra inventory and titles you stock.
   d. Tell them about the usual mix of discount store inventory and the reprints and remainders that you also have or could obtain.
   e. Tell them about your backstock of basic books and former best-sellers, slower-moving classical titles, and new books by new authors that they cannot find at the competition.
   f. Tell them (if they live nearby) about the automobile expenses they save by shopping at your conveniently located store.

I do not recommend discounting all your books, even at just 10–20 percent off. You will be giving up all your store's current profit. Most booksellers do not have the resources to sustain losses incurred by price cutting while figuring out how to achieve a profitable mix of bargain merchandise discounts and regular discounts.

Nor do I recommend selling the twenty, thirty, or forty best-sellers at 30 percent or 40 percent off continuously. Selling books at very large discounts as loss leaders is usually successful only if sales on the regularly priced inventory are increased substantially.

For example, let's take a look at a store with a gross margin of 35 percent and follow it through different pricing policies. Management must decide which policy to follow, perhaps by testing whether or not sales are lost to the discounter. Will more gross dollars be saved by a combination of C and D, or by B, or by E?

A. Selling $1,000 of best-sellers at full price................ $1,000

   Gross margin dollars at 35% 350

B. If a discounter opens up nearby, not all full-price best-seller sales
   will be lost. Let's assume our store maintains full pricing and takes a
   loss of 50% on the original $1,000 sales.
   Selling $500 of best-sellers at full price.................. $500

   Gross margin dollars at 35% 175

This means the store has lost $175 gross margin dollars.

C. The store could discount best-sellers at 30% to compete.
   Cutting prices on $1,000 of best-sellers by 30% $700

   Gross margin dollars at 5% 50

But this still leaves the store with a loss of $300 in gross margin dollars.

D. To make up that difference, the store would have to sell additional
   books at full price.
   $857.15 additional sales.............................. $857.15

   Gross margin dollars at 35% 300

E. If full-price sales cannot be increased, lost gross margin dollars on
   discounted best-sellers can be made up if sales on discounted best-
   sellers increase by seven times.
   $7,000 sales discounted by 30%........................ $500

   Gross margin dollars at 5% 350

With good management and merchandising, C and D are possible, E rarely happens, but B is probably the way to go, while using some of the tips mentioned above. Finally, experimenting with a couple of big titles at special prices for a few days periodically might help the image, too. But when you have savings and very special buys to offer, flaunt them. Don't let them just sit. Your new competition is formidable. Watch it, copy it, better it where you can. You could come out all right in the end.

V
Other Sales and Services

Chapter 40

Institutional Sales

JERRY L. REHM

Institutional sales may be the best-kept secret in retail bookselling. Some stores have been involved in institutional sales for years, but these sales take place behind the scenes and are not much discussed. The pity of this obscurity is that sales to businesses and educational institutions can be the exact ingredient needed to make bookselling truly profitable.

In these days of economic constriction, institutional sales can improve a store's competitive position. They can expand the market geographically. They can lessen the impact of seasonal variation and other consumer-related phenomena. Businesses and institutions, after all, need books during snowstorms and heat waves; research continues even when the market declines. A store willing to operate with special kinds of organization and levels of discipline can compete directly with publishers for the lucrative institutional and corporate market.

Corporate sales are a growing part of bookselling. There may not be a general trade store in the country that has not supplied a book ultimately paid for by a business enterprise. Even these limited transactions reveal the current awareness that information and communication are the lifeblood of success in business. Companies depend on the book industry to keep them current and point the way to future developments. This chapter demonstrates how bookstores can take aggressive steps to capitalize on corporate needs. In particular, it will discuss the knowledge, skills, inventories, and procedures necessary to tap the corporate market.

Finding the Corporate Market

The first step in developing corporate sales is defining your market. As in the analysis for a general store, this definition must take into account store goals, location, and staff aptitudes. The definition must recognize that, geographically, a corporate sales market may be quite large. The market may encompass whole metropolitan areas or major regions because much of the customer contact is by phone, mail, or specialized advertising media. Since this kind of specialized selling is not addressed in all bookstores, those across town may not be competitors for corporate sales in their own "backyards."

The existing store expanding into technical sales should take a close look at current inventories. Potential corporate customers present new opportunities to sell familiar titles. For example, corporate training programs may need quantities of standard self-help titles. The most demanding responsibility for managers of corporate sales is to budget time for this kind of market review. Then a market analysis of corporate needs in your area should be made to determine what new inventory to add to your store. Let your imagination guide you. This is a research project. Start with public and academic libraries, and discover what materials are sought by corporate borrowers on a regular basis. Learn something about the corporate specialties of the area. Identify local professional organizations and talk to key people. Contact business purchasing agents and corporation librarians to find out what would make their jobs easier, save them money, and enable them to acquire books more quickly.

Assemble this market research and develop a plan to tap corporate book business. Expect that your efforts will take time to develop into solid sales. If your market research suggests inventory additions or new concentrations, recognize that real financial commitment is necessary. Review all your steps continuously as expertise increases and becomes more defined, and as the market changes.

Specialized Promoting and Selling the Corporate World

Aggressive promotion is an absolute requirement in developing corporate sales. The potential corporate client has little chance to stumble into your shop and recognize you as a resource. Even if he should stumble in, you may not have the specialized materials he needs, so your value to him is not obvious. The front line is not necessarily a huge inventory. Even those technical stores with the largest inventories know that the corporate world is too diversified to be served only by books in stock. Instead develop a store "posture" that exudes knowledge and helpfulness. Train employees to provide the extra services of research and rapid response to special orders. Recognize that today's obscure inquiry may be tomorrow's established account worth hundreds of dollars a month. Instruct employees on dealing with a request that comes without full or accurate information. Suggest rush shipping options when specific projects are dependent on a book's arrival. Suggest libraries, university departments, or professional societies as sources of information to those customers who do not have specific titles in mind. These suggestions are in themselves promotional devices, and the investment in time will often be rewarded with great word-of-mouth recommendations.

Continuing on the path set in the market analysis, allocate time for contacting companies and offering your service. Personal phone calls by an owner/manager are an investment with potential for long-term results. Even if the return on calls is only one in twenty, realize that one account may produce more sales than twenty walk-in customers. Even a chat with those uninterested in your service helps define market potential and identify possibilities previously not considered. You have let them know you are there to help them with their book needs.

Become familiar with the roles and purposes of professional organizations. Many areas have a special association for corporate librarians. Some of these groups are starved for program ideas that you may be able to supply. Others may welcome your attendance on a regular basis.

Advertising directed to your corporate market will be distinct from other store advertising in style, format, budget, and media. Newspapers or newspaper sections geared to your corporate market have special merit. State or local professional organizations with their own periodicals provide a perfect format for contacting the market. Direct-mail lists exist for highly defined professional groups or administrative levels. Yellow Pages advertising has special significance because many people assigned to acquire materials are not familiar with the book business.

The corporate customer is your "most likely to return" customer. General book buyers have more choices for book acquisition. Thus, the promotional effort to attract a new account and initial activity between store and account is crucial to success. The secretary, librarian, or purchasing agent may be your corporate contact, but they only represent the eventual consumer, who remains unseen. Their needs differ from the consumers you serve within the physical premises of your store. Purchasing agents need to have clear, accurate, instant, and dependable information to report to third parties.

Make honest and reasonable quotations of price and fulfillment time. Be specific about what you can't do, and convey your limitations pleasantly. Technical book departments may not always be able to order from certain publishers, acquire reprints of old journal articles, locate specialized industry institutes, deal with some professional associations, or make recommendations on particular subjects or titles. Be up front about this. The relationship between promotion and selling is familiar in general bookselling. In corporate sales it is even more dramatic because of the predominance of phone and third-party contact. The engineer who receives a vital book one week late may forgive you because he is so satisfied with the material, but the purchasing agent won't forgive you for submitting him to a week of badgering from that same engineer.

One can see that selling books to corporate accounts is an exercise in establishing a good service operation. Ostensibly the bookseller sells books, but he also sells expertise, knowledge, and service. In the corporate world, he is always selling his store as the best resource for their next book need.

There is old-fashioned selling to corporate accounts as well. The most common is accurate title verification so that a sale may be made off the shelf or placed on special order. The other most frequent selling occurs when a professional telephones with a general need but no particular title in mind. This situation must be handled cautiously because the bookseller is not qualified to give recommendations. However, the store can provide some help by noting applicable titles and authors on hand or available. The professional may then recognize the the aptness of a title or the reputation of an author. The clerk provides an additional service by being ready and willing to read parts of the dust jackets, introduction, or table of contents over the phone. Knowledgeable staff may also indicate the sales record of given titles, authors, or the specialized concentration of certain publishers. These services may net a sale without the customer having to travel to the store.

Providing recommendations for things not in stock but listed in catalogs or *Books in Print* is risky business. Identify that risk to the customer. Suggest ways of verifying the selection by library visits and/or consultation with colleagues, professional organizations, or recognized authorities on college campuses. You are selling a book but also selling the concept that your bookstore has knowledgeable ideas about what is important to specialized customers. Given that most of these professionals work in large corporate settings, one truly satisfied customer is a step toward serving the complete corporate acquisitions process.

Opportunities for specific solicitations to established or potential corporate accounts are often overshadowed by day-to-day operations of the store. Even new shipments received every day should be reviewed for promotional possibilities. The new edition of the *National Electric Code*, for example, can be sold in multiples by a few routine phone calls to prospective buyers. Record keeping should be instituted to identify who buys certain major works, handbooks, annuals, or crucial topics. Then calls can be made to notify established customers of the existence of new editions or important new works. Remember that in technical fields the most current information is crucial to job performance. These contacts will usually result in immediate sales and tend to undercut direct-mail competition from publishers, clubs, and national book sources.

Recognize that these publishing events also provide a chance to prospect potential corporate accounts. For example, a new civil engineering handbook could justify calls to construction firms, government offices, and consulting firms, while a new petroleum accounting handbook suggests calls to accounting firms, specialized lawyers, and oil companies. In both these examples, the diversity of customer operations and your ability to respond may establish continuing corporate accounts that far exceed the scope of the original call.

Ordering and Delivery for Corporate Accounts

Corporate accounts come in all shapes and sizes. The trick to maintaining a good relationship is to keep your services and procedures flexible so that they can respond to the rigid conditions that characterize the corporate account. You should convince customers that your adjustment to their policies is the easiest thing imaginable. Gymnastics training is the best skill to bring to this impossible task, but understanding a few principles will ease the burden.

Corporate acquisitions can be divided in two large groups: those done by purchase orders and those done by verbal contract. The verbal contract most resembles general book sales with which we are familiar; an employee calls to request that a book be sent to the office. The purchase order process may begin that same way, with a purchasing agent inquiring about the availability and price of a title. However, the purchase order is a much more formal document of agreement, with all conditions of the purchase written in specific detail. For the purposes of this discussion, concentration on the purchase order method provides us with the opportunity to respond to the nature of the formal document and still see that a verbal agreement requires answering the same group of questions. In fact, the purchase order has the advantage of having everything spelled out by the corporate account, while verbal agreements usually require the bookseller to verify that *all* conditions of sale are enumerated.

Many corporate sales will take place as a series of actions over time. Thus, record keeping at all stages is vital. The first contact will occur when a purchasing agent calls to see if a title is available in a given quantity. If the book is not on the shelf, this inquiry should be seen as a prelude to a special order, and you should begin to keep records at this point. The clerk will assure the agent that the store can respond to purchase orders—that is, to order without cash in advance—and be able to bill the company. He will keep notes that can be referred to when the agent calls back after comparing prices and obtaining approval for the purchase.

The most important item of record is the price quotation. If at all possible, prices should be indicated as approximations. A price quoted on the eve of a new edition of *Books in Print* is well recognized as undependable. However, even "new" publisher's catalogs have been known to contain errors and old information. Unfortunately the typical purchase order process cannot handle a flexible quote. The bookseller is relieved to find that purchasing people are familiar with these problems and can provide guidelines to protect the store. Purchasing agents are equally interested in maintaining a positive relationship between both parties and are well aware of the realities of business. At the same time, the store should make every effort to provide the most accurate price information. This is particularly true when the order consists of a large quantity of the same title. In this situation a call to the publisher/supplier to verify price and availability can be coupled with a check on discounts available to retailers. Furthermore, the accuracy of this information provides the store the opportunity to extend quantity-order discounts to the corporate account with confidence if that extra service is desired.

After price, the time needed to fill an order is most crucial to the purchasing agent and will be part of the purchase order. As with standard trade sales, bookstores have two major sources of supply: publishers and wholesalers. Many technical books are not available from wholesalers or not available at as good a discount as from publishers. However, when wholesalers can be used, they provide speed that can endear booksellers to purchasing agents. Booksellers who are intent on establishing corporate accounts should become familiar with various ways to acquire books speedily from publishers. Frequently, placing orders by phone reduces delivery time dramatically; mail time is eliminated, and the order is directly entered into the publisher's fulfillment process. In addition, United Parcel Service shipment (ground or air) and other truck and air services can reduce delivery time. Recognize that corporate accounts are much more prepared and willing to pay rush transportation and service charges than the average walk-in trade customer.

Now we are ready for order taking and a full look at the purchase order. Having obtained price and time information in the first call and having checked for necessary internal approvals, the purchasing agent calls the bookstore to place the order. The bookstore locates its own records of quotation, making this second call easier. Together they review title, author, publisher, price, and time information. In addition, the wise store records on a predesigned form the account's name, the "ship to" address, the "bill to" address, the person at the company who should receive the books, the purchasing agent's name and telephone number, rush order instructions and charges if any, and the applicability of sales tax to the account. The purchasing agent will want to know the billing terms of the store (such as net thirty) and who will pay shipping (the store or the account). Purchase orders will state "FOB shipping point" when the shipping charges may be added to the bill and "FOB destination" when the bookstore must pay. This information exchanged, the store can begin the order, although in a few cases it may wish to wait for written confirmation of the telephone conversation.

Ordering for corporate accounts should not vary from the principles discussed elsewhere in this manual. However, recognize that special requirements promised, especially speed of fulfillment, require that the order department know the alternatives and respond to these orders expeditiously.

Now the shipping and receiving department becomes the most important link between the store and a satisfied customer. A proper receiving function should check for damaged books, defective copies, and wrong titles or editions. When these standard functions are applied to special orders, they save the corporate consumer endless effort, trouble, and confusion. Thus, it is services like these that guarantee our niche in corporate sales. In addition, the receiving function carries the reputation of the store as it first encounters price variations and out-of-print or out-of-stock reports on publishers' packing lists. The properly trained employee passes such information to the correct area of the store so that the corporate account can be notified in a timely and orderly way.

Generally it is wiser to avoid drop shipments between publisher and customer. On small orders drop shipments make it difficult to obtain acceptable discounts. Also, drop shipments represent invoicing problems, as store invoices must be created and the customer must match them against publisher packing lists. However, the most important reason to avoid drop shipments is that the store is placing its whole reputation in the hands of the publishers, which is downright lunacy. If drop shipments present the types of problems that the store's receiving department is trained to resolve, then the corporate account would do just as well to deal entirely with publishers.

Recognize that all these factors involve satisified customers and image building. These customers may never set foot in the store to see a smiling face or a knowledgeable presence. They are dependent on other clues to determine the quality and professionalism of the store. These customers are making judgments from the first contact through the order and receiving stages. In the final stages it is very important to capitalize on the good beginnings. Invoices should be of a style to express the store's unique nature, and of course, accuracy is a must. The books requiring shipping from store to corporate account must be packed properly to avoid damage. With large orders this requires special care because of the weight of technical books. Shipping labels should be prepared to avoid shipping to incorrect addresses (such as the billing address) and should include purchase order numbers and be directed to the intended employee at the corporate account. A dependable carrier should be selected to transport the books without damage and with acceptable proof-of-delivery procedures. With the store's image intact and the books shipped to the account, half the store's job is completed.

Payment and Credit for Corporate Accounts

In order to develop a large number of corporate accounts, a bookstore must be willing to extend credit. Most corporations that expect to do business regularly with another require credit recognition so that checks may be approved and written after receipt of goods is completed. Extension of credit means a store must be prepared to recognize sales in accounting terms for tax purposes and lease requirements prior to actual receipt of cash. Further, the store must develop policies to determine under what conditions it will extend credit and at what terms. It must also develop a method to record such credit sales and periodically encourage payment.

Generally the terms for corporate accounts should be "net thirty days." This means that the full invoiced amount (no discount for early payment) is due thirty days from the invoice date. Although shorter periods are possible, most companies require that amount of time just to process a check; a few even require longer.

What you communicate by net thirty days is that this is a typical convenience billing, not intended for extended payment.

While offering house accounts for corporations, it is wise to avoid personal accounts, with a few judiciously placed exceptions. Accepting MasterCard, Visa, and American Express provides ample credit options to the average personal shopper. Note that American Express is virtually a requirement for the technical store because so many companies use American Express accounts for business expenses (incurred by their employees).

A formal credit application may be wise in some circumstances but is not typically required. For smaller, less well-known companies, requiring the first transaction to be paid by check in advance will avoid setting up "one-timer" accounts and will prove that both the buyer and the transaction are sanctioned by the company. In establishing credit accounts, ask for a list of people who can charge on the account, the name of the company's bank, and whether or not formal purchase orders are required. The well-intentioned but unauthorized person will hesitate to answer these questions and will almost never know the name of the bank. A permanent billing address should be obtained, as well as contact people for purchase order and accounting problems. This information should be at the ready disposal of appropriate bookstore staff, for example on the Rolodex file placed by the telephone.

The cash flow of the store requires that such credit activity be monitored and periodic statements be sent to summarize invoices and encourage payment. Slow payers must be identified and remedial action taken. Sales tax, percentage rent, transportation costs, cost of goods, and wages associated with credit sales are due on a very current schedule whether or not the invoices have been paid by the corporate customer.

Given these cash-flow needs, it is somewhat reassuring to know that most of the reasons for slow payment are within the control of the bookstore. The three most common reasons for nonpayment are that the invoice did not arrive at accounting, that the purchase lacked proper authorization, or that the invoices did not follow the purchase order agreement. The quicker any of these problems is identified, the quicker the invoice will be paid. A quiet, peaceful inquiry can do wonders.

If any of these irregularities happens on a regular basis, it is a signal for the store to review its internal controls. If the invoice doesn't find its way to accounting, it may help to send invoice copies to accounting with the statement or at the time of shipping. Care should be taken to use appropriate billing addresses. If the purchase lacked proper authorization or was a personal purchase, the previous recording of who initiated the order can quickly resolve the problem. Even when the purchase had proper authorization, the invoice may fail to show that approval through purchase order numbers or authorizing signature. The price may have changed but the change not been approved. Also, shipping charges may not have been sanctioned by the purchase order. A sales tax exemption stated on the purchase order may have been overlooked at invoice time. This inventory of potential errors is obviously intended to show the need to track all important requirements from order through delivery.

There are more difficult credit problems that can give any store manager pause. Let's assume there is no debate about the ordering or receipt of goods; the company just cannot pay or refuses to pay. These more sticky problems may require outside assistance from collection specialists or lawyers, but here again, patience and persistence can do wonders. The owner/manager by making regular personal calls to appropriate counterparts at the problem account may identify and resolve problems as well as indicate that the bill will not be forgotten. Payment may not come as speedily as expected, but eventual payment is better than none at all.

Corporate sales can turn out to be the natural extension of bookselling in a highly competitive environment. Such specialization expands the bookstore's role and its profit. It requires not so much the development of new skills, but rather the fine-tuning of those already practiced by aggressive, independent retailers. Promoting and selling with carefully selected, unusual inventory is old hat. Service is not a new concept. Having mastered all that, there are only a few new techniques to acquire. The challenges, satisfactions, and profits of corporate sales are a natural part of retail bookselling.

Chapter 41

Selling to the Institutional Customer: Educational

CAROLYN B. TEAGUE

What is the most important element in selling children's books to educational institutions? My answer: Knowledge of an experience in the field of children's literature. Institutional selling *is* different from regular over-the-counter selling, yet the principles of good selling remain the same. One must have an interest in what is being sold and concern for the customer's needs. In this chapter I describe briefly some of the methods that have worked for me as a retail bookseller specializing in children's books selling to institutions as well as to the trade. Please do not confuse this type of selling with wholesaling. These are sales the wholesaler would not normally receive and would not be seeking.

My first contact with educational institutions I hoped would buy from my bookstore was a letter sent to all preschools, private schools, and day-care centers in my market area. The letter was simple and direct:

> *School librarians and teachers are telling us that Teague's has one of the best selections of books for children that they have found anywhere in the Fort Worth/Dallas metroplex. We are continuing to build our stock so that you can look to us for the new books that are in step with the interests of today's young readers and prereaders.*
>
> *Our school discount of 10 percent, which is available to private, parochial, and public schools, enables you to buy more with your book funds. The discount applies to all cash purchases by the school, or schools may charge purchases of $50 or more and obtain the discount by paying within ten days. Discounts cannot be offered to individuals even when employed by a school.*

*It will be a pleasure to serve you whenever you are
considering new books for your library or teaching programs. We are open from 10:30 A.M. until 5:30 P.M. daily
except Sundays and Mondays.*

Yours truly,

Carolyn B. Teague

*P.S.: If you will inform us of your reading lists, we will try
to have the required books available for your students.*

What this letter does is introduce the store to the institutional
buyer with the positive comments that have been made on the
quality of our selection. Before a bookseller approaches the institutional market, an inventory has to be in place that will not only
support the bookseller's ability to fulfill orders, but substantiate the
bookseller's apparent knowlege of the field. Content knowledge is
more important in children's-book selling than in any other aspect of
bookselling. Customers, both individual and institutional, look to
the bookseller for guidance, which means children's-book sellers
have to read the books they sell and have an awareness of the classics
as well as the contemporary titles.

The letter also states in a businesslike manner the terms of sale
to institutions, which make it very easy for the interested buyer to
open an account. The final sentence in the second paragraph is
important in that it states in writing that discounts will not be
offered to individuals. Although this is not the policy of all booksellers selling to institutions, it is ours, and it is important that
everyone be aware of it.

The final paragraph is an invitation to visit the store, with the
hours. And, an important P.S., asking for reading lists. Even if these
aren't forthcoming, students will appear in the bookstore and expect
you to have books on those lists. It is a service to everyone to know in
advance so the titles can be in stock.

An important element in selling to institutions is the willingness
to listen and keep learning. Educators are, or should be, continuous
learners, and this certainly applies to booksellers as well. Listen to
your customers. They will teach you a great deal. Read every book
you can and every book review. Be the first to know which are the
outstanding books and the not so good, so that your recommendations come to be respected by teachers, librarians, and parents.
Maintain active memberships in professional organizations where
there is an exchange of ideas and information. These organizations
often open avenues to new prospective institutional customers.

In building our inventory in the store, we gambled that our clientele would prefer hardback books. So we concentrated on these, including many award-winning titles. We keep the Caldecott and Newbery books, as well as other award-winners, in stock at all times. These titles are all presold because of their publicity. In addition, we keep all of the basic backlist titles that we know will be in continuing and constant demand. Some of the classics have to be stocked in several editions because of differing preferences for illustrator or format. Of equal importance are the new titles, which institutional customers expect to see in the store so they can be examined. Publisher's representatives are an essential source of early knowledge about what is coming that might be especially good for our market. Orders are placed well in advance of publication of many of these books, so we try to always see something of the book in the way of unbound sheets in the case of a picture book (or a galley for a nonillustrated book), so we can judge the quality for ourselves.

As the word spread that Teague's had a broad range of children's titles in stock and that we were knowledgeable about the new books, we began to receive calls and orders from local institutions. Through word of mouth, we began to acquire loyal customers. Then we gave book talks before school groups and sent out newsletters.

We had started with the policy of allowing a 10 percent discount to institutions such as schools, churches, and libraries. Soon we realized that we needed to refine this policy. We now allow the discount on sales of any amount if the customer pays cash. However, many institutional buyers request billing, and we are pleased to bill them for sales of $50 or more, provided we receive payment within ten days. Because some customers do not pay within the ten days, we never show the institutional discount as a deduction from the face of the invoice. We invoice for the full retail amount with a note appearing at the bottom of the invoice stating the amount that may be deducted and the final date that the discount is allowed. Our discount is allowed only to the institution itself and not to its employees, such as teachers buying books for their personal use.

In dealing with institutions, it is important to make sure the person ordering books has the authority to do so. Know your institutional customers, their people and their policies. When books are picked up in the store by an individual representing an institution entitled to the discount, we ask the person to sign the sales ticket regardless of whether the sale is cash or charge. As we began to receive orders from larger institutions such as independent school districts, we discovered the importance of conforming to their requirements regarding order filling, invoicing, and delivery. This is not difficult, and handling the paperwork properly can help build confidence in the store and lead to repeat sales. We do not offer delivery service to our regular trade, but when required by an institutional customer we are glad to load their order into the station wagon and make the delivery in person.

Serving the institutional market demands keeping a substantial inventory. Occasionally you may need to fill an order on short notice that could amount to as much as a month's worth of over-the-counter sales. Once we worked almost all night to fill an order for a school district library using grant funds that had an approaching expiration. Always remember, the *service* they receive is the primary incentive for an institution to deal with a retail bookseller rather than with a wholesaler or publisher.

As in almost every business, public relations are important, and each bookseller will have his or her own style. My emphasis is on involvement in community affairs related to education. I am active in the local chapter of the National Association for the Education of Young Children (NAEYC), Texas Elementary, Kindergarten, Nursery Educators (TEKNE), and Kappa Delta Pi, the national honor society in education. Each summer I work with Texas Christian University in their seminar in children's literature. I have conducted workshop sessions for our local school district and for private schools and women's groups. I cooperate with local schools that have sponsored children's authors and illustrators in programs at the schools. This can lead to having guest authors in our store for an autographing session or for our store to provide books for sale at the school. Sometimes public relations activities can be seen to pay off in terms of direct tangible sales, but more often the benefits are long term in building an awareness of your store among the institutional book buyers in the community. Making them not only aware of your existence, but so aware that they think of you first when they need books, is the goal to be sought.

Institutional sales are not only profitable in themselves when properly handled, they lead to a greatly expanded customer base for individual sales. The effort expended can pay off handsomely.

Chapter 42

Book Fairs

ROBERT D. HALE

There are book fairs of every type, size, and purpose—international, antiquarian, educational, and more. The fairs discussed in this chapter are those conducted by bookstores for the purpose of selling books. Such fairs can also create goodwill, provide a community service, and be an excellent way of advertising.

Displaying books anywhere outside the physical confines of a bookstore is worthwhile if it results in sales and/or an increased awareness of the bookstore. A sponsored book fair held within the bookstore, which brings in people who might never otherwise cross the threshold, is another opportunity not to be missed. Book fairs are an active way to sell books. They require careful planning, extra hours of hard work, patience with sponsors, and intelligent post-analysis, but they say forcefully to a community, "This bookshop exists; it aggressively promotes and sells books. We seek your attention."

Book fairs are usually sponsored by community organizations seeking to raise money for a worthy cause or simply to raise the cultural level of a segment of the population. Parent-teacher groups frequently want to expose students and their families to books beyond those required in class. They attempt to stimulate enthusiasm for books by bringing books to the community that may not visit libraries or bookstores. It's a valuable endeavor for everyone involved. Some groups sponsor book fairs to make money to buy books for the library or the school, to supplement scholarship funds, or to contribute to any number of charities. By participating in such an effort, the bookseller becomes known as an involved member of the community, and that alone is sufficient reason to think positively about the potential of book fairs. Successful fairs can build a loyal following for a bookstore by drawing people into the store as regular buyers who first became customers at a fair.

How does a bookseller make a book fair successful? Let's start at the beginning, with the sponsor and the initial conversation. When a bookseller is approached by a group, several things need to be ascertained. Are they official representatives of an organization, empowered to act on its behalf, sign agreements, be responsible for planning and carrying out that organization's part in the fair? Is the organization they represent a recognized entity? Does it consist of people who will support a fair and make it a success? If they are going to make the sales and collect the money, is the organization financially sound and reliable? In other words, will the bookseller be working with serious and responsible people?

A lot of time is required for planning and executing a fair. It may be possible to throw a superfair together in six weeks—the world was created in six days—but this doesn't happen with great regularity. Unless one is feeling extra godly, it's wise to start talking about a book fair several months before it is to be held.

Setting a date requires thought and cooperation. Sponsors will want it at the height of the selling season—how about the Saturday after Thanksgiving when everyone is thinking about books as gifts? True, lots of sales would be made at the fair, but can the bookseller afford to be involved in a fair held on one of the busiest days of the bookstore's year? If there is staff to cope, perhaps. If not, try another date, not as close to the heavy in-store-sales days.

There may be special days for the sponsoring group—an anniversary celebration that will bring in lots of people; a festival of which the book fair is to be only a part. Those events are worth working around because anything that builds traffic helps make the fair successful.

Whatever the date, set it far enough ahead (three months is a desirable minimum) so there will be time to settle on the list of books to be displayed and sold. You need to get the books into the store if they aren't already there and do the promotion and advertising that will assure an audience. You also want to give both the organizers and the bookstore the necessary hours to get unsold books back into stock and accounts straightened out after the fact. It is better not to have a fair at all than to do it in haste and make such a bungle of it that everyone is unhappy.

The sponsors checked out, a great date set, what kind of fair is it to be: paperback only, for children grades K through six, for affluent adults, or for scientists? Ask the sponsors who will be coming to the book fair. If it is just children, then probably just children's books should be displayed, but if parents are going to drop in, too, suggest broadening the variety. Never underestimate the range of interest of any group at a book fair—give them the widest-possible choice of books to buy. If the fair is to be a part of a holiday boutique or bazaar with other merchants displaying, obviously gift books should be included. But you should also include not-so-obvious gift books; all kinds of books are purchased for gift giving. The greater the variety on display, the greater the chance of catching a prospective buyer's eye. A few copies of many titles are usually better than stacks of a limited assortment.

Who chooses the titles that will be taken to the fair once it is clear what kind of fair it is to be? The bookseller does. Don't make enemies over selection. If a member of the sponsors' committee is red hot on a book and desperately wants it included, include it. That person's enthusiasm will probably sell the few copies you take. You might even help it along at the fair by pointing out the books, saying "Mrs. Cumquat thinks very highly of this one." If the committee members say specifically they do *not* want a certain title displayed for a specific reason, respect their wishes. However, do not let any committee or any librarian member of the committee give you an exact list of books that are to be displayed. No matter how knowledgeable the sponsors may be about books, they are not booksellers. Combine their suggestions with your own ideas, but you, the bookseller, should ultimately decide what will be offered at the fair. If you do not display a title they wanted and you have lots of requests for it at the fair, you will learn by mistake. If you have numerous titles they insisted on and none of these sell, you'll learn from that, too.

The final selection has to be the prerogative of the professional bookseller. The books belong to him until they are sold. It is the bookseller's time and money and effort that get the books from the distributor or publisher (and return them if unsold), so it has to be the right of the bookseller to arbitrate selection.

Sponsoring committees with an ongoing history of successful book fairs can be of enormous help in selection and should be listened to. Always listen and learn, but don't get carried away or feel bound by committee requests. Analyze afterward the success or failure of the committee's choices and of your own, so that next time you will know how to do it with that group. Each group will differ. Don't think that because you had a successful selection for the Knights of Midnight fair, you'll sell the same books at the Dames of Pythias boutique.

Once you've made a list of titles to be displayed, where do you get them? If you have enough lead time, you can include the fair books in regular orders sent to publishers, taking advantage of stock plans, dating, and other incentives publishers offer each season. If you are caught short, you will probably have to go to your best distributors and hope they have in stock the titles you want.

Many booksellers do it all through distributors as a matter of policy; they neither take anything from their regular stock nor display any titles beyond the distributors' inventories. Everything comes in at once, and the unsold books can be returned in one shipment. It's neat and fairly simple. The disadvantages here are a restricted title selection and the lost opportunity to increase initial discount through substantial publisher orders.

Booksellers who do book fairs on a regular basis, whether they are a few or many each year, schedule them far in advance and plan much of their buying around fair requirements, adding quantities to regular in-store stock orders. This is the way to realize the most profit on sales, but it demands good organization and intelligent long-range planning.

The old way of setting up books at a book fair was to display a single copy for potential customers to examine; orders were taken from that copy and filled by the bookstore later. It certainly made setting up a book fair relatively simple, but it meant mountains of paperwork with order forms, lists of books, deposits, and/or amounts due upon delivery. It also meant disappointed customers if books ordered never arrived or came too late for whatever purpose they had been purchased.

This is not an effective way to sell books compared with having the titles immediately available. A child or anyone else who sees a book he wants wants it *then*, wants to pick it up, pay for it, and carry it home. To be told you'll have to place an order and wait for six weeks is to say, "Forget it." Those who have done it the old way and have switched to actually having a stock of books right there to be sold on the spot find sales increasing many times over. And the bookkeeping is much easier.

Multiple copies of books mean increased sales. It also means the person planning the fair has to play the same game of roulette that is played when books are bought for display in the store. How many copies of each title should be taken? It is an individual judgment with all the inevitable right-on guesses and ridiculous mistakes. Do the best you can, keeping in mind the customers who will be coming to the fair.

There are several ways of selling at the fair. Sometimes sponsors pick up the cartons of books at the bookstore, cart them to the site, unpack, set up the display, sell, count the money, return the unsold books, and give a financial accounting. Other times a member of the bookstore staff helps out, especially with display and by being present to answer questions. The whole fair can also be done by the bookstore staff, if the book display is a segment of a larger fair, as at a boutique or bazaar. There are advantages and disadvantages to each, most of them obvious.

If the sponsor's committee is going to do it all, the success of the fair will depend on the ability, energy, and enthusiasm of the members of the committee. If they just lay books out on tables (we're assuming the selection is terrific) and then stand back, waiting for the hordes to exchange cash for covers, paper or cloth, the fair may be a bust. Selling is selling, and good display is essential at a fair, even if potential customers are receptive to buying books for a good cause. They will buy more if the books are arranged attractively, artistically, and intelligently. Customers react to the same merchandising techniques at a fair as in a store; the same professional methods should be applied.

If the sponsor is going to do it all, help the committee members with category lists, suggestions for groupings, and selling ideas. Inspire them with enthusiasm just as you try to fire up your own staff. Committees won't sell as well as you might, but they will do a better job if they've been given a pep talk and some definite ideas to spur them on.

If a member of the staff goes with the books, chances are the display will be better, and so will the sales. "What can I buy for a four-year-old?" is more easily answered by someone who knows than by a panicked parent who doesn't see a thing on the table her four-year-old has read. The staff member can also suggest books that might not be on display but could be brought from the store the next day or mailed later. Book knowledge sells books, and having someone at the book fair with knowledge is of incalculable value. That person also says to the milling throng, "The books at this fair came from our store." It identifies the store with the event. Book events managed by members of the bookstore staff are difficult to handle, especially at busy times of the year, but are the most successful. This works, of course, only if the staff is professional—if the staff consists of booksellers and not just book shelvers. A book fair is a microcosm of the world of bookselling, and the top-selling fairs are those run by book*sellers*. People come primed to buy, but they have to be guided, helped, and sold.

Booksellers have to decide what percentage of sales they are going to give the sponsoring organization. This varies from area to area. It also depends on what is required of the bookseller. As an example (not to be taken at all as a scale to use), a bookseller might give the sponsors 20 percent if they do all the work, pick up the books, and return the unsold books with no bookseller involvement at all in the actual setup or sale. The same bookseller might give 15 or perhaps 10 percent if a member of the staff went along to help. The lower percentage is to compensate for the staff member's time. If the bookstore is expected to do everything from beginning to end, then the sponsoring group might get a percentage based on total sales, say, 10 percent if sales are less than $500, 15 percent if between $500 and $1,500, 20 percent if between $1,500 and $3,000, and so on—whatever is mutually agreeable—and of benefit to both the bookseller and the sponsor.

If the fair is part of a boutique or bazaar with many merchants selling, it is far better to pay a percentage of sales to the sponsor than a flat rental fee for space. The incentive to buy for supporters of the sponsor is vastly greater if they know the eventual dollars going to the charity are based on sales. If the sponsor already has its money in the form of rental fees, the selling effort can be dismal indeed.

If the sponsoring committee picks up, sells, and returns the books, they should be packed with a complete and accurate (check it twice) packing slip, the duplicate to be kept by the bookseller. The packing slip should have the quantity of each title and the price. If you want added information for more orders, such as author and publisher, that can be included. But title, quantity, and price are essential. It is helpful to have two blank columns next to the quantity-sent column—one for quantity returned and one for quantity sold. There should be another blank column on the right-hand side of the sheet next to the price column for extending the retail value of the quantity sold for each title. This makes it relatively easy to transfer the information to an invoice.

When the committee returns unsold books, they should see that the packing slip is filled in with the quantity sold and the quantity returned. It is wise for someone from the store to unpack returned books in the presence of the committee, checking them in and marking the store's copy of the packing slip with the quantity returned. It is usual practice for bookstores to consider as sold any books that are not returned. If ten of something went and three came back, seven were sold, no matter what happened to them at the fair, and it is the sponsor's responsibility to pay for them as sold.

In this portal-to-portal method, in which the committee has collected the money, the store should produce an invoice based on figures shown on the packing slip, giving the total amount of sales, less the agreed-on percentage due to the sponsor, and the net amount to be paid to the bookseller. These invoices are usually paid immediately, before the sponsor banks the cash taken in at the fair.

It is impossible to go into the vagaries of sales tax collection because no two states or cities are the same. Whatever sales tax rules apply in a bookstore's locale have to be used. It is also difficult to suggest a rule for charge card sale percentages because factoring rates vary greatly. These have to be worked out between the sponsor and the bookseller on an individual basis.

Whatever the financial arrangement, it is wise to have it in writing prior to the event—a simple contract stipulating the responsibilities of each party and the agreed-on percentages.

Packing slips and a similar payment situation would also be used if the committee did it all but with a staff member helping.

If the store is staffing the fair, whether or not lists are kept is purely personal preference. They are valuable for control of the books before and after as well as an aid in the final accounting. If the bookseller is taking in the money from sales, accounting consists usually of providing duplicates of the sales slips, a total listing of sales, and the bookseller's check for the sponsor's percentage.

One of the greatest potential assets of book fairs is promotion of the bookstore. Schools, libraries, churches, hospitals, whatever the sponsoring nonprofit group is, can get acres of free publicity in local newspapers and hours on radio or television. It's a good cause supported by the community. Every time the fund-raising event is mentioned in the press, the bookstore is cited. Make sure when initial agreements are reached that such involvement in publicity is discussed. If there aren't many dollars of profit from the fair, the bookseller can be soothed by new customers coming in because they heard about the store when it did the Jolly Jumpers Fair.

Sponsoring committees frequently need help with promotion. They may not know how to publicize their event. Give them all the direction you can. The more successful they are, the more successful you will be. Use your professional know-how. Publicize the book fair in your store. Mention it in your paid advertising. The more generous you are with them, the more grateful they will be, and the greater the chance of a successful fair.

Any gimmick that helps boost the fair's potential is worth trying. Posters, parades, on-air interviews—all can work. Authors' appearances at the fair can be great or dismal. A popular personage may draw a crowd and sell his or her book, but the number of times authors bomb at these events is so much more than when they have been roaring successes that it is well to be extremely careful about who and where. Authors and illustrators of children's books are almost always successful, with adults as well as with children.

In-Store Book Fairs

There is a developing trend among booksellers to hold book fairs in the bookstore rather than elsewhere, persuading sponsoring groups to pull their supporters in to see a vast array of books rather than a few gathered especially for an event. These can be done in several ways.

A sponsoring group can give out hundreds—thousands are better—of coupons that say something like "The Sisters of Mutiny will receive __ percent of the retail price of any book or books purchased on Thursday, Friday, and Saturday, October __, at the

Ding Bat Bookstore, 102 Chicory Place. We urge you to buy your Christmas gifts now, reminding you that books are the most economical of gifts because they can be read first and then given away. Support our scholarship fund, and do your Christmas shopping early at Ding Bat. . . ."

No special effort is required of the bookstore in display or merchandising. Coupons are collected on the days of the fair, the customer pays full price, and after the event a total is taken of coupon sales. A previously agreed-on percentage is then sent to the sponsor.

The same kind of outside promotion and publicity can be used as for other kinds of book fairs. If they want, sponsors can take advertising space, including a coupon. Anyone wanting to support their cause can clip the coupon and come into the bookstore. The public isn't getting the books for any less than full retail, and even though the bookseller is paying the sponsor a percentage of the coupon total, the traffic of new customers is greatly increased.

The in-store book fair can also be an event in itself. It can be held on a night when the store is usually closed, with the sponsor sending invitations, providing refreshments, again publicizing and advertising, and thus getting a percentage of the store's sales for that night, Sunday, or whenever.

In-store book fairs are possible to do closer to a gift-giving season than out-of-store fairs simply because they require less extra effort on the part of the bookshop staff. No great lists have to be made or agreed on. No books have to be carted or checked out and in. While the inventory should be good, it doesn't have to be expanded by special titles bought just for a fair. The store's regular inventory, fleshed out in popular areas, is usually sufficient.

No matter how you run your book fair, there must be analysis afterward of the positive values of the fair in terms of dollar profit, public relations, long-range traffic building, and so on. The negative effects of added inventory, the costs of books in and out or absorbed, the effect on the staff, the drain on the bookseller's own energy—all these factors must also be evaluated.

Don't expect to make a killing the first time out—or the first fair in. Everything builds. If it doesn't build after it has been given a good try, or if its effects are continually more negative than positive, drop it and figure out another way to expand your market. Remember, no bookseller can afford to just sit and wait for customers to come to the store. We all have to reach out, and book fairs can be a very good way to improve sales.

Chapter 43

Getting into Mail Order

CRIS POPENOE

Many retailers have an idealized concept of mail order, not realizing that mail order is a business unto itself, quite unlike the traditional retail operation to which they are accustomed. We will begin this brief discussion by first offering some generalized do's and don'ts, insights from our experience, and a summary of how we go about our business.

Our first word of advice to those considering mail order: Don't do it! This might seem like strange advice from Yes!, a company that has been in the mail-order business for more than ten years. If we were beginning again, we probably would not make mail order a significant part of our business. There are certain perks that we receive from publishers as a cataloger account, such as review copies, but obtaining these perks is a time-consuming process, and mail order would never pay for itself without it. To continue as a mail-order account with the publishers, you must produce catalogs and mailing pieces.

Consider the economics: If you sell over the counter, you have the expenses of receiving and stocking the titles and employing a cashier to direct the customers to the books and take their money. If you sell by mail, you still need to receive and stock the books, and you have many other steps, such as opening the mail or taking a phone order, pulling the titles, processing the order, packing it up, and sending it off. Finally, you have to keep complete records of the transaction whether or not there is a problem with the order, and you must keep track of debits and credits.

Perhaps the most critical decision is what merchandise you plan to offer. Titles and subject areas have to be carefully selected. If you try to offer all kinds of books to a general clientele, your mail-order business will simply not succeed. "Specialization" is the key word.

Find a niche and target your business to it. Make sure that it is an area to which you can target mailings. If you don't reach prospective customers, even the most attractive mailings will fail. Don't worry about discounting; mail-order customers are generally more interested in the quality of the offering and service than in price, though bonuses and special offers are popular.

Mass Mailings

How do people hear about you so that they can make their first order? You may advertise, but you will need a direct-mail campaign also. You must design an attractive mailing piece. To reach potential customers, it is advantgeous to buy mailing lists. There are mailing-list brokers who manage and promote lists in many different fields. You can select lists of subscribers to certain magazines, buyers of certain products, even members of selected professions. Utilizing a list broker can be a great help. Names usually cost a minimum of $60 per thousand. Estimate the cost of preparing for the mailing, the cost of producing the mailing piece, and the postage. You have to put out a great deal of money before you can hope to see a single response. A good response is 2–3 percent.

Needless to say, the lists you select are as important as the appeal of your mailing piece. Even the most fantastic offer will be a bust if it is offered to the wrong target audience. This means that magazine subscribers are often not a good target, no matter how interested they are in your subject matter. Proven mail-order buyers are the key market. A direct-response piece to your house list (made up of your previous mail-order customers plus those who have asked to be placed on your list) will always prove the most successful. You can generate income from your house list by selling it to promote offers you feel are worthwhile and noncompetitive. In addition, you can trade your list with other organizations or companies for their list and thereby reduce the cost of your promotion. We generally obtain most of the outside lists we mail to through trades of this kind. As a matter of fact, our most successful outside mailings have been to a list we have been using at least once a year on a trade basis for the last ten years.

Depending on the size of your mass or bulk mailing, you may want to use a mailing service. This can be an invaluable service as it saves you time, money, and hassles with the postal regulations. The mailer will be able to cut your list into labels, affix these to your mailing piece, bundle your pieces according to postal regulations, and take them to the post office and mail them out bulk rate. Four-up Cheshire address labels are standard in the industry. That is, the labels are computer-generated and printed out on 14¾-by-11-inch paper, four names across and eleven names down. Most mail-order software for word processors and small computers provide for generating this kind of list.

In order to mail at the inexpensive bulk rate, you or your mailing house must have a bulk rate account, and you will be issued a bulk rate number. The post office can answer any questions concerning bulk rate accounts and mailings. They will even provide a bulk rate mailing kit free of charge to those who wish to prepare their own mailing.

Once you have a customer, he's not yours forever. It is essential to continue to send out mailings to remind him that you are still there. Constant mailings and new catalogs are a necessary part of any successful mail-order operation.

Catalogs

Initially we concentrated our efforts on producing large catalogs with extensive offerings in a wide number of areas. These provided concise, critical reviews of thousands of books and were packaged as trade book guides, not strictly Yes! Bookshop catalogs. Random House distributed some to bookshops and libraries, and one was even published by Penguin in the United Kingdom. We also sold them in our shop and through the mail and published regular updates, which we sent out periodically to our house list. These update supplements often contained one thousand titles in many fields, most of which were of no particular interest to those receiving the mailing. And the sheer number of listed titles was overwhelming. There also was no way to predict the demand for a particular obscure title, so books had to be back ordered. This created a mountain of extra paperwork, additional postage, and packing charges . . . and customer complaints. I know when I order by mail I eagerly anticipate receiving the goods. And I'm never happy to receive out-of-stock notices.

A few years ago we stopped issuing these general supplements and replaced them with specialized catalogs and with more attractive, periodic mailings of 200–250 bestsellers and unusual remainders, each illustrated with a photograph and a harder sales pitch than we used in the larger, generalized book guides. We only list titles that we expect will sell a minimum of one hundred copies. And we make every effort to have every title in stock. So it's easy to pick and pack the order. The books can be shipped out promptly, no back orders are generated, and happy customers are loyal customers who will order from you again and again.

Fig. 43-1. Yes! Bookshop's mail-order catalog.

Setting Up a Mail-Order Department

Almost every bookshop has the occasional customer who asks for a purchase to be mailed or a special order to be processed and sent to him or someone else. In such cases, there's no need for a separate mail-order department. You just need to have a staff member responsible for tracking the paperwork. Remember that the postal system (whether it be UPS or the U.S. Postal Service) is not infallible; things do get lost and need to be traced and replaced.

If you plan to be actively involved in mail orders, you will need a staff member to head up the department. This may or may not be a full-time position depending on the volume of orders you process, but it should be a full-time employee—there's no way of predicting when a customer will call to inquire about an order, and it's good to be able to respond to the inquiry as expeditiously as possible.

You'll need to devote office space to mail orders: space for one or more file cabinets; a packing table with postage meter, scale, electric stapler, rubber stamps, packing tape, Jiffy bags (we use the bubble-pack kind that are more lightweight and easier to work with), boxes, and packing material (Styrofoam peanuts work best); a desk or two; a typewriter, calculator, and maybe even a computer terminal; and space to stack the books you have pulled and space for those waiting to be packed. And don't forget about room for the postal service mail bags you are filling for fourth-class mail and the shipments waiting for a UPS pickup. As you can see, quite a bit of space is needed, even for a relatively small mail-order operation.

We staff up as needed, depending on the time of year and whether we expect an imminent response to a recent catalog mailing. Our base staff is two full-time people: a department manager and an assistant. When responses to a mailing are coming in heavily (we do mailings of about a hundred thousand pieces three times a year), we hire a lot of part-time staff to pull books, pack the orders, open the mail, answer the phone (we have an 800 number), file the orders, and so on. At this time the manager has his hands full just scheduling bodies and space to work. There are two universities within a few blocks of our shop, so an ad in the university newspaper brings us plenty of energetic, eager part-timers.

Direct-mail sales are a growing business in the United States today and, if handled properly, can be a great boon to your business. If you can target a market and have the space, staff, and desire, then go for it. Just remember that a successful mail-order business is a complicated and expensive art and one at which only the best succeed.

Chapter 44

Special Orders

GINGER CURWEN

Special orders, some theorize, provide a litmus test of the true bookseller. If a store's special-order systems are haphazard and disorganized, they have the potential for alienating customers and demonstrating conclusively that sloppy service is no service at all. If, however, the systems are streamlined and efficient, they reflect the bookseller's talent for management, knowledge of books and publishers, and passion for satisfying the customer.

But who ever said it was easy? In the past couple of years, the numbers of titles that are out of stock, out of print, or greatly elevated in reprint price have increased dramatically, and print-bound references have found it impossible to keep up with all these changes. Among other things, this has resulted in an increase in the "But you told me it would be only $14.95, not $23.95" scenario repeated in store after store across the country, as the customer comes in to pick up that special order.

The first step in establishing a special-order policy is to determine what's appropriate for your staff, your environment, and your customers. Elements of this policy will range from decisions about deposits and service charges to how far you'll go with a special order. Some booksellers will conduct an out-of-print search if the customer and book require it. Others turn up their hands at this point and say simply, "Sorry." Setting your special-order policy will be the cornerstone in its formation. Out of trial and error, many booksellers have established certain limits. Some have selected not to order, for example, mass-market paperbacks that aren't available from whole-sale sources; titles from publishers that do not have retail discount schedules (or they will order but add $2 to the price or encourage the customer to place the order directly); publishers listed in the back of

Books in Print that do not have telephone numbers (how will you complain if something goes wrong?). Some booksellers also choose not to order short discount titles or textbooks; they also avoid STOP forms and prepaid orders to firms whose regular *ABA Book Buyer's Handbook* listing contains a disclaimer on their reliability.

The next consideration: Will you ask for a deposit? Bookseller responses tend to vary tremendously on this question from none at all to 100 percent, but most booksellers find that asking for a deposit of some kind does cut down on the number of special orders that never get picked up. Requiring a full deposit, however, makes less and less sense these days, especially if the book has to be ordered directly from the publisher. If the book comes in with a hefty and unexpected price increase, you are placed in the position of asking the customer to pay more after she already thought she paid it all. Asking for half the ticket price is a common solution. One Texas bookseller asks for 50 percent on a cash sale, but if payment is by credit card, he imprints the MasterCard or Visa number directly onto the order form. If the book is not picked up, the customer is charged its full price by card or forfeits the cash deposit.

Making a decision about a service charge is the next ingredient of your special-order policy, and since it's a competitive element, a survey of the policies of the other stores in the area is crucial. Most booksellers will not charge extra if the special order is available from the wholesaler, though they may pass along the postage. Other booksellers add service charge only on short discount titles. A range of $.50–$2.00 seems to be the norm for service charges. Many booksellers do not charge any fees for special orders at all.

Given the vagaries of publishers and the increasing number of titles that are out of stock, out of print, or have gone way up in price, it makes good sense to ensure that your customer's expectations are in line with reality *when* you're taking the order. Naturally, you'll check the microfiche immediately to see if the title is available at one wholesaler or another; if so, you've an easy and quick response to the customer and can usually assure delivery within a few days. If it's not at the wholesaler, many booksellers tell the customer it will take four to six weeks and try to err on the side of overestimating. Stress that the *Books in Print* price is only approximate, as of the previous year.* After experience you will get to know which publishers have slower service and which publishers tend to substantially increase the prices on their backlist titles and will be able to factor all this in when quoting a price and time length to the customer. Since the

---

*The advent of *Books in Print* updated quarterly on CD-ROM promises to be a great help in quoting prices accurately.

special-order process can take over a month and customers tend to have short memories, many booksellers find it helpful to have their special-order policy imprinted on the customer receipt; it answers many questions in midstream.

Now to the ordering. If the title is available at the local wholesaler, we'll presume that you'll simply add the title to your next order. Or, if you order frequently from the publisher in question, you'll add the title to the next stock order. Either way, it makes sense to flag the order in some fashion to make it easier to identify in the receiving area. Some stores circle the special-order title in red on the purchase order; others attach a copy of the special-order form to the purchase order; those who have special orders on-line generate a variety of reports, including books on order by source. All these devices serve to alert the receiving crew (yourself or a cast of thousands) that a special order has arrived in the shipment from the publisher or wholesaler. To answer customer inquiries on the status of a special order, many find it helpful to keep another copy of the order by the phone or the register, filed alphabetically by customer name.

But what if a desired title comes from a publisher with whom you do little or no business *and* it's not carried by the wholesaler? This dilemma brings us to STOP (the Single Title Order Plan program). Developed cooperatively between the ABA and the Association of American Publishers, this program enables booksellers to earn a 35–40 percent discount on their special orders instead of the 15 or 20 percent that a single-title order would normally earn. The prepayment or open check that accompanies the STOP form provides the incentive to the publisher.

There are two basic approaches to using STOP: an open check system or prepayment (retail price and postage combined). And there are problems with each. Prepayment runs into the problem of price increases. To combat such difficulties, you can call the publisher on the toll-free number to verify the price, then you can consult the STOP information booklet to help estimate the weight (and therefore the postage). Still, one bookseller recently reported that one-third of his STOP orders were returned because of price increases or because the titles were out of stock. The former situation has led many to adopt the open check system. This requires a separate checking account with a balance of anywhere from $100 to $1,000, depending on how many special orders you do. The checks can be preprinted or handwritten with a "Not to exceed (specific dollar amount)"; the publisher then fills in the retail price minus the discount, adds the postage, and sends the book. This avoids the problem of STOP orders returned after six weeks because you were short five cents, but if the publisher doesn't send back to the store the yellow copy of the STOP form with the computed price information and the book has no printed retail price, the bookseller may not know what price to charge the customer unless he receives the canceled check in the mail first or calls the publisher.

STOP forms are available from the ABA in packages of 150 sets. Nonmembers pay a higher fee. Not all publishers participate in the STOP program; some may respond if you send them a STOP form, but success is not guaranteed; mass-market publishers do not accept STOP forms.

Although the inclusion of payment with the STOP order should speed up fulfillment, in that credit checking and the rest is unnecessary, this is infrequently the case. Because these orders are outside the regular routine, they sometimes get put aside to be taken care of "later." This is not universally true. Some publishers fulfill STOP orders with speed, but because they are some rather than all, it is best not to give the customer extravagant promises of early delivery just because the order is prepaid.

When the book finally arrives, it's time to let the customer know. Imprinted postcards come in handy here, especially considering the rise in the number of households with both spouses at work and children in school. It can often take you more time to try phoning the customer three times than it does to address a simple card. Besides, messages have a way of not getting through, or if they do, sometimes not happily. Don't forget that people's personal reading can sometimes be very personal—a stockbroker, for example, might not want his office staff to know he had ordered a copy of *How to Declare Personal Bankruptcy.* (This is a true story!) If the book is unclaimed after a week or so, the customer is generally sent a second notice, again usually written. After the second or third attempt, most booksellers simply claim the deposit and attempt either to stock (and sell) the book or return it.

Telephone notification does have the benefit of providing another personal contact with the customer and can result in questions about other titles. There cannot be a hard-line decision on notification methods because both have to be used for the best-possible service.

Suppose that despite your best efforts, the book does not arrive because it is out of stock or out of print. If the customer still wants the title, the bookseller can provide another service by referring the customer to the nearest used-book dealer or antiquarian bookseller or by conducting an o.p. search for the book.

After all these details, the notion of special ordering may sound more tiresome that it usually is. Once your systems are in place, most booksellers agree, it's really not that time-consuming. And think of the benefits! Special ordering enables you to offer customers a crack at those fifty-five thousand new titles published every year that you surely can't afford to stock; it enables you to check on new titles that might become basic stock; and you can't beat special orders for inspiring customer gratitude and generating repeat visits. In this self-service world of ours, it's a real pleasure for customers to get exactly the book they want—and that's why you went into the business in the first place, isn't it?

Chapter 45

How to Start an Out-of-Print Search Service

JANE E. SHURTLEFF

To customers who have been searching for an elusive out-of-print book, the bookseller who finds it is nothing short of a magician. For booksellers, o.p. book searching is by no means magical, and though it does involve some luck, an o.p. search is basically made up of a lot of paperwork and commitment of time. The following policies and procedures show what is involved in establishing and maintaining an o.p. book search service. These methods are not those used to establish an antiquarian or rare-book department.

AB Bookman's Weekly (P.O. Box AB, Clifton, NJ 07015) is the best marketplace for out-of-print books in North America. This weekly publication contains trade news, reference lists, and special features as well as pages of ads citing titles wanted and titles for sale. For British editions, the equivalent to *AB* is *The Bookfinder*. Before embarking on out-of-print searches, you should obtain a copy of *AB* to get an idea of its advertising formats. The customer policies and advertising procedures that follow all relate to advertising o.p. books in *AB*.

Customer Policies

When to do an out-of-print search. How do you know if a book is really o.p.? If a book is not listed in *Books in Print*, you cannot really assume it is out of print. Unfortunately, *Books in Print* is usually all that a new bookseller has to go by. If you cannot locate a book in *Books in Print* under author or title, then, if the publisher is known, refer to the *Publishers' Trade List Annual* (if you have this tool) or to the publisher's backlist catalog. If the book still cannot be found, try looking it up in a quarterly publication entitled *Best Buys in Print*, put out by Pierian Press (Box 1808, Ann Arbor, MI 48106). *Best Buys* lists thousands of books that have been remaindered and tells where to get them. This checking may sound tedious, but it is well worth it to save the time and expense of an o.p. search.

Obtaining bibliographic information. You will notice in the *AB* ads that some titles listed are followed by a question mark, indicating the advertiser does not know the name of the author. This is fine if it is the only information that you or the customer can gather about a book, but for more positive results, try to get the correct title and author. The best that you can do is to get your customers to give you the most accurate information they have about a book. You should also ask your customers if they want a particular edition of the title. If they specify a first, then you should specify "first edition" in your listing in *AB*.

Charging for an o.p. search. Most booksellers charge the customer the price of listing a book in the *AB*. Any other charges booksellers pass on to their customer depends on how much time and correspondence is involved. Other policies can be made concerning the fees; for example, if the book is found and the customer buys it, a prepaid fee could be deducted from the price of the book. If the customer does not buy a book that is found, then the fee will not be refunded. If the book is not found, then a bookseller could refund the fee (but usually does not). The customer is paying for the initial advertisement. If the customer wishes to advertise for the book more than once, then the customer could pay the fee again, or, if the bookseller wishes, the bookseller could offer to absorb the cost of a second ad. However you do it, it is wise to make the customer realize that there is no guarantee of getting a quote on the book.

Giving a customer a time limit for a book. For the best results from an *AB* ad, run as large an ad as possible and on a regular basis. A small bookstore might advertise once a month. Accumulate enough titles to do a full-page display ad (approximately 136 titles), if that is possible. It will save you some money on advertising in *AB* and will give you better coverage. If not, run small ads, but with some frequency. Ad deadlines are two weeks prior to date of issue, and the magazine suggests you allow two weeks after the ad runs for a good response. Tell your customer it will take at least two weeks from the date that you expect the ad to appear for you to know if the book will be quoted. Most people have been looking so long for a book that they really don't mind waiting.

Procedures for Keeping Records, Advertising in the *AB*, Accepting Quotes, and Pricing

Have a special-order form for preparing o.p. search requests. This form, which ought to contain a copy for the customer and a copy for you, should allow for the following: title, author, publisher, edition, date request was taken, date title will appear in *AB*, and some space on your copy to record quoted prices and sources. Also remember to leave space for the customer's name, address, phone number, and so on.

File your copy of o.p. requests by title and then keep each series of titles grouped by the dates that they will appear in *AB*. Two weeks before you want your ad to appear, prepare your typewritten list of requests either by title or author. Since you may not have authors on some titles, you might want to list them separately from the titles with known authors. (For *AB*'s complete advertising policies, write to them or study a recent issue.) For better results, print the line "All quotes will be answered" at the end of your ad. When a dealer quotes a book to you, that means he is saving it for you until you respond. Even though you should wait two weeks after the ad runs to receive the maximum number of quotes, do not wait any longer than two weeks to answer them. Keep all your quotes together with the copy of the search request until you have actually received the book—just in case the quote you pick does not work out.

Pricing and accepting quotes. When choosing the best quote on a book for your customer, try to pick the cheapest price for the one in the best condition. People will swear up and down that they will pay anything for an o.p. book, but don't believe them. When pricing an average o.p. book, most booksellers double the price that they are quoted. This works out fine, unless you are paying too much for the book initially. You may not have much control over what you are quoted, and the customer will have the final say on what they can pay for a book, so how can you get the book in your customer's hand and still earn a good profit? Try not to pay more than half the cover price, if known, on a regular o.p. book, then mark it up 50 percent or more if you think your customer will pay for it. As you do more and more o.p. searches, you will find cases where the quotes are too high for you and your customer, and the only real question is whether to accept the high quote or keep searching for more reasonable ones. The safest way is to collect all the quotes you receive for a title, double the asking price, then call your customer to report on prices and conditions of the copies offered. Let the customer make the decision, and agree to the price, before you send your check off to the dealer.

If the book arrives and it is not the book you wanted or is in less-than-promised condition, most dealers will refund your money if you send back the book. If your customer is willing to accept a book in poor condition, then you might want to reduce the price a bit, but you can't afford to cut the price too much. Most dealers are very reliable on book condition, but everyone has a different opinion of "fine," "good," and "fair," which makes buying books sight unseen chancy.

After you have received all the quotes you're likely to get from an ad, contact the remaining customers whose books were not quoted and ask them if they wish to repeat their ad. If they don't, offer to keep their requests on file just in case you see the book being advertised for sale in future *AB* ads.

Write to the dealers whose quotes you did not accept and let them know that you do not want the book. Keep their names and addresses on file with the title they quoted you, just in case you get a second request for the book. Also, once you get a large-enough file of dealers and their specialties, you can go directly to the dealer for future out-of-print requests.

Letting the world know that your bookstore offers out-of-print book searches is the easiest part of the whole process. The *AB* will send you free stickers advertising the service that you can display in your store. You can also mention the service in your Yellow Pages ads and your regular bookstore ads. You can even advertise the service on bookmarks and cash register receipts.

There are a lot of ifs, ands, and buts about out-of-print book searches, but it is a good customer service with nice profit margins. If you decide that you want to offer the service, but don't want the hassles of the paperwork, there are many free-lancers who will work with bookstores at offering a book search. Otherwise the best idea is just to dive in and see how it works for your store and your customers.

Chapter 46

Sidelines or Nonbook Merchandise

MARY ANN TENNENHOUSE

Beside the cash register in many bookstores sit displays of book-marks, bookplates, and other small items. These and all nonbook products sold in bookstores are called sidelines. In the economic climate of late-twentieth-century America, most stores find it essential for survival to provide a variety of merchandise in addition to books. This trend does not represent any less dedication to the book but indicates a coming to terms with the reality of business. It is the additional income from sidelines that enables many booksellers to remain in business.

Choosing sidelines merchandise is not an easy task. Products related to books are the most obvious and probably the safest choice when beginning. Where else would a customer look for book covers, totes, racks, magnifiers, bookplates, and bookmarks? And what would be the logical source for book-inspired posters, cards, calendars, games, dolls, toys, T-shirts, paper goods, and more? These items, even without direct tie-ins to books, are good prospects for sales. Actually, with business sense and ingenuity anything can be sold. A prime example is the New England bookseller who sold four hundred down vests in three months a few chilly winters ago. To recommend such a venture would be misleading, but for that bookseller the opportunity and time were right and paid off.

The two most important factors to be considered when planning to buy sidelines are the amount of space to be used for the merchandise and the funds available. Space devoted to sidelines may range from a point-of-purchase rack at the cashier's desk to an entire store within a store. Dollar investment can run from less than one hundred to thousands. The choice of and commitment to sidelines are individual to each store. This cannot be emphasized sufficiently.

What succeeds in one store may not in another, so the decision must be made only after careful research and consideration.

The preliminaries of site selection—checking traffic patterns, interests and needs of the surrounding community, nearby institutions—will all be helpful in determining the types of sidelines for a store. What kinds of people shop in this area? What do the stores nearby sell? Is the bookstore close to schools, a library, hospital, museum, theater, sports facility? Do not overlook the bookstore staff. What strong interests do they have? Does anyone have a specialty that might be utilized? Learn from yourself. Why do *you* go to a particular store? Does your store have special subject sections? Sidelines might be coordinated with some of them. Does the store itself have any features that might lend themselves to the display or sale of a particular item? Be unique. Establish your store as "a source for ____." Are there local artists, artisans, or craftspeople whose work you might display and sell? Taking articles on consignment involves a commitment of space, but no financial investment. If sidelines are being added to an established store, listen to the customers, both children and adults. Ask their opinions. Pay attention to the media, to community events and interests, to shifts in local and national trends, many of which may be short term but lucrative. All bookstores have books, most have sidelines, but no two are identical. Visit other stores, including bookstores, for ideas about what and what *not* to do. Seeing what doesn't work in an existing store may prevent mistakes in your planning.

The good news about sidelines, and one of their major pluses, is that they are usually purchased at 50 percent of retail price. The bad news is that this merchandise is generally not returnable, and some companies have fairly high initial minimum orders. Careful judgment must be exercised when ordering. These merchandise vendors are not as lenient as publishers. Payment *must* be made promptly. Start small, be cautious, and then reorder quickly if the merchandise does well. Before buying, consider what to do if the stock does not sell, so that you have a plan ready to minimize possible disaster.

Once types of merchandise have been considered, how can I find out what is available?

Among the best sources are trade shows such as the twice-yearly gift shows in major cities and the annual stationery shows in New York, San Francisco, and Los Angeles. Suppliers show their lines for the coming season, providing an excellent overview of industry trends. Many firms, including jobbers and reps, have permanent showrooms in major cities. *American Bookseller* and *Publishers Weekly* report regularly on sidelines related to the book business. These articles and advertising are specifically for the bookstore market. Trade journals of industries such as gifts, greeting cards, and toys are good sources for new product information and trends. The *ABA Sidelines Directory* contains lists of sidelines suppliers in all categories as well as helpful essays on how to buy, display, and sell various types of merchandise. The book is free with membership in ABA.

Write to manufacturers and suppliers of sidelines for catalogs, prices, and complete information about terms. Investigate discounts (usually, but not always, 50 percent), returns (usually nonreturnable), and minimums (some have them, some do not). Determine whether the supplier permits replacement of merchandise that does not move. Ask about exclusivity—being, by agreement, the only source for a product line in your vicinity. If possible, it is a distinct advantage to be the only store in the area to carry an unusual or popular item.

Sidelines are usually referred to and written up by product category. These categories are a means of organizing the sometimes bewildering variety of items available. In discussing sidelines, it is more practical to cover these groups according to their proximity to or distance from books, rather than proceeding through categories alphabetically.

Calendars are one of the most popular and best-selling sidelines for many bookstores. So many calendars are produced by publishers that many people think of them as books, although they are frequently available at better-than-book discounts. Calendars require space and good display, but since they are a seasonal item, the space allotted can be used for something else for part of the year.

Book accessories relate directly to books. These include bookplates and bookmarks, book covers, totes, racks, holders, bookends, bookstands, booklights, and more. Although these items are sold in other outlets, the bookstore should be a major source for them. Prices range from $.50 for bookmarks to $100.00 or more for special bookends or bookstands, making it possible to put together a selection of items in several price ranges.

Magazines and periodicals can be an important adjunct to books since they convey information in much the same way as their close relations and are produced in a similar manner. Some booksellers consider them an integral part of their merchandise mix, while others carry them as a service.

Paper and printed materials coordinate well with books. The spectrum includes art prints and posters (naturals with art books and excellent for display), greeting cards and stationery, wrapping materials, pads, office supplies, and more. It is possible to stock

Fig. 46-1. Stationery and blank books are another popular sideline, as evidenced by this counter display at a New York Logos bookstore.
(Photograph by Joan Adelson)

anything from the most inexpensive mass-produced personality poster to expensive, signed, limited-edition prints and lithographs. Posters that tie in with book stock, especially art and photographic subjects, are among the most promising. Storage and display, which require space, are keys to the success of such merchandise. Some posters are individually rolled and sealed, others are flat and shrink-wrapped with cardboard. Display fixtures are often available from manufacturers with orders, or they can be specially made. It is possible to store and display posters on the type of wall-mounted swing-out fixture seen in museum stores or in bins. Both methods encourage browsing. Prints and lithographs should be stored in plastic sleeves and protected with fine-grade paper. Individual posters displayed on the walls above shelving add considerably to the decor and image of the store. Reproductions the size of greeting or postcards can mean additional sales. These are impulse items and as such should be displayed near the register.

Recreational merchandise, including games, toys, puzzles, hobby and craft items, sell well by themselves and are excellent tie-ins to do-it-yourself, craft, and game books. Many stores distinguish between children's and adult items and sell them in separate sections, although there is some overlap, particularly with puzzles, model kits, craft items, and games. Many stores also make a distinction between educational games and toys and the purely fun variety. The increasing selection of book, movie, and TV spin-off merchandise such as Sesame Street, Garfield, Muppets, and other items are excellent sidelines candidates. The same is true of the many children's book characters now available from toy manufacturers. Since there are so many items from which to choose, careful, informed selection is essential. When planning such a selection, be aware that toys need space for display.

Tapes and cassettes are now very popular and can be sold successfully in bookstores. Both fiction and nonfiction have been recorded. Videocassettes are gaining in popularity too and are also available for bookstores. Videotaping has made possible the sale of films based on novels, which could be an important source of income. The exploding software market can be a tempting and profitable venture in the right bookstore. This field is relatively new and should be approached with care.

In some areas the local bookstore is the only source for teacher's aids—workbooks, subject area materials, flash cards, language cards, and charts. Although these are usually sold to bring in extra income, sometimes a store handles them chiefly as a service to the community. If space and customer interest exist, a whole educational section might be established incorporating teaching materials with educational games and projects. Success with this type of venture requires working closely with educators in the community. Religious goods are excellent sidelines in some areas. This is one specialty that demands a thorough knowledge of the community and its needs. It is possible to obtain items for many more than just Christian and Jewish customers since burgeoning interest in Oriental and African beliefs is opening up new possibilities.

Munching and reading seem to go together. Some stores make a good profit selling candy or other food products. A wide range is available from penny candy to exotic gourmet items. Special coffee and tea assortments, jams, even frozen specialty foods can be sold. Storage and refrigeration and other equipment must be considered. Be sure there is no restriction in your lease pertaining to food.

Publishers are now producing many sidelines items spun off from books. These include cards as well as posters, calendars, toys, diaries, and more. Rights to the use of characters, photographs, and

Fig. 46-2. Peter Glassman, co-owner of Books of Wonder, a children's bookstore in New York, with Wild Things dolls.
(Photograph by Joan Adelson)

trademarks are sold to companies that produce an array of products, some as exotic as linens, household goods, and the like. These can be sold in conjunction with books, but care should be taken to choose things that have the most appeal for your market.

The image a store projects is very important. To enhance this image, most stores have a logo that serves as an immediate identification. A design or simply the name of the store in an unusual typeface, when used in advertising and on stationery, wrapping materials, book covers, bookmarks, and totes sold in the shop will familiarize the community with the store and identify it as a source for books and related items. Many firms offer this personalized service to bookstores. From giveaway bookmarks to fine-quality totes, the variety of imprinted products available can bring a store into focus and create a specific image. Promotion and profit combine with the sale of these special sidelines.

Fig. 46-3. For Under Cover Books & Records outside of Cleveland, Ohio, tapes and
CDs are an important sideline. A customer browses at the rack of rock, jazz, and
popular music tapes.
(Photograph by Pamela Turner)

Stores with specialties, such as children's, feminist, religious,
business, theater and film, or whatever, have the opportunity to
carry any number of items that coordinate with the specialty.
Another type of specialty, the bookstore hyphenate, has met with
success. The most popular combination is the bookstore-cafe or
restaurant, where the food business may be a sideline or may
influence the choice of sidelines sold. Galleries, game- or poolrooms,
and other combinations are possible. This is an area that requires
expertise and extra investment of money and time, especially when a
restaurant is involved. Special licenses and additional health and
other city codes are involved, so much advance planning is necessary, and much expert advice should be sought.

It would be wonderful if once sidelines were selected, unpacked, and in place, they sold like hotcakes. This probably will not
happen. As with books, sidelines must be advertised, promoted, and
sold, not simply set out to sell themselves. One method is to display
sidelines and books together, such as crafts materials with crafts

books. Another method is to set up a sidelines department that may be almost another store, for which advertising and promotion might be done apart from books. The staff should be familiar with all merchandise in order to answer customer questions and sell properly. The customer who sees that you know your products and who trusts your judgment will return. Do not underestimate word of mouth, especially with sidelines. If one kid knows that you have the best stickers in town, more will quickly find you. The exquisite card you sold to go with the gift book will not go unnoticed by other potential customers.

What happens if those fine-looking sidelines don't move at all? Reduce them; get them *out.* Then try to determine *why* they did not sell. Perhaps the items were too expensive, or there was not enough interest in the particular product, or your timing was wrong. Peak buying seasons for sidelines coincide with books, but not in all cases. January and February are the top months for hobby and crafts sales, for example. Customers must not be over- or underestimated. It is important to listen to the people who come into the store. One caveat must be added. Even if everything has been done properly, if the merchandise is temptingly displayed, reasonably priced, and well advertised, the sideline may still be a dismal failure. One store may do exceedingly well with an item, and another store may do poorly. The selection and selling of sidelines is a very individual matter, particular to each store. Trial and error is involved to determine what will sell. Some booksellers have found that no sideline, with the exception of bookplates or bookmarks, will succeed. It must also be said that some booksellers consider sidelines to be an intrusion that dilutes book stock. This factor must be considered, but if the alternative to carrying sidelines is not to be in business, is there really a choice?

To minimize the risk, when setting up a sidelines department, the bookseller must know the needs and interests of the community or neighborhood. Money and space should be allocated on that basis. The bookseller should always start small until buying patterns develop, should coordinate books and sidelines for a unified atmosphere, and above all else, should be flexible. Experimentation will be necessary to find a good and successful mix. Sidelines should not be just a means to make money: they should be a positive addition to the store and to the fulfillment of being a bookseller.

More about Several Important Sidelines

Calendars. Some love them, some hate them, but most booksellers stock them. They come in many different sizes and in a variety of packages, take up a lot of space, and can be difficult to display. But they can be purchased at higher discounts than books, are bought by more people, and make excellent gifts. Calendars should be ordered early and displayed months before January 1.

There are hundreds of calendars available on all subjects from dozens of sources. They can be ordered from publishers, wholesalers, stationery manufacturers, museums, foundations, and other organizations. Types include wall calendars, engagement books, desk diaries, pocket-sized calendars, poster calendars. The trick is to select from hundreds the number and types right for your store. Because of the variety of sizes and the fact that most are not free-standing, calendars can be difficult to display. However, they are seasonal, so space is required only for six months, peaking in December and January. Many stores use fixturing that is also suitable for large-format paperbacks. Some stores simply stack them on the floor with sample copies on the wall, some hang them on pegs. Creative displays require a little imagination.

When buying, consider the alternative discounts offered for returnable and nonreturnable. Then decide which calendars should be bought which way. Several years' experience helps with this decision but is by no means infallible.

Games and toys. This very broad category includes everything from baby rattles to the most expensive chess sets. Many stores distinguish between juvenile and adult items and between educational and recreational merchandise. Games include checkers, chess, and other board games as well as fantasy games. Jigsaw and other puzzles also fit in here. The toy category includes stuffed animals and dolls in addition to trucks, robots, toy soldiers, and dollhouse furniture.

The recent phenomenon of character licensing has caused a population explosion in the toy business. Book characters have sprung to three-dimensional plush or fabric life, toy characters are being immortalized in print, and whole groups of new characters are being created for a complete line of products, one portion of which is books. Some care should be exercised in selecting this merchandise since so much is available. Manufacturers sell direct, but since many have high minimums, some stores buy from a local distributor and select a variety of products from one source. The usual terms are 50 percent, no return.

Considerations for toys and games are adequate space for display and stock, possible breakage of mechanical items, disappearance of pieces from unsealed games and puzzles, and keeping dolls, stuffed animals, and other unpackaged merchandise clean. Such a department must be carefully supervised. It is best to select a small number of items for which there is a demand or which will coordinate in some special way with book stock, at least in the beginning, and then expand gradually. The toy business is very competitive, and there are discounters everywhere. Be sure that you have a market for what you buy, and that you select quality items not easily available elsewhere.

Greeting cards. Opinions differ on how involved in the card business a store can and should be. Some stores carry a whole line from one of the major card publishers. Others carry unusual cards from a variety of manufacturers. Cards are sold at 50 percent of list, which makes them attractive. They add color, variety, and interest to a store. One problem with cards is keeping them clean and fresh. They can require more housekeeping than books. Before making a decision about cards, check the neighborhood carefully. If there is a full-line card store down the street, you should probably not stock heavily but should find a limited number of unique cards. Many stores stock cards only for Christmas and Hanukkah, choosing a selection of quality cards suited to their clientele. Some stores do very well with personalized albums that require display space only for the books themselves. This requires a staff person to oversee orders and fulfillment. Advance planning is necessary to obtain sample books in sufficient time for early ordering. If handled properly, this can be a lucrative sideline.

Stationery. Annual trade shows in New York, San Francisco, and Los Angeles are an indication that the stationery business is thriving. A few hundred companies produce everything from strictly formal engraved stationery to outrageous notes and cards. There is something for everyone available from the major companies and a host of small, specialized, innovative firms as well. The problem is to select only what you think can be sold. Experimentation will probably be necessary to find the right mix for your store. Stationery may be big business but may not be the right sideline for every store. Storage, display, and housekeeping are required.

Personalized stationery needs no storage and minimal investment but does require space for the manufacturers' sample books. It is also necessary to make it known that your store offers this service. Care and thoroughness are essential when taking and placing orders to avoid errors in printing and fulfillment. Often one staff person is assigned to the section so that it will be run consistently.

Magazines and periodicals. Considered essential by many and a nuisance by some, magazines and periodicals are a logical adjunct to books. The fact that magazines carry a low discount is countered, according to those who swear by them, by the facts that they provide excellent traffic, bring repeat customers, and have much more rapid turnover than books. In addition, periodicals contribute to the image of your store as an information resource and provide more timely coverage of topics than is often possible in books.

In setting up this department, select good, high-visibility space that can be easily monitored. Magazines should draw into the store people who might not otherwise consider coming in. Decide which types of periodicals best fit your image and clientele. Determine the amount of money you are able to invest. A local magazine wholesaler can take care of most of your needs and will likely provide fixtures. Specialty and foreign periodicals are obtainable from national sources. There are firms that specialize in literary magazines. Just as with other products, if you can't find a supplier for a particular publication, go directly to the publisher for help. One staff person should be given responsibility for the department—to monitor the flow and keep the selections current. Magazine racks require attention, or they can quickly become unsightly.

Some stores offer a subscription service. This involves no inventory but does require careful record keeping and can be a profitable venture. Your wholesaler can advise you on how to set up such a department.

Records, tapes, and video. Some stores consider them heaven sent. Records and tapes can coordinate with book stock, can be handled in much the same way, and require about as much maintenance as books. As with books, there are new releases, backlist and remainders. It is possible to obtain a selection of budget, popular, or classical records and tapes from one source or to maintain a full-scale department stocked by more than one supplier. In this instance, one staff person should manage the department.

Spoken records and tapes are a natural coordinate to books since a variety of material is available—writers reading from their own works, readings of literary works by actors, dramatizations of novels as well as recorded plays, comedy records, radio shows, and more. Many fiction and nonfiction best-sellers are now available on tape cassettes. Not to be overlooked are the many types of educational and self-help records and tapes such as foreign-language courses, lectures, and motivational programs, several of which come with books. The wide variety of children's records is a perfect tie-in to a good selection of books—children's classics read by well-known actors or authors, dramatized stories, television programs, songs, and more.

Videotapes of special material and films can be a good sideline, especially with the many book tie-ins available from mass-market publishers. There are two ways of handling movie videos in the bookstore: selling outright or renting. Both involve obtaining stock from wholesalers. Film rental requires a considerable initial investment to purchase inventory, which is earned back over a period of time by rental fees, after which a profit is realized. Careful record keeping for each individual transaction and ample storage space are both necessary. The rental stock may also be sold off. As initial price per unit drops, it becomes more feasible for bookstores to sell individual tapes. These can be ordered on demand (even ordered in advance) from wholesalers, or an in-store inventory can be maintained. For a store situated near a video outlet of any sort, especially if a substantial outlay is planned, this would not be a suitable sideline.

Software. Although the software explosion has been very profitable for some bookstores, it is a sideline that should be approached with caution. There are many computers and microcomputers available, and there is a lot of software on the market, all of which is not compatible with every computer. Herein lie the problems. This is one sideline that requires knowledge of the field. Some familiarity with the software to be sold is essential, since not all software packaging includes sufficient information about how to use it, what the program contains, and with what it is compatible.

Recreational software, such as fantasy and adventure games, goes in and out of fashion quickly, and it is necessary to stay on top of the market to keep the inventory current. Unlike books, there is virtually no backlist. The titles change rapidly or are updated frequently, as is the case with educational software, making the earlier versions obsolete. Although unimaginative packaging has made display a problem in the past, manufacturers are now creating more attractive and informative packages in better formats. The majority of software now comes packaged to fit book display fixtures. Shrinkage can be a problem since many individual packages are small and easily concealed.

The pluses of software are good discounts, high individual sales, and consumer demand. Some software is packaged with books (automatic double sales), and much software coordinates with books. To sell software, technical support from manufacturers and/or wholesalers is necessary and available, frequently by hotlines.

On the negative side, the fast-changing nature of the business requires continuing effort to anticipate and take advantage of trends. The comparatively higher cost per single unit can cause some initial sales resistance, so it is wise to order from the lower end of the spectrum at first. If there is a computer or software store down the block, look for another sideline. But if the demand from customers, staff interest, money, and space all exist, software can be an excellent sidelines choice.

Chapter 47

Other Services

ALLAN MARSHALL

When is a bookstore more than a bookstore? When is a bookseller more than a bookseller?

Over the years people in this country have come to think of the bookstore as more than just a place to buy books and of booksellers as more than retailers who simply sell books. In part, the book-buying public has gotten that impression because bookstores are reaching out to find ways to increase profit margins. A widely used means to accomplish this is through the sale of sidelines, which carry a higher discount than books; another way is to provide services that complement books and bookselling. Some booksellers offer services not otherwise found in the community whether they are strictly book-related or not. The expanded bookstore is not an entirely new concept—remember the general store!

Let us examine some of the goods and services that a bookstore might consider adding to its operation.

Gift certificates. For a variety of reasons, a customer may not be able to select a particular book as a gift. In order not to lose the sale, the bookseller should be able to turn the situation around and offer the customer an alternative: the opportunity to purchase a gift certificate. There are several ways to provide this service. The hassle-free way is to contact the ABA, which offers a very attractive, nominally priced gift certificate package.

If you have a talent for design and a desire for individuality, it is possible to create your own certificate, or you can ask a commercial artist for help. Most stationery shops and print shops have stock gift certificates on their shelves or in their catalogs. This will save you the task of marshaling the project through the several production phases necessary for the completion of a homemade item. Gift certificates are an important way to increase sales.

There are any number of bookstores that sell blank greeting cards, and when the need for a gift certificate arises, the salesperson can simply take a card from the display rack and inscribe the necessary message for the customer. The salesperson takes in the money and records the transaction for future reference. Some booksellers give the card to the purchaser free of charge, and others add the cost of the card to the sale.

Charge accounts. Credit has become a way of life—for some people it is the only way! Even though we may consider credit cards insidious, as businesspeople we have to admit that their existence is an incentive to buy more than if cash were used as the medium for payment. In fact, the existence of credit may be the *only* incentive for some people to buy; they just don't have the cash.

With the increasing popularity of the national credit cards, internal house charge plans are becoming less and less useful or feasible for the small bookseller. There will always be those favorite steady customers who find it easier to pay once a month. There will also be those customers who will need a monthly statement of their book purchases for tax purposes and certain institutional or corporate customers that need invoices in order to make payment at all. For these accounts, any retailer would be happy to extend the service of "in house" credit.

It is difficult to imagine a store doing without one or more of the popular credit cards: MasterCharge, Visa, American Express, Carte Blanche, or Diners Club. The best way to make contact with any or all of these companies is through your local bank. If it doesn't handle the particular card in question, it will know how to steer you in the right direction. With little more effort than it takes to make your regular bank deposits, you can have the credit card company handling a portion of your accounts receivable problems for you. Of course, these credit card operations charge you for doing business with them. Since the percentage usually varies with your dollar volume, it is best to check the charge with your bank.

If you wish to have your own internal charge plan, you should carefully calculate what it is going to cost to maintain. Is the cost of your time or a bookkeeper's worth it? Are the printing of forms and envelopes, the secretarial time, the record-keeping, postage, and cash-flow problems going to pay off? There's no denying that the availability of credit encourages impulse buying and can add to sales, but go into this service with your eyes open.

Research services. Selling new books, whether they are current or backlist titles, is easy. Selling rare or out-of-print books is something else again (see chapters 37 and 38). Customers will flock to your bookstore if you are willing to at least *try* to find books that are no longer listed anywhere known to the general public. Many readers need books for research, business, for a collection, or just because they "gotta" have it; they will pay almost anything if their local bookstore can get them a copy. They are also willing to wait a long time to receive the book if there is the slightest chance that you can find it.

Although willingness to do research for customers will not always set the cash register ringing, such service will generate goodwill, which often leads to future purchases. Many is the scholar who at a late hour finds his bibliography is missing a publication date or a publisher's name, and with luck the missing information might be found in your copy of *Books in Print*. A neighborhood author might be putting together a reading list for an upcoming project; you can help by allowing her to use your reference books, such as *Subject Guide to Books in Print*, for drawing up the list. Some of those books will be checked out of the library, but some will be bought from you. All you had to do was provide the reference books and a quiet corner where the customer could make a list.

Gift wrapping. Gift-wrapping services are an absolute requirement. Make contact with the company supplying your paper bags to find out if it also sells counter wrapping paper and ribbons. It doesn't cost much to set yourself up with one style of paper, one contrasting ribbon, a roller cutter, some tape, and scissors. Be sure to have a supply of gift cards with your logo on them, of course, and always insert a bookmark or business card, both with your store's name, logo, and services, into the book before wrapping it. Some customers, while taking advantage of your free service, will complain about the commercialism of the bookmark in their gift. Don't make an issue of it; leave the bookmark out. Wrapping a spinning globe can present problems, but a book is easy. Practice a little so that you use as little paper, ribbon, and tape as possible. Every little bit helps when it comes to cutting overhead. Charging for gift wrapping is entirely up to you. Most stores do not.

An extension of gift wrapping is a shipping service. Your local stationery store can supply you with a good scale; your local post office has rate charts for you to use; your bag supplier will most likely have padded mailing bags, reinforced shipping tape, corrugated cardboard rolls, mailing tubes, and heavy-duty staplers, and you already will have plenty of empty boxes. Be sure to calculate carefully the weight of the *wrapped* package (box, stuffing, and books) so that you'll know exactly what to charge your customer. Ask if he wants the package insured, and charge if he does. Also charge for a padded bag if that is to be used. Be sure all your out-of-pocket expenses are covered. Whether you put a service charge on top of that is a decision you will have to make. One more point: Save your empty boxes. Not only will you need good sturdy boxes to mail books for your customers, but they will help when returning books. Customers unfortunately move, and they need boxes to pack their belongings. It is only natural that they should come to you for a supply.

Book repairs. Many fine old books have trouble living through the use or abuse to which they're put. Inveterate book collectors—those who refuse to part with the books they've read—will want to have the book restored or rebound, to give it a second life. This may be true, for example, of children's books that have been in the family for many generations. The *ABA Sidelines Directory* provides a listing of bookbinders who will provide the service. These people are becoming almost as extinct as the dinosaur, but a few of them are still out there. And some of them will even indulge your customer's desire for a *fine* binding of leather, gold tooling, or fancy endpapers and flyleaves. As in the case of rare books, this is a wide-open market, and you can charge as much as the market will bear.

Some nice things to do. A bookstore can provide space for a community bulletin board that has good visibility without encroaching on valuable sales space. All kinds of people will come to you asking if they can put up signs in your window. With a bulletin board, you can allow them to post the signs somewhere without covering up your display. Local dance recitals, house or garage sales, yoga instruction, and the like will all be announced at one time or another within your store. The notices will range from small scribbled notes to glossy multicolored posters large enough to hide everything else that is posted.

A community bulletin board may lead directly to your becoming a kind of ticket agency for local events. Usually there is no commission allowed, but many local groups will appreciate your providing an outlet for the sale of raffle or lottery tickets and general-admission tickets to dances, dinners, and flea markets.

If your space is large enough, allow local organizations to hold their meetings in your store. The space could be provided free or for a small charge and should be arranged so that the noise of the meeting does not conflict with your conducting business. This kind of service is particularly good as a promotional device if the groups and their activities are somehow connected to books or will need them in the future. You might also think of starting your own reading club or encouraging poetry and drama readings in your public areas. Not only will these people begin to think of your store as home, but they will become a captive audience and say to themselves, "Well, as long as I'm here, I might as well buy a book."

As your contribution in the fight against illiteracy, you might consider volunteering space in your store for literacy tutoring. There are many organizations that would welcome rent-free space and a ready access to books for their students. Once the word gets out that you have space available, you'll have no trouble locating groups that wish to avail themselves of your offer. Take my word for it!

Selling postage stamps, whether you do it out of a shoebox or by having a vending-machine supplier furnish a coin-operated machine for your store, will definitely help the late-night letter writers and those too lazy or too rushed to walk to the post office. If you go the machine route, there is a small commission to be made.

Magazines have become a very popular item in bookstores. So why not consider a magazine subscription service? If you wish to find out how to set this up, talk to your magazine jobber or wholesaler. Look through the listing of magazine subscription agencies in *Literary Market Place* at your local library, and make contact with some of the agencies listed there. It should be noted that the competition is pretty stiff these days. You have only to think of the subscription offers you receive in the mail to realize what you're up against. But if you're located outside the urban centers, it's worth a thought.

Copier services. Copying machines have become a necessity in most people's lives. You might want to offer a copying service, if you have the space for the machine and if you have a potential for its use. First check out the area to see what copy services are already available. If the situation seems pretty well under control, stop right there. However, if after investigation you feel that having a copier in your store would bring people in, contact the local representatives of the major copy machine companies. Ask for all their terms after you have described what you have in mind. You will want to know about leasing or purchasing, or a combination of both, about maintenance agreements, supplies, and costs. Analyze all the information before you proceed because there is little point in doing it if it is going to end up as a major expense item with little income and not much activity.

Consider that activity carefully. If the equipment is going to be used a great deal, make sure it is placed in an easily accessible spot in the store where perhaps it can be used by customers and not require constant staff attention. Unless you want to turn into a copy center, keep the "service" aspect of a copier in a controlled perspective. If it can pay for itself from the per-copy fees you charge, and bring customers into the store who might buy something else, and give you the capability of copying your own documents, you are ahead. If it becomes a nuisance that is costing money and not enhancing your business, it's not worth the time and trouble. Think about it carefully before proceeding.

Another one of those services that people can never find when they need it most is that of a notary. Contact the office of your state's secretary of state to get the details. A little study is required before taking the test and paying the fee to get the license. After that, all that's required is a small sign in the window, and you're in business.

There are as many other services that a bookstore can provide as there are creative booksellers. UPS pick-up spot, baby-sitter service, message center, ticket or travel agency, and so on and so forth. Bookselling itself is a service. Anything that enhances that service is worth considering.

VI
Advertising
and
Promotion

Chapter 48

Advertising—An Overview

ROBERT D. HALE

There are times when a bookstore event can be advertised in all the local papers, on the radio stations, and on television channels, with notice of it sent in the bookstore's newsletter to everybody on the mailing list, and then the day after it's all over, a customer will come in and say, "I would have come to see_____if only I'd known. Why didn't you promote it?"

There are other times when you will answer the telephone in your bookstore, and a voice will ask, "Do you have a copy of_____?" You reply that you do and are asked to save it for the caller, who then says, "I'll be coming from about sixty miles away. Where are you exactly?" If you inquire as to how this long-distance caller happened on to you to buy a book, the answer might well be, "I heard your ad on station XYZ," or, "I saw a copy of your newsletter at my sister's house," or, "I checked in the Yellow Pages and found your classified ad."

Advertising is one of the great guessing games of modern commerce. Even the most sophisticated polls and surveys can't be 100 percent sure of why one thing works and another doesn't. For a bookseller to ascertain which advertising is the absolute best is impossible. (Everybody agrees that "word of mouth" is best, but how to get those words into and then out of all those mouths is the challenge.)

To assume that one is so well known, or one's business is so established, that no advertising is necessary is nonsense. There are a variety of statistics that indicate all of us lose a substantial percentage of our customers each year, because they move away, because we didn't give them the service they required, for any number of reasons. If we managed to pick up new customers to replace those we lost, and if the new ones purchased about the same amount of books, we could probably maintain a static sales figure. But nobody in business can maintain a static sales figure and remain in business. Expenses increase, and if sales don't increase at least at the same rate, what profit there was can be wiped out, or if there were already losses, these will increase. What every business needs, bookstores included, is more customers buying more merchandise to provide sufficient growth to keep the business healthy.

To get new customers, and to get old customers to increase their purchases, we need to let them know that we not only exist, but are bringing in new and exciting titles all the time, that we are bringing in authors, participating in community programs, have special value days, and so on. My first temptation when that customer says, "I would have come to see ____ if only I'd known she was going to be here," is to ask if I'm expected to telephone everybody in my market area and give them the message personally. Wouldn't that be nice if it were possible. As much as we all hate telephone solicitation, it must work because so many national companies are doing it. I just wish they wouldn't always do it during my dinner.

Of course everything a store does, from putting a sign up in front, to opening the door, to doing window displays and in-store displays, putting new books face out, and stacking an impulse item next to the cash register, is all advertising, all merchandising. But the purpose of the next several chapters is to discuss classical ways of getting one's name and message out to the public—to get people talking, spreading the word and coming in to buy books. Every bit of advertising a bookseller does should be geared toward that goal— sales. This applies to advertising in high school prom programs as well as in the local newspaper or on the radio station or whatever. Advertising is an investment that should be made wisely. All investments don't pay off, but if none of them do, the investor is wiped out. Even though you may not know exactly what resulted from each of your advertising investments, you can, over a period of time, begin to get the feel of what brings people in to buy and what doesn't seem to have any effect at all.

Melissa Mytinger will tell you about advertising in print, meaning newspapers or other periodicals. J. Rhett Jackson will tell you about advertising on radio with a few comments about television. Gail See has much to say about getting publicity, which is free advertising and frequently the most effective of all. Judy Noyes shares her experience with a very productive newsletter.

In each of those articles there is some mention of the same things, such as cooperative advertising (of which I'll tell you more in just a moment). Don't feel that these overlappings are repetitive, but rather an indication that many of the same principles apply whether one is advertising in print or on the air. Planning advertising over a period of time rather than on a hit-or-miss basis is obvious, no matter what the media. Using one form of advertising to complement another is also obvious. If one has a great newspaper and a marvelous radio station to use, planning campaigns that carry the same message on both more than doubles the impact for the advertiser. This is an instance where a slogan should be part of the store's logo, so that the reader/listener sees it in the print advertisement and then hears it on the air. This repetition truly drives the message home so that it remains in the potential customer's memory and can establish a pattern of sending that person to your store whenever she or he needs or wants a book.

If you are to plan campaigns rather than just drop an ad in the newspaper from time to time, budgeting is essential. It is best to start with an annual amount to be spent, which can then be apportioned throughout the twelve months of the year. Beyond the opening-year advertising expense, which will of necessity be a major portion of the overall budget, there is much discussion of what percentage of annual sales a bookstore's advertising budget should be. It ranges from 2 to 5 percent and in some cases more. Part of that difference can be the result of location and lease expense. If you have a prime location where everybody for miles around can see the store, maybe a gigantic sign and then a few ads for special events will do. If you're down an alley and up the stairs (chapter 3 says location, location, location is important), then only insiders are likely to drop in unless a steady barrage of advertising goes out. If you have a very low rent, the dollars saved might be spent on advertising. If you pay high rent—in a mall, for instance—the advertising percentage might have to be lower, but the greater traffic within the mall offsets the need for more dollars spent on advertising.

It should also be stated that advertising as a percentage of sales will probably be greater in the early years of a bookstore's operation than later, unless a slump requires pumping up the traffic with an advertising barrage. Rather than state specific percentages here, which could not be on target for everyone because of individual circumstances, I suggest that once the opening year is completed and the pattern of growth established, the bookseller should do an analysis of all the forms of advertising used so far, to come up with an assessment of their effectiveness, then undertake an investigation of other forms that might be considered, and then, after compiling the costs and rates for each, devise a year-long advertising program that is affordable. It is easier to start with what you want to do than take an arbitrary figure and try to make the plans fit into it. Now, after that devised plan is all costed out, it may be obvious that the bookstore couldn't pay for it, which means some cutting has to be done. Or it may be, happily, that what one has considered is within the budget dollars as well as the percentage. We always talk about percentages, but it is dollars that we use to pay for things.

Dollars from the bookstore can be increased with cooperative advertising dollars from publishers. These dollars are available to all booksellers, but within very specific guidelines. So as to not be guilty of restraint of trade, every publisher has its own guidelines. There are generalities, however. The two main bases for their contribution to a bookstore's advertising are a percentage of the previous year's purchases from that publisher or a percentage of the purchase of the title or titles to be advertised. Not a generality but an absolute is that permission must always be given by the publisher before any advertising agreement is valid. In other words, a bookseller can't just do a big ad on a Harper & Row title and then send Harper the bill. Nor can a bookseller assume that just because they did $5,000 worth of business with another publisher, that publisher is going to send them whatever percentage for his advertising purposes.

Cooperative advertising means just that—cooperation between the publisher and the bookseller. Publisher's sales representatives are the best way to achieve this cooperation, but barring that, a bookseller can contact the publisher's marketing director for information.

The percentage a publisher allows is also variable. Frequently it is based on a formula of 75 percent of an ad's cost, but that 75 percent is also based on whatever dollar amount the publisher has agreed to give the bookseller. If the publisher agrees to $75 (to keep it simple), then on a 75/25 split, the bookseller should run a $100 ad, for which the publisher will give him 75 percent. If the bookseller says, "Aha, I have $75 from the publisher. I will run a $75 ad and let him pay it all," he may be surprised when the paperwork is submitted (tear sheets or affidavits plus copies of media invoices) to receive $56.25 rather than $75.00, the smaller figure being 75 percent of $75.00. The experienced bookseller will find out how much the publisher will allow before committing to an ad, even though the publisher will want to know how much the ad is to cost before it will approve an amount. If this seems confusing, it simply means there is a jockeying period during the discussion phase of planning cooperative advertising.

It is possible to plan a $1,000 ad and have a publisher reply, "Based on last year's net sales, we'll give you $612," or, "Based on the books purchased for this campaign, we'll give you $46." Don't sign up with any media for any amount until agreement has been reached with a publisher for cooperative advertising *if* you expect cooperation.

Once the deal has been struck and the ads run, then papers have to be submitted as indicated above for payment by the publisher to the bookseller. Again, there are variations in what is required, so we won't go into details, except to say that generally the bookseller pays the media and the publisher pays the bookseller, either in credits or with a check. Do *not* anticipate this payment by automatically deducting what you think your credit will be when paying a statement to that publisher. Wait until their paperwork is done as well as yours. Be patient to a point, but if nothing is forthcoming after a sufficient period of time, jog their memories about what is due you, exactly as they jog yours about what is due them.

Your annual dollar amount is not going to be spent all at once, not if you have any business sense. The total amount should be apportioned to the seasons and months. Most booksellers will have a few set advertising expenses each month, such as the cost of the ad in the Yellow Pages—remember that call from a customer who didn't know where the store is—or the small institutional ad you might run on the book pages every Sunday, or whatever. But beyond that, advertising dollars can be spent in widely different amounts each month depending upon potential sales.

Devising a chart here in this chapter would be easy, but it would reflect my situation, which might be totally different from the reader's. It is a truism that Christmas is bonanza time for most bookstores, so building sales prior to Christmas with lots of advertising is a common practice. Nevertheless, there are some astute booksellers who are convinced they can ride on the crest of the public impulse during that season, advertising minimally to remind everybody to come to their store to buy books and saving their big bucks for other seasons when they need to boost sales. There are booksellers in summer resorts who may be open for Christmas, but it is definitely a secondary season for them.

Whatever the breakdown in your sales pattern, an advertising budget needs to be divided to meet the needs of your particular bookstore. This should be done in advance of spending the money, or you can easily find the total allotment for advertising gone by April. The bookseller planning to use cooperative dollars should count these in the apportionment, but they can't be spread out in any equal percentage per month. In devising what is going to happen for the year ahead, as much as you can, it might quickly become apparent that after allotting money in January for the sale, February for Valentine's Day, May for Mother's Day, June for Father's Day, and so on, March and April have pretty slim pickings. Those are the months to consider advertising some specific titles so that you can boost your budget with publisher's money.

Then you continue, and plan whatever your area calls for in the summer, starting to build in the fall toward Christmas and gift giving. Once again, you will want to supplement what you have to spend with what you can get from publishers. In other words, you start an advertising budget exactly as you do any other budget, first putting down the absolute musts, then fiddling and fussing and planning the rest so, while you may not have all peaks throughout the year, your dips in sales are not deep valleys.

A word in closing about the tone of a bookstore's advertising. Inasmuch as the purpose of advertising is to bring people into your store to buy books, the stronger you can transmit that message, the better. This is where personality in advertising comes in. Whatever the personality or image or ambiance, or whatever you want to call it, of your store, do everything you can to convey that in all your advertising. If you are the colorful personality, consider doing your own radio spots—providing your color and personality achieves the results you seek. If you are the only bookstore around with a thousand cookbook titles in stock and that is your claim to fame, use it over and over in your message. If you gift wrap customer's purchases with a big blue bow—use that as your advertising gimmick and repeat, repeat, repeat. Bookselling is accumulated knowledge. Advertising is accumulated awareness.

Don't just go with title, author, price, location advertising in print or on the air. If you want book buyers to go past all those other bookstores to get to you, you have to give them a reason, whether it be curiosity, fabulous reputation, or whatever. Intrigue them and entice them. Think about what you want your advertising to say and convey, then think about the best way to do it. Allocate your available funds so that it will be said and conveyed on a constant basis. If you do it properly, it can be an investment that pays great dividends.

Chapter 49

Print Advertising

MELISSA MYTINGER

Bookstore advertising in print is a necessary ingredient in any well-rounded promotional program. Although publishers spend a good deal of money in the national media advertising their books, mostly those they hope will become blockbuster best-sellers, these ads are not targeted generally to a specific community. The titles that might do especially well in a bookstore's market may not be those the publisher hopes to sell nationwide. It is therefore in the bookseller's best interest to communicate the singularity of his store and the availability of titles in that store that are a reflection of that particular community.

This advertising of specific titles can in many cases be partially underwritten by publishers through their cooperative advertising programs. The myriad co-op programs available can be quite confusing. Sales reps can usually explain them and are frequently very useful in suggesting titles of local interest to advertise. The point is to advertise those books that have the greatest potential for sales, which means the bookseller must consider several things. For instance, what is the market that will be reached by the publication? Are the readers members of a university community, or vacationers at a resort, or perhaps professionals and businesspeople in an urban area?

In addition, the bookseller should consider any specialties that have been developed and are doing well in the store: cookbooks, for instance, or children's books or computer books, or whatever. It makes no sense to promote books in subject areas where there is little community interest and almost no sales potential, but it is very good business practice to advertise and promote more of what is already selling best.

To continue for a moment with the cooperative advertising possibilities, which cannot be completely covered here simply because they are so varied, there are several basic rules. The first is to get permission in advance to do the advertising. A bookseller can advertise anything he wants anywhere at any time, but if he hopes to have a publisher pay for part of that advertising, an agreement has to be reached between bookseller and publisher before the ad is placed. Publisher's reps are very helpful in arranging this, but even if a bookseller does not see a salesperson from the publisher of a book he wishes to advertise, cooperative monies can be sought by contacting the publisher directly.

Some publishers base their advertising allowances to a bookseller on that bookseller's previous year's net purchases. There are those who leave it completely up to the bookseller as to how those monies will be spent and on which titles. Other publishers have further rules about the use of their money—which is just one more reason to know all the rules before committing any dollars.

Still other publishers base their contribution on the number of copies purchased of whatever title it is the bookseller wants to advertise. Sometimes their percentage of contribution depends upon whether an author appearance is part of the promotion. There are endless wrinkles to be ironed out before the money can be used. Most co-op policies reimburse 75–100 percent of the ad, depending upon all the conditions that have been agreed on initially.

Once a publisher agrees to cooperate with a bookseller on advertising, it will provide materials to be used in the ads—sometimes even completely made-up ads, which only require insertion of the bookstore's name, address and telephone number, hours, and whatever other basic information is desired. Because of the various ways printed materials are produced, publishers will need to know in advance not only what materials will be needed, but in which form. As is by now obvious, cooperative advertising really requires cooperation.

After the advertising has been done, the money doesn't automatically appear on the bookseller's desk. There are forms to be filled out, verifications to be made, and more. Even the easiest require tear sheets showing the advertisement in whatever paper it was placed, copies of the invoice showing the cost of the ad, and copies of the signed contract between publisher and bookseller. Cooperative advertising requires some organization of paperwork if reimbursement is to be prompt and accurate.

A bookstore doesn't just advertise specific titles, however. There is what is called institutional advertising. A basic example of institutional advertising would be the bookstore's listing in the Yellow Pages of the telephone book. Cooperative money from publishers is not available for this, but it can be the most productive advertising a bookseller does. A bookseller may also want to advertise his store's special services, or holiday shopping hours, or the addition of a new department, or the fact that this store has the best mystery section in town. This institutional advertising is always intended to make potential customers aware of that particular business and make them want to come there to buy.

For most independent booksellers the cost of doing either specific title or institutional advertising in large metropolitan daily newspapers is prohibitive—even with cooperative allowances. This forces them to use local weeklies and monthlies and is perhaps one of the few economic barriers that is positive because small newspapers and periodicals generally have a more ardent readership than the big splashy newspapers, which are read once over lightly and then tossed out. Readers tend to keep the weekly newspaper around the house until the next issue comes out, meaning next week—which means that your advertisement placed in that weekly has a much greater chance of being seen and, more important, being read. Because these smaller papers and other periodicals are local, are community-oriented, their readers look to them for local sources. They are a good buy for a bookseller, whether the advertising be institutional or for a specific title.

A sizable chunk of a bookseller's institutional advertising budget can be absorbed by community programs ads. Although the cost of a single ad in the high school football program, the program for the local drama group, the Christmas concert, or whatever can be quite small, in total they can add up to a substantial amount. They can be dollars well spent if the result is increased goodwill, if the people of the community support the merchants who support community programs and projects. Do establish a budget for this type of advertising, however, so it doesn't eat up all the dollars you have to spend. If the demand is great enough, a wise policy might be scheduled alternation of ad placement, advertising in every other community theater program, only the holiday concert program, or some other established policy that will give as much coverage as can be afforded and at the same time protect the bookseller from an endless drain of advertising funds.

The most successful ads in these community programs are those that really catch the eye, either because of their dramatic layout, their humor, or whatever. If money is to be spent, the ad should be noticed. This is as true of goodwill ads as hard business advertising.

A bookstore should establish an identifiable personality in its advertising. The beginning of this is use of a symbol or logo that says to everyone looking at it, even if they are quickly scanning the page, "Ah, this is an ad from the bookstore." Logos should always be professionally designed, simple, and appropriate to the business. The logo should appear in and on all printed matter the store purchases and uses, from newspaper ads to store bags and envelopes and whatever else might be carried about by customers to let the world know that store exists.

Other than the logo, the constants in printed advertising are store name, address, telephone number, and business hours. Obviously, you might think, but notice how many ads do not have these essentials. Some ads may in addition carry a slogan, credit card information, whether a store does special orders or not, gift wrapping, other services, and so on. However, unless you are doing a catalog of reasons why all book buyers should always come to your store, it might be overkill to mention all facts each time. Remember, simple ads have the greatest impact. Never overstuff the space. Design it so the reader can take it in quickly and easily—and remember it. White space is as effective as lots of print. Use it to your advantage. If you do not feel adequate to doing the actual layout of an ad, work with the professionals where the ad is to run, or if it can be afforded, hire someone, a free-lancer, perhaps, to design ads for you. If the result is increased awareness and increased sales, the dollars spent on quality will have been a sound investment.

There are many decisions to be made about print advertising other than just layout. Do you want a full-page spectacular, or would you get more for your money if you did four quarter pages? Should you budget yourself to run small ads each week, or should you save up to run larger ads every other week or once a month? Some booksellers like the repetition of a small ad run constantly, but if an ad is too small, it makes almost no impact, and if it is run always in the same place, after a while nobody sees it.

Investigate all the possibilities in the bookstore's area before committing to just one newspaper or other periodical. There is a chance the store's clientele could be increased by using some advertising dollars in newspapers from adjacent areas. There might be very specialized periodicals available that would fit exactly into the special inventory a store carries. The biggest newspaper in town may not be the best when it comes to selling books. Consider all the alternatives.

Look into rates for all the newspapers in your area. They will probably have one-time rates and rates for regular advertisers, rates for up to so many column inches and a reduced rate over that number. They may have what they call "run of the paper" rates and premium rates for special placement (asking that your ad appear on a certain page). However, premium rates are a best buy sometimes —if, for instance, you want to advertise a new baseball book and ask to have it placed in the sports section. The ad will get more interested readers there than if it appeared in the living section.

Keep track of your record of successes and failures in print advertising. Although it is impossible to know exactly what brought that new person into the bookstore unless you ask her, it is possible to analyze the effectiveness of an advertising program—program, rather than a single ad. If a bookseller advertises regularly in a newspaper, both titles and general ads, and never has any sign that the ads are pulling people into the store and selling books, then it is time to consider another paper or getting some help in making the layouts more effective. If one type of ad seems to sell while there is no response to another type, develop the former and forget the latter.

Advertising is much more than merely spending a specified percentage of one's budget. Successful advertising in print is making an impact that makes a difference in the volume of business you do. As in every other aspect of bookselling, it requires careful planning and execution and constant analysis. Print advertising is visual. It should be simple and direct. It can make a bookstore a well-known part of a community, and it can sell books for that store.

Chapter 50

Radio and Television Advertising

J. RHETT JACKSON

After forty years of buying radio and television advertising, first for a furniture retail business and then for selling books, I feel I've not only gained considerable experience, but picked up a few ideas I'd like to share.

Let me start off by contradicting some of the often-expressed thoughts in this industry about how much we should spend for advertising. Most balance sheet examples suggest that bookstores spend only 2 percent for advertising. I simply do not believe that a bookstore can make any kind of impact on its market with so low a percentage. The first year I had my bookstore I budgeted $10,000 for advertising, as I knew I must build a quick and solid image if I were to compete with seven chain stores that were also opening. I considered this first year's advertising budget part of opening expense.

My total volume the first year was $145,000, so my advertising amounted to about 7 percent. In the years that followed, I have set my goal at 4 percent of sales. When I use all the cooperative money that is available to me, I probably spend about 6 percent of sales, 4 percent coming from my dollars and 2 percent from publishers.

My market is the state's capital city with a population of about 500,000. We have fifteen radio stations, three local TV network stations, an educational TV station, and several cable TV stations. Selection of which radio and/or television station to use for advertising is a very difficult job. At best it is intelligent guesswork, and often mistakes are made. What I strive for is hitting the right programs and stations most of the time. The old merchant prince, John Wanamaker, has been quoted as saying, "I know half of all advertising dollars are wasted; I just don't know which half."

Not many booksellers can afford to do much advertising on television. Rates are generally too prohibitive, except for a few twenty-second announcements, perhaps, on a movie tie-in when offered the use of some publisher co-op money. However, it is possible to get free time on TV, and many booksellers have been successful at that. This is especially true with local public channels or cable stations. We will look more closely at this toward the end of the chapter.

Why Radio Is Best

I think the bulk of a bookstore's advertising budget should be spent in radio with the use of newspapers reserved for special events, autographings, and annual sales. This decision will depend upon which of the media is most important in a bookstore's market. In some places people may not be reached by radio but may be avid newspaper readers. In others, the local radio stations may dominate the market. The trick is to balance costs for a potential audience with the bookstore budget. In my market, newspaper advertising is so expensive I use it sparingly with only a regular institutional ad running on the Sunday book page.

I have discovered that the local radio stations are reaching my potential customers, so I carefully work out advertising campaigns that run on a regular basis and are within my budget range. By choosing the time slots carefully (sometimes this is achieved after trial and error) and repeating an ear-catching ad, often I have built a loyal following of customers for my store. Most of the time when someone is listening to the radio, whatever is being broadcast has that person's complete attention. This is a captured moment in which to tell somebody about your store and the books to be found there. A small ad in a newspaper tends to get lost, but a small ad on the radio can have great impact.

In choosing the best radio station(s) for your advertising, you must make a thorough study of the market reached by the various stations and combine that with the kind of market you hope to reach. You will probably find there is a country station, a rock station, a concert or classical station, and more. High school and college students and young professionals probably listen to the rock stations, and older audiences listen to the rest. Because repetition increases impact, it is better to select one or two radio stations and use them frequently and regularly than to scatter your dollars over all the stations and so make a minimal impression on all the markets.

Not only should you investigate which stations are most likely to reach those you think will become your customers, but you also have to discuss with the stations selected which times of the day are best. Radio stations have time slots such as drive time, early morning, and so on, with rates depending upon their estimated number of listeners in each segment. Drive time may be the most expensive, not only because of the number of listeners, but because of the more complete attention paid by drivers to what is being said on the radio while they are in their cars. If what you want to advertise has appeal for those drivers, then the greater dollars spent may be well worth the bite out of your budget. Perhaps you want to advertise something that you think would be most appealing to late-night listeners or to the legendary housewife at midmorning. Select time slots not only for their costs, but for their particular effectiveness.

Frequently a certain radio personality will be a most effective salesperson for you. If there is a talk-show host who interviews authors, that show is a natural for bookstore advertising. If there is an announcer who reads as well as talks, you might get extra bounce for your buck by using that announcer. You will discover that the longer you advertise on a particular station or spot, the more successful that advertising will be. The effect is cumulative. You can't test the results on short time periods.

However, if your choice of station or time does not seem to be working out for you, don't be afraid to change and try something else. It may take several years before you are completely comfortable with the schedule you have arranged. Even then, don't be afraid to rotate it to make sure you are reaching as many people as possible with the story of your bookstore and what it has to offer.

If you are having a sale or a special promotion, you can often get a package deal from your radio stations. An FM station I use whose spots are about $20 per sixty seconds sometimes has a special of thirty spots for $300. That's half price and is as good a value for me as my sales are for my customers. Most local stations have special offers from time to time.

Preparing a Radio Commercial

You will want two kinds of commercials. The first is a regular, day-in-and-day-out, strong institutional advertisement. In mine I constantly tell my customers why a good, well-run, well-stocked, independent bookstore is a better place to shop. I tell them about our selection, its depth and variety, about our special-order service, hours, location, telephone number, and so on. Frequently I intersperse with this information brief but very clear reviews of books. You can say a lot about a book in forty or fifty seconds. I write my own commercials and send them to the station for their people to edit and produce. On another station I take my material to the station studio and record my own commercials. After a little experience this is not difficult, and the sound of my voice instantly alerts listeners to my bookstore. Personalized commercials of this sort are very successful for any business, but especially so for a personal, independent bookstore.

The second kind of commercial is for the special sales event, for autograph parties or any other promotion. In these commercials your message is more urgent—"You must act now," "Sale ends Thursday," "The author will be here Monday from two to four P.M." While the institutional message is long range and so written and produced to build confidence in and curiosity about your store, the special-event message has to stir listeners to action—*now*. You may want to use many brief messages for this, repeating the same information over and over to impress listeners with the need to respond at once.

Think about what you want your commercial to do for you, and plan each very carefully. In any radio commercial, mention the name of your store at least twice, at the beginning and the end of the message, and give your location—not just in such-and-such a shopping mall, but in the so-and-so mall at the corner of whatever and whatever. Don't assume your listeners have any idea where you or the mall are located. Tell them. There is basic information for any advertising: name, address, telephone number, and hours.

Most independent booksellers can, with the help of the radio stations they are using, create their own commercials. An advertising agency might be used for a special campaign if their costs will be more than made up by an increase in sales. Perhaps the bookseller will want to pay for professional help in producing a music logo. But generally, the bookseller should spend the dollars on air time and not on professional assistance in preparation of material. The time may come when professionals can be afforded within the budget and the right agency for the purpose might produce stunning results, but that is more likely in the future, not in the beginning. And by the time the ability to pay comes around, the personalized advertising created by the bookseller and the radio station staff will probably have been so successful there will be no need to change.

After you have selected the station or stations you think will be of most benefit to you, sit down with representatives of those stations to find out just how much help they are able to give you. In most cases, you will find that your knowledge of what you want and your ideas combined with their technical expertise will result in effective advertising at very low cost. Keep in mind that you can also use the assistance of publishers if you are going to advertise specific titles, and you can also use their cooperative advertising dollars. Most publishers require written approval in advance for this advertising, however, so make sure you have that firmed up before you go ahead.

The important thing about planning an advertising program is not to be afraid of it. It is just one more thing you have to learn as a bookseller. It is not difficult, and media people are not only well trained, but eager to work with you. After a year or two you will find that a few hours spent each month planning and writing your advertising copy will produce the sales for which it is intended.

Television

Because most independents cannot afford it, I am not going to say much about planning and buying television time. The principles would be the same—selecting the station or stations with the viewers who would be most likely to respond to your message, then working out schedules with the station that would be most effective and affordable for you. There may be opportunities to do tie-in advertising when a book has been turned into a miniseries, and for this cooperative money from publishers is frequently available. This is the extent to which most independents would use TV advertising.

With the advent of cable, opportunities are greater than before, and these should be investigated if you are interested in pursuing TV commercials. More production is involved in TV commercials than in radio, and usually more professional assistance is needed. There are some booksellers who use local television much as I use radio—appearing on their own commercials, for instance. Using some of the basic steps outlined above, look into TV if it appeals to you—but with the same care and caution you exercise in any investment of time and money.

Free Air Time

In every community there are countless opportunities for getting free time on radio and television. Television stations are supposed to allocate a certain number of hours each week to local shows of community interest. Frequently these shows include author interviews. If you make friends with the station staff by helping them locate interviewable authors and supply them with information about newsworthy books, for instance, they will often mention you and your store and the availability of the books discussed.

An astute Florida bookseller, Charles Haslam, prepared a sample script of a TV show that interviewed authors and reviewed books and sold his idea first to a public television station and then to a private network. He was the interviewer on these shows, which ran for many years at no cost to him except for time and planning effort. He also had a similar show on one of Florida's leading radio stations. There are numerous booksellers around the country who do similar kinds of shows.

Publisher's representatives are good sources of information about which authors will be in an area and when. Passing on that information to a television or radio station and making the connection for them with the author through the publisher is great public relations and leads to possible free air time for the bookseller. The ABA-produced *Newswire* has several pages of authors' tours each week. It is frequently possible to book additional radio or television appearances for these authors—especially if none are already scheduled for your area. Don't overlook those call-in radio programs that are on at odd hours of the night and day and have enormous listenerships. It is possible the station may want the bookseller as well as the author on the show.

There are many ways for a bookseller, because of the very special nature of the business and because many authors are newsmakers as well as writers, to obtain free air time. Be creative in thinking of ways you can get some of that free time for your bookstore.

In summary, I feel very strongly that you will find radio advertising to be your best investment in the promotion of your bookstore. If you study your market area carefully, you can find the station(s) that will be the most effective in reaching the people you want to become book buyers at your store. After selecting the stations, produce announcements that tell an effective and quality story about your store and your books. Tell this story often, and always give sensible reasons as to why book buyers are better off shopping at your bookstore. Don't forget to always tell them when you are open and how to reach you! Make those announcements personal and attention getting. Remember that radio stations offer a lot of help for you in both scheduling and ad preparation. In addition to the advertising that you pay for, be alert to the many opportunities to get free publicity on both radio and television. Know when authors are available for interviews, and know how to reach those people in the media who can get them "on the air."

Finally, let me caution you not to get all your programs "set" and then forget them. You need to monitor your ads constantly, to be on the alert for needed changes. When times change you may have to change your format, your stations, or your emphasis. Be flexible, and keep creating advertising programs that sell books for you!

Chapter 51

Publicity

GAIL SEE

Publicity... what is it? *Webster's* definition reads: "An act or device designed to attract public attention." As booksellers, we are in a unique position to attract public attention in our communities because the product we sell lends itself to all kinds of community-wide promotion. A bookstore by its very nature can and should be a gathering place, a local meeting spot, a center of information about the community and its activities. Bookstores have this special place because, in dealing with books, we are dealing with ideas, hopes, dreams, entertainment, and information. Everyone in the community can feel at home in the bookstore, the new parent looking for a baby book, the business executive looking for a book on management, the newly moved family looking for a local map, the high school English teacher looking for copies of *Macbeth*, or the closet writer looking for *Writer's Market*.

How does publicity help you attract all these varied and diverse people? *Webster's* definition shows us that publicity begins at our very door, for the signs we use, our window displays are, in fact, "designed to attract public attention." Our public face is carried throughout the store, in displays, lighting, layout, and most important of all, in our attitude toward our customers. But beyond these obvious outward signs, there are specific ways to seek and find public attention.

In-Store Promotions

Autograph parties. There are as many tales of autograph parties as there are booksellers, and many of them tales of woe. But there are also success stories, all of which start with planning: lining up the author, arranging for an adequate number of books (including the author's previous titles), sending out invitations and news releases to the media, and talking with every customer who comes into the store as well as designing eye-catching in-store displays announcing the event. We find it works best if we group our events, planning four to six store events twice a year. We start by asking the publisher reps when we are buying their lists about any authors going on tour who could make an appearance in our store. We look for authors for whom we believe we can attract an audience! In thinking about author events, don't overlook local authors and illustrators. They are thrilled to be asked to come, and most often have a local following. (We always ask these local people for a list of friends, family, and acquaintances, to whom we send personal invitations.) There are events that can tie into books, which do not require an author: a local flower-shop owner has talked about flower arranging and recommended books, the chef from a restaurant demonstrated pasta making and discussed cookbooks.

Planning the actual event involves setting a firm time with the individual and making arrangements for their appearance in the store. Three to four weeks before the day we send a five-by-seven-inch postcard announcing all the spring or fall book-author events to our mailing list. If one author has appeal to a particular group, we will send special invitations to that group. For instance, we had a local author who had a book on education and schools. We contacted, and personally invited, all the members of the local school boards in our area, as well as members of the school's administration and selected faculty members. For a gardening book promotion, we sent invitations to all the garden club members in the area. For a wilderness book, we located the names of the nature conservancy group.

Your local newspaper is one of your most important sources of publicity. In addition to placing ads announcing various events, send news releases, and invite a reporter to cover the story. Best of all, send a copy of the book to your local paper, particularly if it is a local author. If you are featuring a cookbook, invite the food editor of the paper.

A variation on the usual autograph party that has generated good publicity has been our "Breakfast with an Author." For an individual who we know will attract a good crowd, we have held a 7:30 breakfast at a local restaurant. We serve a Continental breakfast, for which we charge a nominal amount. The author speaks and/or answers questions for approximately an hour. Our community is accustomed to early-morning meetings, and we have attracted both men and women on their way to work.

In-store book fairs. Another variation of an old theme is the idea of in-store book fairs. Community and church groups, college alumni groups, and other community organizations looking for fund-raising events find an in-store book fair a simple way to raise money and to attract publicity for their organization. At the same time, you are introducing your store to new people while contributing to the community. Usually, the sponsoring organization handles invitations and publicity releases to the papers, radio, and TV stations and arranges for members of their organization to be in the store to greet people and to help if needed. We compile a list of book suggestions that is included in the invitation. Phone orders are accepted and delivered by members of the participating group. Since most of the organizations go well beyond the borders of our community, we have very good exposure, make new friends and attract new customers. Our cost is a percentage to the sponsors of the event's sales.

Out-of-Store Promotions

We in the book business are in a unique position to widen our market and to generate publicity by working with community groups. Watch for seminars, classes, or special school or civic events that can be tied to books. When you see an interesting announcement, call the sponsoring group, and usually you will find them happy to have you take books to sell at the event. Offer to donate a percentage of sales to the group. That is a small cost for your exposure to potential customers. Once again, you are contributing to your role as an integral part of the community.

Schools. In addition to book fairs (which are covered elsewhere), there are other ways to be connected with schools. We contact school librarians and English teachers to find out which books are being assigned at what time of year. In our community, the teachers cannot require the students to buy books, but many students want their own copies. It is very discouraging to both the student and the bookseller to be out of *Tom Sawyer* when twenty eager readers ask for it. In addition, we call the school librarians and English teachers before we do returns in the spring and fall and offer them a 40 percent discount on the titles we are returning. Also, at the beginning of the school year, we send a card (distributed through the school system) to each teacher offering a 10 percent discount with the presentation of the card. This is to introduce our store to the teachers, especially the new ones, and let them know we are interested in being their bookstore.

Study and book clubs. There are a growing number of individuals starting book and/or study clubs. Your bookstore can be the obvious place for these people to go for help in selecting reading lists. This gives you an opportunity to introduce the reading public to those little-known "gems," books that deserve a wider audience but do not receive the hype of major best-sellers. When a group asks for help, inquire into their interest areas, whether they want to develop a theme for the year or want different types of books for each meeting. Ask one or two of the group to come into the store and go over selections with you. Most groups want from six to ten books a year and will order them from your store. You may be asked to talk to the group about one or two of the selections, which is not as terrifying as it sounds. Unless you are paralyzed at the thought, meet with the group and discuss a book about which you are particularly enthusiastic. Enthusiasm is the secret weapon for publicity. Which brings us to "book talks."

Book talks. Most organizations are thirsty for programs, and once word is out that you are available to do book talks, you may have more requests than you can handle. Again, this is because we are in a business that interests the general public. The most successful book talks combine information about the behind-the-scenes happenings in publishing and bookselling, new trends in the business (will computers replace books?), with an overview of current, unusual, interesting titles. Here again, we, as independent booksellers, have a chance to introduce our audiences to the many fine, well-written, challenging, unusual, thought-provoking titles that we know and appreciate, titles that never see the light of best-sellerdom. The choice of books for discussion should match the group, obviously. Don't choose the latest family saga or movie star biography for the Rotary or Downtown Men's Club luncheon or the hottest management book for a women's support group. These audiences are enthusiastic, supportive, appreciative, and they will become your customers. In addition, your book talks will reinforce your position as a knowledgeable book person.

Newspapers. The editor of your local newspaper can become a good friend and source of excellent publicity. Newspapers are interested in local news, and will usually run news releases sent to them. If you or any of your staff does anything considered newsworthy, send a press release to your paper... if you attend the ABA Convention, if you speak to a local group, certainly when you are having any event in your store. Submit a best-seller list from your store. You may be invited to write a book column for your paper with suggestions of current books. In some areas, booksellers have become book reviewers for local radio and TV stations.

Always remember, bookselling is a fascinating profession to the general public. You can and should be the most knowledgeable and enthusiastic book person in your community, so do all you can to "spread the word." You will discover added joys of bookselling, your books will "attract the public attention" they deserve, and so will your store.

Chapter 52

Newsletters

JUDY NOYES

Booksellers deal in words. Reading and talking are occupational requirements, and it very often follows that booksellers are fairly good wordsmiths. We all like books, and most of us like people, so we dedicate ourselves day after day to encouraging more and more people to buy more and more books. Given these aims and attributes, it is no wonder that many bookstores, small or large, are producing personal newsletters as a major part of their advertising and promotion programs.

A shop newsletter is that something extra: an individual touch in this day of mass, canned, powdered formula approaches that leave us weary and suspicious. Just as people are delighted to be called by name and given other attentions, they respond gratefully to a mailing that is clearly geared to the special group to which they belong. A newsletter is a direct and personal communication between you and your customers, reinforcing the image of your store, reminding your old customers, and informing your new, of the services you offer, telling them about new books and old favorites. Don't assume that everybody reads national book reviews, studies all those zillions of booklists, or follows the TV author interviews. In your community, *you* inform and encourage readers.

The slick, readily available commercial catalogs cannot achieve the personal touch, the "this is written for *you*" quality of the individual bookshop publication. The do-it-yourself newsletter has the advantage of allowing you to choose the books you plan to stock and promote—the titles you and your staff are most enthusiastic about, including unusual titles that would not appear in the mass-produced catalogs. It gives you the opportunity to present your store's unique qualities.

At the Chinook, our newsletter grew out of a monthly book column we wrote for a local FM radio guide when the bookshop was new; the column cost us nothing except time and was a way of introducing ourselves to the book-buying public. When the little FM magazine folded, we decided to expand the column into a brochure of capsule reviews and commentary. We called it *Currents from the Chinook.* (A chinook, we might explain, is a warm, dry wind blowing down the eastern slope of the Rockies, literally a "snow eater" that dramatically raises temperatures and brings a promise of spring.) We chose the word "currents" for its implication of flow and timely comment. This initial effort was one page (one side), professionally printed and mailed to a few hundred customers. *Currents* is now six pages, printed on both sides, and goes to customers all over the world.

For our first brochure, we hired a commercial artist friend to design a masthead and advise on type and layout. It is usually possible to find someone capable who can help you with this part of the job in exchange for books. Make sure, however, that the artwork and layout are clean and professional. Your best friend's drawing of a bookworm may look cute, but if the world at large finds it amateurish, that's the image you'll leave of your store.

We feel strongly that because *Currents* represents our shop, it must be quality in every respect. We choose paper, stock, and ink with care, and we go over proofs meticulously. Typographical errors, mistakes in grammar or punctuation, authors' names or titles misspelled, or other inaccuracies raise doubts about your general knowledge and efficiency and bespeak a sloppiness that your readers could attribute to your whole operation. We have learned enough through the years to be able to do our own layouts, working with the printer. Decorative borders, fancy initial caps, and illustrations can be found in old magazines or in books such as the Dover collections of old advertising art. (Be sure to use only material that is out of copyright.) A solid page of type can be forbidding; it's good to break up the monotony with some kind of artwork. A drawing of your store or your front door or even photographs can be used.

Your printer will show you various types and grades of papers and inks. We have found a seventy-five to eighty-pound stock the best for mailing purposes, and we prefer the appearance of a textured finish. We use what printers call an average high-cost paper primarily because it permits a greater variety of finishes and colors. The color combinations are almost endless: brown ink on gold paper, black on olive, turquoise on white, navy on rose, green on cream. We generally use 8- and 10-point Times Roman type. Make sure the ink is readable. See a sample run before you decide. If

Fig. 52-1. *The Envoy* is the newsletter of the Harvard Book Stores.

the newsletter is difficult to read, you're defeating your purpose. For size, we like an 8½-by-14-inch sheet with a triple fold, printed by offset with Linotype composition.

If you are a new store and your mailing list is small, you may be able to hand address your newsletter. However, as the mailing list grows into the upper thousands, you will need mechanical help. For years we used a label machine that we acquired secondhand, but like other dinosaurs, it finally gasped its last. This was a blessing; we have switched to a local computerized mailing service, which saves a significant amount of time and money. Of course, if your store has a computer you will want to put your mailing list into it.

Doing a quality job on a newsletter is not cheap. And it's difficult to measure the results. It certainly had better be productive if you're going to expend money and time. You can keep track of actual mail-order response; aim for at least 7 percent to make it worthwhile. Of course, you can only guess at the response from customers (gratifying sight) who come into the store, newsletters in hand, with titles checked and circled. Your actual pull is probably going to be considerably beyond what you can measure. No one can put an exact dollar value on goodwill and public relations.

How often you issue a newsletter depends on your own desire, time, and budget. Remember to allow at least a month from the time you get copy to the printer until the actual mailing. If you're aiming for the Christmas trade, you should have everything at the printer's by November 1 at the latest—the earlier, the better. Keep in mind, too, that a mailing list, like a garden, must be constantly pruned, culled, corrected, and enlarged. Be sure to go through your list at least once a year and throw out the known no-buys. With postage so high, you can't afford deadwood.

We cannot stress enough the importance of gearing your mailing piece to the particular interests of the people in your area, using the appealing qualities of the soft sell and personal touch; this contrasts favorably with the hucksterish, noisy prose of most direct-mail advertising. Let yourself go creatively; use limericks, rhymes, puns, or any other device you want to make your point. You may also be negative about a book or subject if you feel it's deserved. If you're weary of wok cookbooks or sick of pop psych, say so. Your honesty will come as a refreshing surprise to your customer-reader.

Keep notes of things that happen in the shop that might add humor and the light touch to your newsletter. Your customers will enjoy reading about the garbled requests: "Do you have *The Scarlet Pumpernickel?*" "*The Rejected Saurus?*" "*The Taming of the Screw?*" Our classic request came from a student who wondered where we kept the books by Ibid: "He must be an important writer since he's quoted in so many footnotes." Tell of how you searched high and low for a book on pansies, later to find it was Pascal's *Pensées* you should have been looking for.

References to regional and local authors, places, and events are always good. Your out-of-state customers who came to know you on a trip to your town will learn of books that might not receive notice or be available in their own communities. At first we were surprised by the number of mail orders we received from people in Philadelphia, Chicago, and Washington, and then we realized that a special book on western Americana might not have been reviewed outside the West.

Make sure you suggest to your readers that shopping by mail is easy, convenient, and painless. Encourage them to telephone their orders if they wish—a great timesaver during the holidays. Print your telephone number prominently. Tell them about your services—gift wrapping, mailing, deliveries, out-of-print searching, whatever you offer—and about your specialties—children's books, regional, religious, technical, cookbooks, paperbacks, bargain books. Your newsletter should be a warm and personal invitation to the reader to use your services and expertise.

As you might guess, there is a great variety of look and style in bookstore newsletters, but one feature they have in common is enthusiastic promotion of the books these booksellers have enjoyed and admired. Children's bookstores, particularly, recognize the service they provide parents and teachers with their knowledgeable evaluations of hundreds of new titles each season, and the newsletter is a key promotional activity for these specialty stores. Jody Fickes of Adventures for Kids in Ventura, California, and Louise Howton of The White Rabbit in La Jolla, collaborate on their children's book newsletter, and to spread the word about their favorites (and also to help with production expenses), they market the newsletter to other bookstores. In reverse of the more usual procedure, Ed and Barbara Morrow's Northshire Bookstore in Manchester Center, Vermont, *features* its children's books, with current adult titles described in an insert. In addition to the emphasis on children's books, there is coverage of special events and services interwoven with charming, mood-setting comments on Vermont seasons. Each issue includes an arresting one-paragraph grammar lesson from the *Oxford American Dictionary*.

Chuck Robinson's Village Books, Bellingham, Washington, "makes an effort to include pictures of the staff to personalize the newsletter," and an especially appealing feature is the section entitled "Young Readers Review Their Favorite Books." Parents will certainly see to it that this particular newsletter gets wide distribution! *The Western Newsletter* from Jean Wilson's Book Shop in Boise, Idaho, is an excellent example of promoting a strong regional department, as are Gail See's mailings from The Bookcase in Wayzata, Minnesota.

Humor and sophistication, both in writing and choice of books to be reviewed, characterize the *Quarterly* from the Waking Owl Book Company in Salt Lake City, a good example of simple and

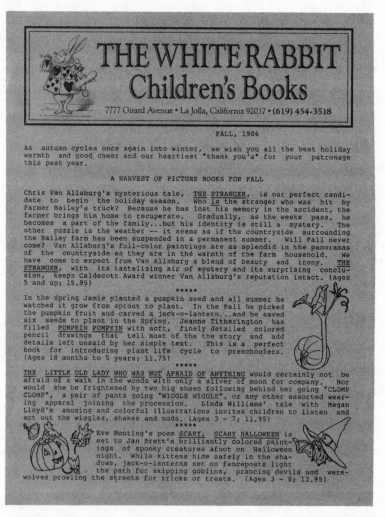

THE WHITE RABBIT
Children's Books

7777 Girard Avenue • La Jolla, California 92037 • (619) 454-3518

FALL, 1986

As autumn cycles once again into winter, we wish you all the best holiday warmth and good cheer and our heartiest "thank you's" for your patronage this past year.

A HARVEST OF PICTURE BOOKS FOR FALL

Chris Van Allsburg's mysterious tale, THE STRANGER, is our perfect candidate to begin the holiday season. Who is the stranger who was hit by Farmer Bailey's truck? Because he has lost his memory in the accident, the farmer brings him home to recuperate. Gradually, as the weeks pass, he becomes a part of the family...but his identity is still a mystery. The other puzzle is the weather -- it seems as if the countryside surrounding the Bailey farm has been suspended in a permanent summer. Will Fall never come? Van Allsburg's full-color paintings are as splendid in the panoramas of the countryside as they are in the warmth of the farm household. We have come to expect from Van Allsburg a blend of beauty and irony. THE STRANGER, with its tantalizing air of mystery and its surprising conclusion, keeps Caldecott Award winner Van Allsburg's reputation intact. (Ages 5 and up; 15.95)

*****

In the Spring Jamie planted a pumpkin seed and all summer he watched it grow from sprout to plant. In the Fall he picked the pumpkin fruit and carved a jack-o-lantern...and he saved six seeds to plant in the Spring. Jeanne Titherington has filled PUMPKIN PUMPKIN with soft, finely detailed colored pencil drawings that tell most of the the story and add details left unsaid by her simple text. This is a perfect book for introducing plant life cycle to preschoolers. (Ages 18 months to 5 years; 11.75)

*****

THE LITTLE OLD LADY WHO WAS NOT AFRAID OF ANYTHING would certainly not be afraid of a walk in the woods with only a sliver of moon for company. Nor would she be frightened by two big shoes following behind her going "CLOMP CLOMP", a pair of pants going "WIGGLE WIGGLE", or any other assorted wearing apparel joining the procession. Linda Williams' tale with Megan Lloyd's amusing and colorful illustrations invites children to listen and act out the wiggles, shakes and nods. (Ages 3 - 7; 11.95)

*****

Eve Bunting's poem SCARY, SCARY HALLOWEEN is set to Jan Brett's brilliantly colored paintings of spooky creatures afoot on Halloween night. While kittens hide safely in the shadows, jack-o-lanterns set on fenceposts light the path for skipping goblins, prancing devils and werewolves prowling the streets for tricks or treats. (Ages 3 - 8; 12.95)

Fig. 52-2. The White Rabbit bookstore newsletter.

effective graphics and layout. Warren Cassell of Just Books in Greenwich, Connecticut, says that his newsletter is "the single most effective selling tool I've had," and "not a day goes by without a customer telling me about the newsletter in a positive and sometimes laudatory manner." His newsletter is discriminating, critical, and makes you want very much to read the books he has chosen to review.

It is helpful to have a model if you're just getting into the newsletter business, and most bookstores are pleased to share samples of their brochures. Contact the ABA or the individual stores for sample newsletters, and when you request a copy, it is a courtesy to enclose a self-addressed, stamped envelope.

All agree that producing a newsletter is extremely time-consuming. But no one would be willing to continue making that effort if it were not an effective way to sell books, create a vivid image, and promote the bookstore.

Chapter 53

Display and Visual Merchandising

CHRISTINE HUFFMAN

The ability to merchandise is an absolute necessity for today's booksellers. Competition is strong, and in many stores service is at a minimum. Merchandising books in easily identified categories and well-signed feature displays is one technique for increasing sales without adding employees. When one considers that almost 45 percent of all sales are generated *within* the store, the old adage, "Books well displayed are half-sold," becomes truer than ever.

Category Placement and Signing

Properly considered, category placement and adjacencies are an integral part of visual merchandising. Some of this theory has been covered in chapter 7 on bookstore planning and design, but it's worthwhile to reiterate that customers should be able to enter the store and very quickly, *unassisted,* be able to tell from signs and placement where the book they want is likely to be. This is not as easy as it sounds. Too often booksellers purchase expensive category signs or labels for the store, then find it too costly or time-consuming to buy more to reflect changes in the store's inventory. It's unreasonable to ask customers to scan twenty feet of shelving without giving them a category and subcategory label. One solution: Use something as simple as Dymo punch tape, which comes in many colors, is inexpensive, and makes it easy to change labels. Whatever interior signing you choose, make sure you can get more of it quickly and cheaply.

Categories change with the times, and these continuing adjustments will give your store a fresh look. Ten years ago, the Fix-It category was clearly for men only, while Decorating meant books just for women. Such divisions of labor now seem archaic, so a category called Lifestyle or Today's Home can serve as umbrella for all those home decorating, repair, and even gardening books. Similarly, establishing a section called Small Pleasures can give you a place for all those appealing little books that aren't new titles, are humorous but not quite Humor, and make wonderful gifts. Such a section can easily entice customers into making impulse purchases.

Don't ignore your customers' sensibility when it comes to devising categories. You may love the concept of Belles Lettres in your store, but your customers may find it aloof and prefer Literary Nonfiction. Make it fun to wander from one section to another; be sure the transitions make sense, and don't overlook the opportunity to refer browsers to other sections. Ann Nelson of Bunch of Grapes Bookstore in Martha's Vineyard, Massachusetts, even tucks small signs with messages such as "More Art Books Upstairs" or "Don't Forget Our Great Sailing Section" into other category headers on tables or gondolas. It's an idea worth adapting. If your store is big enough, you might want to create a store directory for customers to serve as an excellent merchandising tool, store memento, and extra sales clerk all in one.

Shelf Merchandising

Booksellers tend to spend most of their merchandising efforts on the new-release sections and display windows, ignoring all those books in the wall sections and gondolas. Granted, these areas are the homes for your backlist titles, but that's no reason for shelving all those books spine out. After all, any book a customer has not read is a new book to that person. Readers can be as easily tempted by backlist as frontlist if you make them equally appealing. Work your wall and gondola sections regularly, pulling out titles that, for one reason or another, have some currency and display them face out. Pick books with lively colors and strong graphics; the wealth of attractive trade paperbacks today makes that an easy chore. Another technique is to establish a face-out shelf at eye level running throughout the store, with titles changing weekly or as new titles arrive. Every now and then you can also experiment with working a publisher's counter display onto a backlist shelf—not every counter display can fit on your counter, and it really does add interest.

Table Merchandising

The notion of merchandising books on tables was doubtless greeted with real suspicion when first introduced; after all, books belong on shelves, while shirts, sweaters, and other kinds of clothing are the right kind of merchandise to display on tables. Yet tables provide a wonderfully effective setting for showcasing new titles, sale merchandise, theme displays, and so forth in an exciting array of face-ups, face-outs, stacks, and rows.

The ABCs of Stacking Books

Books are among the few retail items that can literally be used as building blocks for display, so a few pointers on stacking books may be helpful here. There are two basic "bases" for book display: with alternating spines (figure 53-1 and, for square books, figure 53-2) and spiral displays (figure 53-3). It's also fun to spiral two or more titles together for a dramatic effect. Use titles of the same or similar categories and formats in two (light and dark) alternating colors.

Two books can also become a substantial base for a display simply by interlocking the books—that is, slipping the backs of the two books into each other (figure 53-4). (To work, the books must be the same size or the same height.) From this base, one can build up by placing a copy of the book (spine out) over the two interlocked books, then adding another interlocked pair of books, and so forth. You can also display books on tables by slanting them on a diagonal with the books supporting each other and a block or wire easel (used facedown to create a forty-five-degree angle) supporting the bottom book (figure 53-5).

Any of these stacking techniques can be used in windows, on tables, on the cash/wrap counter, or as endcaps to island fixtures. Once you've mastered these basic techniques, it will take you little time to build exciting displays. Just remember that book displays should never inhibit sales by being too complicated and thus discouraging customers from handling the books. Loose copies should be available for examination and purchase in all displays.

Endcap Merchandising

Such stacks of books also work very well on endcaps to define the adjacent categories more clearly. Try to use a box or skid under the stacks to keep books from being damaged by customers' feet, mops, and other hazards of the lower depths. If possible, build height on endcaps. If the display is low, because you have only a few copies of the book, use point-of-purchase posters about the book or the related category above the display on the endcap.

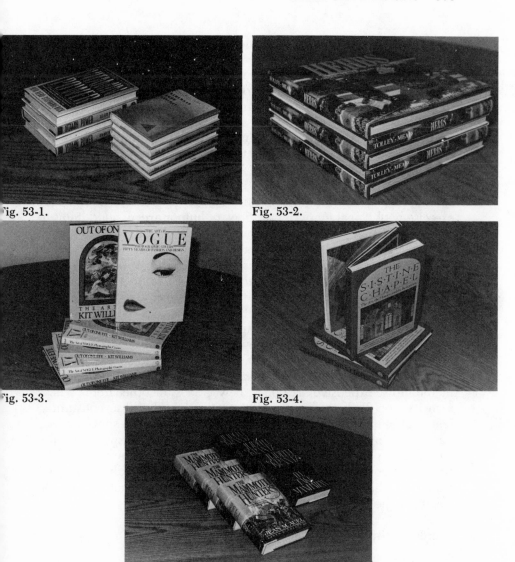

Fig. 53-1.

Fig. 53-2.

Fig. 53-3.

Fig. 53-4.

Fig. 53-5.

Incidentally, if your store layout features all island fixtures end to end in long lines, you may want to break these by using a herringbone or diagonal placement of fixtures. This placement takes additional floor space but offers a more interesting traffic flow; it also exposes the customer to more merchandise and provides space for endcap display whether for racks, publisher's floor display, stacks of major titles, boxed sets, or a calendar rack.

Merchandising the Cash/Wrap Counter

The cash/wrap area is literally the last place in the store to encourage your customer to spend a few extra dollars. As such, the area demands your best merchandising efforts. Just as you have picked up additional odd items at the drugstore or grocery store simply because they were displayed near the register, so too your customers will respond to items that are both appealing and low enough in price to be considered an appropriate additional item to the merchandise already intended for purchase. Bookmarks, enclosure cards, bookplates, restaurant guides, the latest inexpensive exercise book, local maps, a new book of humor are all good items to display here. So are certain trade paperbacks, if the books are exciting in format, color, design, and subject matter. Make sure that the selection looks logical. The cash/wrap should not be a collection of unrelated items that look as though they wound up there only because there was no other place for them in the store.

A grid combining face-out titles and prepacks with face-ups of additional titles in front of the standing merchandise maximizes the potential for additional sales. Leave plenty of space for sales transactions on either side of the register, and be sure to display new titles on the shelves behind the cash/wrap—it's an excellent way to merchandise expensive art books, new videos, or other items whose security you'd like to ensure. Rotate this merchandise constantly, featuring numerous titles. The front of the cash/wrap should either have shelving or floor displays, leaving plenty of space for the customer to shop, yet offering enough merchandise to give the browser plenty to look at while waiting to have his or her purchase rung up. This one area should never be static. It should give the customer the chance to finish shopping in your store.

Window Displays

There's a good reason why retailers consider window displays key to their advertising and promotion effort. Windows give the community a preview of the store, its atmosphere, and its selection. They telegraph your taste, your emphasis on what's current, they reinforce your advertising. And even more effectively than advertising, a good window display can prompt the passersby to change their plans and walk into your store. Once you get them inside, you have the opportunity to sell them books and other merchandise.

Regardless of size, all windows need exciting contrasts in color, arrangement, and a message or theme (figure 53-6). Use a bold graphic, whether a photograph, publisher's poster, or your own

Fig. 53-6. Seasonal props set the tone for a summer window display at Pinocchio's Books and Toys in Morgantown, West Virginia.
(Photograph by E. J. Goodman)

blow-up of the jacket of a major title to attract attention and unify the window. Build the theme of the window around this graphic. Place the graphic at eye level and arrange the books around it. Your focal point could also be a three-dimensional object that relates to the theme or a well-designed sign stating your theme—"Fall into Fiction" or "Back to School with Books" are a few examples. A set of signs for basic seasonal and special-event themes is a good investment. ABA offers a good-looking set of seasonal posters with backup suggestions and camera-ready ads and bookmarks at a reasonable price.

Your arrangement should emphasize each title in the window, even if there is only one copy of the book. This can be achieved by angling the books differently and, where possible, using a three-dimensional object beside the single copy—a cooking utensil by a cookbook, a vase by a book on flower arrangements, a child's toy beside a picture book, and so forth. It's also effective to choose an item that resembles an object on the cover of the book.

To avoid that monotonous books-lined-up-like-soldiers look, build height in your windows. Stack or place books on cartons or boxes of differing sizes or use glass shelves with metal standards holding the glass. Standards come in many lengths, and some twist to adjust exactly to the space between the ceiling and the floor of the window. These metal supports or standards use the same shelf brackets often used for bookshelves and have the added advantage of being useful inside the store as well. Unless you have a backdrop for the window display, you must merchandise the window from both sides, inside and out.

Repeated use of the same jacket or an item used as a focal point attracts attention. Place the featured title in an interesting geometric pattern. A few examples:

- A diagonal pattern worked across the window
- One item deliberately placed out of traditional sequence
- A pyramid of the title built slightly to the right or left of the suspended graphic
- The creation of a mirror effect by placing titles in two symmetrical arrangements
- The use of multiples of such props as plants, trees, lamps, or other items
- The use of sideline items such as five Garfield cats in a row for a humor window

Don't forget to maximize the power of color. Much contemporary retail store design uses primarily contrasting colors such as red and white, yellow and green, red and yellow. Color can come from crepe-paper streamers, three-dimensional items used for emphasis, or structural elements used to give the window its framework. Plastic boxes or crates in bright colors can be used to display as well as give a display a base or home.

A word about holiday windows: The holiday season is a long one, starting in early November in many communities and often going through New Year's. This means whatever theme you pick—A Child's Christmas, A Winter Wonderland, and A Country Christmas are a few suggestions—your initial window setting should be created and executed so that the structure can remain up for six to eight weeks while the book selection will be changed regularly. Create your own schedule of when to merchandise specific categories in your display, remembering to focus on the more costly books during the Thanksgiving weekend and later in December. Customers usually spend more on a specific title later in the season after all those ads and reviews have given them the last needed nudge to buy.

From shelves to windows, endcaps to cash/wrap, the time and attention you pay to displays and visual merchandising throughout the store will be repaid time and time again. It is a strong part of successful bookselling.

Chapter 54

Authors Sell Books

RON WATSON

Once a book is written, you would think the author could rely on the publishing house to sell it. Each year a few especially successful authors/promoters manage to help push their titles to the tops of best-seller lists; as a result, most writers nowadays are willing to participate personally in the promotion and sale of their books. Some writers refuse to do this, considering it either demeaning or simply not their job; others wisely realize they are better at writing than making personal appearances. In many cases, however, an author, through touring and media appearances, becomes an effective marketing tool for the bookseller.

Some writers have personalities that blossom in the spotlight. They become celebrities, and their celebrity sells books. Some would be well advised to remain aloof and perhaps acquire a sense of mystery that would be more appealing than their presence. Success even for the extroverted author depends on being booked on the most suitable shows, appearing in the best stores in the best markets, or speaking to carefully targeted groups.

In general, authors who do tour are articulate, accommodating, and considerate of the reading public. They recognize book buyers as their livelihood and are aware that booksellers are the all-important connecting link. Booksellers should utilize that awareness and goodwill through in-store appearances by authors, both increasing sales and garnering excellent publicity for the store. It is also beneficial to the bookseller that author appearances in a bookstore are seen by the public as community service rather than promotion. These appearances focus attention on books in general and on the sponsoring bookstore in particular.

The first step after deciding to promote authors in your bookstore is to select those you would like to have. Not every writer is available, and even those who are interested in appearing may not be able to fit you into their schedule. Well-known writers on national tours, if you can get them, are great because they are almost presold. The local media clamors for interviews, and crowds of customers are almost (almost, not always) assured. The bookseller's primary promotion role here is to adequately inform the public as to time and place of appearance.

Less well-known writers require a different approach. The subject of the book or perhaps the special quality of the as-yet-unknown writer may have to be promoted. Although these authors with no fame to fan the fires of public enthusiasm are more work to "sell," they can be (and frequently are) very willing promoters. The events can prove quite successful.

Local authors can provide some of the most successful promotions if everything falls into place, or they can be complete duds. It is necessary to develop strategies carefully. Locals have the advantage of flexibility in terms of being available for publicity and for establishing the best date for a promotion. They may have a good reputation or be extremely popular in the community. Play on all of these factors.

No matter what type of author you decide to promote, the success of the event depends on the planning and effort put into it. Good promotions don't just happen. They are the result of thoughtful preparation and proper follow-through on all the details. Bring the members of your staff into the planning from the very start, including the decision of which author to attract. This is good management in that employees feel directly involved in important store decisions. It also allows the bookseller to delegate chores. Keep in mind that one person needs to be in charge of and responsible for the overall promotion and planning.

Involve your publisher's sales representatives in the planning of author promotions. They may have suggestions for authors to be invited; certainly those reps from the houses publishing the books of the featured author have to make sure books arrive when you need them. Sales reps can be a liaison with publicity departments. The bookseller should also call to make sure books are available and determine the ship date.

Selecting an author or authors for a promotion or a series of events is only the beginning. It is a good idea to make a list of things that have to be done. Then consider all the ways a particular author and/or book can be promoted to get best results based on the author's or the book's special qualities. If you have an author or illustrator of a children's book, you might decide National Children's Book Week is the time to schedule the promotion. Perhaps the author of a book on the American Revolution might be brought in around the Fourth of July. Do a lot of thinking about ways to tie in your promotion with other things that will be getting public attention to ride along on a wave of interest. In some cases you might want to bring in an author when there is absolutely nothing else going on anywhere in town so your program will stand out like a gala. Think about the best scheduling.

Next, put on your list all the ways to implement your scheduling decision. Note when to make the announcement and how. List what you will do to get media attention, known as publicity (which is free), and to supplement your advertising campaign (which costs money). Very early in the planning discuss with the publisher's publicity department the possibility of setting up local interviews with the press, appearances on television, and radio interviews. The media often respond favorably to calls from publicity departments. Follow up by checking with the publicity department to make sure that the needed publicity has been scheduled. Make every effort to get a newspaper story that will run the day of or before the promotion date. This may involve an advance telephone interview between author and reporter. Book review editors are often cooperative about scheduling reviews to coincide with author appearances. Involve your local media people through your own contacts. Get them enthused about the person who is coming to town.

Plan your advertising campaign carefully to get the best mileage for your money. You should use whatever cooperative advertising money is available from the publisher. Whatever the amount, decide how to use it. Will a blockbuster ad do the trick, or might flyers mailed to your customers be better? Perhaps a combination of both. How about spot ads on the radio station? You will want to spend some money on signs for the store, maybe posters to place elsewhere if the budget is large enough and the occasion warrants. Knowing how much money you will have to spend is important because you must keep to a budget. It is easy to blow the works and not have much to show for it afterward. Saying that it was an investment in audience recognition is fine for a time or two, but as a regular thing it can bankrupt the store. Some promotions will be much more profitable in actual dollars than others, but the goal should always be sales as well as satisfaction.

Plan the in-store displays and the windows you will create to engender enthusiasm. All of this will become second nature eventually, but it is still a good idea to use the laundry-list system. When you're displaying quantities of the author's new book, the one that occasions all the excitement, also display some of the author's earlier works, especially those that made his or her reputation if this is a well-known writer. The title of the new book may not mean anything to the public, but the famous books will attract their attention and focus interest on that person's latest title. You will frequently sell copies of the older titles almost as well as the new if the author is present to sign them. Don't lose those extra sales.

Mailing individual invitations to customers on your list is a generally sound way to get response. It is essential for a local author promotion, as the author's friends are likely to be the best customers. When discussing an appearance with a local author, always ask for a list of people who should be invited. Better yet, suggest that the author might like to address and mail out a substantial batch of invitations. Get these invitations out early enough so recipients can plan to attend, but not so far in advance that they will have forgotten about it when the event comes around.

Concentrate all your efforts on the in-store appearance and the autographing. No matter what else the author is going to do in town, the main event should be seen as the autographing. Play it up by emphasizing that individuals have a chance to actually meet and talk to the writer in person. If done haphazardly, you might get lots of publicity for the author, some for the store, but a poor attendance at the event that is meant to be the climax, and upon which you will eventually judge the success or failure of your efforts. Obviously you are going to spend weeks or months of planning for an event that will last only an hour or two. To make that appear less onerous, realize that there will be sales of the author's book after the event—if public interest has been aroused. Always have the author sign, but not date, copies of books to be sold afterward. Promote these signed copies to get as much business as possible out of your initial effort. Putting a sign with the books marked "Autographed Copies" is sufficient and inexpensive.

As part of your planning, pay some attention to getting the author around town. Publishers will usually see that an author gets in and gets out, but the bookseller may be responsible for transportation and entertainment while the person is in town. Writing down a timetable is the most efficient way to make sure it all happens when it should. Getting the author to a television studio twenty minutes late for an appearance won't work, nor will the newspaper be happy if the interview was scheduled for noon and the author shows up at 1:45 P.M. If the promotion appearance schedule is tight, someone who knows the city might be able to keep on schedule more easily.

Allow time for meals and maybe a few minutes of relaxation. Whatever you do, get the author to the store on time. People who take the trouble to get to the store to buy a book and meet an author should have the author there when he's supposed to be and should

Fig. 54-1. Martha Stewart at an autographing session at B. Dalton for her book *Weddings.*

also have time to at least exchange greetings. Some authors are better than others at giving each individual undivided attention. You may judge the success of the appearance on how many books were sold, while the customers will judge it on how satisfied they were with the seconds or minutes they spent face to face with the author. Plan for their success as well as yours. Control the flow of people approaching the author. Single file seems military sometimes, but it works best. If you have a mob, lines give everyone a chance to say hello. If you have only a few show up, single file makes it seem like more people than there actually are. Eliminate hassles and frustration for both the author and the customers, and you'll send them away remembering how well you do things at your store.

Even though publishing houses have entire publicity departments to attract attention to their authors and their books, they cannot be expected to do everything in every locale. No matter how much your chosen author's publisher plans to do in town to publicize your event, make sure you are involved and help in every way possible. You may be expected to do it all with the publisher providing only the author and books. Whichever way, stay on top of it. Remember: The success of an author event depends upon the carefully planned and coordinated efforts of the hosting bookseller.

Don't be afraid to share the glory afterward, however, if there is glory to share. Take time to thank the publisher for all the help given. Send clippings of press reports. You will need to send copies of advertisements if you used cooperative money. Make the publisher aware of your success with an author event so the company will be eager to work with you again. If it wasn't successful, tell them why. Author promotions are a joint effort between writer, publisher, and bookseller. Exchanges between them should not stop with the conclusion of the planned event.

Authors sell books in other ways than by coming to a bookstore. They sell books by being on national television shows or by appearing on the covers of magazines or in feature stories. Any and all publicity authors get attracts attention to their books. Alert booksellers are aware of this and take advantage of it by prominently displaying titles that are in the public eye.

Authors also sell books when they appear locally at a convention or before a professional group or speak at a college. It is sometimes possible for a bookseller to actually sell books where the author is speaking, especially if the author will agree to a signing following the talk. These arrangements should be made with the sponsor of the event. Sometimes this type of promotion is more happily agreed to if the bookseller offers to make a donation to the sponsor through a percentage of the sale of the books. Make sure all the arrangements, including the percentage, are agreed upon in advance to save everyone bad feelings afterward. Once again, you want the result to be positive even if the basic gain is nothing more than goodwill—of which no business can have too much.

If you cannot sell books at such an event, and if you cannot get the author to visit the store for a signing, you might see if you could have some time with the author so that books could be signed to be sold later in the store. And, at the very least, the savvy bookseller will prominently display the books of any author who is getting coverage in the local press no matter where or what the event might be.

Authors not only write books—they sell books. Booksellers and authors working together are an effective team.

Chapter 55

Seasonal Promotions

DIANE BROOM

When we think of seasonal promotions we think of Christmas, which is logical. That holiday season is our busiest time of year. Customers select gifts from our expanded inventory as we booksellers decorate, display, advertise, and promote to the best of our ability. How can we generate the same kind of enthusiasm and resulting sales figures throughout the year? One way is to take advantage of all the other seasonal opportunities. With a little ingenuity, we can capitalize on all holidays from New Year's Day through Thanksgiving. Here are a few practical suggestions.

First, prepare a calendar for seasonal promotions. Mark any holidays or special events that might be turned into promotions. Remember to include community events, and watch out for those "floating" holidays. Go over your annual advertising budget to learn how much is available, where it is committed, and how many dollars might be used for seasonal promotions. Write those rough figures on your calendar. Go over the new-books lists to see when they will be coming and what the publishers plan to do to promote them. There might be a terrific new book for Halloween, for example, that could figure prominently in your seasonal campaign. Jot down on your seasonal calendar the publication dates of forthcoming important books.

Coordinate special events based on publication dates with what already exists—a schedule of holidays, community affairs, and so on. Then begin to plan. Long-range detailed planning is the best way to have successful, smooth-running, and profitable promotions.

First, consult with your staff. See how many ideas you can capture and use. Make sure there are no conflicts, such as previous commitments for an out-of-store display, an autograph party, or a sick leave. Find out what other plans are under way in your community. You may have good luck joining forces with others for special programs. Librarians, teachers, and many similar professionals are usually glad to help—sometimes with money if it will bring an author to town, sometimes with art, printing, display, or promotion, and always with ideas and advice. Use them.

Check the bookstore merchandising calendar that appears frequently in *American Bookseller*. Keep track of success stories in *Publishers Weekly, The Horn Book,* and other trade publications. Booksellers are always glad to share their expertise and advice.

Next, discuss the project with your publisher's sales representatives. Even if you plan to promote several books, you can often get promotional bookmarks or posters. If you feature one book, you may qualify for co-op money from its publisher. Some publishers will supply co-op funds for their own titles no matter how many other books you promote. You can use this money in a variety of ways—to prepare radio or newspaper ads, produce your own handouts or bookmarks, or to make posters. If your advertising allowance is large, it might stretch to television advertising. Some publishers will even help defray the costs of refreshments, napkins, and the like when an author visits your store. Keep checking your store's own advertising budget. Knowing what money is available is essential as you make your plans.

When all decisions are made, you are set to go. Order your books, organize your staff, and delegate tasks. Prepare your in-store advertising and displays. Distribute posters, flyers, bookmarks, or whatever you have through the community. Submit your advertising copy to the media. Send direct mail to your target audience. You probably have a file of names—charge customers or people you invite to autographings. Keep it current, and keep using it.

Notify local news media. Press people appreciate knowing in advance and in detail what you have planned. Coverage will vary according to lots of factors: sometimes you'll get great free publicity for your promotion and for your store in general, but don't be discouraged if you fail to get on the ten o'clock news. Do always invite the press.

Not every seasonal promotion needs to be a major event. Sometimes a window display or a table is sufficient to pique your customers' curiosity. Take advantage of the promotional aids and display merchandisers available from publishers.

It's easy to plan things for Christmas, but everybody promotes that holiday. Your bookstore will stand out stronger, with less time and money spent, if you publicize another holiday. Be creative. Don't be afraid of something you haven't done before. How about a best-costume party for Halloween, puppet shows for Children's Book Week, or "hidden" discounts for Easter? Here are a few month-by-month suggestions for seasonal events:

January. After Christmas Clean-up Sale: reduce seasonal or shopworn titles. New Year's Resolutions can make a great promotion; it's a perfect time to feature diet, health, and exercise titles. Martin Luther King Day. Calendar Promotion; not everyone gets one for Christmas!

February. Groundhog Day. Lincoln's Birthday. Valentine's Day. Washington's Birthday: do a display of biographies of all presidents. Chinese New Year: how about a "fortune cookies" discount?

March. St. Patrick's Day. Early gardening display.

April. April Fool's Day. Easter/Passover. Income Tax Time: showcase those tax preparation books. National Library Week. Secretary's Day.

May. Mother's Day. Graduation. Memorial Day.

June. Father's Day. Summer Solstice. Travel Promotion: you can get props from local travel agents or unfold a couple of maps to help you sell travel guides.

July. Independence Day: promote history, biography, and the John Jakes series all at once! Bastille Day. Summer Reading Promotion: for a window idea, use the Reading Rainbow theme. Theater or Dance Festivals. Sports: sailing, swimming, tennis—you name it.

August. Summer Reading Continues. State Fair Display: a great opportunity to sell books on food preservation, needle crafts, art techniques, and more.

September. Labor Day. Back to School display. Jewish New Year. Banned Books Week.

October. Crafts for Christmas Promotion. Columbus Day. Football Season Promotion. Good Bears' Day; in connection with Teddy Roosevelt's birthday, this is fun for promoting bear books. Halloween.

November. Election Day: feature current-affairs titles under a red, white, and blue bunting; if you are short on time, you can easily leave this display up through...Veteran's Day. Children's Book Week. Thanksgiving.

December. Christmas/Hanukkah. New Year's Eve: if you have the energy, you can promote entertaining titles and cookbooks for this holiday.

Chapter 56

Promotion through Creative Events

CYD ROSENBERG and BARBARA LIVINGSTON

Promotion is a special event or series of events that increases sales and enhances the bookstore's position in the community. Promotions can be extremely simple or very sophisticated. This chapter will examine several promotions that various booksellers have done, ranging from exhibiting books at a computer show and academic conference to major promotional campaigns for single titles focusing on a celebrity or author. These promotions were in stores of different sizes and in different parts of the country. Even though your store may not be able to duplicate the Pavarotti promotion of the Book Market stores in Illinois or the Robert Bateman promotion done by A Different Drummer in Burlington, Ontario, Canada, there are elements in each of those two promotions that you can adapt for use in your own store.

Promotions can be built around a specific title, a category, seasonal or regional theme, a special occasion, or just because it's time to do something different and have some fun. Staff members might have ideas and should always be solicited for promotional concepts.

A promotion should have well-defined goals. Increased sales are hoped for at all times, but this may not necessarily be the central focus of a specific promotional effort. You might wish simply to increase your exposure in the community or to attract new customers. A promotion reinforces the image and purpose of your store, its special feeling. What's happening with books is reflected and reinforced in the minds of your regular customers with successful, well-planned promotion. It also lures people past competing stores and brings them to you. A well-planned promotion can generate a good deal of free publicity. In a small town or even within the neighborhood of a large metropolitan area, the promotion taking place in your store can become a newsworthy event.

Planning, as already mentioned, is essential if the promotional event is to be successful. If it is a communitywide effort, the support of other merchants is essential. In several of the children's books promotions we'll be discussing, successful results came about through close coordination among the bookstore, the libraries, and the elementary schools. Key questions to be answered whether the promotion is a communitywide event or involves only your store relate to areas of time, money, and space. Will extra staff be needed, or is overtime involved for regular staff? If the promotion is to be held away from the store, will covering both locations be a problem? Will you require extra inventory? Have you a realistic idea of what sales to project for the event? Will you require the rental of a community room or auditorium in your area, or is there adequate space in the store? Will there be problems with display or storage of excess inventory? Have you planned appropriate advertising and publicity? Have you coordinated co-op advertising with the sales representative? In addition, you must evaluate the promotion at its conclusion. Did it meet your goals? Sales should be measured, even if increased sales was not the main purpose of the event. You should also examine aspects that did not work, and look for alternatives for the next time. Don't forget to include your staff's evaluation of the event. They may come up with positive suggestions because of their firsthand involvement.

Now on to some specific promotions!

For the past several years, ABA has co-sponsored a Banned Books Week in cooperation with the National Association of College Stores, the American Library Association, the Association of American Publishers, and the American Society of Journalists and Authors. The event also has had the endorsement of the Center for the Book and the Library of Congress. Its purpose is a national consciousness-raising effort to make the public more aware of the threat of censorship and to call attention to specific titles that are targeted by pressure groups from all sides of the political spectrum. Many stores participated in the week-long event by creating in-store and/or window displays and sending out press releases using materials from a kit distributed to all member ABA and NACS stores.

Bookstores reported tremendous interest in the displays and in the overall theme of the promotion. At the University Center Bookstore in Missoula, Montana, Barbara Theroux declared, "Banned Books Week displays created more conversation, goodwill, and exposure than any other single event we've done." Lynn Clark of The Bookworm in Jackson, Mississippi, offered 20 percent off to

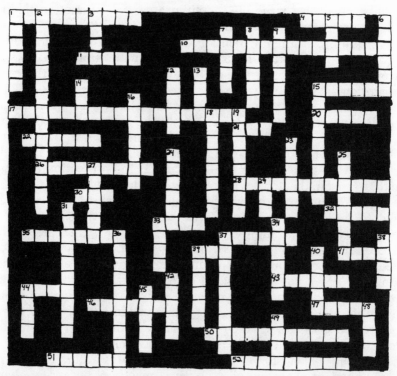

PUZZLED BY BANNED BOOKS?

ACROSS

1. *American Heritage* _____
4. Dorian's creator
10. Bogart/Bacall film
11. *Go Ask* _____
15. *Emma* _____
17. *Boston Collective's book*
20. *O'Hara's War*
21. *Naked* _____
22. Sue Lyon role
26. Diary author
28. _____ *de Maupin*
30. Word from Salinger title
32. *The Living* _____
33. Author of *Soup*
35. Kurt _____
37. Matthew, Mark, Luke and

John each wrote
39. Hemingway character's milieu
41. Gervaise's daughter
43. Eugene _____
44. Plath's jar
46. Lara's lover
47. *Adam Bede* author
50. One flew over it
51. Part of E.B. Browning title
52. Darwin's theory

DOWN

1. Charles B. _____
2. "A _____," Kubrick film
3. Author of *Human Body*

5. _____ *Story*
6. Jay _____
7. Goethe bestseller
8. Woman with the scarlet letter
9. Maya _____
12. Michigan-born author
13. Gave us *The Giving Tree*
14. *Are You There* _____, *It's Me Margaret*
15. *Decameron* author
16. Studs Terkel's labor
18. Author of *Candide*
19. Loman's profession
23. Orwell's farm
24. Robinson's last name
25. _____ *Tragedy*
27. Erica's fear

29. Alias for Doris Kappelhoff
31. Where Alice had her adventures
33. Corleone's creator
34. Infamous place in early soap
36. *Bridge to* _____
37. Rabelais' largest title
38. Below Benchley's gums
39. Sex education book for children
40. _____ Zola
42. _____ *Fishing in America*
44. Royko title
45. *Little Black* _____
48. Hardy character
49. _____ *Flanders*

As part of its promotion for Banned Books Week 1983, the two Community Newscenter stores in Ann Arbor, Michigan, created this Banned Books crossword and encouraged its customers to complete the puzzle and compete for a prize of $15 worth of banned books. Although customers seemed enthusiastic, the two stores received fewer entries than expected—perhaps because customers were embarrassed at not knowing 12 Down, our sticking point. Still, concocting a puzzle was fun, reports Nita Krygier-Fox, who created this puzzle with her colleagues, Sue Gordon, Dave Bowman, and Michael Hirsch. P.S. All the books and authors used in this puzzle are cited in the historic list of 500 banned books that ABA made available this fall. P.P.S. Cheaters: The answers are on p. 31. □

Fig. 56-1. As part of its promotion for Banned Books Week 1983, the two Community Newscenter stores in Ann Arbor, Michigan, created a crossword puzzle. Customers who completed it got to compete for $15 worth of banned books. (Answers on following page)

Fig. 56-2. Images from Banned Books '86.

customers brave enough to purchase a banned book. Nelle and Don Frisch of Downtown Books in Grand Rapids, Michigan, invited community members to a program to read aloud from their favorite banned book. Participants included a Congregational minister who read from the Bible, a children's librarian who read from *Where the Sidewalk Ends*, and others reading parts of *Alice in Wonderland* and *Grapes of Wrath*.

Printers Ink, in Palo Alto, California, silk-screened their plain white bookstore bags with original art related to the theme of banned books. The demand for the bags was so great, they had to go back to press and ultimately distributed 2,500.

As part of their Banned Books Week promotion, the two Community Newscenter Stores in Ann Arbor, Michigan, created a banned books crossword puzzle (Figure 56-1). Customers were encouraged to complete the puzzle and compete for a prize of $15 worth of banned books. All the books and authors used in the puzzle came from the list of five hundred banned books made available to booksellers with the promotional materials supplied by ABA. Although customers were enthusiastic, the store reported receiving fewer submissions than expected. Perhaps customers did not want to be embarrassed by incorrect answers!

Banned Books Week is a national occasion where booksellers are given the concept and materials with which to work. However, some of the most innovative and exciting promotional events are those created by the booksellers themselves.

Jocundry's Books, in East Lansing, Michigan, has sponsored a week-long festival of events, culminating in their traditional Halloween costume party and contest. The results were spectacular. Although good sales are always hoped for and did result, they were not the main focus or effort of this series. Using a different theme or event daily, Jocundry attracted different audiences for each day and thus exposed the store's varied sections to many new customers. Jocundry's calendar of special events is always varied and stimulating, such as a workshop on writing historical romance novels, an old-fashioned spelling bee, a local author's reception, a mystery contest, a decorated chocolate cake contest, a storytelling gala, a computer contest, a "Sometimes a Great Needle" quilt contest, and an annual Halloween costume contest. They have a special sale in connection with each promotion, discounting books 15 percent in the appropriate categories. Frequently this store's programs are co-sponsored by local merchants who donate merchandise to be used as prizes or give gift certificates. Sharing prizes with other local merchants lowers the cost of a promotion for the bookstore. Co-sponsoring merchants also share the cost of printing flyers and advertising in the local newspapers. Such occasions generate a good deal of free publicity, including stories in newspapers and sometimes on television.

The Blue Marble, a children's bookstore in Ft. Thomas, Kentucky, became excited about promoting *The Read-Aloud Handbook* by Jim Trelease. Because it was a natural for their store, they wanted to sponsor a two-day community event in which parents could learn about using books and become involved in reading with their children. They decided to offer a two-part workshop, given by Professor Rosemary Ingham of Northern Kentucky University, in the Municipal Auditorium, which was available at no cost and was a few short blocks from the store, which meant registrants could come to the bookstore following the session to purchase books. No registration fee was charged, although participants were required to buy a copy of the Trelease book. Professor Ingham used material from the book and provided handouts with additional information.

The event was promoted in the store's newsletter and in the "Events" section of the local newspaper. Although the program didn't generate as much publicity as the owner, Pilar Moore, would have liked, she found that many of the attendees who had not been customers previously soon became regular book buyers at the Blue Marble.

A more elaborate promotion focusing on one title was Chicago's Book Market promotion of *Pavarotti, My Own Story*. At the time of the promotion, there were five Book Market stores in operation throughout the state of Illinois. Steve Cogil, general manager, decided that this was a book they could heavily promote because Pavarotti had been receiving a tremendous amount of media exposure. He had recently announced that he would do a benefit concert on behalf of the Italian earthquake victims. The Book Market saw an opportunity to support a worthy cause while at the same time promoting and selling books. It would also introduce Book Market to new customers and get potential buyers to bypass other stores in order to purchase the book at Book Market, where $2 of the price of each book sold would be given as a donation to the Italian Earthquake Relief Fund. Book Market announced that a matching $2 contribution would be made by the bookstore. The effort was coordinated through the local office of the Italian Earthquake Relief Fund and through the publisher after receiving an endorsement from Pavarotti. The endorsement was used in all print and radio advertising. Ten thousand dollars was spent on the promotion, including advertising in all major newspapers in their market area, on radio, and nationwide in *Attenzione* magazine, where a coupon ad was placed. End result—2,500 books sold at $14.95, a major contribution to a worthwhile cause, lots of great publicity, and many new friends and customers.

A Different Drummer Books, in Burlington, Ontario, Canada, is known for its well-planned and innovative promotions. In a nine-month campaign for *The Art of Robert Bateman*, they sold 2,500 plus copies of a $40 art book. It took well-coordinated planning and detailed effort, but it was certainly worthwhile. The book was the perfect choice for that store to promote.

The right selection is essential to success. Do not plan to promote a book that you normally wouldn't sell. To create a promotion such as the Bateman project, you have to have a strong feeling about who comprises the market for a book and why. Then you must plan how to make customers aware that your store is the place to buy that title. *The Art of Robert Bateman* was ideal for A Different Drummer for several reasons. The author is an extremely well-known and popular nature artist who lives in the store's area. He had taught at the local high school and exhibited his work in the community for the previous fifteen years. He was a customer of the store and was eager to help in the promotion. Knowing that the book would sell well anywhere, the goal was to link *The Art of Robert Bateman* with A Different Drummer in the mind of the public and make sure that they purchased it there and not from Bookstore X or Art Gallery Y.

The store launched a campaign in February for the book, which was not to be published until September. As John Richardson, then the store manager, explained, "Since our ad budget is slightly lower than Ma Bell's, saturation advertising was out of the question, so we decided to offer a few extras to attract people to our store. First, we promised everyone who ordered the book ahead of time an autographed copy. Second, we bought one of Bateman's limited-edition prints and offered it as a prize in a drawing. Everyone ordering the book *before* publication was entitled to a chance to win this valuable print." The store first announced the book and the extras in their spring newsletter, which was sent to 3,500 mailing-list customers. In less than two weeks, they received advance orders for three hundred copies. Next, they ran a coupon ad once a week in their local newspaper from April through June. In May, another mailing was sent to the store's regular customers. By the end of June they had accumulated one thousand orders for the September book.

An in-store display was created with a dummy of the book, a blow-up of the newspaper ad, contest entry forms, and special-order forms highlighted by a continuous showing of slides of Bateman's work. The display was set up in March and remained until finished books arrived.

Thinking that the book was an ideal gift, the store did an extra promotional mailing to 2,500 corporations, doctors, dentists, and lawyers in the area, resulting in two substantial corporate orders (one for 250, one for 275 copies). By the middle of September, the total advance commitment for the book was 1,600 copies. The store had placed an order for 2,500 copies at the publisher's maximum discount of 46 percent.

Because of the emphasis the store was putting into the book, they wanted to do more than the traditional store autograph party. They decided to sponsor "An Evening with Robert Bateman" at a local auditorium. They sold tickets at $4 per person, after promoting the event in the newspaper and on in-store bookmarks. A total of 425 tickets were sold. At the "Evening," they showed a thirty-minute film about the artist, displayed prints supplied by a local art gallery, and served refreshments. Bateman spoke, answered questions, and autographed books.

By the time the author began his national publisher-sponsored publicity tour in mid-November, the store had eight hundred copies left on hand. Bateman's press promoted the book heavily, and the store again began selling twenty to twenty-five copies a day. Other bookstores ran out, as did the publisher. A Different Drummer was in the happy position of selling its 2,500th copy a few days prior to Christmas.

The annual Father's Day promotion is another success for A Different Drummer, although not as elaborate as the Bateman promotion. Actually, it's a fun concept that has translated into a good advertising campaign and in-store display, resulting in increased sales. Capitalizing on the idea that the traditional Father's Day gift is a tie, the store's promotion one year was that everyone who bought either a gift certificate or a book for over $10 could choose a free tie for Father. A Different Drummer acquired a collection of out-of-style and truly ugly ties from a Toronto wholesaler for $1 each. A newspaper ad and mailing piece capturing the whimsical spirit of the promotion were created, and an in-store display of the ties carried out the theme. Customer reaction was wonderful, with many outrageous comments. Sales were equally good. The week before Father's Day was up 40 percent over a typical spring week, and sales for the Saturday before that Father's Day were double what they had been the previous year.

You don't need a holiday or the opportunity to work with a celebrity to get on the promotion bandwagon. You can promote your entire inventory or a specific section by exhibiting at a conference or trade show. There are conferences and shows in all interest categories. Listings are usually available from the local Chamber of

Commerce. If you are a college store, or located in a college town, you should always be aware of the seminars and events taking place on campus, so you can tie in with many of them.

Computer shows for both the professional and the hobbyist are occurring everywhere on the horizon, and it's an ideal place for booksellers to display. A computer fair would expose you to a new group of customers who may not be aware of your store. According to Gloria Weiner, formerly of the Harcourt Brace Jovanovich Bookstore in San Diego, California, "Customers are part of a specialized market, and you must reach them on their own ground." Exhibiting at computer fairs may result in extra sales there, of course, but booksellers find it's even more useful for building customer in-store traffic and for expanding mail-order business. Jack Feyock of McGraw-Hill Bookstore in New York City takes booth space at computer shows because they offer his store broad exposure and provide an opportunity to aggressively solicit corporate accounts.

Barbara Theroux, formerly of University Center Bookstore, is constantly involved with conferences taking place at her Missoula, Montana, school. When the Pacific Northwest Regional group of the Medical Library Association met, the bookstore was there. Rather than taking a tabletop exhibit (cost of $75), they decided to offer a convention coffee service (cost of $35) and invite the registrants into the bookstore, offering them a 10 percent discount coupon. Along with the coffee, an introductory letter was included in registration packets, and the registrants were supplied with a directional map and campus bus token. The results were excellent. Many of those attending the conference came to the bookstore and bought books not only in their special subject areas, but from the store's entire inventory. It was a good opportunity for the registrants to purchase sideline and gift items that would not have been available had the store just purchased a tabletop in the exhibit area. It was a simple idea that worked well and produced good results because of planning.

Sometimes a promotional opportunity arises from an unlikely source. Barbara Theroux was once invited to speak on children's books to parents and staff at her son's day-care center. The attendees became interested in purchasing some of the books, so she arranged delivery of a box of books, with prices and other title lists, for what has since become a monthly event. This led to a request for a table display at the state convention of day-care centers. After the first year's involvement with the state conference, funding became available from the state government to set up three regional resource centers. Because of the store's prior involvement, most of the money that was budgeted was spent at the University Center Bookstore.

Every November, Children's Book Week is sponsored by the

Children's Book Council and is a good opportunity to do a major promotion. At The Book Shop in Boise, Idaho, Diane Broom, the children's book buyer, decided to promote Children's Book Week by celebrating Pinocchio's birthday. The idea originated from the design of a spectacular poster of a newly illustrated edition of *The Adventures of Pinocchio.*

The first step in planning the specifics of the book promotion was to contact the publisher and the publisher's sales representative to ascertain the availability of the illustrator for appearances in conjunction with the event. Artist Gerald McDermott was available, and Four Winds, his publisher, agreed to pay the travel costs.

To ensure a good audience, a committee was formed with three area librarians. This bookstore committee decided to sponsor a statewide poster contest to include children of all ages. That way, children who were too young to read *The Adventures of Pinocchio* on their own, or those who weren't particularly good readers, could participate on an equal basis with excellent readers. Everyone would be encouraged to enjoy the Pinocchio stories and to create an original art piece. The contest would be statewide so children from all areas could compete. There would be prizes for each region, and then each region would forward their finalist's entries to The Book Shop, so the grand-prize winners could be selected by Mr. McDermott.

In addition to the wide enthusiasm and excitement generated by the poster contest, the committee arranged for several speaking programs by the artist, an appearance on a local television program, a reception, and the presentation of a Pinocchio puppet show. The puppet show had to be canceled when the puppeteer was called to jury duty, and the television appearance was canceled because the person involved failed to make proper arrangements. When planning major promotional events, it is wise to have some type of contingency planning for unforeseen circumstances.

The promotion was a great success. At each Gerald McDermott appearance attendance was at least triple what had been expected. Over one thousand posters were submitted in the contest. Everyone in the area was aware of Pinocchio and children's books in general, but most specifically of The Bookstore in Boise.

Jan Bruton and Lynn Kelly of A Children's Place in Portland, Oregon, took advantage of Tomie dePaola's appearance at a West Coast ABA Convention by inviting him to participate in a community event that their store would organize and sponsor. The goal was to get as many people as possible interested in and excited by dePaola's books. In order to do this, they had to get out of the bookstore and into the community.

Many people contributing ideas resulted in a program that

brought hundreds of children together with the author-artist and his books. He was grand marshal of a parade of his characters. Along with city dignitaries and news media, he dedicated a community-built play park. He appeared on the top-rated local TV talk show, where the children in the audience honored him with a book *they* had written. There were three autograph sessions, one being a special reception for book lovers that included interpretive presentations of two of the author's stories by a local children's drama class.

Planning for the event involved four schools in the store's immediate vicinity. Each school chose the books it wanted to represent and began preparations for the parade, which included the making of banners, signs, and costumes and the choosing of one hundred children from each school to march in the parade. A mailing was sent to all preschools in the area, so that they could participate by lining the parade route to the park dedication ceremony. This included one class of deaf children, who during the parade signed their delight at the passing spectacle.

The event was promoted through posters in the central and branch libraries, announcements to everyone on the store's mailing list, notices to all private and public schools in Portland and suburban areas, flyers sent home with children in the participating schools and given out to customers in the store, and press releases that were sent to all newspapers and television and radio stations. As a result of this effort the park dedication ceremony received media attention, and a neighborhood event became citywide news.

As the store is only 650 square feet, the owners realized they would need additional space in which to hold the autographing sessions and the reception. They decided to use an old garage behind the store. They got permission and transformed the space with hung sheets on which slides of dePaola illustrations could be projected. Friends baked cookies in shapes of dePaola's characters. To accommodate as many people as possible, the store had a presale of books so people could arrange to have copies autographed even if they couldn't attend the event. Mr. dePaola signed all those books the night before. To sum up, this event really did reach beyond the store's own regular customers and offered something that was fun and at the same time worthwhile to the community as a whole.

Although several of the promotions discussed here featured big-name authors, having a big-name author is not essential to a successful promotion. The most important element of any of these promotions is planning. Think about the goals, and then plan the promotion step by step. If outside assistance is needed to ensure a successful event, then take the proper steps to organize a committee, either other book people in the community or other merchants.

Contact the publisher(s) and see what type of assistance they might provide—either co-op dollars for advertising or for author expenses or money for invitations, flyers, and refreshments. Find out if the publisher's sales representative will be on hand for assistance. Organize and plan your advertising and publicity. Order the appropriate quantity of books needed for the event. Plan for the unforeseen—a contingency scheme if something goes wrong. Finally, have a critical eye for the post-event evaluation with staff to determine how successful the event was in meeting its goals and whether or not it should be repeated in the future.

In all promotions imagination is an essential ingredient. Even if you copy something someone else has done, give it your own touch, something that will identify it as yours. Remember, promotions should always make more people aware of your store and its special qualities. That builds business and makes all the effort worthwhile.

VII
Changes in
the Business

Chapter 57

Moving and Expanding

JOYCE KNAUER

Making any kind of substantial physical change in an existing business can occasion stress and anxiety, particularly if the decision to change involves a move in location or the expansion of existing premises. The risks loom large, and the financial burden seems awesome. Worry sets in as to whether customers will approve of the change. Will they maintain their loyalty? Will enough new patrons be coaxed in to warrant the additional expenses incurred?

Although the element of risk can never be completely eliminated, careful analysis and organization should serve to reduce it. A good sense of direction and understanding of the goals of your store helps. Perhaps this is the time to make a reassessment of those goals and to address some long-range questions. Has the marketplace changed? If the renewal of your lease is less than two years away, it's none too early to begin an examination of your choices. If the lease is renewed, are the terms likely to be favorable? If you expand at a later date, what are your options likely to be? Is the amount of space you're likely to need generally available in the immediate area? If your store is 1,500 square feet now and you're considering 3,500 square feet but most of the availability around you is 1,200 square feet, it may prove difficult to find the exact amount of space in the best place at the right time. Beginning the scouting process early is even more important in such neighborhoods. Would you prefer to rent, to buy, or to build? What can you afford? If you rent, is an existing building preferable, or would a new development offer more advantages?

Giving yourself plenty of time for analysis is one of the biggest favors you can do for your business. The correct responses to the questions of when, where, and how to expand can prove elusive. Some signals are very apparent. Customers may come in the door, see a packed house, turn, and leave. Comments can be overheard as to the customer's discomfort. Returns have just been pulled ruthlessly throughout the store, but there are still books on the floor in ones and twos that are *not* overstock, with 98 percent of the remaining stock packed on the shelves spine out. Are you getting a lot of requests from customers for a certain sideline item or a special service that could be incorporated into your operation? Expanded quarters may be in order to enable your store to take on these additional responsibilities.

Other clues are more subtle. The space may seem sufficient every month of the year except December. If the store normally grosses 25 percent of its yearly business during the holiday season, but floor space is becoming less and less able to accommodate the increasing crowds of people, sales will drop even if the books are available. If you notice a decline or leveling off of the percentage of growth in all months, but your good sense tells you that there is no decline or leveling off of the marketplace, expansion may be the key.

What about the competition? What are your immediate competitors doing to upgrade their operations? Are there any gaps in the marketplace that your store might fill? Even the closing of a store across town where you have had no or very little competitive involvement can sometimes affect your business. This is especially true if that shop had an area of specialization that could be nurtured in your own store, enabling you to pick up the dropped sales.

An examination of the growth history of your business is absolutely essential at this time. Graphically charting the years month by month can offer visual impact to the importance of the holiday period or other seasonal variations in your area. At the least, a review of the month-by-month percentage of growth should be undertaken, with particular notice given to the effect on business when a new sideline was added in the past or a section expanded. If more exposure tends to sell more books in your store, you have good reason to believe that larger quarters will enhance sales.

You may be to the point in your thinking where expansion is a definite possibility, but the exact form it takes is elusive.

One of your best resources here is your customers. Now is the time to ask them some questions. Although a professional polling service can offer useful data, you don't need to hire expensive help to find out about your customers. A questionnaire can be devised that will provide valuable information. It's important to keep it short (no more than ten to fifteen questions). Do the sampling to cover as broad a spectrum as possible, each time of the day, each day of the week, and so on. The survey can be passed out for the customer to complete on the spot, or a personal interview can be made. Both methods have their advantages. The former gives the customer more privacy to convey candid opinions; the latter offers a more personal touch, sometimes enabling the interviewer to gather other important information through conversation if the customer is apt to chat. Care should be taken with either method not to be unduly intrusive on the customers' time or goodwill as well as to offer special thanks in appreciation for their time and attention.

Upon compiling the results of the survey, you should have a sense of where most of your customers live, if there are a substantial number coming from a secondary area, where to advertise to most effectively reach these existing customers, as well as where to advertise if you want to experiment with expanding your clientele base. It can also offer an assessment of what your customers like best and least about your store (thereby helping to determine what should be emphasized in your new store) and other things pertinent to your own operation.

Take time to visit other bookstores. Even other types of retail establishments can offer ideas that might be incorporated into your new operation. Floor covering, signs, lighting, telephone systems, and color are universal items. There is much to be gained (as well as avoided) by spending the time now looking at the efforts of others.

Unless the neighborhood is changing, you would probably prefer to expand the existing premises. This can sometimes be done in less obvious ways than by taking over the vacant storefront next door. Can an empty office be converted to receiving space? A dead-end hall refitted for storage? Is there space available above or below? A vertical move can be quite a bit trickier but more rewarding financially since rents are often considerably less for space away from the ground floor retail level. If the move is vertical, you'll of course have to put in a staircase, which eats square footage and is in itself costly. Yet the benefits accrued in expanding in the same location are not to be negated.

Placement of a staircase is of prime importance. It should be broad (at least wide enough for two people carrying an armload of books to pass comfortably), visible, inviting, and as safe as possible for young and old alike. Depending on the height of the ceiling, more than one landing should be considered to lessen the psychological (and physical) barrier of a long flight of stairs. Access for the handicapped should be arranged if at all possible. In order to transport books up and down, the cost of a two-way conveyor, dumbwaiter, and/or elevator should be investigated. Generally, the least expensive and most versatile of the three is the conveyor belt.

Your budget and your needs will determine the advisability of purchasing any of these work savers.

Don't be daunted by the apparent confusion and mess generated by an expansion of the premises. Certainly you need to keep the noise down as much as possible and the debris contained, but many customers return more frequently just to keep abreast of the construction progress. Upon completion, it shouldn't be necessary to close even for a day unless you have an extremely complicated or large project. With good advance planning your expansion should be able to be structured so that the relocation of sections happens in domino fashion.

Moving away from your existing location presents added problems. Most of the time it means giving up one place for another, and the timing must be perfect. Expenses increase astronomically, as do the decisions.

Enlisting the aid of a real estate agent as well as that of an architect or space planner should be the next order of business. These individuals can be of inestimable help to you at this time, the latter particularly if you are moving into a new building. Special care should be taken in choosing these professionals. Ideally, they should be familiar with the needs of bookstores. At the least, they should be well versed with retailing. Good rapport between you is essential.

It's to be emphasized that their job is to aid you: they should not be a substitute for you. They will bring their expertise and their suggestions, but the final decision rests with you and your staff. You and your staff have created a successful business; now you want to move it, making improvements in the expansion of that thriving venture.

Deciding on a new site often proves to be among the more difficult of these decisions. Unless there are very obvious reasons to relocate some distance away from the area you're in now, your business would probably be best served by staying close by, preferably within sight. Continued foot traffic is of prime importance, as is parking. No matter what the benefits of a new location, there are always disadvantages to weigh into the balance. The net result should tip substantially in favor of a move if you are to head in that direction.

Having made the decision to relocate and having decided on the exact spot, there is much to attend to regarding the details of reestablishing your business. No item is too small or too large for consideration or reconsideration. Attention must be given to floor covering, colors, signs, shelving, and spatial arrangement, as well as to the minutiae of new bags, stationery, bookmarks, and business cards. Weightier consideration will be directed to advertising budgets for the promotion of the new store, the possibility of a name change (to consider with the greatest degree of caution), as well as Yellow Pages advertising, new telephone lines, and the like.

Plan to the last detail, but prepare for less-than-perfect results. Loose ends should be kept to a minimun. Too often, we learn to live with the halfway measures we established to accomplish a difficult decision.

Staff and customer preparation for the impending move should begin as soon as the new lease is signed. Problems related to resistance as well as misplaced euphoria resulting from the misguided perception that a move will solve all problems should be anticipated and dealt with. Instruction on using new equipment such as cash registers and telephone systems should be offered well before the actual move takes place. If you anticipate the need for additional staff, hire them now so they will be well trained by the time the new store opens for business.

The physical process of moving warrants careful attention and planning. If you're just expanding a section or two, you might be able to get away with reshuffling the stock by putting in a bit of overtime after the store closes, but anything more extensive will assuredly tax your wits and your strength.

If you're expanding the existing premises, you will need a domino plan accompanied by time and materials estimates. Physically, the new space should be completely ready to accommodate the books. Shelving should be measured for height and in place. A count of the number of books to be moved, an average of how many will fit per box (which should be of uniform manageable size packed spine up, in shelf order, to facilitate packing and reshelving), and an analysis of how many people can comfortably move about the space accomplishing the move should all be made. The extent and configuration of your project will determine whether you need to consider hiring extra help (or asking for volunteers), gathering a few extra dollies, renting roller conveyors, or conscripting the local high school's graduating senior class to hand over hand the boxes from one part of the store to the next.

Moving to another location requires all of the above and then some. Will trucks have to be rented? Do any streets need to be crossed and, as a result, possibly closed off to traffic? If so, be sure to contact your local police department well in advance; you may need to collect permission from neighborhood businesses that would be affected by such closing.

Alleviating the physical hardship on the staff that such an enormous project entails should be of primary concern. To be sure, it will mean a lot of work, but it should not be exhausting; after all, you need to be ready to serve your customers when it's all over, and simply adjusting to the new location once you're in will require a lot of energy.

Labor-saving devices, dollies, trucks, book trucks borrowed from your local library or jobber, rented roller ramps or conveyors, and the extra hands offered by volunteer or temporary paid help can reduce the burden placed on the staff.

Once it's determined how many books are to be packed, in what number of boxes, and by how many people, schedules can be drawn up to determine how long the move will take. Now is the time to make adjustments as to whether more or less help should be solicited as well as assessing the benefits of beginning the packing process the evening before the day of the move. Using regular staff to pack and unpack boxes while the extra help attends to the actual physical moving can facilitate a more orderly reshelving procedure. Carefully marking and color-coding boxes according to department will help assure their accurate relocation. Consideration should be given to the advance moving of supplies, overstock, and furniture. If you have special moving needs relating to large pieces of furniture, you might be money ahead to hire professional movers or, perhaps more economically, the folks who deliver for the local antique or furniture store. They are used to handling large, heavy, awkwardly shaped objects.

If fixtures from the old location are to be used in the new one, care will have to be given to the logistics of moving and installing them. It might be more expeditious and economical in the long run to leave most of them behind, retaining only the old standard adjustable shelves (if they are of the same style and in reasonably good condition) for use in the new bookcases. Having a carpenter on hand on moving day to refit shelves and attend to other minor adjustments might prove helpful.

Don't forget to make arrangements for refueling your mighty moving crew. If you can afford it, arrange for food and drink to be on hand, or at least forewarn the crew that a sack lunch is in order.

Once the move is basically completed, your attention will need to be given over to what's been left behind as well as to the myriad details of settling in. If you're not keeping your old location, you will need, perhaps, to sell off old fixtures, clean out debris, and, most important, arrange the signs notifying your customers that you've moved. You may already have begun the advertising campaign about your new location, and perhaps the press release you sent out about the move generated some media attention. Despite that, for months henceforth, you will need to apprise vast numbers of people about the change. Maintaining a good relationship with your old landlord as well as the new tenant occupying your old space is a good idea.

Settling in after such a major event will feel like a big relief, but it will bring with it readjustment problems for staff as well as customers. Some will like the old store better; some may feel disappointed that the new store is not quite up to their expectations. Communication and patience are the essential ingredients here. Set aside time for more staff meetings or, better yet, individual meetings. Then work together to create that very special bookstore. Moving it was only the beginning; now, it's time to bring it to life.

Chapter 58

The Branch Store

GINGER CURWEN

Whether or not to branch out to a second site is a question that sparks fierce debate among booksellers. Some veterans frankly doubt the worth of multiple locations, contending that overhead costs are not reduced significantly, problems only multiply, and the additional net profit is not sufficiently commensurate with the effort. Still, others argue, opening a branch store can bring added economies, give firsthand experience with a new neighborhood, and help hedge your bets in a changing economic environment. The following questions may help in the decision-making process.

- Exactly why do you want your business to grow? Is it the lure of added volume and extra discount, or the desire to give a key employee or a partner or, in fact, yourself more challenging work? Growth and new problems seem to go together, so it's important to analyze your desire for expansion.
- Is your current business structure appropriate to handle a second store? Booksellers who are set up as sole proprietors may find that a limited partnership or small corporation is better in terms of taxes and financing. Ask your accountant and lawyer to review your current structure in light of your proposed expansion plans.
- How will you finance the branch store? Obviously, it's important to have already developed a good relationship with your bank loan officer. If you're adding another partner instead, make sure that partner has appropriate expectations about return on investment. Wholesalers and publishers may extend your credit limit if they know you are opening a new store, thus partly financing your expanded inventory.

- Have you explored the new location thoroughly? Are you well versed in the demographics of the neighborhood, the shopping patterns and tastes of your prospective clientele? Is the new location sufficiently far away so that the main store's sales will not be affected?
- Is your current store in good shape, with all systems functioning, staff fully trained and operating well without extraordinary management attention? When you open a branch store, your main store is likely to suffer, at least slightly, from the extra attention you'll need to pay to the branch—make sure it can stand the distraction.
- Are you good at delegating responsibilities? When you open a branch store, management changes are almost identical going from one to ten stores as from one to two. Inevitably your time will become more focused on administration. You have enjoyed doing the buying but may need to hire a buyer for the store; regardless of the distance between the two stores, you may well want to hire a manager (or manager/partner) for the second store. You'll have to worry much more about training, shipping, fixturing. Added employees may prompt you to review general policies, expand your insurance coverage, even write an employee policy manual.
- Are you being realistic about the economies of scale you predict? Assuming centralized frontlist buying for both stores, there will be increased publisher discounts, and certain overhead costs, such as bookkeeping, can be spread over two stores, but hidden costs exist. Knowledge and style are hard to transfer precisely from one location to another. Training a new manager is a real cost factor. If you've delegated buying to the new branch manager, your returns will probably increase until he or she gets to know the neighborhood and clientele.
- Are your systems ready for expansion? Do you have an inventory control that works well now? Will the change to multiple sites prompt the change to a computerized inventory system? And if so, have you allowed time to put it in place? Do you want to set up a central buying location, central receiving or different ship-tos, centralized advertising and promotion? What amount of autonomy do you wish the branch store to have? Many retailers structure their operations for maximum efficiency but encourage the branch manager to give input into the buying decisions. Have you rethought your cash-flow projections?
- Have you considered what kind of interaction should go on between the stores? Do you want to encourage stock transfer on a

regular basis? If the stores are near each other, do you want to rotate employees among the stores?

Certainly the establishment of branch stores enables you to get in on the ground floor of a neighborhood going upscale, monitor other changes and trends in the community at large, and practice some economies of scale in terms of buying and advertising. Whatever your decision, however, make sure that the move does not jeopardize the success of the original store. Answer all the above questions and any others that might affect opening a branch store *before* you start the actual planning.

Chapter 59

Getting Out: Liquidating or Selling Your Bookstore

ELIOT LEONARD

A bookseller makes the decision to retire from bookselling or for some other reason to dispose of his/her store. What are the steps to be taken to close shop or sell the business? There is a lot of thinking and planning ahead.

Selling the business will usually bring a greater return to the owner than liquidating the inventory and other assets, paying off the creditors, cleaning up, and closing the doors. If there is some potential for future success, or if it is already a very good and profitable bookstore, chances are prospective buyers will be attracted to bid on the business.

But if changes in the customer market and business area have affected the bookstore operation, causing a fall in sales and profit, there might be little chance that a buyer will come along to rescue the owner. Severe economic conditions or tough competition can put a store on the ropes, forcing liquidation by selling out, because no one else will take a chance with that situation.

An active retail store with consistent growth of sales and profit should attract a price greater than any amount that could be realized by a piecemeal selling of inventory, fixtures, equipment, supplies, and so on. The operating expense of a slow liquidation, usually under distress conditions, could offset any advantage of a sales promotion to retail customers. There is usually a large segment of books in stock that are not salable at high-enough prices to pay for the time and expense involved to maintain the business while disposing of them.

It is wise always to have a sound concept of the worth of your bookstore business. An occasional analysis of the balance sheet and profit and loss statements will offer a ballpark figure of its value, if you also take into consideration recent trends. The worth varies with changes in market demographics and competition. However, some independent booksellers who have built great store reputations have proven that they can still increase their business in spite of deteriorating conditions. The current status of the business should be known because:

1. You might want or need to sell the store suddenly.
2. In case of emergency, your beneficiary should know the value of the store.
3. It is an important aspect of your estate planning arrangements.
4. You might need to borrow money.

A professional appraisal may be needed to obtain a precise valuation. It might cost only $100 for a small operation, with a perusal of most recent financial statements, or it could cost hundreds of dollars for a detailed inspection of all assets, liabilities, operating and merchandising factors, and trends that might relate to future business. A written report should be made explaining the advantages and disadvantages existing for a potential buyer and suggesting a selling price.

If there is more than one owner of the store, there should be an agreement, preferably in writing, if the business will be sold or closed out, under what conditions and terms. If an outside agency is to be involved, there should be an agreement on selling terms, including commission and other fees or expenses involved.

Liquidation

If no buyer can be found to buy and continue the bookstore, the owner should prepare a procedure and schedule for closing out the business. There are two ways to go, and both should be examined before one plan is chosen for disposing of the assets. One way is to sell off the merchandise, fixtures, equipment, and supplies bit by bit to retail customers in the market. The other is to try and find one or two people or companies who would offer to purchase the bulk of these assets at a wholesale price. Booksellers and other retailers in the region might be interested in bidding for the books and other items.

However, before any action is taken, the current lease for the store space should be examined for restrictions on closing the store for business. Must you wait for the lease term to end before closing the store? Are there penalties involved? Is prior notice to a landlord required, and how much? In what condition must the store space be left? Who owns the improvements you installed, and even the fixtures? All clauses and phrases that relate to store closure and leaving should be inspected carefully.

When legalities are understood, the owner should get in touch with other booksellers and wholesalers in the region and inform them of the intention to close and that merchandise and other items are for sale. If acceptable bids are not made, classified advertisements could then be placed in industry periodicals and local papers. The chances are that any bids from these sources will be in the 20–40 percent of retail range, depending on stock age and condition. Rarely does closeout merchandise and equipment bring offers close to replacement or original value, unless an inexperienced buyer appears.

If the bookseller feels that the highest bids for disposing of these assets in bulk are not sufficient, a clearance or going-out-of-business sale should be prepared. Elements of the promotion should be thought out and scheduled. Local ads, new signs, window and interior displays, and direct-mail pieces should be used to let retail customers know about the closeout, with the wonderful bargains available. If this is the route chosen, price the books to move them, while getting as much as possible. Analyze the titles one by one, and decide how much of a markdown will move each of them. Perhaps about one-third of the inventory will be at 20–30 percent off, about one-third will be 35–50 percent off, and most of the others will sell only at 60–80 percent off. There will always be a small percentage of items that must be priced at $.59 or given away.

Operating expenses must be reduced to a minimum to make this disposal method pay. An up-to-date inventory should move out fairly fast, allowing payroll and other fixed expenses to be kept at an acceptable level of sales dollars that will return more than would selling of these assets at wholesale. Speed of disposal is desired. Only one to three months should be considered for the total clearance. It might be necessary to order in copies of some current best-sellers during this period to be sold at a discount, to keep the clientele interested and to attract them back until the end. Slow-moving stock should be marked down again and again as the days pass, to find the market for them.

If a deal has not been made for some other retailer to buy the fixtures, equipment, and other items, they should be marked with "for sale" signs during the clearance, with a large sign in the window. Everything left at closing day could be donated to a library, school, or other nonprofit user and thus shown as a donation on the final P & L statement.

Selling the Business

A bookseller selling a successful operation should aim to recoup the current value of the tangible assets, with compensation for building the shop and its reputation over the years. The premium amount for "goodwill," or "key" money to be determined and paid, is usually the important negotiating factor that can make or break a sale. The value of the physical assets of the business can be ascertained more easily.

If it is just a poor or fair bookselling operation and a buyer is found, the selling price might be the actual value of the assets to be transferred, with other balance sheet items such as accounts receivable and payable taken into account. Usually the seller has the advantage of having actual facts and figures, knowing the market and trends, and having more bookselling experience than the potential buyer. A better price might result if there is careful long-range planning for the disposition of the business. The owner should attempt to show buyers a fairly complete inventory selection, cleaned of damaged and defective books, with returns of dead titles made to publishers and attractive, well-signed displays throughout the store.

Whatever kind of book business it is, large or small, very profitable or just breaking even, all financial statements should be complete and up-to-date. Any buyer will be interested in examining results of the past couple of years, to get a picture of potential opportunities and pitfalls.

Most of the time, there seems to be a ready market of bookstore buyers who are anxious to be booksellers and are willing to plunk down a few thousand dollars or their life savings. If they have any retail experience, or have professional help in finding a shop to buy, they will want a store that looks in good order, is showing profitable results, or has the potential to be successful in the near future. An inexperienced buyer will rely on the seller's facts, figures, and oral tidings, which might result in little negotiation and a higher selling price.

Here are some ideas to keep in mind when you are ready to offer the bookstore for sale:

1. Do not procrastinate during any negotiations and communications with prospective buyers. You have made the decision to get out, so deal honestly, be straightforward, and come to an agreement that will be good for both parties.

2. The best time to sell is probably when the business is going well, recent profits have been recorded, and you can show future potential. If it is a distress situation, you will just have to push the store's best characteristics and get the best return possible out of the sale. Just after Christmas might be a target date for transfer, taking advantage of highest sales, cash flow, low inventory, and the best profit period of the year.

3. Involve a lawyer, accountant, and/or other professional people in all phases of the sale, such as pricing, timing, tax implications, and the like. Bookkeeping records should be ready for examination and should be separate from personal and family finances.

4. The inventory on the shelves is probably the most important factor involved in the selling and transferring of the store. Be sure that the bookkeeping figure for books on hand relates closely to the actual physical inventory that probably will be taken before the sale is consummated. A clean, accurate inventory, well displayed, can help sell the bookstore.

5. Get to know a prospective buyer as well as possible, both personally and through others. Try to ascertain that the buyer will be capable of running the business, especially if you will be partly paid out of future earnings of the store. Even if you will be getting cash in full, you still have pride of former ownership and would not want to see the operation fail. Of course, if you are happy just to get out of a poor situation, you might not care what happens once you have been paid for the bookstore. But passing the business on to family, friends, nearby competition, and other successful retailers would be best for ensuring continuation of a good store.

6. How much do you tell prospective buyers? Everything advantageous and favorable about the store, but do not mislead or lie about problems. Obvious shortcomings should be pointed out, or a potential sale could be lost when your credibility is questioned. A reasonably good deal must be had on both sides. Along with the financial facts, you should offer a history of the store, the employees, the clientele, and the competition and provide a reason for selling.

7. If you use specialists to help you sell the store, have an understanding about fees and commissions you will have to pay for their advice and help. In most cases, an accountant, lawyer, banker, or other professional person can help you save money and avoid troubles.

8. Negotiate! And expect the prospective buyer to negotiate. Do

not be cold to any offers made, no matter how much the difference between an offer and your asking price. Getting to know each other and the facts often brings a deal together when least expected. Find out why prospects want to buy your store, feel your way, and negotiate!

9. When a deal is ready to be finalized, make sure the written agreement spells out exactly which assets are to be transferred, which liabilities are to be handled by whom, how taxes, insurance, and other fees and payments will be prorated, and so on. The actual transaction is usually completed with the help of an attorney or accountant.

10. Although family, friends, customers, and others in the area know that your bookstore is up for sale, and one of them might make an offer to buy, it might be best to advertise the shop publicly in the classified-ad sections of *ABA Newswire, American Bookseller, Publishers Weekly,* local or city newspaper, and the like. You might thereby get a better idea of the market for your store and a better price.

All employees in your store should know your intention to sell or liquidate. They should be kept up-to-date on anything that might affect their future in the business, but do not make any promises to them that might hinge on the future owner's decisions.

During negotiation, a buyer might ask if the owner will stay on to help the novice bookseller get started. Agreeing to do so might help complete a sale, but it is usually best if the former owner breaks away almost immediately. If you do agree to stay on, it should not be for more than four to eight weeks. This is long enough to break in a new manager in all areas, to learn the stock, the customers, and the resources. Staying on too long might bring up discovered problems and claims that could be very unpleasant.

Selling Price

There is no single or simple formula to determine the selling prices of bookstores. The net worth of the business could be a determining factor depending upon the strength of the elements that make up the assets and liabilities that appear on the balance sheet. In reality, tangible assets to be transferred, such as inventory, equipment, and fixtures, are the most important considerations, plus profitability, that will establish the selling price. "Goodwill" is the hardest component to agree on when negotiating the deal. A good-to-excellent bookstore should bring in some goodwill money for past results and future potential that can be forecasted. A store's reputation, competitive comparison, special location, earnings trend, and fast return of a buyer's investment should all be considered in this goodwill category. A fair or poor operation might only bring the total value of the depreciated assets that will be transferred and nothing for goodwill, and the former owner must pay off all debts.

Bookstores have sold under all kinds of formulas, such as an amount equal to inventory plus a sum of some thousands of dollars that the owner decides he wants, or a sum equal to three or five or ten times last year's net profit plus cost of inventory, and so on. The problem is, how does the owner determine the amount to ask for the key, or goodwill, or how accurate a figure is the net profit shown? It has been noticed that many book and other retail stores have sold for about half of last year's sales in recent years.

A reasonable and satisfactory formula should be based on the assumption that a bookstore is worth the value of its tangible assets that will be transferred, plus a bonus related to profitability over recent years, called goodwill. An evaluation of the bookstore and market for selling purposes may be made step by step as suggested in the following formula:

1. Establish a reasonable profit figure for the upcoming year by using an average of the last three years, adjusted for extraordinary, nonrecurring, and unusual bookkeeping entries. The profit figure should be realistic. Allowing salary compensation for the owner/manager, assume a $150,000 volume store attains a net profit of $7,500.
2. Figure current value of the tangible assets. Using a recent balance sheet, assume:

Merchandise Inventory at Cost	$40,000
Depreciated Equipment & Fixtures, etc.	25,000
Total	$65,000

3. Estimate and establish a profit multiple to put a value on earnings, historic and future. This is actually establishing a goodwill or key amount to be paid for a good-to-excellent bookselling operation. For a fair or poor operation, little or no amount should be paid for the key. The store characteristics that may be evaluated for this figure are shown in the following example, using a scale of 1 to 5:

1. The Store—established, good reputation 4
2. Industry—bookselling has average growth rate 3
3. Competition—minor now, little chance of more 4
4. Sales Growth—steady, little above inflation........... 3½
5. Profit Growth—rising with increasing sales........... 4
6. Market—middle to high income and education,
   in growing numbers............................... 4½
7. Desirability—respected profession with high status
   and pleasant atmosphere......................... 5

Total 7| 28

Divide by 7 items for multiple = 4

4. Figure selling price. The formula is:

Reasonable Profit × Multiple + Tangible Assets
$7,500   ×   4   + $65,000

Selling Price = $95,000 (suggested asking price)

   The above is a very logical and reasonable method to estimate a selling price that might be accepted by both parties in the transaction. The steadier the growth of sales and profit over recent years, the easier it should be to attain a realistic figure for goodwill. It is important to realize that not all stores with about the same annual sales and tangible assets can be sold at the same price. Recent announcements in a trade magazine offered two bookstores in the same category of figures, but one was asking almost $100,000 more than the other. Individual store characteristics and trends must be analyzed carefully.

Bankruptcy

   Sometimes a bookstore can no longer meet its obligations, pay its bills, and the owner sees no way to improve the situation. It can only get worse. A petition of voluntary bankruptcy can be filed by the owner before the store might be hit with involuntary bankruptcy by one or more creditors. The owner wants to go out of business, and by declaring bankruptcy voluntarily, he or she will be given time to plan and conduct liquidation of all assets and settle all liabilities to the satisfaction of creditors, with the approval of a referee or trustee who will supervise the liquidation.

Checklist

In addition to the general "getting out" procedures covered above, there are many other business items that must be attended to during and even after the store is closed or sold:

1. All utility and service companies should be notified in writing about the changes to take place, and when. Check the bills to be paid for utility, trash, telephone, and so on, and check prepaid deposits. Set cutoff dates with each.
2. Charge account customers should be notified about payment of bills and where to send checks after store closing. It might pay to stop new charges thirty to sixty days before closing, if possible. Send reminder statements faster than usual.
3. Notify all resources—publishers, wholesalers, and other suppliers —about the changes to take place and when. Request final statements, and be sure returns to resources are up-to-date in the bookkeeping department. Do everything in writing, including cutoff dates sent to both the publishers' offices and shipping departments. If there is a problem in paying creditors, arrange for a schedule for paying off all debts. Request checks instead of credit when you have credit balances with resources. Do not forget to cancel open stock and special orders. Return any customer deposits for books.
4. Notify bank, insurance, and especially your lawyer about all facts as you plan the liquidation or transfer, and keep the latter informed of all steps as they take place. Talk about protecting your personal assets from any outstanding debts, especially if you have operated as a proprietorship. Bank accounts should have cutoff dates. Insurance contracts should be inspected for any benefits or rebates.
5. Check out all federal, state, and local licenses, fees, permits, and tax situations. File final legal and financial reports required.
6. Personnel records should be up-to-date and complete. All employee compensation should be paid up, including Social Security and other benefits.
7. Above all, keep in touch with your attorney and accountant on any questionable closing-out actions.

Selling or liquidating your bookstore can be an emotional experience. Once the process is set in motion, it is important to follow through as smoothly as possible. It is also wise to leave the business with a good reputation in the minds of the store customers, resources, and professional people with whom you have been in contact over your bookselling years.

VIII
Beyond the Bookstore

Chapter 60

What Is ABA and What Can It Do for You?

BERNARD E. RATH

The ABA was founded on November 15, 1900, to represent the interests of the retail booksellers of America. Today, almost ninety years later, the organization is stronger than ever and accomplishes its mission in a variety of ways by providing both tangible and intangible services. Its objectives are far-reaching and ambitious:

- To bring together in one organization, for their mutual benefit, persons and firms engaged in the retail sale of books in the United States of America.
- To provide services, conduct studies, disseminate information, hold meetings and conferences, and provide educative programs for the enlightenment and improvement of its membership.
- To stimulate in every possible way the retail sale of books in this country.
- To promote high standards of professional competence, conduct, and ethics, and to combat unfair trade practices by all legal means.
- To encourage association activities on a regional as well as a national basis, and to assure that the composition of the board of directors be such that the broadest segment of the regular membership, geographically and by size and type of enterprise, is represented.
- To foster communication and cooperation among publishers, wholesalers, retailers, and others in the American book industry.
- To work toward the establishment, maintenance, and improvement of favorable trade conditions, and to maintain a careful

watch over, so as to support or oppose, legislation affecting the
bookseller's interests.

- To aid booksellers in the encouragement of reading of all kinds at
  all age levels.
- To assist booksellers in recognizing and responding to their unusual
  cultural and educative responsibilities to their communities.
- To contest actively all encroachments upon the free expression of
  ideas in this country, by persons or groups seeking to impose
  their own standards or tastes upon the community at large.

ABA's best-known tangible services are its publications, its
educational meetings, and its retail aids, each of which has come
into being to meet a stated need of the membership. These needs
have been interpreted and met by the hundreds of booksellers who,
over the years, have volunteered to serve on such association committees as publications, marketing, basic booklist, and education,
among others.

A Manual on Bookselling: How to Open and Run a Bookstore is
designed to be a textbook for setting up and maintaining a successful
bookstore, based on the hard-won experience of professional booksellers. Revised and updated every few years, the manual is now in
its fourth edition. Previous editions have sold over 60,000 copies
since the first printing in 1969. ABA members receive a free copy of
each revised edition.

ABA's oldest and most constantly used publication is the *ABA
Book Buyer's Handbook,* or "the Red Book," as it is affectionately
known in the book trade. Published each September in loose-leaf
format, and available exclusively to ABA members, it provides the
addresses, phone numbers, discount schedules, returns policies, and
cooperative advertising policies of hundreds of American publishers
and wholesalers.

The most widely circulated publication of the ABA is *American
Bookseller,* a monthly magazine for retail booksellers that has a
circulation of approximately eight thousand people in the book
industry. Regular features include news of association and regional
activity, articles on merchandising and management, analysis of
trends, and bookstore profiles. Although subscriptions are available
for nonmembers, all ABA members receive a free subscription with
their membership and are eligible for special rate reductions on
additional subscriptions for themselves, friends, and staff.

"The first ten thousand titles are the hardest," quip experienced
booksellers. In response to one of the most frequently asked questions by future booksellers—"Which books should comprise the
opening inventory for my new store?"—ABA produces the *Basic
Book List.* Updated and published biennially, it contains titles

recommended as a possible nucleus of basic stock as selected by a committee of active booksellers from across the United States based on their personal experience. Sales rate is an important criterion for the selection of stocked titles, but this committee also takes great care to choose titles that will stand the test of time.

Since many booksellers sell products other than books, such as calendars, cards, toys, audio- and videotapes—every few years the association publishes the *ABA Sidelines Directory*, a comprehensive listing of sources for nonbook merchandise that has been sold successfully in bookstores.

Among ABA's most useful publications is *ABA Newswire*, a weekly newsletter featuring timely, front-page news reports about issues relevant to booksellers, from industry mergers and censorship legislation to changing terms. To help booksellers anticipate public demand, *Newswire* also contains listings of upcoming publicity tours, forthcoming book reviews, and ad campaigns. The publication is delivered each week by first-class mail to all members and is available, by subscription, to nonmembers.

Meeting the educational needs of booksellers is a prime goal of ABA, accomplished through ABA Prospective and Professional Booksellers Schools (described in chapter 62) and at panel discussions at the annual ABA Convention. Cassette tapes of these ABA Convention sessions are available for purchase.

Members are also able to purchase, at favorable prices, other products useful in the everyday operation of a bookstore. The most popular of these items is the STOP order form for single book titles, which was developed by the ABA in cooperation with the Association of American Publishers. This handy three-part form, when filled in and accompanied by a check, allows a bookseller to receive a single copy or multiple copies of a single title at a trade discount, when that book by itself might not qualify for the publisher's trade terms. Other popular items include purchase order forms, handsome gift certificates for bookstore customers who may not be able to choose an appropriate gift title, and the ABA forms kit, which provides the retailer with thirteen handy camera-ready forms from which to print multiple copies of problem sheets, charge-back forms, returns forms, inventory cards, and special-order postcards.

A new ABA service, the ABA Bookstore Site Location Analysis, has been designed to help those interested in opening bookstores to find suitable locations. The analysis offers a statistical demographic profile on a site being considered. Twenty-five key indicators, including population, income, households, education, occupation, age, sex, and race, show the characteristics of prospective customers and provide information about the economic strengths and weaknesses of a proposed site. The service is also useful for existing bookstores; it can be used for analyzing the present location to determine if it is meeting the area's current needs, when seeking to relocate, or if planning to open a branch store.

ABA members are eligible for reduced rates at the annual convention, the largest English-language trade book fair in the world, special prices on group insurance plans, and low service fees on Visa redemptions through a group plan. Only ABA members may join the ABA Bookstore Merchandising Group and receive display and merchandising materials and information at a nominal cost.

As important as all of these tangible benefits of membership are, there are also many intangibles that serve the needs of the retail bookselling community. ABA has been a guardian of bookseller interests in matters of governmental action, lobbying against postal increases and First Amendment abuses. Through its membership in a group known as the Media Coalition, the ABA has argued before the Supreme Court in censorship cases. Twice a year, members of the ABA board of directors visit the chief executives of major publishing houses to reassert the importance of the retail bookselling community to the publishing process and to suggest ways in which publishing houses can cooperate to improve the competitive position of the bookseller in the marketplace. ABA also maintains liaison committees with the Association of American Publishers, the National Association of College Stores, the Children's Book Council, the Canadian Booksellers Association, and the Center for the Book at the Library of Congress.

Even today, with its multimillion-dollar operating budget and a staff of thirty, the ABA remains primarily an organization for, by, and about the retail bookseller. The twenty-member board of directors and the fifteen committees comprising dozens of additional volunteers work hard to ensure that ABA's programs and projects help to make a career in retail bookselling a professional and profitable experience. The positions that ABA takes give the bookseller a powerful voice in the industry. Legislation or trade practices that affect one bookseller affect all booksellers. ABA is ever alert to all these matters.

For the ABA to function effectively, it must have the support of all booksellers. Not only does it assess an annual dues contribution, which is the tangible expression of a bookseller's commitment to the goals and objectives of the association, but it requires enthusiasm and cooperation from all member stores. Only united can the ABA help ensure that retail booksellers maintain and enhance their rightful place as a vital link in that complex chain that brings reader and writer together.

Chapter 61

Belonging: The Value of Regionals and Other Local Organizations

BARBARA THEROUX

A sense of community is important in the bookselling world. Before opening a new store, you were probably involved with a market study, finding out about the people, politics, and organizations in your area. In a successful store you constantly identify customers and look for new ways to meet a changing market. The image of the store is reflected in your buying decisions, which should be a direct result of listening to your customers. Personal booksellers know that interests in and of their community help sell books.

Every parent is familiar with the volunteer efforts of school, band, scouts, and sports teams as a way to identify local issues and people. In much the same way, you need to seek out other booksellers and businesspeople to enhance and increase your business. Belonging to professional and business organizations can strengthen the bookseller's position and make the bookstore an active community center.

The first organizations to consider are regional bookseller associations. In recent years these groups have become active in providing services to members such as trade shows, catalogs, newsletters, rep lists, and cooperative ways to promote local authors or literary efforts. For people who cannot attend the ABA Convention, a regional trade show can serve some of the same purposes. In fact, a regional show could be especially useful because local sales reps are in attendance there, and regional titles will be highlighted. Since most regional shows are in the fall, finished books can be seen—so you can adjust an original buy or finalize author and other promotions. Regional shows are also good places to meet local wholesalers and perhaps tour their facilities. Seminars or panels identify booksellers in your area who share similar problems and frustrations.

Christmas catalogs have grown out of regional booksellers needing (and demanding) advertising for local-interest books and authors. Regional newletters and local rep lists are good ways to keep in contact. Time and distance do not always allow attendance at all meetings, dinners, seminars, or shows, but newsletters and visiting sales reps can keep us up-to-date.

Several regionals now have literacy programs, book awards, and other merchandising campaigns. These are good ways to bring your store into community, state, and regional projects. Personal bookselling campaigns are what keep booksellers unique, so look for those opportunities. If you live in an area surrounded by strong regionals, decide on one to actively support, but consider also being on the mailing list for other groups. Most regionals are focused on one major city in the area. Join the one where most of your sales reps live. Regional associations are only as strong as the members make them. Every group needs active people and new ideas—so booksellers should join and contribute their knowledge.

Other bookseller associations to consider center around specialties. These include NACS (National Association of College Stores), CBA (Christian Booksellers Association), and ABC (Association of Booksellers for Children). These groups grow out of special needs and share publisher, wholesaler, and bookstore-related problems through newletters and journals. There are other possibilities— mystery bookstores may want to consider joining the Mystery Writers of America. Look around for groups that reflect your store's interest. Writers, illustrators, publishers, wholesalers, and booksellers all have a stake in bringing books and the public together.

In your own community many opportunities exist both in book and nonbook organizations. Library groups, reading associations, and book discussion clubs can provide programs and ways to involve both bookseller and bookstore in community events. Authors often attend conferences or talk at libraries—the bookseller could help bring someone to town in exchange for an in-store autograph session. The bookseller shares a mutual interest with these groups, and perhaps working together could strengthen a local literacy effort.

As a community business consider organizations such as the Chamber of Commerce, Downtown Merchants, or Mall Associates that promote your market area. All stores need customers and can work together on promotions and advertising. The commercial groups can bring in speakers to address financial or security concerns. Seminars on advertising could be offered as well as referral services and community networking.

Belonging does cost money and time. To sign up for all the groups mentioned here would be ridiculous. Before joining an organization, find out what that group does or represents. Ways to obtain firsthand information are attending a meeting as a guest (or speaker) and being on the mailing list. Consider joining first as an associate member or nonvoting member. This classification usually pays a cheaper dues rate. Finally, do not overlook belonging to a service club or theater group, something totally outside your business interest. Take time to relax and escape—but keep on the lookout for ways and opportunities to sell books!

Chapter 62

Booksellers Schools and Workshops

CYD ROSENBERG and BARBARA THEROUX

Everyone knows that a better-educated bookseller is a better bookseller, but not everyone knows where to look for bookseller education opportunities. ABA offers formal booksellers schools and workshops, convention panels, and publications such as this manual and the *American Bookseller* magazine. In addition, there are an array of courses, seminars, and workshops available in your community or through the mail.

There was no formal instruction in retail bookselling prior to 1966. You learned by experience, either working in someone else's store or plunging ahead blindly and opening the doors to your own business. Russell Reynolds, then general manager of the National Association of College Stores, was concerned with the need for inproving trade book departments in college bookstores and charged Marge Goodman of the University of California at Riverside and G. Royce Smith, then of the Yale Co-op, with the task of designing a curriculum for a three-day seminar in retail bookselling. The first such seminar was held in Oberlin, Ohio, in 1966, and from that initial effort has come the very successful bookseller educational program, co-sponsored since 1969 by the ABA. More than nine thousand booksellers have completed the course, and the school itself has undergone numerous evolutionary changes.

At present there are two kinds of booksellers schools, professional and prospective. The Professional Booksellers School is suggested for those already in the business with up to approximately three years' experience, both owner-managers and staff members. More experienced booksellers frequently attend for the opportunity to learn what other booksellers are presently doing and to sharpen their own skills.

Curriculum for the professional school includes all aspects of retail bookselling—from reviewing the use of basic tools to staff management; budgeting and financial management; inventory control; display and visual merchandising; advertising, publicity, and promotion; selling books ouside the store; and so on. Classes are led by experienced booksellers, many of whom are former students of the school, coming from stores of all sizes and geographic areas to share what they have learned with colleagues.

The Professional Booksellers School is presently held four times each year in different parts of the country, one session in each time zone, with each session limited to eighty students. The school is an intensive experience with three and a half days of nonstop bookselling-related talk. Booksellers from all over the United States and Canada come together to exchange ideas and experiences. Classes are structured but informal; discussion is encouraged by the volunteer bookseller instructors, who explain aspects of book retailing with which they have had particular success.

Several years ago the ever-increasing number of students attending the school who had no experience whatsoever and were considering opening their own bookstore brought about the formation of the Prospective Booksellers School, separate from the basic school. Courses are geared specifically to those entering the book business, with an emphasis on the information necessary to start a business and then an overview of bookstore operations, similar in nature to the curriculum of the professional school. Detailed classes are held on selecting a site and negotiating a lease, financing a bookstore, physical planning, inventory selections, hiring a staff, and grand-opening promotion and advertising. Faculty for the Prospective Booksellers School is made up of experienced booksellers who have been through the opening-a-bookstore experience themselves, plus experienced ABA staff members who regularly counsel prospective booksellers. Some students who attend the school are just casually thinking about the possibility of going into the retail book business, while others are far along in their store planning and are able to share experiences already acquired.

Anyone seriously considering opening a bookstore is urged to attend a prospective school as early in his or her planning program as possible. Expensive mistakes can be avoided with information acquired at the school. Prospective Booksellers School sessions are held presently twice a year in varying locations around the country. Enrollment is limited to eighty students.

Every year at the ABA Convention, a series of timely and informative panels are held, covering a wide range of subjects. Selected panel topics might include "A Kaleidoscope of Ways to Sell

Children's Books," "Used Books in the Trade Store," and "Selling Computer Software." Cassette tapes are made of these panel sessions and are available for purchase. The cassettes are valuable for those who cannot attend every convention, and even for those who do, in that the information can be heard by all staff members. A cassette library can be maintained by a bookstore for constant reference.

Regional bookseller associations can also be a valuable source for educational programs, as they offer panel sessions and workshops in conjunction with their meetings and trade shows. These panel sessions usually address topics of current regional concern or interest, and the workshops frequently involve a practical hands-on experience or discussion group, more feasible in the smaller regional association gatherings than in the national ABA Convention. On occasion, ABA offers one-day workshops held in conjunction with regional meetings. These workshops usually focus on one specific topic, such as children's books or financial record keeping.

Not all educational opportunities have to come from ABA or regional associations. Some surprisingly good sources can be found without leaving your home or store. The Small Business Administration field office is a good place to begin looking for community-based learning resources. The SBA offers free counseling by experts through its SCORE program (Service Corps of Retired Executives) and ACE program (Active Corps of Executives). Any businessperson can use these human resources without being the recipient of an SBA loan. The SBA also runs institute programs throughout the country, in which university faculty members, SBA officials, and graduate students in business administration work with owners of small businesses. The national office will send lists on request, one of free publications and one of booklets for sale. These cover the brass tacks of financial management as well as specific issues, such as preventing theft and advertising techniques.

Another source of local community business education is the Chamber of Commerce. Most chambers have a division for small businesses as well as a publication to promote local business. It's helpful to own this guide to area goods and services. Also look into Chamber of Commerce seminars and other low-cost local classes as well as small-business libraries in the area.

If located near a college or university, you can drop into classes fairly easily and audit courses. At the local community college or university, you might look into night courses or extension courses if you are too far away from the institution's main campus. In addition to business and computer courses, check literature and history listings for courses that might be helpful. Sometimes you can benefit—offer your store for on-the-job experience and learn as you are teaching. Begin looking within your area for courses by contacting the department of continuing education on campus or the adult education office at the local high school.

In the past two decades, an interest in accessible information has led to new, informal educational "networks" that offer noncredit, short courses on a variety of subjects, from arts and crafts to business management. These educational networks operate throughout the country. For a listing in your area, contact the national offices of the Learning Resources Network and the Learning Exchange.

Correspondence courses are a natural choice for booksellers who are short of the free time it takes to attend a regular class. For correspondence courses that are related to the business of bookselling, try children's literature, accounting, bookkeeping, communications, advertising, computer science, data processing, or English literature. Most courses are usually based on a high-quality text, divided into preprogrammed lessons. There really is no way to choose one correspondence course over another without actually seeing the materials, but fortunately many schools will allow you to review the materials before signing up and sending the check.

A wonderful source for correspondence courses that offer academic credit is the Guide to Independent Study through Correspondence. It lists about twelve thousand courses from sixty-nine accredited colleges and universities and gives complete information on costs, financial aid, credit, prerequisites, and applications. For vocational schools, which offer noncredit correspondence courses on subjects ranging from accident prevention to zookeeping, try the National Home Study Council. They will send you a packet of information with a directory of accredited vocational schools. Business-oriented vocational courses include business administration, computer programming, data processing, management of small businesses, and personnel management. A word of warning about correspondence courses. The freedom from regular classroom hours that makes correspondence study attractive can also be a curse. Most programs allow a period of six months to two years for course completion. Watch out for your tendency to procrastinate.

Opportunities to learn can lurk in some unlikely places. Banks, for instance, will often let you sit in on training courses offered to their employees. Computer stores will give you lessons in accounting, payroll, or point-of-purchase inventory systems—just be prepared for the inevitable sales pitch that will follow. On the government level, the IRS offers tax seminars for business owners, and your local job service or employment office offers publications and workshops on such topics as employer/employee relations and state requirements on pay benefits. Be on the lookout for one-time seminars sponsored by radio, TV, or newspaper advertising departments. Community awareness can go a long way toward broadening educational horizons.

Addresses for further information:

Correspondence Courses

Guide to Independent Study
  through Correspondence
c/o Peterson Guides
Box 2123
Princeton, NJ 08540

National Home Study Council
1601 18th St. NW
Washington, DC 20009
(for vocational courses)

Seminars

These national organizations coordinate short, business-related seminars throughout the country; write and ask for a catalog, which will provide details on course content, price, and location.

Applied Management Institute
623 Great Jones St.
Fairfield, CA 94533

American Management Associations
135 West 50th St.
New York, NY 10020
(212) 586-8100

Educational Networks

The Learning Exchange
P.O. Box 920
Evanston, IL 60204
(312) 273-3383

Learning Resources Network
P.O. Box 1425
1221 Thurston
Manhattan, KS 66502
(912) 532-5866

General

U.S. Small Business Administration
P.O. Box 15434
Fort Worth, TX 76119
(800) 433-7212
In Texas: (800) 792-8901

This book, A *Manual on Bookselling*, is a continuing-educational tool that should be kept at easy access within your store.

It should be thought of as the first place to check for additional information about a new area of bookselling into which you might be looking or new type of event you're planning to offer. Staff people should always be encouraged to read the manual.

Issues of *American Bookseller* should be circulated throughout the staff as well and filed for future reference, especially if staff people do not have subscriptions to the magazine at their home address (a nice service for the owner-manager to provide). You might develop a loose-leaf binder of articles in different areas of interest or simply collect the annual index to back issues published every year. The magazine has articles focusing on special areas of current concern or publishes groups of articles about a particular topic, such as special ordering or used books, which can be a valuable source of information; it also provides tips on ways to solve a particular problem. The "Bookseller News" column has features on bookstore promotions where it's always possible to pick up an idea worth trying out in your own store.

ABA strongly believes that an interchange of ideas and continuing education is vital for a growing, successful business. The educational programs and valuable information in the publications offered by ABA, as well as educational opportunities offered outside the store through other sources, provide the retailer with the opportunity for such growth.

Chapter 63

The ABA Convention

GINGER CURWEN

My first ABA Convention was a shocker. I was twenty-three, just promoted to the position of publicity manager for a small independent publishing house. My timing was perfect. Getting that new job in April meant that I would get to go to the ABA Convention in May. On the big day, I walked into the Shoreham Hotel in Washington, D.C., down to the exhibit floor, ready to be as grown-up and businesslike as my years and experience would allow. Instead of literary decorum, I found the Big Top: hundreds of exhibits, thousands of people (all of whom seemed to know each other) milling in the aisles. Some booths offered free popcorn to promote their new books. And over in one of the rows, I spotted my first convention author: Mickey Spillane. He was busy autographing the flyleaf of his new book, some crime thriller with a stunning, near naked blonde on the cover, then handing each copy over to his wife, the spitting image of that blonde, who, in turn, autographed the cleavage on the cover.

This was publishing?

This was—and is—the ABA Convention, an annual rite for the publishing and bookselling industry, where the intersection of literature and commerce produces interesting incongruities. A three-and-a-half-day event, generally held over the Memorial Day weekend in some large convention hall in some large city, the ABA Convention has been the birthplace for more trends in publishing, more book deals, author launchings, job switches, marriages, divorces, friendships, mergers, and distribution deals than anything else you can think of. How this exhibit and trade show, which is sponsored by the American Booksellers Association, came to be synonymous with the association itself is lost in the sands of publishing history, but synonymous it is. Everyone simply refers to the convention as the ABA. For at least five months of each year, the publishing industry prepares for ABA, decides whom to send, what books to feature, what parties to host, what guests to invite, what reading copies to give away, what new terms to announce, what clothes to wear, and which vacations to take afterward. For booksellers, the agenda is a near mirror image: how long to stay, which book and author breakfast to attend, which parties to go to, which reading copies to get, and so forth. It is a wonderful, productive, exhilarating, but often overwhelming experience.

What is now the largest English-speaking gathering of book people and exhibit of English-language books in the world began modestly in 1947 with a simple collection of displays set out for booksellers to browse through on the last day of their annual convention. The number of exhibits swelled to 117 more formal booths for most of the following years, then mushroomed. In 1985, the convention boasted 1,500 booths of 800 exhibitors displaying books, computers, video- and audiocassettes, calendars, store supplies, and an attendant throng of some 17,500 publishers, booksellers, agents, and the like. And 1986 was even larger.

For years the standard litany to first-timers was this: Prepare in advance; wear sensible shoes; make sure you make a tour of the entire exhibit before going back to see the booths that really interest you. Well, times have changed. The bit about the shoes still holds. Walking each aisle is hard to do these days, thanks to the sheer size of the exhibit (more advice on this later). Advance preparation? More necessary than ever.

Establishing your priorities for the convention is the first step in advance preparation. Getting a good look at the fall books is usually on everyone's agenda, and by this we mean taking a look at books that *must* be seen before buying decisions can be made; getting a good overview of the fall season, its upcoming trends and likely best-sellers; and scanning the offerings not just from major publishers, but also from small presses and regional houses. A walk through the small press section of the convention is a must for discovering wonderful, truly one-of-a-kind books. With the overview of the fall season in mind, you'll be able to start making preliminary plans for co-op advertising and author promotions. The people you'll need to talk to are likely to be in the booths.

You may also decide to use the convention as the place to finally start up a children's section, complete with foreign-language books, or research the now-booming audiocassette field, or make that final decision about a computerized inventory program. The wealth of exhibitors in various areas makes it an excellent place to do market

Fig. 63-1. An overview of the 1986 ABA Convention in New Orleans, Louisiana. (Photograph by Lawrence Migdale)

research, and you'll find that one of the many educational panels probably covers the topic in which you need to acquire expertise.

No bookseller should neglect to study the publishers' convention stock offers that are announced in *American Bookseller's* annual convention issue. Take inventory beforehand and figure out what you need and can afford to spend. Many booksellers claim they can save enough by taking advantage of these stock offers to pay for their airfare, hotel room, and meals. Problem-solving is another goal on many booksellers' lists, and in this arena the traditional advice is still good. If there are ongoing specific problems with certain vendors, bring documentation and try to schedule an appointment in advance.

In preparation for all these goals, study the exhibitor offerings and features mentioned in the hefty preconvention issues put out by *American Bookseller* and *Publishers Weekly,* and make notes of the booths at which you must stop. One bookseller takes the trouble to organize all the booths of interest to her geographically. She studies the map of the convention floor that is in the preconvention issues of the trade magazines, notes the location of particular exhibits, and transfers the information to a small black notebook, putting the booth numbers into geographical clusters on tab labels, one cluster to a page. It takes some time, but it's an excellent way to organize her time at the trade show, and ever since *American Bookseller* ran an article on her system, booksellers with little black notebooks are seen stalking the floor. They seem less tired than the rest of us.

Naturally, you'll want to save time for education and recreation. The panels, previously mentioned, usually feature savvy booksellers sharing their experiences on a wide range of topics; the topics for panels can range from getting into used books or sidelines to improving inventory control and turnover, from making the decision to expand or start a branch to organizing author promotions. You should also save time on your calendar for the ABA's annual membership meeting. Although some of it is devoted to obligatory reports, the new business section of the meeting has been an exceedingly lively forum for all concerns of booksellers across the country. You'll want to scan who's appearing on the book and author breakfasts. In the past such notables as Jimmy Carter, Lee Iacocca, and Shirley MacLaine have been the headliners, and naturally tickets go fast. You may also want to check out the autographing schedule to see which of your favorite authors is signing his new book. (Tip: For popular authors, you may have to stand in line for thirty minutes or so.) The ABA cocktail party and buffet is usually on Sunday night, and there is a closing banquet on Tuesday night. There are plenty of publishers' parties, large and small, in between.

Booksellers who have attended more than one ABA Convention take care to bring plenty of business cards with them to save time when talking to publishers. Many bring an empty suitcase or collapsible luggage cart for trekking around samples and catalogs and vow not to take catalogs from publishers that already mail to them lest their arms or suitcase break. And no matter how organized they are, all attendees always make notes on how to do it better next year.

Chapter 64

When Is It a Crime to Sell a Book?: A Review of Laws Seeking to Regulate Sexually Explicit Books and Magazines

MAXWELL LILLIENSTEIN

Booksellers are faced with jail every day in every state for selling books they cannot possibly know are unlawful. At this writing, the trend is for laws regulating morality in the print media to become more severe. Why?

More than twenty-five years have passed since the Supreme Court in *Roth* v. *United States*, 354 U.S. 476 (1957), first held that (a) "obscenity is not within the area of constitutionally protected speech or press"; and (b) proof that "obscene material will perceptibly create a clear and present danger of antisocial conduct" is not required by the Constitution.

A cornerstone of the monumental decision was the assertion that statutes using such words as "filthy," "indecent," or "obscene" can "mark boundaries sufficiently distinct for judges and juries fairly to administer the law." Yet today, after numerous judicial attempts, a definition of obscenity with such sufficiently distinct boundaries has eluded the Court despite its promulgation of several significantly different obscenity definitions.

Close scrutiny of case law, statutes, and sociological studies dealing with possession, publication, production, dissemination, and display of pornographic books, magazines, and motion pictures reveals a muddled diversity of opinions as to a workable definition of obscenity, the causal relationship between obscenity and antisocial conduct, the constitutionality of legislation regulating obscenity, and the most appropriate means of preventing its spread.

Despite this diversity of opinion—highlighted by a consistent split (five to four) among the justices of the Supreme Court as to the constitutionality of obscenity laws—booksellers all over the country continue to be shock troops on the firing line. Since June 23, 1973, the date of the most recent Supreme Court attempt to redefine obscenity, there has been a proliferation of obscenity laws enacted in most states. Currently in force in many states are laws making it unlawful not only to sell obscene books and magazines, but to sell or display in areas of the store accessible to minors books and magazines containing sexually explicit materials that are not obscene as that term has been defined by the Supreme Court. In a period of heightened public interest in sex-oriented books, it is vital that booksellers have a basic knowledge of the laws that might make them criminals for selling books they have no reason to believe are unlawful.

What is obscenity?
Strangely, this word, employed in almost all obscenity legislation, is erroneously used. In fact, whenever the word is used in legislation, it is intended to mean "pornography." The Supreme Court definition of obscenity, still evolving, contains a three-pronged test:

> (a) whether the average person, applying contemporary community standards, would find that work, taken as a whole, appeals to the prurient interest; (b) whether the work depicts or describes in a patently offensive way, sexual conduct specifically defined by the applicable state law; and (c) whether the work, taken as a whole, lacks serious literary, artistic, political, or scientific value. *Miller* v. *California*, 413 U.S. 15 at 24 (1973).

Justice Brennan, writing for the majority in *Roth*, expressly rejected the standard used in the time-honored case, *Regina* v. *Hicklin*, 3 Q.B. 360 (1868), because the "Hicklin test, judging obscenity by the effect of an isolated passage upon the most susceptible person, might well encompass material legitimately treating sex, and so it must be rejected as unconstitutionally restrictive of the freedoms of speech and press."

In 1964, the Supreme Court, by Justice Brennan, in *Jacobellis* v. *Ohio*, 378 U.S. 184 (1964), recognized the ambiguity and shortcomings of the *Roth* obscenity standards but stated: "We think any substitute would raise equally difficult problems, and we therefore adhere to that standard."

A distressing but amusing question discussed in *Jacobellis* v. *Ohio* was whether only "hard-core" pornography should be banned by the legal test for obscenity. "Yes," said Justice Stewart, "I have reached the conclusion, which I think is confirmed at least by negative implications in the Court's decisions since *Roth* and *Alberts* [the companion case to *Roth*] that under the First and Fourteenth amendments, criminal laws in this area are constitutionally limited to hard-core pornography." "No," replied Chief Justice Warren, along with Justice Clark, "we are told that only 'hard-core pornography' should be denied the protection of the First Amendment. But who can define 'hard-core pornography' with any greater clarity than 'obscenity'?"

Justice Stewart volunteered one pathway through the definitional thicket: "I shall not today attempt to further define the kinds of material I understand to be embraced within that shorthand description [of hard-core pornography]; and perhaps I could never succeed in intelligibly doing so. But I know it when I see it. . . ."

However, Justice Stewart's personal obscenity divining rod will not assist potential violators of obscenity statutes or policemen whose job it is to make obscenity arrests in determining what matter is obscene.

In 1973, the *Miller* decision was handed down by a sharply divided (five to four) court. Justice Brennan, the author of the landmark opinion in *Roth* declaring obscenity to be unworthy of First Amendment protection, dissented in *Miller*. After sixteen years of groping for a definition that would give fair warning to potential violators, he reconsidered his original view and concluded that no obscenity statute could be clear enough to be constitutionally valid.

In the companion case of *Paris Adult Theatre* v. *Slaton*, 413 U.S. 48 (1973), he concluded that no definition of obscenity could give the constitutionally required fair warning.

Since *Miller*, Justice Brennan has consistently been joined in his obscenity dissents by Justice Stewart, Justice Marshall, and, more recently, Justice Stevens.

Average Person

The Supreme Court, in *Miller* v. *California*, defined obscenity for the third time in sixteen years. Since that decision, almost every state legislature and the United States Congress have enacted, or are in the process of enacting, legislation patterning the definition of obscenity after *Miller*. Thus, it is a matter of self-interest for every bookseller to understand that definition (to the extent that it is possible) so as to avoid committing a crime. A dissection of the *Miller* definition into its component parts should assist you, the bookseller, in better understanding the problems you face.

Miller requires a jury to determine whether the average person applying contemporary community standards would find that a work, "taken as a whole, appeals to the prurient interest. . . ."

Does "average person" include minors? If so, wouldn't the standard set for the entire community be reduced to standards permissible for minors? Fortunately a recent Supreme Court decision, *Pincus* v. *United States* (1978), appears to have established the principle that children are not to be included in the hypothetical concept of average person.

Average in what community? Where the court is located? Where the work is published? Where the work is disseminated? Can a jury know what the average person thinks about erotica, a subject obscured by social taboos? Can the average person know what "contemporary community standards" prevail with regard to such a subject? If not, then the jury will use purely subjective standards that provide no advance warning as to which books are obscene.

Thus, "average person" is an ambiguous concept to which *Roth* v. *United States* and *Miller* v. *California* failed to give a meaning that would permit a jury to make an objective distinction between materials under First Amendment protection and those whose publication and dissemination would subject publishers and booksellers to prosecution.

Prurient Interest Appeal

First applied in *Roth*, this test requires a jury determination that objectionable material appeals to the "prurient interest" of the average person in the community. *The Oxford Dictionary of the English Language* (unabridged, 1971) defines "prurient" as an "itching desire or curiosity, or an uneasy morbid craving" and "given to lasciviousness of thought or mind." In *Jacobellis* v. *Ohio*, cited earlier, the Court narrowed the meaning of prurient interest to matters tending to "excite lustful thoughts."

What is wrong with appealing to prurient interest in consenting adults?

Dr. Willard Gaylin, an eminent psychoanalyst, observed, "Appeals to the other senses are not considered vulgar. Yet our puritan tradition at one time interdicted those appeals as well, and the delights of the palate, ear, and eye were held obscene in their day."* Supporting the idea that pornography may have socially redeeming value is a recent observation made by Professor John Money, a respected sex researcher, at the sixty-first annual symposium of the American Pathological Association:

> It is important to emphasize that it's normal to be aroused by erotic stimuli even when they're in pictures in picture books that you may buy in the sleazy part of town. . . .

*W. Gaylin, "The Prickly Problems of Pornography," 77 *Yale Law Journal* (1968), 584–86.

Now, on a somewhat different note, and a positive one, exposure to pornography, and considering one's own reactions to it, does in fact lead to the possibility of bettering one's own sex life, leading one to have less guilt and fewer "hang ups," and more honesty and freedom about sex.

It also helps one better to define one's own standards and, therefore, to guide one's own children or other people that one may be responsible for—especially those whose lives are devoted to medical treatment. *

Patent Offensiveness

Miller declared that appeal to prurient interest must be accompanied by depiction of sexual conduct in a patently offensive manner before material could be considered obscene.

First employed in *Manual Enterprises* v. *Day,* 370 U.S. at 482 (1962), the "patently offensive" test has since been retained in each new Supreme Court definition of obscenity as an essential prerequisite to a finding that material is obscene. But can the tests of prurient appeal and patent offensiveness be reconciled? The apparent inconsistency of these two tests was suggested in *United States* v. *Klaw,* 350 F.2d 155, at 166–67 (2d Cir.1965), in which Judge Moore observed:

> Most of the witnesses testified that they found the material disgusting or revolting, but that lascivious and lecherous thoughts had not been aroused in them. . . .
> If the witnesses presented in this case provided any sampling, these pamphlets and pictures stimulated no one's prurient interest.

Judge Moore concluded:

> Too easily the jury could aid suppression simply on the basis of speculations and suspicions about the prurient appeal of the material to some unknown, unidentified person whose psyche is not known.
> With the First Amendment in the background this cannot be abided.

Simply stated, something that is disgusting to one person will not excite lustful thoughts. If the same material excites lustful thoughts in another person, it is not disgusting to that person. Modern psychology assures us that such conflicting reactions to pornography are the norm. Dr. Money has said in a book on con-

*J. Zubin and J. Money, *Contemporary Sexual Behavior* (Baltimore: Johns Hopkins University Press, 1973), 418–19.

temporary sexual behavior published by Johns Hopkins University Press, "I would suspect that every single human being alive is able to feel some kind of disgust at the pornography that is sexually arousing to certain other people but not to one's self."*

Thus, if we define *patently offensive* as "disgusting," it would be absurd to look for coalescence of appeal to prurient interest and patent offensiveness. Nevertheless, the *Miller* decision requires precisely such a coalescence.

Defining obscenity in such a manner is an invitation to jurors to determine subjectively what they believe should be censored. Ironically, in *Hamling* v. *United States*, 418 U.S. at 107 (1974), Justice Rehnquist declared in the majority decision that a principal concern " . . . is that the material is judged neither on the basis of a juror's personal opinion nor by its effect on a particularly sensitive person or group."

The LAPS Test

This test actually is an exception to the rule that if a work is prurient and patently offensive, it is obscene. Thus, a work may appeal to prurient interest and be patently offensive but may be entitled to First Amendment protection if, "taken as a whole," it contains serious "literary, artistic, political or scientific value."

However, the LAPS exception is somewhat limited. No provision is made for material that is educational or has entertainment value and that might otherwise be considered obscene. That pornography has entertainment value is attested to by the fact that it is a multimillion-dollar industry and that *Playboy* and *Penthouse* magazines, two of the most conservative magazines of that ilk, together distribute more than ten million copies monthly

That pornography may be a valuable tool in sex education is evidenced by a quarterly periodical** subscribed to by prestigious hospitals and devoted principally to a description of pornographic materials available for purchase by institutions or persons "engaged in education, research, therapy, or counseling." If we accept the LAPS exception literally, even such educational uses of pornography may, under present law, be criminal in nature. How incongruous this is, in the light of pornographic films used as standard tools in the sex education of medical students and physicians.†

*Zubin and Money, op. cit.
**Multi-Media Research Guide. Published quarterly by Multi-Media Resource Center, 1525 Franklin St., San Francisco, CA 94109.
†See H. Lief, M.D., "Obstacles to the Complete Sex Education of the Medical Student and Physician," in Zubin and Money, op. cit.

Community Standards

However difficult it might be to define the concepts of average person, prurient interest appeal, patent offensiveness, and the LAPS test, a definition of "community standards" is the most elusive.

Miller did not make it clear whether the community could be the nation, a state, a county, a city, a village, or a judicial district or whether, perhaps, it was none of these. *Jenkins v. Georgia*, 418 U.S. 153 (1974), and its companion case, *Hamling v. United States*, 418 U.S. 87, each dealt in part with the meaning of community standards. *Jenkins* held that neither national nor statewide standards were required and approved the trial court's instructions directing jurors to apply community standards without specifying *what* community.

The majority in *Hamling* declared, "Since this case was tried in the Southern District of California, and presumably jurors from throughout the judicial district were available . . . it would be the standards of that 'community' upon which the jurors would draw."

Such a conclusion, reached despite the fact that the trial court's instructions to the California jury made "occasional references to the 'community standards' of the nation as a whole," makes the judicial definition of community standards less than comprehensible to any jury responsible for the application of such standards. Since it cannot be clear to an average juror just what community standards are, the specter of purely subjective standards being unconstitutionally applied looms large.

United States Postal Service statutes, as well as interstate transportation and conspiracy statutes, have been used regularly by United States attorneys to prosecute the disseminators and sellers of obscene materials. Crusading U.S. prosecutors have used these statutes to shop for the venue with the most puritanical standards in order to obtain convictions. This is possible because prosecutors can select any community in which books are received, whether in the mail or by shipment in interstate commerce. The application of community standards to such federal statutes creates a dangerous definitional and constitutional problem, which must inevitably result in self-censorship by booksellers and publishers.

In *Hamling*, Justice Brennan, citing *Smith v. California* (361 U.S. 147–154) in support of his position, concisely but powerfully set forth the First Amendment arguments against employment of local community standards as defined by the Supreme Court majority:

Under today's "local standards" construction . . . the guilt or innocence of distributors of identical materials mailed from the same locale can now turn on the chancy course of transit or place of delivery of materials. . . . National distributors choosing to send their products in interstate travels will be forced to cope with community standards of every hamlet into which their goods may wander. Because these variegated standards are impossible to discern, national distributors, fearful of risking the expense and difficulty of defending against prosecution in any of several removed communities, must inevitably be left to retreat to debilitating self-censorship that abridges the First Amendment rights of the People. *Hamling* (Brennan dissenting).

The Problem with "Minors' Access" Statutes

Recent years have seen a flourishing of state and municipal "minors access" statutes and ordinances in response to a perceived need for limiting the availability to minors of sexually explicit materials. Typically, such legislation proscribes the display of materials deemed harmful to minors and occasionally bans their sale to minors—often without regard to whether such materials are obscene as to adults or to minors.

The Supreme Court has upheld the constitutionality of "minors" legislation limited in scope to the prohibition of sales to minors of materials found to be obscene as to minors. However, the special problems of determining what books and periodicals may be harmful to minors—combined with the recent tendency of state legislatures to include statutory provisions criminalizing the display of materials with sexual content in a store to which minors are permitted access—lead to the conclusion that minors' access statutes are inherently unconstitutional because of their inevitable tendency to restrict the availability to both adults and minors of materials safeguarded by the First and Fourteenth amendments.

The constitutional boundaries of valid minors' access legislation have been delineated by two Supreme Court cases. In *Butler* v. *Michigan*,* the Court unanimously invalidated a statute that subjected to criminal penalties any person who made available to the general public books or other materials "containing obscene, immoral, lewd, lascivious language or description tending to invite minors to violent or depraved or immoral acts, manifestly tending to the corruption of the morals of youth." Justice Frankfurter wasted few words in an opinion striking down the act, noting that its effect "is to reduce the adult population of Michigan to reading only what is fit for children [and that to do so] is to burn the house to roast the pig."

*353 U.S. 380 (1957)

In *Ginsberg v. New York,* * by contrast, the Court scrutinized a statute that criminalized sales to minors, as opposed to the general public, of materials meeting the then-prevailing *Roth-Memoirs* obscenity standard as adopted to accommodate the sensitivity of minors to sexually explicit materials. Noting that the statute erected no barrier to the sale of such materials to adults, the Court focused on whether the First Amendment rights of minors were infringed by a content-based regulation restricting their access to materials potentially available to adults. The Court answered this question in the negative, agreeing with the concept that the definition of obscenity "may vary according to the group to whom the questionable material is directed or from whom it is quarantined." Having determined that, it held that the First Amendment accords minors "a more restricted right than that assured to adults to judge and determine for themselves what sexually explicit materials they may read or see."

Because the materials regulated by the statute were obscene as to minors, they were beyond the scope of First Amendment guarantees, and according to the *Ginsberg* Court, the statute could stand if it survived substantive due process rationality analysis. The Court noted that the New York legislature's finding that obscene material has had a deleterious effect on youths, though not supported by sufficient scientific consensus to meet the "clear and present danger" test prerequisite to content-based regulation of materials protected by the First Amendment, could not be classified as irrational, and upheld the statute.

Read together, *Butler* and *Ginsberg* stand for the unstartling principle that the scope of what may be deemed obscene as to minors may encompass more than that which may be deemed obscene as to adults, as long as the First Amendment rights of adults are not abridged by the more restrictive regulation. Even when the rights of adults are unaffected, however, *Ginsberg* and subsequent cases do not give state legislatures carte blanche to regulate the access of minors to sexually explicit materials.

Although more extensive curtailment of the availability of "objectionable" materials to minors has been justified on the ground that minors lack "that full capacity for individual choice which is the presupposition of First Amendment guarantees," the Supreme Court recognized in *Tinker v. Des Moines* ** that minors are entitled to invoke First Amendment guarantees, and noted in *Erznoznik v. Jacksonville*† that "[s]peech that is neither obscene as to youths nor

*390 U.S. 629 (1968)
**393 U.S. 503
†422 U.S. 205

subject to some other legitimate proscription cannot be suppressed solely to protect the young from ideas or images that a legislative body thinks unsuitable for them."

Minors, then, like adults, have a constitutional right to receive nonobscene expressive materials. However, a single formula for defining obscenity as to all minors regardless of age, such as the standards upheld in *Ginsberg*, presents troublesome constitutional questions. Such a formula appears to curtail the First Amendment rights of minors at the upper end of the age and maturity spectrums.

In *Pincus* v. *United States*,* the Supreme Court found reversible error in a jury instruction incorporating "children" in the "community" whose standards were to be applied in determining whether materials were obscene as to adults. The Court noted that a jury following the instruction in attempting to apply the standards of an "average person" in the community "would reach a much lower 'average' when children are part of the equation than it would if it restricted its consideration to the effect of allegedly obscene materials on adults." The Court found this potential lowered average to be a violation, albeit a less drastic one, of the *Butler* principle that adults should not be reduced to reading what is fit for minors.

The *Pincus* rationale appears equally applicable to a determination of what is "obscene" for minors. By lumping seventeen-year-old college freshmen in the same category as thirteen-year-old high school students and five-year-olds, a unitary obscenity standard for minors reduces all minors to reading that which is fit for younger minors, without taking into account the differing maturity levels of children at college, high school, elementary school and nursery school levels. It bears noting that "minors" may include married persons and college students.

To the extent that reduced First Amendment protection for minors is warranted by their reduced ability to exercise First Amendment choices, minors' access statutes must allow for consideration of the different maturity levels of minors. Indeed, the Court in *Erznoznik* commented that "[in] assessing whether a minor has the requisite capacity for individual choice the age of the minor is a significant factor."

Irrespective of whether the statutory obscenity standard is unitary or takes into account the differing sensitivities among minors, minors' access statutes present in aggravated fashion the definitional problems inherent in all obscenity legislation. To ask a bookseller to screen all materials sold to minors and anticipate what a fact finder would determine to be obscene for a ten-year-old child is

*436 U.S. 293

to invite a refusal to sell any books with sexual descriptions or depictions, regardless of merit, rather than risk criminal prosecution. This is a form of self-censorship that the First Amendment, as interpreted by *Smith* v. *California*, will not abide. Furthermore, booksellers will receive little consolation from the knowledge that the enforcement problems of minors' access statutes may be so great as to render meaningless the *scienter* (knowledge) element required by the prosecution for a criminal conviction. How many would dare to expose themselves to criminal prosecution?

The all but inevitable effect of minors' access legislation is to deprive minors not only of materials that are deemed obscene, but of materials protected as to minors by the First Amendment. The chilling effect of minors' access legislation gives special pungency to Justice Fortas's dissenting observation in *Ginsberg* that denial to minors of access to "girlie" magazines of the type involved in that case "is also denial of access to great works of art and literature."

Are displays taboo?

The unconstitutionality of minors' access statutes that prohibit the mere display of materials deemed obscene as to minors is more flagrant. The Supreme Court has yet to review such a statute, but lower courts have held that display provisions unconstitutionally restrict the First Amendment rights of both adults and minors.

Georgia's minors' access statute, invalidated in a federal district court opinion,* contained the following display provisions:

It shall be unlawful for any person knowingly to... display in public or at newsstands or any other business establishment frequented by minors or where minors are or may be invited as a part of the general public, any motion picture or live show, or any still picture, drawing, sculpture, photograph, or any book, pocket book, pamphlet, or magazine the cover or content of which contains descriptions or depictions of illicit sex or sexual immorality or which is lewd, lascivious, or indecent.

The court found such terms as "sexual immorality" and "lewd, lascivious, or indecent" to be impermissibly vague and also noted that the statute was overbroad because it contained no requirement that the proscribed materials be obscene as to minors. Although such flaws are easily remedied by more careful drafting, the inherent unconstitutionality of such a statute remains. A recent Colorado statute, also invalidated, simply traced the "variable obscenity" standard approved in *Ginsberg* but made it applicable to displays.

ABA v. McAulliffe, 533 F.Supp. 58

The trial court held that the effect of such an infirmity (such as abridging the rights of adults) was incurable.

The fundamental, and irremediable, flaw of display provisions is that compliance can be attained only through unconstitutional means. Assuming, for the sake of argument, that a bookseller were capable of screening thousands of pages of incoming materials in an attempt to discern what might be considered obscene as to minors and were to remove all such materials from the bookshelves, compliance would squarely violate *Butler's* command that minors' access legislation must avoid the abridgment of adult First Amendment rights.

An alternative avenue of compliance is exclusion of all minors from establishments covered by the statute, a solution that, in addition to being impracticable in many instances, constitutes an unconstitutional prior restraint on the exercise by minors of their First Amendment rights to peruse or purchase nonobscene materials. A compromise solution, involving the creation of separate "adults only" sections in bookstores containing materials considered harmful to minors but nonobscene for adults, would face insurmountable economic and practical barriers. Moreover, under a literal reading of most display statutes, a bookseller could be convicted of displaying materials harmful to minors, in an establishment frequented by minors, even if the materials were displayed in a separate section for adults. A bookseller could avoid this result by not "displaying" any questionable materials but, instead, hiding them behind a counter and making them available to adults only upon request.

Purchasers of books and other materials frequently become cognizant of specific items only through browsing, however. To permit access to such materials only to a requesting adult is tantamount to rendering unavailable to adults a substantial proportion of First Amendment–protected material, a result incompatible with *Butler.* Since there does not exist a feasible means of compliance that does not burden the First Amendment rights of adults or minors, minors' access statutes barring the mere display of books or publications deemed harmful to minors are inherently unconstitutional.

The prohibitions of "harmful to minors" legislation target persons or businesses stocking, selling, or distributing sexually explicit materials, thereby creating a "chilling effect" on the dissemination of constitutionally protected materials by making them substantially, if not totally, inaccessible to potential minor and/or adult readers, viewers, or listeners. Attempts to exempt from liability such specific sources as libraries, schools, and museums are not likely to survive equal protection scrutiny. As a practical matter, therefore, most, if not all, "harmful to minors" statutes, if allowed to become

effective, would result in statewide suppression of First Amendment–protected materials.

The constitutionality of minors' access statutes will be decided
by the Supreme Court during its 1987-88 term. Briefs were submitted in the spring of 1987, and oral argument in the case of *ABA et al.*
v. *Virginia* was heard the following fall.

Women's Rights versus the First Amendment

In May 1984, the City/County Council of Indianapolis enacted
a "human rights" ordinance outlawing allegedly pornographic books
and magazines that do not fit within the definition of "obscenity" set
forth in the landmark Supreme Court decision in *Miller* v. *California.* * In so doing, it has posed the most serious censorship threat to
sexually explicit books and magazines since the days when the works
of D. H. Lawrence, James Joyce, and Henry Miller were banned in
the United States.

The ordinance** is based on the expressly stated premise that
"pornography is a systematic practice of exploitation and subordination based on sex, which differentially harms women," and that "the
bigotry and contempt it promotes, with the acts of aggression and
frustration, harms women's opportunities for equal rights in employment, education, access to and use of public accommodations." It
makes it unlawful to produce, sell, exhibit, or distribute "pornography," to coerce, intimidate, or fraudulently force any person to
perform in "pornography," or to force "pornography" upon anyone
in a place of employment.

The ordinance authorizes the establishment of a board to
review complaints about such "pornography" and to make findings.
Certain administrative sanctions are available to the board, including the issuance of a cease and desist order and the cancellation of
city licenses. In addition, this board is authorized to proceed to
court for the purpose of obtaining an injunction against the violators
of the ordinance. Not only may the board enforce the ordinance, but
"any woman has a cause of action as a woman against the subordination of women," leaving the possibility that the board and one or
more women may simultaneously institute legal proceedings against
a book or magazine publisher, distributor, or retailer.

Proponents of this type of legislation have appeared on national
television programs and newscasts in connection with a similar
ordinance that was introduced in Minneapolis and have indicated
an intention to foster similar legislation throughout the country.

*413 U.S. 14 (1973)
**Ind. Proposal No. 228, 1984 (chapter 16), enacted into law on April 23, 1984

Thus, the content and the ramifications of this Indianapolis ordinance are worthy of careful scrutiny, since it will most likely serve as a model for similar legislation seeking to outlaw books, magazines, motion pictures, and television programs that are "pornographic," as defined by this new ordinance, but not "obscene," as that term has been defined by the Supreme Court.

More than a quarter century has elapsed since the Supreme Court held that "obscenity is not within the area of constitutionally protected speech or press."* Although precise definition has been somewhat elusive, the Supreme Court in *Miller* v. *California* defined "obscenity" in accordance with a three-pronged test, set forth above.

The three-pronged test has been modified only with respect to legislation regulating the availability of materials to minors,** or when children are depicted as objects of sexual abuse in photographic materials.†

The Indianapolis ordinance created a board empowered to make determinations as to what materials constitute "pornography" without taking into account the *Miller* three-pronged test. Instead, the legislation defines pornography as the "sexually implicit subordination of women, graphically depicted, whether in pictures or in words, that also includes one or more of the following:

(1) women are presented as sexual objects who enjoy pain or humiliation; or
(2) women are presented as sexual objects who experience sexual pleasure in being raped; or...
(3) women are presented as sexual objects for domination, conquest, violation, exploitation, possession, or use, through postures or positions of servility or submission or display."

However, by defining pornography in this manner, and totally ignoring the *Miller* definition, the legislation opens the door to the censorship of such works as Shakespeare's *The Taming of the Shrew*, Boccaccio's *Decameron*, the Marquis de Sade's *Justine*, Emile Zola's *Nana*, Margaret Mitchell's *Gone With the Wind*, and many popular novels and historical romances by many noted authors, including some feminist authors.††

Only under extraordinary circumstances will any system of

Roth v. *United States, supra*
**Ginsberg* v. *New York, supra*
†*New York* v. *Ferber*, 102 S.Ct. 33, 48 (1982)
††*The Female Eunuch* by Germaine Greer comes to mind.

prior restraint of expression be held constitutional.* Such a system
has been tolerated only where it operated under judicial supervision
and guaranteed an immediate judicial determination of the validity
of the restraint.** In *Bantam Books, Inc.,* v. *Sullivan,* the state of
Rhode Island had created a commission that subjected the distribution of publications to a system of prior review for the purpose of
establishing particular publications as objectionable if the publication was deemed to encourage immorality in youth. The Court
found the lack of judicial supervision before notices could be issued
and lack of immediate judicial review of the commission's findings
to be constitutionally fatal defects.† The legislation in Indianapolis
suffers from the same constitutional infirmities. A board has been
established by the city council that has the power, after a lengthy
administrative hearing and appellate procedure, to issue cease and
desist orders. In the first instance, appeal may be made only to an
appellate board created by the legislation. There is no provision
whatever for judicial supervision before notice is issued or even for
judicial review of the commission's determinations until this lengthy
administrative procedure has been complied with.

The actions of the board created by the ordinance will have the
affect of censoring materials without benefit of judicial supervision
or a judicial hearing of any kind. This follows from the reality that if
any particular book or magazine is singled out for a complaint by the
board, it would be the path of least resistance for the retailer or
distributor simply to discontinue the sale or distribution of the
publication in question. The First Amendment cannot abide such a
form of self-censorship.†† Adding to the danger of self-censorship is
the prospect that following an expensive and perhaps administrative
hearing and appeal, the retailer or distributor will be faced with a
legal proceeding in the courts, to be instituted by the board. Since
the average retailer or wholesaler of books and magazines carries
thousands of titles at any given time, the removal of a single title will
not cause her or him serious monetary loss. However, such removal
will constitute a serious blow to the right of Americans to publish,
distribute, and read constitutionally protected materials.

The Indiana ordinance, before it was amended, stated that it
shall not be a defense that the defendant did not know or intend the
materials were pornography or sex discriminatory. Such provision,

---

Bantam Books, Inc., v. *Sullivan,* 373 U.S. 58, 70 (1963); *Near* v. *The State of Minnesota,* ex
rel. Olson, 283 U.S. 697; *Kingsley Books, Inc.,* v. *Brown,* 354 U.S. 436
**Kingsley, supra; Bantam Books, supra*
†*Bantam, supra,* at 71
††*Smith* v. *California,* 361 U.S. 147 (1959)

dispensing with the defense of *scienter*, is patently in violation of the First Amendment.* The Indiana amendment was made only after ABA and a number of other plaintiffs brought suit to declare the ordinance unconstitutional.

Statutes or ordinances that affect First Amendment rights are particularly vulnerable to attack on the "due process" ground that they are void for vagueness and must meet much stricter standards of clarity to be constitutionally valid.** The Indianapolis ordinance is especially replete with vague and inconsistent terms and definitions. For example, "trafficking in pornography," prohibited by the ordinance, includes "coercion into pornography performance." However, included within the definition of "coercion" is the statement that one or more of thirteen enumerated facts or conditions "shall not, without more, negate a finding of coercion." Reviewing some of the facts and conditions enumerated, one could reach the preposterous conclusion that coercion did exist in a case where the alleged subject of the coercion is a prostitute, who has attained the age of majority, who demonstrated no resistance and cooperated actively in the photographic sessions, who signed a contract agreeing to cooperate, who was paid for her services, and where no evidence existed of physical force or threats. One provision of the ordinance permits any woman, man, child, or transsexual who has been injured by an assault or physical attack due to pornography to sue for damages against the publisher, distributor, and/or retailers of the book or magazine in question. No standards or criteria are set forth for ascertaining how one may determine whether a particular book or article or photograph caused an individual to assault or physically attack another person. Such vagueness is impermissible in legislation that regulates the publishing and dissemination of materials protected by the First Amendment.

Such ambiguous provisions will trap the innocent and will lend themselves to arbitrary and discriminatory enforcement. Even more important, such an ordinance will lead book and magazine retailers, wholesalers, and distributors to steer far wider of the unlawful zone than if the boundaries of the forbidden areas were clearly marked. Such an inhibition of the First Amendment freedoms may not be tolerated.†

Books, magazines, motion pictures, and television programs representing women or, for that matter, any group, in an unfavorable or demeaning light are to be decried. Some of the most

---

*Smith v. California, supra; Hamling v. United States, 418 U.S. 87 (1974); see Ferber v. New York, supra
**Bantam Books, supra; NAACP v. Button, 371 U.S. 415 (1963); Smith v. California, supra
†Grayned v. City of Rockford, 409 U.S. 104 (1972)

important literary works in history may be considered flawed for this reason—works like *The Merchant of Venice*, the great novels of Fyodor Dostoevsky (whose pages are replete with anti-Semitic remarks), and in the view of some, the Bible. Nevertheless, the solution to the problem must surely not be censorship.

In *ABA et al.* v. *Hudnut et al.* the Supreme Court declared in 1986 the Indianapolis ordinance to be in violation of the First Amendment.

If your state or city is considering the adoption of a statute making it a crime for booksellers to sell obscene books or to sell or display sexually explicit books or magazines to minors, please notify the ABA immediately. Although the ABA is a member of the Media Coalition, which normally notifies us of such impending legislation, the cooperation of each bookseller is vital.

When is it a crime to sell a book? Will the sale of *The Joy of Sex* or the *Decameron* constitute a crime? If it is unlawful in Indianapolis, will it also be a crime in New York City or San Francisco? Will it be a crime to sell or merely stock sexually explicit books that are not obscene, simply because minors have access to the store?

At this writing all these questions are being tested in the courts. We don't know the answers yet.

Chapter 65

Publisher–Bookseller Relations

EDWARD A. MORROW, JR.

The Eighties are well established as a decade of change and transition for the publishing and bookselling community. New trends have been sweeping away established patterns and forcing self-examination upon every segment of the industry. The prodigious growth of chains, the advent of massive discounting, the accelerated harnessing of computer technology, the proliferation of titles competing for exposure, the shift of influence from erudite editors to number-crunching comptrollers, the expansion of publishers' lists to include software on magnetic media, books on tape, and videocassettes, are all part of this vast, uncomfortable, but exciting shake-up of our industry.

We are learning firsthand the import of the ancient curse about living in interesting times. These interesting times in the book industry can indeed be uncomfortable and livelihood threatening, but they also offer opportunity. It is the nimble who survive and thrive in times of radical change, so we must learn to be nimble. We must examine trends to see how they impact on our own spheres of activity. We must look at the big picture to see where we fit into it. This means constant reeducation: staying current with the trade press, including awareness of articles about areas not directly related to our specific niche in the industry; attendance at trade shows, seminars and workshops, both about the book world and business and technology in general; and constant communication with a view to deeper understanding of all parts of the bookselling process.

The bookseller, more than ever, needs regular cross-fertilization of ideas with other booksellers, with association staffs, with middlemen such as wholesalers, and, most important, with publishing houses. The bookseller must be aggressive in fostering constructive communication with reps and customer relations staff, of course, but also with sales managers, marketing directors, editors, operations heads, and publishing house executives. The successful bookseller today needs to make every effort to understand the publishing industry in its full complexity from manuscript to register receipt.

Bookselling has long had many unique characteristics, a number of which result in built-in friction points between publisher and bookseller. Maintaining healthy relations with publishers involves identifying the most common areas of friction, analyzing them to discover the best way to lubricate hot spots, and learning how to cope with the sores that will inevitably develop from time to time. Building a foundation of common concern—understanding the other person's perspective—is the first step in assuring healthy communication.

There are two broad areas that foster the "them versus us" mentality between bookseller and publisher. There are *systemic irritants* and there are *solvable incidents*. Understanding which frustrations are systemic—that is, just part of the way the industry does business—and which result from particular problems that can be solved through proper communication can go a long way to diminishing antagonistic feelings. The more integrated one's knowledge of how the industry functions, the better prepared one will be to achieve significant efficiencies, provide superior service, and avoid time-consuming and useless arguments.

Examples of systemic irritants are the complexity and lack of uniformity in discount, co-op, and returns policies; appallingly long fulfillment delays; the continuing inability of many publishers to use the Single Title Order Plan as it is designed to be used; the buying frustrations caused by overpublishing and publishing redundancy prompted by the cash-in-on-a-successful-idea phenomenon. The truth is, all of this simply goes with the territory and thus should be treated with a degree of magnanimity. The bookseller must recognize the difficulties caused by such industry irritants and deal with them in as organized and creative a fashion as possible while trying to keep the resultant frustrations from poisoning his overall feeling about publishers. Most of these systemic problems are just as frustrating to publishers.

It is worth pointing out, however, that individual booksellers can sometimes help eliminate systemic irritants. A bookseller who perceives a detrimental policy or method of operation by a publisher should calmly and constructively point out the drawbacks of the offending policy and forward copies of several alternative policies (selected from the *ABA Book Buyer's Handbook*) that make better sense to the bookseller. The publisher may simply have been unaware of the difficulty his practice was causing. It is important, with such a message, to be sure communication is with the proper decision maker in the publisher's chain of command.

The publisher–bookseller friction we are categorizing as *solvable incidents* is best ameliorated by a sophisticated program of communication. But the sheer volume of incidents that require solution deserves some comment before a discussion of appropriate action.

We start from the premise that an error ratio is built in to all human endeavor. All human enterprises generate mistakes. If we are resigned to dealing with a certain *permanent* error ratio, we will save a lot of heartache. Also, because mistakes are, by definition, "nonroutine"—that is, they are not planned to happen—their exceptional nature often causes additional mistakes in the effort to correct the first. These compounded errors are the most frustrating and time-consuming. (Understanding that some publishers are better organized in dealing with their error factor than others will aid in helping the less efficient publishers make the necessary corrections while minimizing the effort involved.)

A further point about the volume of errors is germane. Error ratios work further to the disadvantage of our industry because of (1) the fragmentation of sources of supply to the book retailer; and (2) the vast number of discrete items being dealt with. The greater the number of different items being handled and the greater the number of supplier transactions, the greater the number of mistakes that will be created. This all works to throw many more errors at a bookseller than at other retailers who deal mostly in case lots of fewer items.

Because of the volume of errors the bookseller faces, a carefully thought-out, written communications policy and procedures guidelines will pay big dividends.

Exceptions to shipments, charge-back disputes, and *co-op documentation* form the bulk of this friction area. Clarity, completeness, and timeliness of documentation is the key to maximizing rapid resolution of these incidents.

The preprinted forms designed for use with window envelopes are big timesavers. Such forms help in several ways: (1) clarity—a well-designed form leaves no ambiguity on the part of the receiver as to what the problem is and what action is desired; (2) completeness—a form reminds the user of all the key data that should be included in the communication; (3) timeliness—because a form requires less writing and is prestructured, it is easy to fill out and is thus less likely to be put off; (4) documentation—it provides a complete written record in the bookseller's files. (Forms with multiple copies make it easier to research those problems that don't get solved right away; copies can be filed to suit any clerical or book-keeping system.) A cash investment in such forms will pay for itself many times over in time saved and frustrations eliminated. Toll-free customer-service numbers are a great way to deal with such prob-lems (especially where time is a consideration, such as a special order). But the bookseller still needs complete documentation of both the problem *and* the solution promised over the phone for further follow-up.

Just as the window envelope is a small timesaver that, multi-plied by many communications, becomes an important timesaver, thinking through and preplanning the action requested of the publisher is critical to saving valuable bookseller time. The retailer should design his first communication about the problem to be the *only* one needed to clear it up. He or she can do this by simplifying the requested action. To illustrate: If one out of five copies of a $2.95 backlist young-adult title arrives mangled, don't ask for permission to return it. With all appropriate documentation, merely ask for credit of $1.77 (assuming the invoice came in at 40 percent) and state that you will hold the book for forty-five days should the publisher wish to have it picked up by UPS call tag. It is the rare publisher who will pay to have a valueless book returned. The credit will come through, and the book can be tossed in the rubbish. No further action is required by the bookseller. If the credit doesn't come through in sixty days, deduct it from the next payment and send a photocopy of your original exception (and/or reference the exception number) with that payment. There are a dozen or so repeat problems like this one that can be structured to minimize time and expense. The point is to place the ball in the publisher's court in such a way as to assure that they'll return it where you want it.

Forms for standard co-op documentation work the same way. Make them clear, complete, timely, and easy to use. They should be designed to meet the most demanding co-op documentation require-ments.

Credit problems cannot be solved with standardized forms. If they could, someone would be making a fortune supplying them. Credit situations must be worked out on an ad hoc basis. But they should be addressed coherently to assure continued healthy publisher–bookseller relations. Depending on the severity of the problem, a long-range plan may be necessary as well as a form-letter communication to many publishers. In the severest of cases, an outside consultant, such as an accountant, may be needed to work out an effective plan. A plan is necessary because the bookseller should be able to fulfill his commitment to the publisher. Therefore he has to know what can reasonably be promised. In less severe cases, the bookseller need only decide how and when he or she will solve the problem (or even partially solve it) and communicate with the credit people involved. Regular communication works wonders. Everybody is reassured if they know what's happening and where they stand.

This discussion of publisher–bookseller relations has concentrated on friction areas. We've focused on how to avoid disputes and manage misunderstandings. Fortunately friction is not the only thing that occurs between publisher and bookseller. Although frustrations may loom large in the bookseller's mind, most of what publishers do is beneficial. In fact, publishers do many things that delight booksellers, starting with publishing good books. Communication should play a much larger role than it does in this positive area.

An exceptional seasonal list might generate a complimentary letter to the head of the house that produced it. The realization that a publishing house, in all its policies and dealings, strives to make relations with booksellers easy and mutually profitable deserves a special letter or a searching out of executives at ABA to thank them. They need to know their efforts are noticed and make a difference. A change in discount, co-op, or returns policy that benefits the bookseller should produce an immediate positive reaction—a call, a letter, even a postcard.

If a bookseller recognizes a void in a given category that some publisher should fill, he or she should think about which publisher is best oriented in that direction and suggest a new title to that sales manager. A bookseller who recognizes consistently good and/or salable books coming from a specific editor might want to let that editor hear from the front lines.

There is a great deal of room for communication beyond problem solving, and it should be fostered. Whatever the area of interaction between publisher and bookseller, the crux of positive publisher–bookseller communication is a sense of common purpose and professional relationships.

Chapter 66

The Publishing Process

CHARLES E. HAYWARD

During the years I spent as a publisher's sales representative, I was asked many questions by book buyers about the publishing process:

- Why are you publishing *this* book?
- How could anyone with two eyes and any sense of taste design that jacket?
- Why is the list price on this book so high?
- Where do you expect to sell the fifty thousand copies that your company is printing?
- Do you know that this is the sixth new title on houseplants I have been sold this season?
- Isn't this the third time you have sold me this title?

This list could go on and on, and I am certain that every bookseller could compile another. Publishing trade books is a detail-intensive process that most booksellers know well because of the number of titles in their inventory, the constant price changes, the number of special orders they process, and so on. Clearly, an entire book of this size could be written on the publishing process. Therefore, this chapter will attempt to deal only with aspects of publishing that are of most interest to booksellers: how publishers acquire books, the marketing and selling of new titles, and a brief look at how and if publishers make a profit. For the purpose of this chapter, these points will be discussed from the perspective of a general publisher of hardcover books and original trade paperbacks. Mass-market publishers clearly are major suppliers to the bookselling community and increasingly have become powerful forces in original publishing. The distinction between mass-market and traditional trade houses continues to diminish, and the issues discussed in this chapter face all publishers of original works.

The process of acquiring new titles varies from publisher to publisher, but in general over 90 percent of all new titles are bought by publishers from literary agents or book packagers. Many books bought by publishers are purchased on the basis of an outline and a sample chapter or two. For authors with previous publishing experience this is especially true, but many first-time authors are often able to sell their book through agents with a good outline, a sample chapter or two, and a strong marketing statement including aggressive representation of the author's credentials.

A constantly debated question in acquiring new books is the influence of booksellers on publishers' decisions. Successful publishers are in tune with what is selling, and this is particularly true of publishers who are competing for paperback reprint rights of hardcover books. However, monitoring retail selling trends does not necessarily translate into successful new title acquisitions. In general, it takes a publisher eighteen to twenty-four months from the time of acquisition to publication date. In recent years, retail bookselling has become very trendy, much like the fashion business. A hot new acquisition today can be yesterday's news by the time it is published. This has been true recently for humor books and celebrity fitness titles.

The most difficult judgment for the publisher in following retail sales is to differentiate between short-lived fads and legitimate long-term trends. The best example in the 1980s of publishers following a perceived trend was the computer book explosion. Computers have made a significant impact on business and personal life-styles, but publishers reacted to this opportunity with uprecedented enthusiasm. In the early stages of the computer book explosion, the technical and subject-specific publishers had the editorial and marketing resources to publish new titles quickly and knowledgeably. Then the general trade publishers moved in to take advantage of what appeared to be an insatiable demand from booksellers.

Publishers made a number of assumptions about computer books that are often made when publishing for fads or trends:

- They assumed that any well-written and timely book would sell.
- Even though the best-selling titles were machine specific, it was assumed that general-interest titles would be received by a large audience.

• Author advances were paid for titles or series of titles that were not justified by the current rates of sale for existing titles. Computer books had to pay their way by retail sales since the traditional subsidiary rights avenues of paperback reprint, foreign, and book club sales did not offer any significant revenue opportunities. Many publishers had to write off extraordinary author advances.

The result was the publication of many more titles than the market was able to absorb. Certainly there were many titles that generated profits for publishers, and computer books represent an ongoing publishing opportunity. However, a great number of publishers wish that they had not responded to early computer book retail sales so enthusiastically.

Although the computer books experience was an extreme case, most retailers wonder why so many books appear suddenly on a particular subject in the same season. Because most publishers are driven by their new-title or frontlist programs, editors are constantly pressured to acquire books and increase their title output. Although there are many exceptions, the average trade editor spends much more time and effort acquiring books than he/she spends line editing. Therefore, when a new trend or event is written about in the media, any number of agents or editors react to this information. Many diffferent proposals on the same subject will then circulate through trade editorial offices. Since each publisher works independently and keeps acquisition decisions privileged information, a number of books on the same subject can be signed up by different publishers. In addition, sales and marketing management has taken an increasing role in acquisition of new titles. Sales and marketing executives can provide insight into developing trends, but they also react to what is selling now, and this may not be what will sell two years from now.

In sum, the acquisition of new titles is a process fraught with difficulty because of the limited number of new titles that are successful among the forty thousand plus new titles that are published each year. However, the publisher that is sensitive to the marketplace and allows its proven editors to pursue their instincts and judgment will be successful in the long run.

Marketing and Sales Planning

When a sales representative calls on a bookseller to present a new seasonal list, a tremendous number of individual decisions have already been made for those books: trim size, format, title, dust jacket, catalog copy, list price, marketing budget, publication date, and so on. The most successful publishers have devised a method of giving each of these individual decisions due consideration without reinventing the wheel for each book.

The books that are sold to a buyer on a fall list are presented to the sales organization by the editorial and marketing staff sometime between late April and early June. Although some of the books may have been under contract for a number of years, the formal planning for this list begins in January with some type of "launch" or "concept" meeting for the fall list. The critical elements for a book that are established during this process are projected advance sale figure, tentative first printing, list price, and marketing strategy and budget.

There are many factors that determine the relative emphasis any title will receive on a publisher's list:

• Amount of investment that the company has made in the project.
• Publishing history of the author.
• Ability of the editor to generated enthusiasm among influential decision makers and the editor's credibility based on past performance.
• Current market appeal and promotability of the subject.
• General strength of the overall list.

Each new title published competes for very limited financial resources within the publishing company.

Equally important, each publisher has a limited amount of human resources to devote to marketing and sales effort for a new title. Therefore, priorities that are established in the early planning stages will determine how aggressively the publisher will present a new title to the trade. It would be nice to think that every book receives an appropriate amount of individual attention and financial support when it is published, but this simply is not so. Books compete for attention within a publishing list just as they compete for shelf space and attention at retail.

This is not to say that publishers always make the right choices of titles for the major marketing effort and funds. I can recall many occasions as a sales rep when a buyer discovered a book that he/she correctly recognized as having much greater potential than my publisher did. As as example, I recall presenting Julian Jaynes's excellent book *Origins of Consciousness in the Breakdown of the Bicameral Mind* to a major chain buyer approximately ten years ago. When the buyer wanted to order 1,500 copies, I gulped because I knew that was twice as many orders as we currently had in house and would represent approximately 40 percent of the scheduled first printing. Try as I might, it was impossible to convince the buyer to *lower* his order. In the end the book went on to become a best-seller and classic in its field.

Of course, the publisher often has a number of markets in mind when a book is published. Many a bookseller questioned the wisdom of publishing the tremendous amount of British category fiction that I sold while at St. Martin's Press. Very few of those titles were intended for retail sales but were targeted for libraries and for paperback reprint. Some of the reasons a publisher might publish a book that does not appear to have hardcover retail sales appeal include paperback reprint sales, book club or other direct-mail applications, foreign sales, library or academic markets, other non-book retail outlets such as gift, gourmet, and the like, and finally, a publisher may be publishing a modest effort of an author with an eye toward a second or third book down the road. In fact, because of the competitive nature of book trade publishing today, every successful publisher has to develop expertise in selling beyond the book trade to balance the financial ups and downs of the traditional retail marketplace.

From the launch or concept meeting in January to the sales meeting, the key elements are carefully decided. Cover design is finalized for all titles, and this art often becomes the focus for the marketing campaign. Advertising schedules and budgets are set; titles and cities for author tours are determined; prepacks, counter displays, and other point-of-sale materials are developed; advance quotes of praise are solicited; submissions are made to book clubs and paperback houses to get indications of interest; advance galleys are circulated to key buyers; and sales projected by title (and often by title by territory) are established. The planning for publication of a new title has become increasingly more important because of the decreasing amount of time that a book has to succeed in the marketplace. Retailers certainly know better than publishers, but in general if a book is not working at retail within four to six weeks after publication date, the prospects for successful sales of that title are slim. This makes it imperative for the publisher to plan carefully and intensively for the presentation of its new titles to the trade. Clearly some publishers do this better than others, and these publishers generally are supported more enthusiastically by booksellers because their presentations demonstrate why the booksellers are going to sell the book once they have bought it.

For the publisher, one of the most critical financial elements in the planning stages for new titles is establishing the "suggested" retail price. "Suggested," of course, is only in the legal sense (since publishers cannot legally fix prices) because this suggested price is what is used as the basis for calculating discounts to booksellers. If the publishing industry should go to true net pricing with volume discounts calculated on *true* cost savings to the publisher, the retailer and wholesaler would establish individual margin requirements. This issue could fill the pages of a book and is a topic of great discussion in the industry.

The retail price of any new original title is the function of four factors:

- Plant or origination cost. This is the cost of all the production components that are involved in getting the book ready to be printed. These include copyediting, typesetting, proofreading, jacket design, internal design, separating and stripping of any illustrative material, and so on. This is a one-time expense that does not vary whether the publisher prints five thousand or fifty thousand copies. Since most publishers charge the plant cost against the first printing, the plant cost per book printed varies directly with the quantity first printed.
- Paper, printing, and binding cost, or p.p.b. This is the actual cost of press time and materials to print the book. On straight type books such as a novel or a biography, the per-unit cost decreases only marginally as the printing/quantity increases.
- Royalty. This is the royalty the publisher pays the author(s) on all copies sold. Royalties are *generally* paid on the "suggested" retail selling price, and for hardcover books the standard trade royalty is 10 percent on the first five thousand copies sold, 12.5 percent for the next five thousand, and 15 percent for all sales over ten thousand. Trade paperback and mass-market royalties generally are lower and average in the 6–10 percent of list price range.
- Publisher's perceived elasticity of demand. That is, what will the market bear? The question here is not what price will sell the most copies, but rather what price will generate the most gross margin. Pricing formulas vary significantly from publisher to publisher, but most realize that they have to compete side by side with other publishers' titles in the marketplace.

To demonstrate the impact of the various factors, consider the following model: The title is *Idiot's Guide to Baseball*, an original trade paperback 6½ by 9¼ inches.

IDIOT'S GUIDE TO BASEBALL

Print Quantity	10,000		25,000	
List Price	6.95	8.95	6.95	8.95
Average Discount	× .53*	× .53	× .53	× .53
Cash Received	3.68	4.74	3.68	4.74
Less (*per book*)				
Plant ($10,000)	1.00	1.00	.40	.40
P.P.B.	.63	.63	.58	.58
Royalty	.56	.72	.56	.72
(8% of list)				
Total Costs	$2.19	$2.35	$1.54	$1.70
Gross Margin	$1.49	$2.39	$2.14	$3.04
Gross Margin %	40.5%	50.4%	58%	63%

*Assume average 47 percent discount to wholesalers/retailers

As one can see, we examined this title with two different first-print quantities at two retail prices. This is a simple model that assumes the publisher sells all copies that are printed, but it will serve to illustrate various pricing issues. The plant cost to produce this title was $10,000. Clearly as the print quantity increases, the per-book plant cost diminishes significantly from $1.00 per book at ten thousand to only $.40 at twenty-five thousand copies. Please note that gross margin and gross margin percentages have been included, because trade publishers have to generate a minimum of a 50 percent gross margin on the sale of a book to generate a profit. Therefore, in reviewing the plant cost impact on gross margin, it is clear that a first printing of ten thousand copies on a trade paperback book even with the higher price of $8.95 for a 224-page all-type book will not generate an acceptable return.

However, it is clear that a twenty-five thousand printing would generate an acceptable profit at both price points. Plant cost per book has dropped significantly, manufacturing cost (p.p.b.) has decreased marginally, and the royalty fluctuates with the list price. If a twenty-five-thousand-copy printing can be justified by advance sales projections, a subjective judgment has to be made about how much can be charged for this title.

The objective of this type of analysis is to find the maximum retail price, at the most realistic printing level, that generates the maximum gross margin contribution.

The pricing of new titles represents a great financial and marketing opportunity for publishers, and in general not enough attention is paid to this important decision. Often, when a title fails to sell according to projection, price is blamed as a predominant factor. On the other hand, when a book takes off very little is said about price, and publishers often seek the first opportunity to raise the price. My conclusion is that in general, hardcover and trade paperback publishers tend to underprice their books because of fear of rejection in the marketplace. Because of the number of titles published, a large percentage of new books will fail, not because of price resistance, but because of other, more important market factors.

Bookselling and trade book publishing are not highly profitable businesses. Why is that? Both deal in a product that has a high cost relative to what one can charge for it, so it is a low-margin business. In addition, both are plagued with a detail- and labor-intensive overhead structure resulting in limited profits even when business is strong.

Below, I have outlined the income statement for a prospering middle-size trade publisher, Breakthrough Books. The income statement is very simplistic but will suffice for the purposes of this analysis. This company has annual net sales of $20 million with a returns percentage of 20 percent and subsidiary rights revenue of $800,000, or 4 percent of net sales. This company has a gross margin percentage of 54 percent, which as was mentioned earlier is a favorable gross margin and should result in a profit for the publisher. Breakthrough Books had a good year with an operating profit of $1,768,000, or 8.5 percent of sales. This is a favorable return on sales for a trade publisher. Many publishers have a percentage of sales returns of less than 5 percent, and only the rare exception exceeds 10 percent.

OPERATING INCOME STATEMENT FOR BREAKTHROUGH BOOKS, INC.
(000's)

Gross Sales	$25,000	*Operating Expenses*	
Returns	5,000	Sales	$1,768
Net Sales	20,000	Marketing	1,664
Subsidiary Rights	800	Fulfillment	1,976
Net Sales and Revenues	20,800	General & Admin.	2,080
Cost of Goods Sold	6,448	Editorial	1,976
Royalty	3,120	Total Operating Expense	$9,464
Gross Margin	11,232	Operating Profit	$1,768

Trade book publishing is a constant frustration for financial analysts who place high priority on stable, predictable growth. Most general trade publishers experience highs and lows in profit performance primarily because of the success or lack of success of their new-title publishing program each season. Even the strongest backlist publisher depends on new titles to generate important volume and profits. Clearly the lack of financial predictability reflects the uncertainty and risk that surrounds the publication of new titles. Breakthrough Books could pay $100,000 in author advance and $75,000 to market a new title, sell 150,000 books, generate $300,000 in profit, and contribute significantly to overhead expenses. Conversely, the book could bomb, forcing the publisher to remainder most of the 50,000-copy first printing and resulting in a loss of $150,000 + . Welcome to publishing.

An income statement tells only *part* of the financial picture for a book publisher because the balance sheet and the valuation of important assets such as author advance and inventory are critical. In the short term, a publisher can appear to be more profitable than it truly is by not recognizing that it will have to remainder books at a loss or that it has author advances that will never be earned back because of a shortfall in projected sales. Therefore, many publishers choose to evaluate their financial performance by measuring profit as a return on investment or assets as opposed to sales.

Because of the inherent low margin in trade books and the tremendous amount of detail in the publishing process, many factors other than poor sales can create financial problems for publishers. As mentioned above, publishers that do not have a full grasp of their pricing decisions can produce and sell a book but not make any profit because of a bad pricing decision. Poor inventory management can give publishers the illusion they are making money until they can't pay their bills because their resources are tied up in inventory. Although most publishing executives would rather concentrate on acquisition decisions or marketing strategies, many a publishing house has been brought down by poor fulfillment abilities or inadequate information systems. Booksellers can often identify these publishers from day-to-day contact they have with the actual book shipments and customer-service department. These areas are critically important to a publisher's financial state because of the tremendous amount of detail that has to be managed and the importance in knowing what books are selling when, to whom, and why.

Publishing is a dynamic process that requires imaginative and creative resources to develop programs, and it demands sophisticated analytical skills to manage the sales and operations issues. The titles that are currently selling and the correct insight into today's trends may change entirely in a matter of months. After spending most of my publishing career in marketing and sales areas of publishing, I believe there is no question that the ability of the editorial group to develop books that deliver on their intended goal is the key to a successful publisher. A sound sales and marketing campaign can enhance the sale of a good book, but it cannot transform a poor or ill-conceived title into a solid seller. Similarly, strong financial and operational executives can save a company a great deal of money, but rarely can they *make* money for the company. In the end, a publishing house is only as successful as the books it publishes.

Chapter 67

Books in Our Lives— Now and in the Future

JOHN Y. COLE

We Americans have a habit of writing premature obituaries. Our love of novelty and our speedy pace of change tempt us to imagine that the new technology buries the old. A century ago some predicted that the telegraph and the telephone would spell the end of the postal system. Television, of course, brought prophecies of the demise of radio. In this century more than once we have heard enthusiasts for a new technology predict the demise of the book. When the automobile first became popular, some actually said that few Americans would stay home reading when they could be riding the countryside in their flivvers. The rise of photography, phonography, and the movies led others to foresee the disappearance of the book from the classroom. It would be displaced, they said, by the latest "audiovisual aids." But today textbooks still dominate the classroom.

The Culture of the Book

Meanwhile, books in their traditional form encompass us in a thousand ways. Each of our major religions is a religion of the book, with sacred texts that are the source and the vehicle of theology, morality, and hopes for the future. Our education has been built around books. The structure of our political life rests on our books of law, history, geography, and biography. Books are the main source of our knowledge, our reservoir of faith, memory, wisdom, morality, poetry, philosophy, history, and science.

The book-stored wisdom of the Bible, Locke, Burke, Blackstone, and the great authors of the European liberal tradition was the foundation for the grand experiment of our Founding Fathers.

They put the free access to printed matter, along with freedom of religion, among the first items of the first article in the Bill of Rights of our Constitution. "I cannot live without books," declared Thomas Jefferson after his books were shipped from Monticello to become the foundation of the renewed Library of Congress in 1815. And at once he began building a new personal library. Without books we might be tempted to believe that our civilization was born yesterday—or when the latest newsmagazine went to press. The very omnipresence of books leads us to underestimate their power and influence. One measure of their meaning to mankind is the desperate hunger of people in unfree societies to read everything that is not government-authorized pap.

It is no accident that people everywhere have considered books sacred and have made them the source and the vehicle of their religious faith. For the power of the book has been uncanny, mysterious, inestimable, overpowering, and infinite—just as the activity of reading has a unique individuality, intimacy, and privacy.

Our civilization is a product of the Culture of the Book. Of course, the book itself—the printed, bound volume—is a triumph of technology. But when we speculate on the future of the traditional book, we are not thinking about a single product of technology. Not since the discovery of fire and the invention of the wheel has any other innovation had so pervasive and so enduring an influence on ways of thinking, feeling, worshiping, teaching, governing, and discovering. The revolution since Gutenberg is without precedent. Its consequences are yet to be seen in much of the world. This effect, in Thomas Carlyle's familiar words, was "disbanding hired armies, and cashiering most kings and senates, and creating a whole new democratic world."

We see books everywhere, of every conceivable variety, in homes and schools, in offices and workshops. Not only Bibles, prayer books, dictionaries, encyclopedias, and textbooks, but also novels, books of mystery, romance, travel, nature, and adventure, and children's books, along with how-to-do-it books on sewing, car repair, home maintenance, computers, gardening, athletics, and health, not to mention telephone books, mail-order catalogs, and company directories. Books are everyday fixtures of our lives, guides and measures of our civilization. To try to extract the book from our lives would be fatal. but luckily this is impossible.

Our long investment in books is only one reason to expect the book to remain a fertile resource in the America of the next decades. The proverbial convenience, accessibility, and individuality of the book are unrivaled now or by any new technology in sight. The book is independent of outside power sources and offers unique opportunities for freedom of choice. "One reads at one's own speed," Vincent Canby reminds us, "in short snatches on the subway or in long, voluptuous withdrawals from the world. One proceeds through a big, complex novel, say, *War and Peace*, or *Crime and Punishment*, like an exceptionally well-heeled tourist in a foreign landscape, going slowly or fast depending on the roads, on one's own mood, and on the attractions along the way. If one loses something, one can always go back to pick it up." For all these reasons, books are messengers of freedom. They can be hidden under a mattress or smuggled into slave nations.

We Americans have never been inclined to underestimate new technologies, nor have we held on sentimentally to the ways of our grandparents. Our faith in obsolescence comes from the amazingly speedy changes in our ways of life. Naturally, then, we enjoy science-fiction fantasies of a world of microchips, where our library store of books has become obsolete and our personal bookshelves unnecessary. For we eagerly discard the old if there seems a newer, more interesting—even if more complicated—way of doing the same task. Rube Goldberg gave us an eloquent slogan for our national way of life: "Do It the Hard Way!"

The Twin Menaces: Illiteracy and Aliteracy

New technologies are new allies in our national effort to inform and educate Americans. We must enlist the new technologies with cautious enthusiasm. The threat to a knowledgeable citizenry is not from new technology. But there is a threat from our hasty readiness to exaggerate or misconceive the promise of new technologies, which carries the assumption that the Culture of the Book is a thing of the past. Today we are failing to do all we should do to qualify young Americans to read and so draw on the main storehouse of our civilization. We are failing to provide enough access to books. And we can do much more to increase the motivation to read.

We must face and defeat the twin menaces of illiteracy and aliteracy—the inability to read and lack of the will to read—if our citizens are to remain free and qualified to govern themselves. We must aim to abolish illiteracy in the United States before the end of this century.

The Alliance of Technologies

The same human ingenuity that produced the book has produced later technologies, and they are all allies. Our task is to recognize and promote their alliance. We must see the role that the computer is already playing and that which it is likely to play. Then we will not underestimate or abandon book literacy. The enemy of the book is not technology but the illusion that we could or would abolish the Culture of the Book.

A Bookseller's Glossary

Expressions, Abbreviations, Addresses, and Financial Terms of the Trade

CHARLES B. ANDERSON
and ROBERT DIKE BLAIR

AAP Association of American Publishers (220 East 23rd St., New York, NY 10010).

AAUP Association of American University Presses (1 Park Ave., New York, NY 10016).

AB Originally *American Bookman*, but now accepted as the abbreviation of the merged publication *AB Bookman's Weekly* (also known as *Antiquarian Bookman*), a journal of the antiquarian book trade published by AB Bookman Publications, Inc. (Box AB, Clifton, NJ 07015).

ABA American Booksellers Association (137 West 25th St., New York, NY 10001).

ABA Book Buyer's Handbook An annually revised reference work giving discount schedules, returns policies, and other trade terms of most U.S. publishers, as well as other essential information. An invaluable tool for any bookseller.

ABA Newswire A comprehensive weekly newsletter, featuring front-page news reports of such issues as industry mergers, changing terms, and censorship legislation. To help booksellers anticipate public demand, it also contains timely listings of forthcoming publicity tours, lectures, articles, book reviews, plus major advertising and promotional offers.

ABAA Antiquarian Booksellers Association of America (50 Rockefeller Plaza, New York, NY 10020).

ABC *See* Association of Booksellers for Children.

academic reprints New printings of scholarly works issued by a publisher other than the original; generally reproduced by a photographic process and intended to satisfy a relatively small, specialized academic market.

accounts payable A debit account in a balance sheet, showing amounts owed to others.

accounts receivable   An asset account in a balance sheet, showing amounts due from customers or clients.

addenda   Material added to the original text of a book, usually printed on a slip of paper; a *tip-in* that is pasted in the finished book at the time of binding. The singular is *addendum. See also* errata.

adult bookshop   A store that makes a specialty of selling sexually explicit materials.

advance copies   *See* review copies.

advance order   An order placed for titles in advance of publication.

advance royalty   A sum paid to an author by a publisher in advance of the receipt of a finished manuscript or in advance of publication, to be deducted later from earned royalties.

agate line   A space one column wide and a fourteenth of an inch deep, used as a measurement in newspaper advertising. There are fourteen agate lines in one *column inch.*

ALA   American Library Association (50 East Huron St., Chicago, IL 60611).

allowance   (*advertising*) A sum of money or quantity of merchandise committed by a publisher to assist a bookseller in advertising or promoting a single title or group of titles. *See* cooperative advertising.

allowance   (*freight*) Partial payment by a publisher of the cost of transporting books to a bookseller.

all rights reserved   A printed notice in a book that any use of the material in it will not be permitted without the consent of the copyright owner.

Americana   Books on American history, geography, biography, and the like.

American Book Awards   *See* National Book Awards.

American Bookseller   A monthly magazine of news and features vital to booksellers. Topics range from store managment and bookseller/publisher relations to merchandising and promotion. Regular departments cover current media tie-ins, regional association news, and association activities.

American National Standards Institute   This organization coordinates and promotes the United States's voluntary standardization program. Accredited Standards Committee X3 is responsible for computer standards; National Information Standards Organization (Z39) is responsible for standards related to the book industry. ANSI standards from NISO (Z39) include the ISBN (Z39.21) and SAN (Z39.43) (1430 Broadway, New York, NY 10018).

Hans Christian Andersen Awards   International awards given annually to an author and an illustrator of children's books in recognition of the entire body of their work. Supervised by the International Board on Books for Young People.

annotated   Provided with critical notes and explanations, as, for example, *The Annotated Shakespeare.*

ANSI   *See* American National Standards Institute.

anticipation   or **anticipation discount**   A discount sometimes offered by some suppliers for payment in advance of the due date on an invoice.

Antiquarian Bookman   *See AB.*

antiquarian bookseller   A dealer in old and rare books.

apocryphal   Of questionable authorship or authenticity.

appendix   Supplementary material at the end of a book. A supplement is typically more extensive than an appendix. The plural is *appendixes* or *appendices.*

Association of Booksellers for Children   (ABC) A trade organization of booksellers and others interested in children's books. ABC holds its annual meeting during the ABA Convention, publishes a newsletter, and offers its members materials and support on issues relating to the sale of children's books.

Atticus, Titus Pomponius   (109–32 B.C.) A bookseller and patron of the arts, as well as the possessor of great wealth, he was able to convince censoring Roman emperors not to destroy documents that have come down to us as major landmarks in our literary heritage. Reputedly, he started the first chain operation with branches in the provinces.

auction house   Auction houses which deal in a wide range of items—furniture, sculpture, paintings, and the like—sometimes also handle sales of rare books and private libraries.

audiovisual materials   Supplementary nonbook teaching aids, such as charts, slides, tapes, and filmstrips.

author's copies   Complimentary copies of the first edition of a book given to the author by the publisher, usually ten in number.

autograph   The signature of an author, usually on the title page or *flyleaf* of a book. Authors are often willing to make public or informal appearances in bookstores to autograph books for purchasers.

automatic distribution   The practice whereby the publisher determines the titles and quantities of the books that are thought to be appropriate for the store.

avant-garde   Literally "vanguard" in French. Describes literature that is experimental or unorthodox, as avant-garde poetry or fiction.

backbone   *See* spine.

backlist   A publisher's list of older titles kept in print because of continued demand.

back order   The unfilled portion of an order promised for future delivery.

backstrap   or **backstrip** *See* spine.

Baker & Taylor Company, The   (652 East Main St., Bridgewater, NJ 08807-0920) A major wholesaler of books, a division of W. R. Grace & Co.

bar code   *See* universal product code, Bookland EAN.

Basic Book List   A periodically revised list of hardbound and paperbound titles recommended as a nucleus for a bookstore's *basic stock*. Chosen by a committee of booksellers on the basis of actual sales in their own stores, this list is useful in planning stock of a new business or as a buying and inventory guide in established stores.

basic stock   The titles from various publishers' backlists that a bookseller decides to carry continuously in stock. Most booksellers find the ABA's *Basic Book List* helpful in determining their basic stock.

Bay Psalm Book   A hymnal of the Massachusetts Bay Colony, regarded as the earliest book printed in what is now the United States (1640).

bds.   Abbreviation for *boards*.

belles lettres   Literature that has aesthetic appeal rather than instructional or informational value. It may be fiction or nonfiction, poetry or drama.

best-seller   A term coined in 1895 by the *American Bookman*, which published each month a list of six best-sellers in bookstores around the country. This American expression is now common in Great Britain and the principal European countries.

biblio-   A prefix from the Greek, meaning "book." A bibliography is a listing of books; a bibliophile, a lover of books; a bibliopole, a bookseller. The Bible, from the same root, is "the book."

BISAC   *See* Book Industry Systems Advisory Committee.

BISG   *See* Book Industry Study Group.

bleed   In printing, extending an illustration to the very edge of the page so that no margin shows.

blurb   A term coined by American humorist Gelett Burgess. It is a short quotation or commendatory description of a book that appears on its jacket or in its advertising.

BMI   Book Manufacturers' Institute, the trade association of book manufacturers (11 Prospect St., Stamford, CT 06901).

b.o.   Abbreviation for *back order*. *See also* invoice symbols.

boards   The stiff material—cardboard or pressed board—used for the front and back of a book and usually covered with leather, paper, cloth, or plastic-coated cloth.

boldface   A heavy-faced type in which, for example, the key words in this glossary are set.

book   The word derives from the German word for the "beech," the bark of which was used for runic inscriptions. A book may now be defined as material printed in page form and bound between covers. In order to qualify for *book rate*, the U.S. Postal Service requires that a book be at least twenty-four pages, permanently bound.

book club edition   Books sold by the various book clubs often—but not always—are more cheaply produced. The list price usually does not appear on the jacket. The words "Book Club Edition" sometimes will appear on the inside front flap of the *dust jacket* or on the copyright page. Customers sometimes present these editions for exchange in a bookstore, so it behooves a bookseller to recognize them. One clue is a small spot or dot (sometimes a small debossed maple leaf) on the lower right-hand corner of the back board—usually debossed, sometimes colored, most often black. Depending on the quality of the cloth used on the cover, the pressure applied in making the dot, or the forgetfulness of someone at the bindery, the dot may not be visible or may be missing altogether.

book fair   An exhibition for the display and sale of books that developed in Europe as the printing of books became widespread. Although several countries in the world sponsor book fairs today, the largest by far is the International Book Fair, held each fall in Frankfurt, West Germany. Its nearest American equivalent is the Trade Exhibit at the annual ABA Convention. Book fairs at the local level, sponsored by schools or other groups, are fairly common in various parts of the United States. Booksellers often work with the fair sponsors by providing the books to be displayed and sold.

Book Industry Study Group   A not-for-profit research organization for the book industry and parent organization of BISAC (160 Fifth Ave., New York, NY 10010).

Book Industry Systems Advisory Committee   An ad hoc group of book publishers, booksellers, librarians, wholesalers, and representatives of school systems, brought together by the common goal of utilizing the ISBN to increase efficiency and decrease costs for the industry. BISAC is a committee of the Book Industry Study Group. They have developed standardized computer formats for the placing of orders, invoicing for shipments, and updating of computer databases (160 Fifth Ave., New York, NY 10010).

Bookland EAN   In November 1985, BISAC recommended that publishers print the *bar code* symbology known as the Bookland EAN on all their publications. Eventually the EAN will replace the use of the ISBN in OCR-A. The EAN is the International Article Number (formerly the European Article Number). The first digits designate the country of origin (with 00 through 09 representing the United States). The prefixes 978 and 979 were set aside as a prefix to indicate that the product is from a "country" known as "Bookland." That prefix is followed by the ISBN without its usual check digit, which is replaced by the EAN check digit to verify all preceding numbers including the 978. The Bookland EAN may be followed by an optional add-on symbol representing the suggested retail price in which the lead digit 0 refers to the British pound and 5 to the U.S. dollar. The important advantage of using the EAN is that electronic scanners that read it will also read the *universal product code (UPC)* now printed on so many nonbook products sold in bookstores.

Book Manufacturers' Institute   *See* BMI.

book rate, book post   Special fourth-class postage rate, flat unzoned rate applicable to books and other educational materials, which allows national distribution of books to libraries and bookstores without penalty for geographical location.

Booksellers Publishing Incorporated   *See* BPI.

Books in Print   An annual publication issued by the R. R. Bowker Company listing all American books in print.

book scout   A person who travels around the country, visiting book and antique shops and the like, buying items which might be desired by dealers, librarians, and collectors.

book sizes   The various terms for book sizes (folio, quarto, and so on) derive from the page size resulting from the number of times a standard-sized printed sheet was folded. In present practice, the size is usually determined by the height of the binding, not the size of the leaf.

> *folio*, approximately 15 inches high (Fo)
> *quarto*, approximately 12 inches high (4to)
> *octavo*, approximately 9¾ inches high (8vo)
> *duodecimo*, approximately 7¾ inches high (12mo)
> *sixteenmo*, approximately 6¾ inches high (16mo)
> *twentyfourmo*, approximately 5¾ inches high (24mo)

Other sizes include:
> *double elephant folio*, approximately 50 inches high
> *atlas folio*, approximately 25 inches high
> *elephant folio*, approximately 23 inches high
> *thirtytwomo*, approximately 5 inches high (32mo)
> *fortyeightmo*, approximately 4 inches high (48mo)
> *sixtyfourmo*, approximately 3 inches high (64mo)

Any book that is wider than it is high is designated as *oblong* (obl. or ob.). If a book is much taller than it is wide, it is designated as *narrow* (nar).

book trade   Retail bookselling and its practices.

book traveler   *See* traveler.

bookworm   The larva of various insects that feed on the binding and paste and often the leaves of books. Also, of course, a passionate reader.

Boston Globe–Horn Book Award   Prize given annually for children's books in the categories of fiction, nonfiction, and illustration. *See also Horn Book Magazine.*

bound galley A prepublication sample of a book, consisting of uncorrected page or galley proofs bound in a plain paper cover, for advance publicity and sales purposes.

bowdlerization A text altered to remove passages offensive to the editor or the era. The word derives from Thomas Bowdler (1754–1825), an English editor who published *expurgated* editions of Shakespeare and others.

R. R. Bowker Company (245 West 17th St., New York, NY 10011) A major publisher of books, periodicals, and reports about the publishing industry, including *Books in Print, LMP,* and *Publishers Weekly.*

BPI Booksellers Publishing Incorporated, the ABA subsidiary that produces *American Bookseller* magazine.

braille A system of printing for the blind using patterns of raised dots. It was invented by the French educator Louis Braille (1809–1852).

broadside or **broadsheet** A sheet of paper printed on only one side intended to be publicly displayed or distributed.

brochure A pamphlet or booklet containing only a few printed pages stitched together. The word derives from the French *brocher,* meaning "to stitch."

bulk A book's thickness without the cover. A book may be "bulked up" by the use of thick but lightweight paper to make it appear larger. Book paper may vary from two hundred to two thousand pages to the inch.

buying around The practice of ordering from a foreign publisher or wholesaler a cheaper edition than the same book in the domestic edition.

Caldecott, Randolph (1846–1886) An eminent English illustrator of children's books. The Caldecott Medal for the best American picture book of the year is named for him. The award is supervised by the Association for Library Services to Children of the American Library Association. *See* ALA.

Canadian Booksellers Association *See* CBA.

cancel back order (CBO) Instructions from bookseller to vendor to cancel any previous orders placed for a title. Often used to be sure a postponed title is not double-shipped because of two or more sets of orders.

caps Capital letters, also called *upper case* letters.

Carey, Mathew (1760–1839) An emigrant from Ireland to Philadelphia shortly after the Revolutionary War, he became a publisher and organized new ways of selling books, including subscription and itinerant bookselling. He helped found the first American booksellers' association in 1806. The firm he ran with his son, Carey & Lea, survives today as Lea & Febiger in Philadelphia. The Carey-Thomas Award, given annually to the publisher of the most distinguished book of the year, is named for him and for Isaiah Thomas (1749–1831), American printer, publisher, and bookseller.

carriage Cost of transportation from publisher to bookseller.

case binding In everyday parlance, a *casebound* book is any hardback as contrasted with a paperback. *See also* clothbound.

cash discount Additional discount for payment within a specific time period.

Caxton, William (1422?–1491?) The printer and publisher of the first books in the English language, the most famous of which was Chaucer's *Canterbury Tales.*

CBA Canadian Booksellers Association (49 Laing St., Toronto, Ontario M4L 2N4 Canada).

CBA Christian Booksellers Association (Box 200, 2620 Venetucci Blvd., Colorado Springs, CO 80901), an organization of booksellers dealing in religious books.

CBC Children's Book Council (67 Irving Place, New York, NY 10003) is a nonprofit trade association of children's book publishers.

CBI Cumulative Book Index, a comprehensive index of all books published in English anywhere in the world, published by the H. W. Wilson Company.

chapbook A small book or pamphlet, usually paperback, containing a religious tract, poetry, or other material. They were once distributed by peddlers, or chapmen.

check digit A digit used to validate by computer the digits in the preceding numerical field. For instance, the last digit of an ISBN or a SAN is its check digit. Contact the Book Industry Study Group for exact programming details.

Children's Book Council *See* CBC.

Children's Book Week A week in November during which attention is focused on children's books, organized by the Children's Book Council.

Christian Booksellers Association *See* CBA.

cloth, clothbound Commonly used to mean hardcover books as opposed to paperbacks, because until recent years most hardcover books were bound in cloth over stiff boards. In trade books now a full cloth cover is unusual, most being bound with paper over *boards*, with a cloth strip over the *spine*.

codex An ancient manuscript volume.

collated Compared critically, as writing or facts; in bookbinding, the sheets verified as to their proper sequential arrangement; the pages of a manuscript put in their proper order.

colophon From the Greek, meaning "finishing stroke." An inscription, usually at the end of a book, giving facts about its publication. Also, a publisher's emblem or trademark—such as Knopf's borzoi or Bantam's rooster—usually placed on the title page and spine.

colporteur A peddler of books. *See* traveler.

column inch A space one inch deep and one column wide in newspaper advertising. Although column width may vary, it is usually about two inches. *See also* agate line.

comb binding   A plastic strip with teeth shaped roughly like a comb is bent so that the teeth passing through slots hold the cover and pages of a book together. Sometimes inaccurately called a *spiral binding*.

concordance   An alphabetical index of the words in a text showing where each may be found. In frequent use with the Bible and Shakespeare.

conglomerate   A holding company, which has acquired ownership of other companies. In recent years a number of large publishing companies, such as Simon & Schuster and Random House, have been bought by conglomerates.

Congress of Young Booksellers   *See* International Congress of Young Booksellers.

consignment   Stock that remains the property of the publisher but is shipped (or consigned) to a bookseller, usually for promotional purposes, with payment to be made only after the books are sold.

cooperative advertising   (co-op) A formal plan through which the bookseller and publisher share a specified percentage of the local advertising for a book or group of books.

copyright   The right, granted by federal law, to the creator or distributor of literary or artistic material, for exclusive publication, distribution, or sale of such property. To secure a copyright for a book, the author must deposit two copies with the copyright office in the Library of Congress in Washington, D.C., together with a registration fee. For most works created—fixed in tangible form—after January 1, 1978, the term of protection begins at the moment of creation, lasts during the author's lifetime, and continues for fifty years after the author's death. Copyrights secured before January 1, 1978, provide for a term of twenty-eight years from the copyright date, which may be extended by another forty-seven years. Works that have no copyright protection are said to be in the public domain and may be reprinted without payment of royalty.

Council for Periodical Distributors Associations   The trade organization representing regional associations of independent distributors of magazines and mass-market paperback books. They administer the BIPAD number system, which issues identification numbers to publishers. These numbers are the first half of the information encoded in the universal product code (488 Madison Ave., New York, NY 10022).

counter display   A small rack or poster with a pocket for the display of books to create impulse sales at a checkout counter or on a sales table.

CPDA *See*   Council for Periodical Distributors Associations.

Cumulative Book Index   *See CBI.*

cuneiform writing   Wedge-shaped characters used by the ancient Babylonians, Syrians, and others in many inscriptions. It is thought to have originated more than four thousand years before Christ.

cut   Any printed illustration or the engraving from which it is printed. *See also* line cut.

c.w.o.   *See* invoice symbols.

data   Factual information that is used as a basis for calculation, discussion, or analysis.

data communications   The transfer of information from one computer to another, most often using telephone lines.

database   An organization of related computer data files containing information or reference material on a particular subject or subjects. It is typically structured so that headings or key words can be referenced easily, allowing for efficient and simple access to, and retrieval of, records.

dating   An extension of credit offered by a publisher to a bookseller. For example, books may sometimes be purchased in the summer with the invoices bearing a December or January due date, even though the books were shipped in the intervening months.

definitive edition   An edition considered the most authoritative version of a work.

dele, delete   A proofreader's mark, meaning remove or omit.

desiderata   A list of books wanted.

Dewey Decimal System   A numerical classification of books into ten major categories with many subdivisions, the system most widely used by public and institutional libraries to classify and shelve their books. It was devised by Melvil Dewey, a librarian, in 1876.

direct mail   Advertising material mailed to a specific list of potential customers, soliciting orders from them by mail.

discount   A percentage of the retail price of a book or books allowed by the publisher or the wholesaler as compensation for the store's acting as distributor. To determine the percent of discount, divide the difference between the retail price and the bookseller's cost by the retail price: $10 (retail price) minus $6 (cost to bookseller) equals $4, divided by $10, equals .40—a 40 percent discount. Discount schedules may be found in the *ABA Book Buyer's Handbook*.

drop ship   Delivery to an address other than the one to which the invoice is sent. In the interest of saving time and additional postage charges, a bookseller, for example, may direct a publisher to *drop ship* a special order directly to the customer.

dual pricing   Illegally offering preferred prices or terms to a few customers in a given business category. All similar customers must be sold on the same discount schedule.

dust jacket or **dust wrapper**   (d.j., d.w.) The paper cover placed around a book not so much to protect the book from dust as to afford the publisher space for promotional copy and eye-catching cover artwork.

Edgar Award   Prize given annually to works of mystery, crime, or suspense fiction in ten categories, including novel, first novel, short story, and so on, by the Mystery Writers of America, Inc. (105 East 19th St., New York, NY 10003).

edition   All copies of a book printed from a single setting of type (excluding minor corrections). Any substantial alterations to the text make a new edition. Any number of printings (or *impressions*) without substantial alterations may be made over any period of time, and all the printings will be of the same edition. *See* first edition. Edition may also refer to a difference in physical format, binding, and the like—the deluxe edition, the limited edition, and so on.

el-hi   A term used to indicate books intended for elementary and high school use.

elite   A size of typewriter type equivalent to 10 *point*, somewhat smaller than *pica*, which is 12 point.

embossing   Raised ornamentation on paper, leather, cloth, and so forth.

endpapers   Paper at the beginning and end of a book, half of which is pasted to the inside of the *case binding* to conceal the raw boards and the binding tape. The other half becomes the first or last leaf of a book and is normally an unnumbered page.

engravings   *See* halftone; line cut.

e.o.m.   End of the month. *See also* invoice symbols.

ephemera   Material of only transitory interest or importance, such as pamphlets or clippings.

erotica   Literature that is sexually explicit.

errata   Corrections of errors found in a book after it has been printed, usually on a page or slip inserted into the volume. *See* tip-in. The singular is *erratum*.

ex libris   "From the books of," a Latin phrase used on bookplates, followed by the owner's name.

expurgated edition   A book from which certain original material considered objectionable has been deleted. *See also* bowdlerization.

face-out display   Arrangement of books with jackets or front covers facing the customer, contrasted with *spine-out display.*

facsimile edition   An exact reproduction of an original book.

fiche   Same as microfiche. *See* microform.

first edition   For book collectors, this is short for "first printing of the first edition." *See* edition. There can be any number of printings within the first edition, but only the first printing in most cases has a value to collectors.

fixtures   Shelves, tables, racks, and other devices on which books are displayed in a store.

flats   Books intended for *face-out display*, usually children's books or art books.

flyleaf   (plural, *flyleaves*) The unprinted page or pages at the beginning or end of a book that are not the *endpapers*.

FOB   "Free on board," an *invoice symbol*. Delivery from the warehouse to the carrier is free, but the rest of the trip is at the buyer's expense. Originally it referred to the transport of goods from the warehouse to the railroad terminal in the days before truck freight. Now it means simply that the buyer pays the freight from the shipping point.

folio   A book approximately fifteen inches high. *See* book sizes. It also may mean page number; *even* folios are on the left-hand pages, and *odd* folios on the right.

fore edge   The edge of a book opposite its *spine*.

fore-edge painting   A picture hand-painted on the fore edge of a book that becomes visible only when the pages are fanned. This form of book decoration flourished in the late eighteenth century. Books with these paintings are collector's items. It is not unusual, however, to find counterfeit, recent paintings on older books.

format   The shape, size, design, and general makeup of a book.

FPT   *See* freight pass-through.

Franklin, Benjamin   (1706–1790) As a young man in Philadelphia, Franklin was printer, author, and publisher. His *Poor Richard's Almanack* was by far the best-selling publication in the Colonies, with an average sale of more than ten thousand copies. In 1731 he established what may have been the first circulating library in America.

freight allowance   *See* allowance (freight).

freight pass-through (FPT)   A system to help booksellers regain some of the margin between cost and selling price that gradually has been lost as transportation costs have risen. Not all publishers use FPT, and among those who do, the amounts and methods of calculation may vary. Basically, however, the publisher sets the cover price of a title higher than the invoice (list) price (before discount) to the retailer. The difference is passed through to the customer and helps pay the cost of transportation.

frontispiece   An illustration facing the title page.

galley proof   Printer's proof taken from type before it has been arranged in page form.

goffered, gauffered, or **deckled edges**   Ragged page edges that add decorative effect to a book. Goffered books are sometimes collector's items in the antiquarian trade.

gothic   A romantic-historical novel of suspense. Also known euphemistically as a "bodice-ripper."

Kate Greenaway Medal   Award given annually by the British Library Association to an illustrator of children's books published in the United Kingdom. Its American counterpart is the Caldecott Medal. *See also* Caldecott, Randolph.

gross profit   The difference between total receipts and the actual cost of goods sold. *See* net profit.

Gutenberg, Johann   (1398?–1468?) The man generally credited with inventing printing from movable metal type. His Bible was one of the earliest and certainly one of the most famous of large printed books.

gutter   The inner margin or white space between the facing pages of a book.

halftone   Reproduction of a photograph or painting using a series of dots so tiny as to be almost invisible. A halftone is made by photographing the original art through a screen. The screened photograph is then used to make a printing plate. Fine reproductions require paper of high quality and make use of 150, and more, dots to the square inch. *See also* line cut.

hardback, hardbound, hardcover   *See clothbound.*

headband   Small band of silk or other material at top and/or bottom of *spine* to add to the appearance of a book.

hieroglyphics   Characters used in the picture writing of the ancient Egyptians or Mexicans.

holograph   A document entirely in the handwriting of the purported author.

hornbook   A primer, usually in the shape of a paddle protected by a sheet of transparent horn, having on it the alphabet and other rudiments, such as the Lord's Prayer. Hornbooks were used in England and colonial America to teach children to read. Though they were common at one time, authentic examples are very rare today.

Horn Book Magazine   A bimonthly publication prepared by The Horn Book, Inc. (Park Square Building, 31 St. James Ave., Boston, MA 02116). It contains reviews of and articles about children's books. *See also* Boston Globe–Horn Book Award.

Hugo Award   Prize for a work of science fiction given annually by readers attending the World Science Fiction Conference.

hurt book   A damaged or shopworn book that is still readable with all the pages intact. Some publishers from time to time make hurt books available to booksellers at greatly reduced prices.

IBF   International Booksellers Federation (Grunangergasse 4, A-1010 Vienna, Austria). The international association of national bookselling associations.

iconography   The art of illustration by means of pictures, images, or symbols.

ID   *See* independent distributor.

illuminated   Decorated with ornamental letters or colored illustrations, a feature of old manuscripts and early printed books.

impression   Synonym for the noun "printing" and being the number of books printed in one press run. There can be any number of impressions within an *edition* of a book.

imprimatur   From Latin, meaning "let it be printed." Official approval, especially that of the Roman Catholic church, to print and publish a book.

imprint   The publisher's name, or the name of a subsidiary or special series, placed on the title page and spine of a book.

incunabula   The plural of a Latin word meaning "cradle," used to describe books issued before A.D. 1500, in the early days of printing. Singular is *incunabulum*.

independent distributor   (ID) Wholesaler whose primary customers for its magazines and paperback books are nonbookstore accounts.

index   A list of the names, places, and topics mentioned in a book listed alphabetically at the end with the numbers of the pages on which they appear.

India paper   A thin, sturdy, opaque paper often used in Bibles and dictionaries. Less brittle than ordinary paper, it will not eventually break if creased.

Ingram Book Company   (347 Reedwood Dr., Nashville, TN 37217) A major wholesaler of books.

inserts   Illustrations or other special material added to the already printed portions of a book before it is bound.

International Booksellers Federation   *See* IBF.

International Congress of Young Booksellers   A project of the IBF. An annual gathering of booksellers under the age of forty from around the world meets for a week in different European cities to exchange ideas and report on progress in the book industry in their respective countries. Anyone may attend; however, the ABA sends a representative through the awarding of the Charley Haslam International Scholarship (International Booksellers Federation, Grunangergasse 4, A-1010 Vienna, Austria).

International Standard Book Number   The international and national standard number that uniquely identifies the binding, edition, and publisher of a given work. Publisher prefix sections of the ISBN are controlled by the ISBN Agency; title identifier sections are assigned by each publisher to their works. The ISBN is the basis for identifying book titles in all industrywide automated systems (R. R. Bowker Co., 245 West 17th St., New York, NY 10011).

inventory   The total stock in trade of a retailer. "Taking inventory" is the process of determining the value and number of goods on hand.

invoice   A detailed list, with prices, terms of payment, and other information, of an individual shipment from a publisher or supplier; the publisher's bill.

invoice symbols   The symbols below are often used on publishers' invoices:

> *b.o.* back order
> *C, CC* order canceled
> *c.w.o.* cash with order
> *e.o.m.* end of month
> *FOB* free on board
> *NE, NEP* new edition pending
> *n.o.p.* not our publication
> *n.y.p.* not yet published
> *o.c.* order canceled
> *o.p.* out of print
> *o.s.* out of stock
> *o.s.c.* out of stock, canceled
> *o.s.f.* out of stock, to follow
> *o.s.i.* out of stock indefinitely
> *p.p.* parcel post
> *t.o.p.* temporarily out of print (A contradiction in terms. "Out of print" by definition is not a temporary condition, but some publishers can't make up their minds.)
> *t.o.s.* temporarily out of stock

ISBN   *See* International Standard Book Number.

issue   A portion of the books printed as an *impression* but differing in some respect and offered for sale as a planned unit of that edition. There may be a different title page, added or corrected text, or any number of variants. Important only to antiquarian booksellers, but in that field of endeavor, a state may be a whole continent of difference in the value of a book.

italics (ital.)   A slanted type as distinct from roman. *This sentence is set in italics.* This sentence is in roman.

jacket   *See* dust jacket.

Jiffy bag   A padded envelope used to mail books, commonly available in a wide range of sizes from wholesale paper and stationery supply companies.

jobber   A book distributor who sells at a discount, usually stocking mass-market paperbacks.

kill   Instruction to a printer to destroy or set aside type that has been set but is no longer needed.

Kirkus Reviews   (200 Park Avenue South, New York, NY 10003) Advance review service provided weekly to librarians and the book trade.

laminated   Literally "in layers." Book jackets are commonly laminated—that is, covered with a clear plastic sheeting that provides them with a glossy appearance and adds to their durability.

l.c.   *See* lower case.

LCCN   Library of Congress Catalog Card Number.

letterpress   A method of printing that involves a direct impression from type or a printing plate made from type. *See also* offset.

library binding   A specially reinforced binding for library use. Because of the higher cost of manufacture, books with library bindings usually carry a smaller discount. Some titles are available only in a library binding.

limited edition   A special printing of a book limited to a stated number of copies, usually numbered consecutively and signed by the author.

line cut   An unscreened photoengraving on metal, usually zinc, for reproducing black-and-white drawings. Known also as line etching, line engraving, or zinc etching. *See also* halftone.

list   All the titles a publisher has available for sale.

list price   The retail price of a book set by the publisher. Often shortened to *list*, as in the phrase "40 percent off list."

literary agent   An intermediary between author and publisher, paid on a commission basis by the author. It is often as difficult for an unpublished author to find a competent literary agent willing to work with him as it is to find a publisher.

Literary Market Place   *See LMP.*

LJ   *Library Journal*, published for public and private libraries by R. R. Bowker Company.

LMP   *Literary Market Place*, an annual publication of R. R. Bowker Company, listing names, addresses, and key personnel of book, magazine, and newspaper publishers and publishing-related agencies and associations.

loss leader   A book or other merchandise advertised and sold below or near actual cost to attract customers into a store. Because they have an established list price, books have long been regarded as being among the most effective merchandise for such promotions.

lower case   (l.c.) Small letters as distinguished from *upper case* or capital letters.

machine readable   Printed in a typeface able to be read by an optical scanning device. *See* optical character recognition.

markup   Difference, expressed as a percentage, between the cost of a book and the selling price. Correctly, it is the percentage by which the cost is increased (the difference divided by the cost figure), but commonly "markup" is used as a synonym for "discount." Better ask for a definition of terms when someone discusses this with you.

mass market   Paperbacks widely distributed in outlets other than bookstores (supermarkets, newsstands, variety stores, and so on). Format usually is "rack size" to fit pockets of wire racks designed for their display ($4^3/16$ by $6^7/8$ inches). Unlike *trade paperbacks*, "stripped covers" (the torn-off front cover) may be returned for credit instead of returning the whole book.

microfiche   *See* microform.

microfilm   *See* microform.

microform   The general term for a photographic reproduction of material stored so that it can be read only with magnification. The two main types of microforms are **microfilm** (images appear on a roll of film that must be viewed sequentially) and **microfiche** (images appear on a flat surface and can be viewed either sequentially or by going directly to the location shown in the fiche index as appropriate for the material of interest).

mint   or **mint condition** A book so described is "like new."

morocco   A durable leather make from goatskin, commonly used for bookbinding.

Morris, William   (1834–1896) English poet, artist, and craftsman, founder of the Kelmscott Press, which produced many books that are still regarded as among the finest ever printed.

ms.   Manuscript. The plural is *mss.*

NACS   National Association of College Stores (528 East Lorain St., Oberlin, OH 44074).

National Information Standards Organization   (Z39) NISO is a standards-developing organization. NISO's members are interested in the best and most economical practices in information-based activities such as librarianship, publishing, bookselling, indexing, and on-line information services (National Bureau of Standards, Administration 101, Library E-106, Gaithersburg, MD 20899).

National Retail Merchants Association   The trade organization representing most of the department stores and many retail establishments in the country (100 West 31st St., New York, NY 10001).

NBA   National Book Awards. Begun in 1950, this is the country's most visible book awards program. From 1980 through 1986, the program was known as The American Book Awards (TABA) (155 Bank St., Studio 1002-D, New York, NY 10014).

NBC   National Book Committee, an organization made up of prominent individuals interested in the support of books and reading. In addition to bestowing the National Medal for Literature, the NBC has undertaken other important projects designed to stimulate the wide distribution and use of books.

Nebula Awards   Science-fiction prizes given annually in the categories of novel, novelette, novella, and short story. Sponsored by the Science Fiction Writers of America (68 Countryside Apts., Hackettstown, NJ 07840).

net   Not subject to discount or other reduction. Can refer to book prices that carry no discount to the retailer or to indicate that the invoiced amount is not subject to cash discount for prompt payment, as in "net thirty days."

net pricing   A method for setting the wholesale price of an item so as to have no relation to any retail or suggested retail price. In net pricing, the publisher establishes the cost price of a book to the retailers and wholesalers, who in turn decide on their selling price to determine their own margin of profit. No cover price is printed on the book, and the catalog price is *net*. The system still is controversial and first was used to any extent in 1979 in the textbook market where the discount generally is 20 percent and the margin therefore considered inadequate by many stores.

net profit   The actual profit made by a store owner after all costs, such as merchandise, rent, and wages, have been deducted from gross receipts. *See also* gross profit.

Newbery, John   (1713–1767) English publisher and bookseller whose efforts made juvenile literature an important branch of the publishing business. In 1922, the Newbery Medal was established in his honor by Frederic Melcher. It is awarded each year to the author of the most distinguished children's book written by an American. Supervised by the Association for Library Services to Children of the American Library Association.

NISO   (Z39) *See* National Information Standards Organization.

NLW   National Library Week, a promotion under the direction of the ALA to encourage reading in general. Many booksellers also participate in NLW.

nom de plume   A pen name, pseudonym.

n.o.p.   Not our publication, an *invoice symbol.*

NRMA   *See* National Retail Merchants Association.

n.y.p.   Not yet published, an *invoice symbol.*

o.c.   Order canceled, an *invoice symbol.*

occult   Describes books that relate to mysticism, magic, clairvoyance, and the like.

OCR   *See* optical character recognition.

OCR-A   A style of type, or font, that can be read by the human eye and by automatic light scanners or wands. Its use as a means of identifying the ISBNs on a book is being slowly phased out and replaced by the use of the *Bookland EAN.*

octavo   A book approximately 9¾ inches high. *See also* book sizes.

offset   or **photo-offset** A method of printing that involves the indirect transfer of an impression from a printing plate to paper as contrasted with *letterpress.* Offset printing, once used mainly for large editions, is now used for printing most books.

on consignment   or **on sale** *See* consignment.

on demand books   or **on demand printing** Books are manufactured a single copy at a time, as a customer demands. The process is used mainly to produce reprints of scholarly works (for which there is not sufficient demand to print in large quantities) from a master file of microfilms. These scholarly reprints sometimes are expensive and poorly printed, but do fill a need, and the technology is improving rapidly. *See* academic reprints.

o.p.   Out of print. When a book is out of print, the publisher has no more copies for sale and does not intend to reprint the work. *See also* invoice symbols.

opacity or **opaque**   Opaque paper is not transparent. It is important that *India paper* or any thin paper have a high quantity of opacity so that the printing on one page does not show through on the other side.

open-to-buy   or *OTB* The dollar amount in a store's budget available for new and replacement purchases in a given period of time.

optical character recognition   The technique of using light-sensitive devices, scanners, or wands to optically identify characters, symbols, or marks in a document and input that information into a computer. *See* Bookland EAN, universal product code.

option   The right to buy or sell a property, as a manuscript or a book, within a specified time, in a specific market, and/or perhaps at a specified price. Not a retailing term, it refers most often to *subsidiary rights*.

o.s.   Out of stock. The publisher or distributor has no copies in stock and is, usually, awaiting delivery of a new printing or shipment. *See also* invoice symbols.

out-of-print dealer   *See* antiquarian dealer.

overhead   The costs involved in the running of a business, such as rent, wages, utilities, and so on. *See also* gross profit, net profit.

p.   Abbreviation for page. The plural is *pp*.

packing slip   A list, enclosed with a shipment, indicating its contents. Frequently, it is a partial copy of the invoice. It generally shows the list price of the titles shipped but not the discount or net price.

page proof   After the *galley proof* has been read and corrected, the type is then arranged by pages, and a new proof is pulled and resubmitted for final correcting.

paperback   A book bound in flexible paper covers without boards. *See also* mass market.

parchment   A writing material made from the inner side of the split skin of a sheep. *See also* vellum.

partial remainders   *See* remainders.

perfect binding   A glued binding, using newly developed, strong adhesives, not sewn or stitched, employed for most paperbacks and sometimes, in order to cut costs, for hardcover books also.

photo-offset   *See* offset.

pica   A type size: 12 point, or about one-quarter inch. Typewriters use two sizes of type: pica and *elite*, the smaller of the two. The first syllable of pica is pronounced like "pie."

pied type   Type that is completely mixed up and must be re-sorted before it can be used. This is a very old printing term, originating in the idea that the type was "knocked into a pie."

pigskin   The sturdy skin of a pig, used in bookbinding.

pirated edition   A book reproduced and sold without legal authorization or permission of the copyright owner. *See also* unauthorized edition.

plus sale   The sale of a second or third book by recommendation of the salesperson to a customer who has requested a specific title. An additional sale. A nonimpulse sale.

pocket book   Frequently used as a synonym for *paperback*. Pocket Books is also the name of Simon & Schuster's mass-market subsidiary. The confusion is understandable since Pocket Books was the first of the American companies to produce mass-market paperbacks and was a pioneer in what is often called the paperback revolution.

point   A measurement of type, approximately $1/72$ inch in height. The main text in this book is 11-point type; the chapter titles are 24-point type. The smallest type in general use for text in books is 6 point; the largest, 14 point.

point-of-sale terminal   An electronic cash register linked to a computer so that sales can be deducted from inventory and/or analyzed based on terminal input by sales clerks.

POS   *See* point-of-sale terminal.

p.p.   Abbreviation for parcel post.

preface   An explanation by the author in a page or a few pages preceding the text of a book of the purpose, scope, and background of the book. A *foreword* covers pretty much the same ground but is written by someone other than the author. An *introduction* defines the organization and limits of the text to follow.

prepub   A special price for a new (usually expensive) book offered for orders in advance of publication date. Often such prices are in effect through the Christmas season until the new year. Example: "$25.00 to January 1; $27.50 thereafter."

printer's proof   *See* galley proof.

pro forma   From the Latin, meaning "for the sake of form." A pro forma invoice from a publisher requires payment in advance of shipment.

protected or **fully protected**   Books so designated may be returned, if unsold, for full credit.

PTLA   Publishers' Trade List Annual A collection, in multiple volumes, of the trade lists of all the principal American publishers, issued each year in the fall by the R. R. Bowker Company.

publisher's rep   A publisher's representative who travels to make sales calls on booksellers in a defined region. *See also* traveler.

pulps   *See* slicks.

purchase order   Instructions, written or verbal, to a vendor specifying conditions of sale. It generally represents a contract with commitment to accept and pay for merchandise on the part of the buyer and commitment to accept the specified conditions on the part of the seller.

PW   Publishers Weekly. A publication for the entire book trade: publishers, booksellers, and book manufacturers. Published by the R. R. Bowker Company.

quality paperbacks   *See* trade paperbacks.

quarto   A book approximately twelve inches high. *See* book sizes.

quire   A measure of paper consisting of twenty-four sheets. *See also* ream.

rag paper   Paper that is made from cotton or linen rags rather than from commercial pulp. Fine stationery or fine book paper has a high degree of rag content. Because it is thought to have maximum durability, 100 percent rag is used for all U.S. paper currency and most stock and bond certificates.

rare-book dealer   *See* antiquarian bookseller.

ream   A ream of paper is now usually 500 sheets. Formerly it was 200 *quires*, or 480 sheets.

recto   The right-hand page of a book. The left-hand page is the *verso*.

remainders   After substantially all potential sales have been made, the books that remain in the publisher's warehouse. These are sold at reduced prices to booksellers usually through remainder houses, though "self-remaindering" directly by the publisher has become more common. A remaindered title, of course, becomes *out of print*, except when the publisher decides to "partially remainder" the title—that is, to sell off some of the stock but still retain some to supply at full price, a practice many consider to be a bad trade practice. The term "remainder" is sometimes incorrectly applied to sale books of all kinds: reprints, imports, and other promotional merchandise.

returns   Unsold books returned to the publisher for cash or more usually for credit. *See also* protected or fully protected.

review copies   Complimentary copies of a newly published title sent by a publisher to book reviewers.

revised edition   When substantial text changes are made to a book, the *edition* designation changes and is a *new* or *revised* or *enlarged* edition. Numbers rather than names often are applied (second edition). A useful text or technical title will go through many editions, perhaps with many printings of each.

rights The claims related to the printing, publishing, and selling of a book, including, for example, the right to distribute the book in particular parts of the world; to produce a reprint edition; and to let a movie studio use the book. *See also* subsidiary rights.

roman *See* italics.

royalty The commission paid by a publisher to an author, usually a percentage of the list price of all copies of the book sold.

RSV Revised standard version (of the Bible).

saddle-stitched or **saddle wire–stitched** Binding method for thin books with folded pages stapled together along the center fold.

SAN *See* standard address number.

science fiction Writing dealing with the impact of contemporary science on people or events, for example, life in the future, interplanetary travel, and so on. Sometimes abbreviated as "sci-fi" or "SF."

SCOP *See* STOP.

script A typeface having certain characteristics of handwriting.

search service The business of searching for out-of-print books wanted by customers, either conducted by a regular dealer of old and rare books or by a specialized searcher who advertises the services and obtains orders by mail.

shorts Those books not shipped on an order because they are currently unavailable.

signature Sixteen, thirty-two, or more pages are printed on a large sheet that when folded many times becomes a signature. The various signatures are gathered, stitched, or glued together and trimmed to become a book. A common defect occurs when the gathering machine takes two of a signature and misses the next one so that in the finished book some pages repeat and some are omitted.

skid A wooden platform on which paper or books are delivered. A skid of books weighs about three thousand pounds.

slicks Magazines printed on slick or coated paper. Those printed on cheaper paper, similar to newsprint, are known as "pulps."

slipcase A protective container with one open end into which a book or books can be inserted.

slit card A card that is slit so that it may fit into or around a book for purposes of display.

special order An order for a single copy of a book not in stock in a bookstore.

spine   The back of a book connecting the two covers. Also known as the backbone or backstrap.

spine-out display   An arrangement of books with spines facing the customer contrasted with "face-out" display.

spiral binding   A metal wire formed into a spiral of appropriate diameter passing through holes in the pages and cover binding them all together. *See also* comb binding.

standard account number   *See* standard address number.

standard address number   The national standard for identifying the names and addresses of all organizations involved in buying and selling books on a regular basis. Formerly called the standard account number, these numbers are assigned by the ISBN Agency (R. R. Bowker Co., 245 West 17th St., New York, NY 10011).

standing order   An order that holds good until it is filled. Also an order for succeeding issues of a publication. Most booksellers, for example, have established a standing order with R. R. Bowker Company for *Books in Print* and other reference works.

state   Minor text variations in books from the same *impression* classify them as different states. Variant states are caused by changes while a book is on press (correcting broken type or errors) while *issues* come from changes made after publication.

statement stuffers   Publishers' advertising designed to be mailed by a bookseller with monthly statements to charge customers.

stet   From Latin, meaning "let it stand." A common printers' and proofreaders' mark denoting that a word or passage previously deleted or changed is to be retained in its original form.

STOP   Single Title Order Plan. A system worked out by the ABA and the AAP through which booksellers may order one or more copies of a title from a publisher by sending payment with the order, using a specially devised order form. STOP replace SCOP, Single Copy Order Plan.

subsidiary   A publishing company owned by a parent company. *See also* conglomerate.

subsidiary rights   All those rights other than the original rights to publish a book, such as the rights to sell the book to reprint publishers, movie studios, book clubs, and magazines.

subsidy publishing   *See* vanity publisher.

TABA   *See* NBA.

telecommunications   *See* data communications.

text edition   A book intended for classroom use, usually without a jacket and carrying a discount lower than that for a *trade edition*.

thesaurus   From Greek, meaning "treasure house." A collection of words or concepts relating to a particular field, as a thesaurus of medical terminology. Also, specifically, a book of synonyms and antonyms, as *Roget's Thesaurus*.

Thomas, Isaiah   *See* Carey, Mathew.

thumb index   An alphabetical or subject index cut into the front edges of a book to aid in quick reference, most commonly seen on dictionaries.

tie-in   A book published in connection with an event in another medium—a movie or TV program, for example.

tip-in   An illustration or leaf pasted or "tipped" into a book, often by hand.

title   A book, its physical and metaphysical aspects, as in, "Booksellers could stand fewer titles from publishers."

tooling   Impressions made on the cover of a book using gold leaf or other decorative material.

TOS   Temporarily out of stock, an *invoice symbol*.

trade edition   An edition of a book intended for general distribution through bookstores, contrasted with *text, library*, and *book club editions*.

trade list   A publisher's list of titles with prices. The trade lists of most American publishers are collected annually into the multiple-volume *Publisher's Trade List Annual*, published by R. R. Bowker Company.

trade paperbacks   Those paperbacks not intended or suitable for the mass market but chiefly for sale in bookstores, as opposed to mass-market outlets, such as newsstands, variety stores, and supermarkets. Generally they are more expensive than mass-market paperbacks.

traveler or **book traveler**   A publisher's salesperson. Also *publisher's representative* or *rep*.

typo   An informal expression for "typographical error."

typographer   A typesetter, printer, or printing designer.

typophile   A lover of printing or typography.

unauthorized edition   An edition published without the permission of the author or the original publisher, or the copyright owner. *See also* pirated edition.

universal product code   The bar coding on merchandise purchased at convenience, grocery, drugstores, and increasingly at bookstores. The first section of the UPC is the publisher's or distributor's number as assigned by the Uniform Product Code Council; the second section is the list price (also known in some circles as "price point") of the book; smaller bars following the UPC symbol represent the title identifier section of the book's ISBN. The UPC will most often be found on mass-market books. For programming details contact the Book Industry Study Group.

UPC   *See* universal product code.

upper case   (u.c.) Capital letters, as distinguished from *lower case* or small letters. *See also* caps.

used-book dealer   *See* antiquarian bookseller.

vanity publisher   A publisher who issues books at the author's risk and expense. Also called a subsidy publisher.

vellum   A calfskin, finer than *parchment*, treated for use in writing or printing or for binding books. Most medieval manuscripts were written on vellum.

verso   The left-hand page of a book. The right-hand page is called the *recto*.

Webster, Noah   (1758–1843) American lexicographer, author, teacher, and—in order to promote the sale of his own books—itinerant bookseller. His *Speller*, one of the most successful books ever published in America, had total sales variously estimated at sixty to one hundred million copies. His first dictionary, published in 1806, was the earliest American English dictionary.

wholesaler   A *jobber*.

widow   A short single line or a word at the top or bottom of a column or page, the existence of which is avoided in good typography.

H. W. Wilson Company   (950 University Ave., Bronx, NY 10452) Publisher of reference tools for libraries and the book trade.

WNBA   *See* Women's National Book Association.

Women's National Book Association   Founded in 1917, it is a professional membership organization of women and men employed in all phases of the book industry with the goal of enhancing the role of women in the industry. Also publishes *The Bookwoman* and awards the Lucile Micheels Pannell Award annually to a bookseller and the WNBA Award biennially. (160 Fifth Ave., New York, NY 10010).

woodcut   In printing, an engraved block of wood or the design from such a block.

word processing   The implementation of word-processor software on a computer for writing, editing, revising, manipulating, formatting, and printing text for letters, reports, and manuscripts.

zinc etching   *See* line cut.

Bibliography

BOOKS ABOUT BOOKS:
A Bookman's Library

JERRY N. SHOWALTER

Most bibliographies are made up of the book titles that were used to prepare the text of a book. This bibliography is different. This one includes books that are mentioned in the text in addition to an annotated list of books on books, books about the history of bookselling, bookmaking, reading, the publishing industry from its beginnings to the present day, and a few books about book and manuscript collecting.

The original list of "Books about Books" was prepared in 1969 for the first edition of *A Manual on Bookselling* by the late Charles B. Anderson, gentleman bookseller from Larchmont, New York, and avid book collector. With some assistance from my editors, I have updated his list and made a few additions of newer titles that have since appeared on the scene. This bibliography is directed to the dedicated bookseller who wants to learn more about our profession, its history, and its inner makings, and who enjoys reading about bookselling and its allied arts. As this edition goes to press a substantial number of the books are in print, though several are not and have been so indicated by "o.p." after the title. Still, all are considered to be classic studies in their respective fields.

If you've never thought about collecting books before, you may want to consider a collection of books about books. It is certainly appropriate to our profession and rewarding as a hobby. You will join the company of many booksellers who have already made the discovery. You might also consider creating a section in your store devoted to this subject. Your customers might be very appreciative, and you could turn your hobby into a lucrative source of income.

ADLER, MORTIMER J., and VAN DOREN, CHARLES. *How to Read a Book.* New York: Simon & Schuster, 1972, paper. Practical information about how to become a better reader.

ANDERSON, CHARLES B., ed. *Bookselling in America and the World.* New York: Quadrangle/The New York Times Book Co., 1975, o.p. Published to celebrate the ABA's seventy-fifth anniversary.

APPLEBAUM, JUDITH, and EVANS, NANCY. *How to Get Happily Published.* New York: Harper & Row, 1978, o.p. An in-depth look at the mechanics of publishing with solid, practical advice. Available in paperback from New American Library/Plume.

ARBUTHNOT, MAY HILL, and SUTHERLAND, ZENA. *Children and Books.* 6th ed. New York: Scott, Foresman and Co., 1981, o.p. A discussion by children's book specialists about the importance of books for children.

BAILEY, HERBERT S., JR. *The Art and Science of Book Publishing.* Austin: University of Texas Press, 1980, paper, o.p. Book publishing from the point of view of a prominent university press publisher.

BENNETT, JAMES O. *Much Loved Books.* New York: Liveright, 1927, o.p. A lively discussion about many books, classic and modern.

BENNETT, PAUL A., ed. *Books and Printing: A Treasury for Typophiles.* Gloucester, MA, and New York: Peter Smith/World Publishing Co., 1952, o.p. A collection of essays about fine printing selected by one of America's typophiles.

BERG, SCOTT A. *Max Perkins: Editor of Genius,* o.p. New York: E. P. Dutton, 1978. A lively biography of one of America's most revered editors. Also available in paperback from Washington Square Press.

BERKELEY, EDMUND, JR. *Autographs and Manuscripts: A Collector's Manual.* New York: Scribner Book Co., 1978.

BLAND, DAVID. *A History of Book Illustration: The Illuminated Manuscript and the Printed Book.* Berkeley: University of California Press, 1969, o.p. An account of book illustration before and after Gutenberg.

BURGESS, WILLIAM E. *Collector's Guide to Antiquarian Bookstores.* New York: Macmillan Publishing Co., 1984.

BUTLER, DOROTHY. *Babies Need Books.* New York: Atheneum, 1980.

CANFIELD, CASS. *Up and Down and Around: A Publisher Recollects the Time of His Life.* New York: Harper's Magazine Press, 1971, o.p. A highly esteemed publisher and editor tells of his life with books and the people who write them.

CERF, BENNETT. *At Random: The Reminiscences of Bennett Cerf.* New York: Random House, 1977. The fascinating autobiography of the co-founder of Random House.

CHAPPELL, WARREN. *A Short History of the Printed Word.* New York: Alfred A. Knopf, 1970, o.p. An engrossing history of printing by a prominent designer and artist. Also available in paperback, David Godine, 1980.

CHARVAT, WILLIAM. *Literary Publishing in America, 1790–1850.* Philadelphia: University of Pennsylvania Press, 1959, o.p. A scholarly account of book publishing of an earlier day.

CHILDREN'S BOOK COUNCIL, INC. *Children's Books: Awards & Prizes.* New York, 1986. The major compilation of children's book awards including U.S., British Commonwealth, international, and multinational awards. Awards classification section; person and title indices.

COLBY, JEAN POINDEXTER. *Writing, Illustrating, and Editing Children's Books.* New York: Hastings House, 1974, o.p. An author, illustrator, and editor writes about producing children's books.

COLE, JOHN. *Books in Our Future.* Washington D.C.: Joint Committee on the Library, Congress of the United States, 1984.

COMMINS, DOROTHY. *What Is an Editor? Saxe Commins at Work.* Chicago: University of Chicago Press, 1978, paper. Biography of the great Random House editor, whose authors included William Faulkner, James Michener, Eugene O'Neill, and John O'Hara.

COSNER, LEWIS A., et al. *Books—The Culture and Commerce of Publishing.* Chicago: University of Chicago Press, 1982; paper, 1985, o.p.

COTT, JONATHAN. *Pipers at the Gates of Dawn: The Wisdom of Children's Literature.* New York: Alfred A. Knopf, 1983, o.p. Available in paperback from McGraw-Hill.

COURTNEY, WINIFRED F. *The Reader's Adviser.* 3 vols. New York: R. R. Bowker Co., 1974, 1977, o.p. A standard reference about authors and books.

DESSAUER, JOHN. *Book Publishing: What It Is, What It Does.* 2nd ed. New York: R. R. Bowker Co., 1981, paper. An informative and readable book about publishing.

DOWNS, ROBERT B. *Books That Changed the World.* 2nd ed. New York: New American Library, 1978. Cloth ed. by American Library Association. Evidence aplenty that the pen is mightier than the sword.

DUFF, ANNIS. *Bequest of Wings: A Family's Pleasures with Books.* New York: Viking Press, 1944, o.p. An eminent children's book editor talks about books in her home.

———. *Longer Flight: A Family Grows Up with Books.* New York: Viking Press, 1955, o.p. A companion volume to *Bequest of Wings.*

FLESCH, RUDOLF. *Why Johnny Can't Read: And What You Can Do About It.* Rev. ed. New York: Harper & Row, 1986, paper. An examination of how grade school teaching techniques don't teach children how to read or comprehend.

———. *Why Johnny Still Can't Read: A New Look at the Scandal of Our Schools.* New York: Harper & Row, 1983, paper. A follow-up study to Flesch's first book.

FOSTER, JOANNA. *Pages, Pictures and Print: A Book in the Making.* New York: Harcourt Brace Jovanovich, 1958, o.p. A specialist in children's books writes entertainingly about how a book is put together.

GRANNIS, CHANDLER B., ed. *The Heritage of the Graphic Arts.* New York: R. R. Bowker Co., 1972, o.p. A collection of articles about prominent typographers, selected and edited by a devoted typophile and amateur typographer.

———. *What Happens in Book Publishing.* 2nd ed. New York: Columbia

University Press, 1967. Articles by specialists about various aspects of the book trade, edited by the former editor-in-chief of *Publishers Weekly.*

GREENFIELD, HOWARD. *Books: From Writer to Reader.* New York: Crown Publishers, 1976, o.p. An interesting account of how books are produced and sold.

GROSS, SIDNEY, and STECKLER, PHYLLIS B., eds. *How to Run a Paperback Bookshop.* New York: R. R. Bowker Co., 1963, o.p. Useful, though dated, information about running any kind of bookstore.

GUINZBURG, HAROLD K., et al. *Books and the Mass Market.* Urbana: University of Illinois Press, 1953, o.p. A president of Viking Press writes about the marketing of books in America.

HACKETT, ALICE PAYNE, and BURKE, HENRY JAMES. *Eighty Years of Best Sellers.* New York: R. R. Bowker Co., 1977, o.p. A fascinating account of book sales and reading habits in America from 1895 to 1975.

HAIGHT, ANNE LYON. *Banned Books.* New York: R. R. Bowker Co., 1978, o.p. A history of hundreds of books that have been banned during the last twenty-five centuries.

HAINES, HELEN E. *Living with Books: The Art of Book Selection.* 2nd ed. New York: Columbia University Press, 1950. Choosing books for a home library.

HART, JAMES D. *The Popular Book: A History of America's Literary Taste.* Berkeley: University of California Press, 1950, o.p. American bestsellers from early colonial times to the twentieth century.

HEARNE, BETSY. *Choosing Books for Children: A Common Sense Guide.* New York: Delacorte, 1986, paper. A relaxed and entertaining guide for adults, especially parents, who wish to know the what, when, and how of sharing books with children.

———, and KAYE, MARILYN. *Celebrating Children's Books.* New York: Lothrop, Lee & Shepard, 1986, paper.

HENDERSON, BILL, ed. *The Publish It Yourself Handbook: Literary Tradition and How-To.* Rev. ed. Wainscott, NY: Pushcart Press, 1979. Practical information about publishing a book on your own and on the history of self-publishing.

HIGHET, GILBERT. *People, Places and Books.* New York: Oxford University Press, 1953. The late, distinguished author and classical scholar writes with enthusiasm and charm about the literary world.

JOVANOVICH, WILLIAM. *Now, Barabbas.* New York: Harcourt Brace Jovanovich, 1966, o.p. An autobiography by one of our leading publishers.

KERR, CHESTER. *American University as Publisher.* Norman: University of Oklahoma Press, 1949, o.p. A digest of a report on American university presses.

KNOPF, ALFRED A. *Publishing Then and Now: 1912–1964.* New York: New York Public Library, 1965, o.p. Reminiscences by one who was regarded as the dean of American publishers.

KOZOL, JONATHAN. *Illiterate America.* Garden City, NY: Anchor Press/

Doubleday, 1985. The author of *Death at an Early Age* tells us that one out of every three Americans cannot read his book, and that is a national disgrace. He proposes a specific program to conquer illiteracy.

KUNITZ, STANLEY J., and HAYCRAFT, HOWARD, eds. *American Authors (1600–1900).* 8th ed. New York: H. W. Wilson Co., 1977. A standard reference book about American literary history.

———. *Twentieth Century Authors.* New York: H. W. Wilson Co., 1942. A companion volume to the one preceding. Supplement, 1955.

LARRICK, NANCY. *A Parent's Guide to Children's Reading.* 5th rev. ed. Philadelphia: Westminster Press, 1983. A useful guide for buyers of children's books.

LEHMANN-HAUPT, HELMUT, et al. *The Book in America.* 2nd ed. New York: R. R. Bowker Co., 1951, o.p. A history of the making and selling of books in the United States.

MCMULLAN, KATE. *How to Choose Good Books for Kids.* Reading, MA: Addison-Wesley, 1984, o.p. Provides criteria that help parents select titles for children. Each of the four chapters spans three years of a child's development from infancy through age eleven. A clear and accessible guide.

MCMURTRIE, DOUGLAS C. *The Book: The Story of Printing and Bookmaking.* 3rd ed. New York: Oxford University Press, 1943. An excellent account of how a book is produced.

MADISON, CHARLES A. *Book Publishing in America.* New York: McGraw-Hill Book Co., 1966, o.p. A prominent editor discusses the influence of book publishing on the American cultural scene.

MALKIN, SOL M. *ABC of the Book Trade: New and Used, Old and Rare, Out-of-Print and Specialist.* Newark, NJ: Antiquarian Bookman, 1966, o.p. The late founder of the magazine *Antiquarian Bookman* talks about the antiquarian field.

MANSFIELD, KATHERINE. *Novels and Novelists.* New York: Somerset Publishers, 1975. An informal and informative book by one of the great writers of the short story.

MEIGS, CORNELIA, et al. *A Critical History of Children's Literature.* Rev. ed. New York: Macmillan Publishing Co., 1969. A survey of children's books in English from the earliest time to the mid-1950s.

MORLEY, CHRISTOPHER. *The Haunted Bookshop.* Philadelphia: J. B. Lippincott Co., 1955, o.p. A classic American novel about an antiquarian bookstore. Available in paperback from Avon.

———. *Parnassus on Wheels.* Philadelphia: J. B. Lippincott Co., 1955, o.p. A standard work available in paperback from Avon.

MOTT, FRANK L. *Golden Multitudes.* New York: R. R. Bowker Co., 1960, o.p. America's favorite books from 1662 to 1945.

MUMBY, FRANK A., and NORRIE, IAN. *Publishing and Bookselling: A History from the Earliest Times to the Present Day.* 5th ed. New York: R. R. Bowker Co., 1974, o.p. The standard British work on the subject.

NEMEYER, CAROL A. *Scholarly Reprint Publishing in the United States.*

New York: R. R. Bowker Co., 1972, o.p. A guide to the selection, acquisition, and use of scholarly books.

NILSEN, ALLEEN PACE, and DONELSON, KENNETH L. *Literature for Today's Young Adults.* 2nd ed. Glenview, IL: Scott, Foresman and Co., 1985. Designed for teachers of young-adult literature in library science, English, and education departments, this textbook is useful for all who are interested in writing for young adults.

PETERS, JEAN, ed. *Book Collecting: A Modern Guide.* New York: R. R. Bowker Co., 1977. A collection of essays by authorities in the field.

———. *The Bookman's Glossary.* 6th ed. New York: R. R. Bowker Co., 1983. Entirely revised and greatly expanded, this volume defines more than 1,600 terms used in the book trade.

PETERSEN, CLARENCE. *The Bantam Story: Thirty Years of Paperback Publishing.* New York: Bantam Books, 1975, o.p. A lively history of the largest paperback publisher.

RANDALL, DAVID A. *Dukedom Large Enough: Reminiscences of a Rare Book Dealer.* New York: Random House, 1969, o.p. The former head of the rare books department at Scribner's Bookstore in New York writes about his life with books.

READING IS FUNDAMENTAL, Ruth Graves, ed. *The RIF Guide to Encouraging Young Readers.* Garden City, NY: Doubleday & Co., 1987. Based on twenty years' experience in stimulating children to read, this guide is a valuable tool that offers hundreds of ways to get youngsters caught up in the fun of words and reading.

SHATZKIN, LEONARD. *In Cold Type: Overcoming the Book Crisis.* Boston: Houghton Mifflin, 1983, paper. An iconoclast's view of the industry today and thoughts on what can be done to improve it.

SMITH, DATUS C., JR. *A Guide to Book Publishing.* New York: R. R. Bowker Co., 1966, o.p. A basic guide to the principles of book publishing. Available from Demand Books UMI.

SMITH, ROGER H. *The American Reading Public: What It Reads—Why It Reads.* New York: R. R. Bowker Co., 1964, o.p. The publishing industry and its relationship to the reading public.

SPEED, ELDON, et al. *Principles of College Bookstore Management.* Oberlin, OH: National Association of College Stores/Harper, 1983. Available only from NACS.

SPILLER, ROBERT E., et al. *Literary History of the United States.* New York: Macmillan Publishing Co., 1974, o.p. Revised edition in one volume, originally published in three.

SUTHERLAND, ZENA, et al. *Children and Books.* Glenview, IL: Scott, Foresman and Co., 7th ed., 1985. A textbook used primarily in courses in children's literature, but meant for all adults who are interested in bringing children and books together.

TARG, WILLIAM, ed. *Bibliophile in the Nursery; A Bookman's Treasury of Collector's Lore on Old and Rare Children's Books.* Metuchen, NJ: Scarecrow Press, 1957, o.p. Informative articles on collecting old and rare children's books.

———. *Indecent Pleasures.* New York: Macmillan Publishing Co., 1975, o.p. A highly entertaining story of the life and times of an eminent editor who once owned a bookstore in Chicago.

TAUBERT, SIGFRED. *Bibliopola: Pictures and Texts About the Book Trade.* 2 vols. New York: R. R. Bowker Co., 1966, o.p. A splendid set of books in three languages—English, French, and German—about the world of bookselling from its beginnings to the present. Many spectacular illustrations in full color.

———. *The Book Trade of the World.* 4 vols. New York: R. R. Bowker Co., 1972, 1976, 1981. A country-by-country survey of bookselling and publishing today.

TEBBEL, JOHN. *A History of Book Publishing in the United States.* 4 vols. New York: R. R. Bowker Co., 1972, 1975, 1978, 1981. On publication of the first volume it was immediately hailed as the definitive history of American book publishing.

TRELEASE, JIM. *The Read-Aloud Handbook.* New York: Penguin Books, 1985. Revised paperback edition of this volume encourages adults to read aloud to young people as the most practical way to encourage independent reading.

UHLAN, EDWARD. *The Rogue of Publishers' Row.* Hicksville, NY: Exposition Press, 9th ed., 1956. A "vanity" publisher defends vanity publishing.

UNWIN, SIR STANLEY. *The Truth about a Publisher.* New York: R. R. Bowker Co., 1976, o.p. The autobiography of a renowned British publisher.

———. *The Truth about Publishing.* 8th ed. New York: R. R. Bowker Co., 1976. The eminent British publisher discusses his profession.

VERVLIET, HENDRIK D. L., ed. *The Book through Five Thousand Years.* New York: Praeger Publishers, 1972, o.p. A bulky, handsome, and expensive book with lavish illustrations, mostly about the book before Gutenberg and Caxton.

WOLFE, THOMAS. *The Story of a Novel.* New York: Charles Scribner's Sons, 1936. The author of *Look Homeward, Angel* talks about writing fiction.

Notes on the Contributors

ALLAN MARSHALL

CHARLES B. ANDERSON ("A Bookseller's Glossary"): Charles Anderson served books and bookselling most of his life and in most imaginable ways. He was a coeditor of the first and second editions of *A Manual on Bookselling* and edited *Bookselling in America and the World* (Quadrangle, 1975). In his spare time, he was a president of the American Booksellers Association and was, until shortly before his death, chairman of the board of Anderson's Book Shop in Larchmont, New York.

ROBERT DIKE BLAIR ("A Bookseller's Glossary"): After five years in the U.S. Army, Mr. Blair served an apprenticeship with the Doubleday Bookshops. He then opened The Vermont Book Shop, sharing selling space in a house with an antique shop in Middlebury, Vermont. Mr. Blair has been an ABA director or officer on and off for fifteen years.

DIANE BROOM ("Seasonal Promotions"): Ms. Broom's bookselling career began at The Book Shop in Boise, Idaho, in 1971. Since then she has directed workshops and participated in panel discussions on many subjects related to books and reading. In 1981 and 1982, Ms. Broom was a judge in the children's book division for the American Book Awards. She currently manages a small, independent store called Charing Cross, Ltd., in Boise.

WARREN CASSELL ("Computers in the Bookstore"): Mr. Cassell is owner, manager, and general factotum of Just Books, a personal service bookstore that caters to the "aristocratic" population of downtown Greenwich, Connecticut. He also served for a short time on the board of directors of the now-defunct Booksellers Order Service.

JACOB L. CHERNOFSKY ("Antiquarian Bookselling in America"): Jake Chernofsky is editor and publisher of *AB Bookman's Weekly*, where he has been on the staff for over thirteen years. He is also co-director of the

Antiquarian Book Trade Seminar-Workshop, presented for the past eight years at the University of Denver.

DAVID CIOFFI ("Computer Books, Magazines, and Software"): Mr. Cioffi is currently manager and vice-president of Dartmouth Bookstore, Inc., in Hanover, New Hampshire. His experience includes being a marketing analyst and a sales training manager for Pepsi-Cola and a supermarket manager for Martin's Foods, Inc. He has contributed articles to ABA's *American Bookseller* magazine and has frequently appeared on panels at the ABA Convention.

STEPHEN COGIL ("Promoting the New Store," "Basic Record Keeping," "Buying from Wholesalers," "Paperbacks in the Bookstore"): Mr. Cogil is president of the Chicago-based SLC Enterprises, Inc. He is an experienced consultant and has taught on numerous occasions at ABA Booksellers Schools and has lectured nationwide on the subjects of bookselling and retailing. Mr. Cogil was ABA's director of education in the early 1970s.

JOHN Y. COLE ("Books in Our Lives—Now and in the Future"): Dr. Cole held several administrative positions in the Library of Congress prior to becoming the first director of The Center for the Book, which was established in 1977.

DAVID COLEN ("Basic Record Keeping"): Mr. Colen is currently the manager of corporate administration for Aura Promotions, Ltd., and is on the consulting staff of SLC Enterprises. Mr. Colen previously worked as a consultant to Bookmarket, Inc., a division of the Charles Levy Circulating Co.

GINGER CURWEN ("Special Orders," "The Branch Store," "The ABA Convention"): Ms. Curwen is editor of *American Bookseller* and director of publications for ABA. Before joining ABA, she worked at Bantam Books, Random House, George Braziller, and the University of California Press.

MICHAEL ALAN FOX ("Inventory Management"): Mr. Fox served as ABA's education director prior to occupying buying and merchandise management positions with Waldenbooks. His past experience also includes managing the general book department of the University Book Store in Seattle, Washington and acting as the merchandise manager of the six Stacey's bookstores in California.

ROBERT D. HALE (Preface, "Buying from Wholesalers," "Hardcover Bookselling," "Paperbacks in the Bookstore," "Specialization," "Book Fairs," "Advertising—An Overview"): Robert D. Hale is the owner of Westwinds Bookshop in Duxbury, Massachusetts. From 1977 to 1983 he was the associate executive director of ABA, and prior to that he was president of the association for two years. He was president and general manager of Hathaway House Bookshop in Wellesley, Massachusetts, for seven years and before that was general manager of the Connecticut College Bookshop in New London for eight years. For many years, Mr. Hale served as dean of the ABA Booksellers Schools.

ELIZABETH HASLAM ("Selling Religious Books in a General Trade Store"): Elizabeth Haslam is owner of Haslam's Bookstore in St. Petersburg, Florida, where she has been in charge of children's book buying for forty years. She is also a member of the Joint Committee of the ABA and the Children's Book Council and serves on the faculty of the ABA Booksellers Schools.

MARY KATHRYN HASSETT ("Technical–Professional Books"): Ms. Hassett is currently a book buyer for Dillard's Department Stores in Fort Worth, Texas. She was associated with The Book Merchant in Dallas for nine years as a partner and had primary responsibility for development of corporate accounts. She is also a former president of the Southwestern Booksellers Association.

CHARLES E. HAYWARD ("The Publishing Process"): Since mid-1986 Mr. Hayward has been vice-president and publisher, trade division, Simon & Schuster. His career began at Houghton Mifflin as a sales representative; he has held sales and marketing management positions at Crown Publishers, St. Martin's, and Macmillan and was president of HPBooks.

SUZANNE HASLAM HINST ("Selling Books"): Ms. Hinst is a third-generation bookseller at Haslam's Bookstore, established in 1933 in St. Petersburg, Florida.

CHRISTINE HUFFMAN ("Paperbacks in the Bookstore," "Display and Visual Merchandising"): Ms. Huffman has held numerous positions in the book industry over the past twenty years. She has also served on the ABA Marketing Committee and written extensively for *American Bookseller* magazine.

J. RHETT JACKSON ("Bibles in the General Bookstore," "Radio and Television Advertising"): Mr. Jackson has been on the ABA board of directors for five years and is currently president of the association. With his wife, Betty, he owns and operates The Happy Bookseller in Columbia, South Carolina. Prior to that he was in the furniture busines for thirty years. He has also been a member of the South Carolina Parole Board, on the board of trustees of a black college (Claflin College), and past chairman of its board.

LYNNE JACOBS ("Bargain Books Basics"): Ms. Jacobs was formerly the marketing coordinator for the ABA and is currently a sales representative for HPBooks. Prior to joining the ABA, she was sales manager for the West Coast wholesaler Pacific Pipeline and in charge of marketing matters for the Pacific Northwest Booksellers Association.

JOYCE KNAUER ("Moving and Expanding"): In 1974 Joyce Knauer closed The Parker Book Shop and moved its stock twenty miles to their newly acquired 950-square-foot Tattered Cover in Denver, Colorado. Since then, Joyce and her husband, Rudy, have experienced eight expansions, the most recent of which saw the consolidation of two locations into one new location with 40,000 square feet of selling space.

ELIOT LEONARD ("Financing the New Bookstore," "Location and Lease," "Negotiating the Lease," "Budgeting," "Discount Bookselling," "Getting Out: Liquidating or Selling Your Bookstore"): Eliot Leonard began his bookselling career at the Harvard Cooperative Society and by the end of his twenty-nine years there had become the general merchandise manager for the Coop's main store and all its branches. He was president of the Pickwick Bookshops, and when the chain merged with B. Dalton, he became that company's senior vice-president and director of western stores until his retirement. Mr. Leonard is a past president and director of the ABA and is currently a bookstore consultant.

MAXWELL LILLIENSTEIN ("Legal Concerns," "When Is It a Crime to Sell a Book?: A Review of Laws Seeking to Regulate Sexually Explicit Books and Magazines"): As general counsel to the ABA and a senior partner in the law firm of Rich, Lillienstein, Krinsly, Dorman & Hochhauser, Mr. Lillienstein has been involved on numerous occasions with the leasing and opening of commercial property and has been heavily committed to the defense of the printed word and the media in cases of censorship.

BARBARA LIVINGSTON ("Promotion through Creative Events"): Ms. Livingston is currently a free-lance writer and editor. Previously, she was an assistant editor for *Library Journal*. While on the staff at ABA, Ms. Livingston was a contributing editor for *American Bookseller* and editor of the *ABA Newswire*.

ADRIEN V. LORENTZ ("Insurance and Protection"): Mr. Lorentz recently retired as owner-manager of the Peninsula Book Shop in Palo Alto, California. He served six years as a member of ABA's board of directors and two years as treasurer. He has had firsthand experience in obtaining insurance and business protection during the thirty-eight years when he was self-employed in wholesaling and retailing endeavors.

FRANK LOWE ("Hiring and Staff Training," "Hardcover Bookselling"): Frank Lowe began his bookselling career at the Doubleday Book Shops and managed several of their New York City stores during the nine years he was there. Following his tenure at Doubleday, he moved to the Scribner Bookstore on Fifth Avenue and became vice-president of operations. He was with that organization for seventeen years.

ALLAN MARSHALL ("The Mechanics of Ordering," "Other Services"): Most recently, Mr. Marshall has been the president of Booksellers Ordering Service and ABA's Director of Professional Development and Education, after serving for several years as the Association's Special Projects Director. Prior to joining the ABA, he owned and operated a general trade bookstore in the Chelsea area of Manhattan.

EDWARD A. MORROW, JR. ("Publisher–Bookseller Relations"): With his wife, Barbara, Ed Morrow owns and operates The Northshire Bookstore in Manchester Center, Vermont. It is the largest bookstore in the state and receives special recognition for its children's book department. Mr. Morrow is a past president of the New England Booksellers Association and is currently a director of the ABA. He has contributed to *American Bookseller* and teaches at the ABA Booksellers Schools.

BETTY E. MUNGER ("Trade Books on Campus"): After sixteen years on the job, Ms. Munger recently retired as manager of the Washington & Lee University Bookstore in Lexington, Virginia. During her tenure there, she exhibited her strong commitment to trade books by offering them for sale on the street level of the store, while texts were stocked on the basement level.

MELISSA MYTINGER ("Print Advertising"): Ms. Mytinger co-founded Unicorn Books in Santa Barbara, California, which began her bookselling career in 1966. She spent time as a small-press publisher, an antiquarian bibliographic researcher, and has worked with several West Coast publishers. At present, she is the executive secretary of the Northern California Booksellers Association and is the business director and advertising/promotion manager at Cody's Books, Berkeley, California.

JUDY NOYES ("Newsletters"): Since 1959, Ms. Noyes has been co-owner with her husband, Dick, of the Chinook Bookshop in Colorado Springs, Colorado. She counts among her many responsibilities the buying of the children's books and the management of the store's advertising program, which includes the highly successful newsletter *Currents from the Chinook*.

CRIS POPENOE ("Getting into Mail Order"): Cris Popenoe is co-owner with her husband, Ollie, of Yes! Bookshop in the Georgetown area of Washington, D.C. Open since 1972, the store specializes in books on self-development, emphasizing philosophy, psychology, and religion. The store's mail order catalogs boast of having over thirty-five thousand names on the mailing lists. Ms. Popenoe has produced catalogs-as-books, notably *Wellness, Inner Development,* and *Book Bytes,* published in the United States by Random House and abroad by Penguin.

MICHAEL POWELL ("Used Books for Fun and Profit"): Mr. Powell has served as a director for both the ABA and Booksellers Order Service. He was originally a used-book dealer and, as the owner of Powell's Bookstores in Portland, Oregon, and Chicago, Illinois, has now integrated new books into his inventory.

BERNARD E. RATH (Foreword: "The Climate of the Book Industry Today," "What Is ABA and What Can It Do for You?"): Bernie Rath has been executive director of the ABA since April 1984. Prior to that, he was the executive director of the Canadian Booksellers Association from 1978 to 1983.

JERRY L. REHM ("Institutional Sales"): Since 1977, Mr. Rehm has been a partner in The Book Merchant in Dallas, Texas. He also has been a faculty member of numerous ABA schools, served on several ABA committees—most notably as chairperson of the education committee, and has served on the ABA board of directors.

JOAN RIPLEY ("Behind the Scenes: Supplies and Equipment," "Receiving Procedures," "Processing Returns"): Ms. Ripley is the owner of The Second Story in Chappaqua, New York. She has been on the faculty of ABA Booksellers Schools, has been a member of or chaired almost every ABA committee, has served on the board of directors of ABA, and was president of the association from 1980 to 1982. Upon leaving the board in 1984, she was appointed director of marketing for ABA's Booksellers Order Service.

CHARLES ROBINSON ("Stock Selection"): Chuck Robinson is co-owner with his wife, Dee, of Village Books in Bellingham, Washington. He is a frequent faculty member at ABA Prospective Booksellers Schools and is a member of the education committee. He is a past president of the Pacific Northwest Booksellers Association.

CYD ROSENBERG ("Opening a Bookstore," "Bookstore Layout," "Trade Tools for a Bookstore," "Promotion through Creative Events," "Booksellers Schools and Workshops"): For many years, Ms. Rosenberg was director of education for the ABA. Teaching and running the Booksellers Schools were her main responsibilities. She was adviser to hundreds of potential new bookstore owners who call in or write to the ABA. She previously managed the Fleetbooks Division of Feffer and Simons and worked in sales at Simon & Schuster.

ANDY ROSS ("Small Press and Self-Published Books in the Bookstore"): Mr. Ross's bookselling career began in 1972, and in 1977 he became owner of Cody's Books in Berkeley, California. He has served as president of the Northern California Booksellers Association and is a director of the ABA.

A. DAVID SCHWARTZ ("Buying from Wholesalers"): Mr. Schwartz was very nearly born in the family bookstore, Harry W. Schwartz Booksellers, in Milwaukee, Wisconsin. After stints managing two Doubleday stores, he returned home to take over the family business in 1972. In 1984, he merged his operation with Dickens Books and is now the president of the combined firms. He has served on the ABA board of directors and has been treasurer of the ABA for three terms.

GAIL SEE ("Publicity"): Gail See has owned and managed The Bookcase in Wayzata, Minnesota, since 1974. She has been a regular member on the faculty of the ABA Booksellers Schools, for a time headed the education committee, and served as ABA president for two terms. She was instrumental in establishing the Upper Midwest Booksellers Association, Give the Gift of Literacy Foundation, and the Minnesota Center for Book Arts.

JERRY N. SHOWALTER (Bibliography: "Books about Books: A Bookman's Library"): Mr. Showalter is director of the Newcomb Hall Bookstore at the University of Virginia in Charlottesville and a former member of the ABA board of directors. He is a past president of the Virginia College Stores Association and served on the advisory board of the Center for the Book of the Library of Congress from 1980 to 1984.

JANE E. SHURTLEFF ("How to Start an Out-of-Print Search Service"): At Cosmic Aeroplane Books in Salt Lake City, Utah, where Ms. Shurtleff was trade buyer, the book specializations were science fiction, metaphysics, and alternate life-styles. Recently Ms. Shurtleff moved to the East Coast and left the book business.

G. ROYSCE SMITH ("Reading, Understanding, and Using Financial Statements"): Mr. Smith was executive director of the ABA from 1972 to 1984. Before that, he was the association's director of education and co-founded the ABA Booksellers Schools. Mr. Smith was book department manager at the Yale Co-op for fifteen years, after leaving the position of buyer in Davison's book department in Atlanta, Georgia. He is now retired and living in southern California.

CAROLYN B. TEAGUE ("Selling to the Institutional Customer: Educational"): Ms. Teague presently owns and operates two locations of Teague's Books for Children in Arlington, Texas. Prior to that, she was the owner and director of her own preschool for twenty years. Ms. Teague often speaks before small groups on the importance of books as the building blocks of life.

MARY ANN TENNENHOUSE ("Sidelines or Nonbook Merchandise"): As ABA's editor of publications, she has walked miles of aisles at gift and stationery shows preparing each edition of the Sidelines Directory. Ms. Tennenhouse also edits the ABA Book Buyer's Handbook, the ABA Basic Book List, and the Guide to the Exhibit for the annual ABA Convention. For a change of pace, she organizes the convention author autograph sessions.

BARBARA THEROUX ("Belonging: The Value of Regionals and Other Local Organizations," "Booksellers Schools and Workshops"): Ms. Theroux is currently owner/manager of Fact & Fiction, a general bookstore in Missoula, Montana. She has fourteen combined years of experience as trade book buyer and manager at the U Center Bookstore, University of Montana, and at the Students Book Corporation, Washington State University. Ms. Theroux was an ABA board member, served on several committees, taught at ABA Booksellers Schools, and often appeared as a speaker on various ABA programs.

BARBARA THOMAS ("Children's Books"): Ms. Thomas, a former teacher and children's book librarian, is founder and co-owner of Toad Hall Children's Books in Austin, Texas, which opened in 1978.

KAY VAIL-HAYDEN ("Foreign Books for the American Bookseller"): Ms. Vail-Hayden currently runs the computer system for the University Bookstore in Seattle, Washington. Formerly, she was the store's foreign book buyer for both the trade and textbook departments.

RON WATSON ("Authors Sell Books"): Mr. Watson is general manager of the Mills Bookstores in Nashville, Tennessee, and was the winner of the 1986 Charley Haslam International Scholarship. He has served on several ABA committees and been active in the Southeast Booksellers Association.

KEN WHITE ("Bookstore Layout"): Mr. White is president of Ken White Associates in Hillsdale, New Jersey, and has designed more than one thousand bookstores in the United States and other countries. He is the author of *Bookstore Planning and Design* (McGraw-Hill).

JEAN B. WILSON ("Buying Directly from Publishers," "Hardcover Bookselling," "Regional Books"): Ms. Wilson has been in the book business for more than twenty-five years and is presently the owner/manager of The Book Shop in Boise, Idaho. She has been a member of the ABA board of directors and has served on the education, publications, and *Basic Book List* committees. Ms. Wilson has taught at many ABA Booksellers Schools.

Index